Inspiring
Australian Women

Kathryn Spurling

Portraiture by Margaret Hadfield (Zorgdrager)

To my wonderful, intelligent, athletic and proud granddaughters
Anastasia Light Spurling
Stephanie Anne Leslie
Emily Beth Leslie
May the opportunities be endless and the future amazing.

Acknowledgements

This book depended entirely on the willingness of: Matilda House-Williams, Helen Reddy, Geraldine Cox, Natasha Stott Despoja, Fiona Wood and Lauren Jackson agreeing to participate. Their lives are incredibly busy and touch so many here and overseas. I am deeply grateful for how they graciously submitted to my intrusion. My questions often seemed banal and unimportant to me, but they showed great patience, over what became years.

I appreciate the Chief Minister of the Australian Capital Territory, the Hon. Katy Gallagher, adding her name to this book by way of the Foreword – she is herself an inspiring woman.

My motivation to write came from the women in my life, none more so than the youngest generation. Margaret Hadfield (Zorgdrager) kept prodding me onwards and her portraits of these inspiring women, added such vitality.

My long-time friend Elizabeth Van Der Hor put a totally excessive number of hours editing my bad prose and I am very appreciative. Also to Len for allowing his wife to be so consumed.

My daughter Jennie Leslie spent considerable time and effort proof-reading and offering another perspective.

Cath Brinkley, Beeline Partnerships, Collaborative Publications (C-Pubs) has needed to weather my protracted writing attempt – thank you Cath.

Nicola Matthews and addcolour digital staff so very expertly turned *Inspiring Australian Women* into an actual book.

I am also indebted to the staff of the School of History, Australian National University (ANU), Canberra, for assistance rendered and believing enough to retain me as a Visiting Scholar. ANU is indeed a welcoming and supportive institution.

Kathryn Spurling

Foreword

Katy Gallagher MLA

CHIEF MINISTER

MINISTER FOR HEALTH

MINISTER FOR REGIONAL DEVELOPMENT

MINISTER FOR HIGHER EDUCATION

MEMBER FOR MOLONGLO

It is an honour to provide the foreword to Dr Kathryn Spurling's book, *Inspiring Australian Women*.

Our Centenary year has provided a unique opportunity to reflect on the story of Canberra, and in particular to acknowledge the contribution that so many exceptional women have made.

A sense of community has always been something women have been instrumental in developing. The earliest Canberrans, the Indigenous women in the Canberra region, to the women who came to the nation's capital from 1913 onwards, built a sense of community as the new city developed.

To this end, women worked together to meet challenges, tackle problems and bring about change. They worked with conviction and courage to realise the true potential of our nation's capital.

From our city's earliest days women have made an enormous contribution to Canberra. Lady Gertrude Denman, who announced the name of Australia's new federal capital city, Canberra, on 12 March 1913 was not simply "the wife of the Governor-General". 'Trudie' Denman was one of the first professional women to make a mark on Canberra. She was a staunch advocate for women's right, a businesswoman, a sporting enthusiast and a patron of the arts.

Over the past century Canberra has been home to countless inspirational women - activists, artists, academics, politicians, sportswomen and entrepreneurs.

Women such as Rosemary Follett, the ACT's first Chief Minister and the first woman to lead an Australian State or Territory; Sylvia Curley who tended to the people of Canberra through her long and distinguished nursing career; Indigenous leaders including Matilda House-Williams whose story is featured in this book and Aunty Agnes Shea, who has made an enormous contribution to the health and social equity of Indigenous peoples in the region.

As a city recognised for its world-class tertiary institutions, we have been home to eminent academics such as the ANU's Hanna Neumann, the university's first female professor, and radiologist Gwen Pinner, one of the founders of John James Memorial Hospital. Internationally renowned artists such as sculptor Jan Brown and poet Rosemary Dobson have also developed their craft in the ACT.

These are just a few of the remarkable women who have left a legacy of achievement of which all Canberrans can be proud.

However, it's not just our inspirational leaders, our eminent academics, or our gifted artists that have made Canberra what it is today.

It is also about the unsung heroes. Those who don't necessarily receive notoriety or public accolade but who have been instrumental in developing and nurturing the social and spiritual side of our city. In particular, it's the tens of thousands of volunteers who give back to the community in so many different ways, many of whom are women.

In telling the stories of Matilda House-Williams, Helen Reddy, Geraldine Cox, Natasha Stott Despoja, Fiona Wood and Lauren Jackson, *Inspiring Australian Women* portrays the strength, passion and commitment of Australian women. Dr Spurling's subjects all epitomise individuals who have demonstrated a genuine desire to make our world a better place.

I hope you enjoy reading these stories and that you find these women as inspiring as I have.

Katy Gallagher MLA
Chief Minister

Contents

Introduction

Each of us needs inspiration, it powers us along, keeps us from dwelling on the insignificant and encourages us to believe we can do better, achieve more, be happier. Hopefully this is not entirely egocentric, not merely translating into bigger and better for oneself, but results also in giving something back to society.

Like every woman, I have spent countless hours in doctors' and dentists' waiting rooms and at hairdressers flicking through magazines. Unfortunately they appear eerily similar – a strange mixture of diets and food recipes. But mostly it is the focus I find uncomfortable. Not just the sensationalism and embellishment but who is touted as worthy of attention and pushed forward as role models. Reality is the first victim when glamorous, self-absorbed pop and film stars are constantly lauded. And of course it is only the extremes of behaviour which are publicised. Most women feel enormous pressure to juggle family life with a successful career; to be always perfectly groomed and don't forget "thin" and "sexy".

A 2008 United Kingdom survey showed there was "an unhealthy obsession with celebrity culture" which was "damaging the academic success" of students.[1] Teenagers were ignoring long-term and tangible career aspirations to pursue fame. Sports and pop stars were the people they wished to emulate; the emphasis was on "me" and "now". The media fixation on reality television and celebrities had, according to that survey, resulted in teenagers wishing "to be famous for being famous". British students most aspired to be like David and Victoria Beckham. American heiress and socialite Paris Hilton was close behind in the most admired stakes.[2] Apparently in Britain: "Paris Hilton coming out of jail interrupted coverage of fighting in Iraq".[3]

Another British survey in 2012 reported: "A lack of positive female role models is damaging the future prospects of girls and young women". The study of girls aged between seven and 21 revealed that "many use reality television and celebrities as a blueprint for how they should live their lives".[4] Around 55 per cent of the girls and young women surveyed believed there was a lack of strong inspirational women. In this pre-Olympics study:

> Many of those interviewed struggled to name a single female sports star, even in the run up to the London 2012 Olympic Games, but could name several singers and actresses.[5]

I have been unable to find similar surveys of Australian teenagers and we are left to ponder if Australian results would be similar. Given the popularity of reality television, television music and talent contests, and social media, it is likely results would not be very different. The media focus here as in the UK tends towards sensationalism and negativity – a world of 60 second media bites which offers the shallowest of impressions. It was ill-informed popular primary source material and the dearth of inspirational women in that media which encouraged me to commence this book in 2008.

Australia can boast amazing women; they could fill many books. Many have been neglected by academics, authors and journalists because they are not deemed powerful enough, they are not public enough and sadly because they may not fit the stereotype accorded "woman". Pre-eminent historian and Harvard University professor, Laurel Thatcher Ulrich, said "well-behaved women seldom make history".[6] It is an opinion which has started many a debate on "what is woman?".

One of the most interesting questions one can ask is "whom do you see as inspiring?" and, "if you could talk to one Australian woman who would it be?". In the first stage of my research I received some fascinating answers, and plenty of "there are so many women out there who don't make headlines". There were quite a few "I saw this documentary on … can't remember her name but she was amazing". It was one of these statements which dropped me feet first into this book. An email came with the forgotten name from that earlier conversation with a friend and although she rarely visited Australia, Dr Catherine Hamlin was going to be in Canberra the very next week, giving a lecture at Canberra Girls' Grammar School to raise funds for her hospital and midwifery school.

I contacted the Hamlin Fistula Relief and Aid Fund and asked if I could interview Catherine during her short stay. She agreed. This gracious lady had a wonderful and uplifting story. Catherine and her late husband Reginald gave up a comfortable Sydney lifestyle and potentially lucrative careers as gynaecologist obstetricians in 1959, to devote their lives to helping the most damaged women of Ethiopia. After perfecting corrective fistula surgery, the Hamlins, with the help of charitable donations, set up a hospital to treat women who had previously gone untreated and were forced to live isolated from their families. The poorest of women would walk for days to arrive at the hospital, desperate for a cure to a problem caused by pregnancy, childbirth and lack of medical care. When I spoke with Catherine the then 84-year-old was exceedingly modest; she wondered why I thought her "special"?

She stretched out her hands and said: "My hands do not shake so I can still operate". Her gentle manner and the words "if only I had more time and energy, there are so many women who need help, who need the operation", provided the motivation I needed.

I listened spell-bound to her presentation. Catherine looked frail but I remember walking very lightly back to my car knowing I had been in the company of a giant. She was totally inspiring and I realised this book should celebrate six Australian women, only six, to allow for in-depth examinations of their lives.

Unfortunately the lack of further opportunity to interview Catherine in ensuing years meant I was unable to continue her chapter. It was pleasing that the book *Catherine's Gift: Inside the World of Dr Catherine Hamlin* was published in 2008,[7] adding to Catherine's own 2004 best-selling book *The Hospital by the River: A Story of Hope*.[8] Catherine has been described as a modern day "Mother Teresa"; she has been the recipient of many awards including, in 2009, the Right Livelihood Award, also called the "Alternate Nobel Prize". She was among the 50 prominent Australians invited by the Governor-General of Australia, the Hon Quentin Bryce, to have lunch with Queen Elizabeth II and the Duke of Edinburgh, Prince Phillip, at Government House, Australia, on 23 October 2011, to mark the Queen's Golden Jubilee. On 24 January 2013, Dr Catherine Hamlin, AC, turned 89. She continues to live in Ethiopia.

I was nonetheless still spoilt for choice for this book, and I hope studies of the lives of Matilda House-Williams, Helen Reddy, Geraldine Cox, Natasha Stott Despoja, Fiona Wood and Lauren Jackson, will not only demonstrate their exceptional qualities but enable an exploration of life in Australia now and in the past; and what it is to be an Australian woman overseas. I make no apology for preferring to write about inspiring women who give back to society. Catherine's influence also was responsible for the idea that each woman featured would nominate a charity or other non-profit organisation of her choice; and a portion of the proceeds of this book will go to charity.

Matilda House-Williams was separated from her parents and grew up on an Aboriginal reserve named "Hollywood". There was absolutely nothing fanciful or glamorous about this "Hollywood". When she believed it could not get worse it did, and she was sent to the infamous Parramatta Girls Home. Matilda was a survivor. Most of all she is "a proud Aboriginal woman". Her upbringing and that pride propelled her into public affairs. She knew the opportunities for her children and grandchildren needed to be much better and the nightmares fewer. She knew she had to say what had to be said. On 12 February 2008, indigenous elder, Matilda House, wearing a possum skin coat, walked barefoot into the Great Hall of Australia's Parliament House. She proceeded to give a traditional "Welcome to country" to a new prime minister, the hundreds of others who filled the hall, and the many more on the parliamentary lawns outside.

To examine the life of Matilda House means a journey into the bleak history of Aboriginal women; to what it was to be discriminated against, dispossessed and abused. For me her chapter resulted in a personal apology. As Matilda is fond of saying: "Our nation is marked by great success and honourable deeds, and some not so, some made right and some yet to be made right" but together we can forge "a united Australia" assuming we are "so committed to succeeding that we will not be denied". Spending time with Matilda House is challenging, definitely inspiring, and a lot of fun.

Contact with Helen Reddy meant the words of her song "I Am Woman" quickly danced back from the nether regions of my brain; that song was a call to arms for a generation of women. I wasn't sure what sort of chapter would emerge from interviews with a singer best known in the 1960s and 1970s. Helen's story led me in a direction I never envisaged. It was the story of women born in the 1940s who pushed against the social resistance preventing them from being who they truly were. Helen just went about it in a louder, more melodic, more colourful manner than most of us. Now she is a member of one of the most invisible in our society, post-menopausal women. But Helen Reddy has no intention of assuming that stereotype either.

Cambodia is a world apart from life in suburban Adelaide. It is a journey Geraldine Cox took many years ago. Geraldine is larger than life. She questioned the values and beliefs of her conservative

Australian upbringing. When she broke free and joined the Department of Foreign Affairs in the 1960s she found there also a female stereotype she did not fit. Geraldine continued to beat against walls and challenge everything. She admits she took everything to dangerous extremes. Geraldine finally decided that the country of her birth and the role she was supposed to assume were no longer part of her future. Her heart was stolen by another land and particularly its children. She founded an orphanage in Cambodia, and then two and now three Sunrise children's villages. Geraldine is "Big Mum" to around 400 children. She fights to safeguard them and the Sunrise villages from everything from military coup to natural disaster. Geraldine believes she would not have been awarded her Australia Medal had her autobiography come out before the investiture rather than a week later. No one has deserved it more. In 2009 she faced another battle, a very personal one, breast cancer. Geraldine may not be quite as big a "Big Mum" today, but her spirit is undiminished.

Politicians are not favourites of the Australian people. But there have been many who have served the public to the best of their ability and who truly believe in what they do and whom they represent. Natasha Stott Despoja was one such politician. No other politician introduced more legislation or was behind more debate in a dozen years on issues which directly affected women and families. No one championed education more. The trouble was that few Australians were privy to this. Few Australians read Hansard. We are dependent on the mass media for our information and that media fails us. Natasha was usually written about because of her age, gender and dress – not for her commitment to Australians or for her legislature. My first interview with Natasha took place as she approached retirement from politics in mid–2008 and she and I both struggled to comprehend all that she had undertaken. Later contact occurred as she eased herself into a post-politics life as wife and mother to two small children. But the fire to work for the community still burns.

Professor Fiona Wood hurtled into the media forefront following a shocking event in the aftermath of "9/11". She went on to be named Australian of the Year. For years in a row she was the "Most Trusted Australian". In 2012 she remained the most trusted woman but was beaten for the most trusted Australian title by Dr Charlie Teo, AM. In typical fashion Fiona telephoned Charlie Teo and said: "I am glad it was you". Fiona finds it all bewildering really; she just thinks she is "ordinary". Clearly Australians think otherwise. I expected Fiona's chapter would take me into the post "9/11" world and some icky medical bits. She took me much further. I journeyed to the blackness of a Yorkshire pit, learnt a great deal about Quakerism, discovered the barriers facing the first women medical practitioners and surgeons, travelled into the worst misadventures of fellow Australians; and yes I learnt a great deal more than I needed to know about skin. All these contributed to the making of Fiona Wood. She is anchored by a wonderful sense of humour and six children. I also discovered more about adversity and the human spirit. I totally disagreed with Fiona – she is not "ordinary".

Lauren Jackson is simply the best of the best at what she does – basketball. Australia is a country where sport is a religion, but only sport played by men. Women's sport is found in the inner regions of the sports pages, if at all. It makes for less than 3 per cent of Australian sports media coverage. It is not that Australian sportswomen are not good enough. Olympics history alone confirms that they have consistently outshone their male counterparts. Their achievements are deemed secondary because "women" are not supposed to be physical, to show the competitive and physical aggression required to excel at sport. Lauren Jackson is the best in the world, Most Valuable Player (MVP) of Australia, the United States, Asia and Europe, yet she is commonly delegated by her country's media behind male footballers, even those who play a code only played in this country. And the neglect is not confined to Australia. Lauren has won MVP of the

United States' Women's National Basketball Association (WNBA), the only non-American player to do so.

She has won this award not once, but three times, but the maximum she earns in a US season is around $98,000 (USD). The top players in the men's competition earn in the vicinity of ten million USD. I followed Lauren through the course of her non-stop 2008 and struggled to keep up as the ensuing years and her achievements sped by. I am amazed at what she means to thousands of people. Lauren Jackson personifies the best qualities of an Australian, is a wonderful role model and attempts to use this for the betterment of others.

The life journey undertaken by each of these Australian women is as inspiring and fascinating as it was challenging for me to keep pace with. I can but hope that my words have done them justice. But at least if a picture can paint a thousand words this book speaks volumes through the insightful portraits by Margaret Hadfield (Zorgdrager).

1. *The Canberra Times*, 14 March 2008.
2. ibid.
3. *www.timeshighereducation.co.uk*
4. *News UK, BBC*, 11 May 2012.
5. www.bbc.co.uk/news/uk-18033198
6. Ulrich, Laurel Thatcher. *Well- Behaved Women Seldom Make History*, Vintage, 2008.
7. Little, John. *Catherine's Gift: Inside the World of Dr Catherine Hamlin*, Pan Macmillan, 2008.
8. Hamlin, Catherine. *The Hospital by the River: A Story of Hope*, Monarch, 2004.

15

Matilda House

Her opening statement says a lot about Matilda House-Williams: "I'm a tough little bugger, I always have been ... and a very proud Aboriginal woman", and because her heritage and extended family is her essence she is quick to add:

> Of the Ngambri Ngunnawal Wiradjuri people; of the country of my great grandfather "Black Harry" Williams, and the daughter of Pearly Simpson-Williams a Ngunnawal-speaking woman of the Wallabalooa people.

I was sitting next to Matilda House-Williams at barbeque at the Artists Shed, Queanbeyan, New South Wales. Friends were amused that mosquitoes were winging their way past them to alight on the Ngambri elder and me. We were not amused and traded insect repellent. One blood-laden mosquito sluggishly left Matilda's arm to land on mine and I had no qualms in destroying this life form. Matilda congratulated me, laughed out loud and said "we have the same blood, sister". I laughed also. Our heritage could not have been more different, nor the genes we carried, but yes, the mosquito had not discriminated. And I was complimented by the carefree comment.

When I first asked Matilda if I might include her in my book I detected uncertainty. I had watched the Ngambri elder bravely offer a "Welcome to Country" at the opening of the 42nd Parliament on 12 February 2008. She was the first Indigenous Australian to be so asked – a poor reflection on Australia and our governments. Matilda was guarded. As I grew to know her better, learnt more of her life and those of her people, I understood – Matilda was a survivor and the layer of reserve was derived from self-preservation. I could never truly appreciate her life as hard as I tried. My grandmother spoke of the "gins" who did her housework and who helped care for my father when he was a baby. She was the wife of the bank manager in Normanton in far north Queensland. She was a tireless worker for the Presbyterian Women's Association which raised money to separate Aboriginal children from their mothers so the children "could be given a proper Christian upbringing". Like most non-Indigenous Australians I considered the 2008 "Welcome to Country" and the apology which followed and struggled with the paradox: could I be proud of my forebears without endorsing their beliefs and actions? Should those of us of British ancestry suffer discomfort when we face our history? I understood this dilemma at a very personal level. Clearly the questions needed to be answered; perhaps, they were unanswerable.

Previously the pomp and circumstance inherited from another nation was closely observed but protocol had changed for this the 42nd Parliament. A large audience filled the imposing marble surrounds of the Great Hall of Parliament House and a new prime minister stood awaiting Aboriginal elder Matilda House. With the haunting tones of a didgeridoo heralding her entrance the Ngambri woman approached slowly. She wore a full length possum coat, the out-turned orange collar bearing the artwork of her people. Two grandchildren accompanied her. They represented another generation – one who it was hoped would face greater opportunities and fewer nightmares. One carried a message stick and this was presented to Prime Minister Kevin Rudd. The elder commenced the "Welcome to Country". Her words and those spoken the following day, a day which would be known as "Sorry Day", were intended to bridge a chasm within a nation.

"I would like to welcome you to the land of my ancestors, the land of the Ngambri people." Matilda's voice faltered slightly;

perhaps it was nerves and for that she could be forgiven because never before had an Aboriginal woman or man spoken in front of such an assembly. The Ngambri people believe their ancestral land, this place now called the Australian Capital Territory, is in the shape of a woman. Mount Ainslie and Black Mountain are the breasts. The land another civilisation chose for the nation's Parliament House rests in the womb. Few Australians realise this. It is disappointing that this belief was not appreciated when white men in stiff starched collars and heavy suits settled on the site for their capital. It was a shame they did not consult those whose traditional land this was. It would have been a most fitting rationale for the siting of Canberra rather than the jealousies of opposing officialdom in Sydney and Melbourne making it necessary to settle on neutral ground between the two major cities.

"Welcome to today's ceremony in this great building that houses the Australian Parliament", Matilda continued graciously on that summer's day in 2008. The silence was profound. Hundreds of people were gathered for this momentous event. Those unable to find seating or standing room inside hovered outside in the Canberra morning sunshine. Matilda looked up and it was as if all were as nervous as she. "And like all houses, it leaks." Before she could explain there was much exhaling of nervous breath and a ripple of laughter. Matilda was chuckling herself; "I won't say no more about that" – more laughter. "I mean the water", she delivered with consummate timing. It was vintage Matilda House Williams. Matilda would never miss an opportunity for humour based on where she was or to whom she spoke, be they parliamentarians or members of the 600 nations of Australian Aboriginal people. She never misses an opportunity to say it how it is. Her laughter was infectious and the stilted atmosphere simply dissolved. This meeting place of Australia's elected representatives "has been known to my people as a meeting place for thousands of years". Matilda spoke of how at the opening of the original Parliament

House in 1927, an elderly Aboriginal, barefoot and wearing his only suit – a worn, frayed garment – was denied entry. The police moved Billy Clements on because his appearance offended the sensibilities of the gathered dignitaries. He was reluctant, this was his ancestral land, but they did not agree. Matilda now stood barefoot and in ceremonial dress and acknowledged that she was honoured and welcome.

> Our nation is marked by great success and honourable deeds, and some not so, some made right and some yet to be made right, like tomorrow's apology.

The Ngambri elder spoke of the great pride she felt for Aboriginal and Torres Strait Islanders, and acknowledged the importance of the day's ceremony. She spoke about how this Prime Minister had shown:

> proper respect to us, to his fellow parliamentarians, and to all Australians. A welcome to country acknowledges our people, it pays respect to our ancestors, the spirits who created the lands. This then allows safe passage to all visitors. For thousands of years our peoples have observed this protocol. It is a good and honest and decent and very human act to reach out to make sure everyone has a place and is welcome. On behalf of the first people of this land, Prime Minister, I now return this honour. On this occasion of the opening of the first parliament of the new Australian Government I welcome you the elected representatives of every part of this nation. I acknowledge the trust given to you by all Australians to represent our interests, to make wise and just decisions and to honour the ancestors in whose footsteps you will follow. With this welcome comes a great symbolism, the

hope of a united nation through reconciliation. We can join together the people of the oldest living culture in the world with others who have come from all over the globe and who continue to come. And together forging a united Australia, so committed to succeeding that we will not be denied.

The message stick was a tangible symbol of the day's ceremony. The message stick was the means of communication of the Aboriginal people. This one bore the hope and pride of the original inhabitants of the nation and "like our ancestors we can reach new heights soaring on the wings of the eagle", Matilda concluded.

The Ngambri elder invited Prime Minister Kevin Rudd and the Leader of the Opposition, Dr Brendon Nelson, to remove her possum skin cloak and replace it on her shoulders with the inside facing outwards. Ceremonial cloaks have a drawing of the country of the Aboriginal tribe inside so this was of great significance because Matilda was inviting everyone that day to be part of the Ngambri people. Decades earlier this tribal elder would never have believed that she would stand here in front of the highest authorities in the nation and this ceremony, her address, beamed by media across the length and breadth of Australia. Decades earlier Matilda House was simply intent on surviving.

Matilda House was born in 1945 on Erambie, an Aboriginal reserve on the fringe of the New South Wales country town Cowra. One of ten children, she was sent to her grandfather's house on the Hollywood Aboriginal Reserve in the Yass precincts. There was absolutely nothing fanciful or glamorous about this "Hollywood" but Matilda was settled and life seemed normal. She remembers the mission attempts to "Christianise" her. Sunday school attendance indelibly imprinted a song:

"Hear them pennies dropping, dropping one by one, they are all for Jesus he needs them every one." It went on and on about how he needed these pennies and I wasn't sure who needed the pennies most, him or us.

Later in life Matilda could laugh about such memories but it was puzzling at the time for an Aboriginal child trying to make sense of it all. "Those pennies" recalls Matilda, "were helping the Inland Mission and other religious groups separate Aboriginal children from their families".

Matilda as child (front) with Aunty Violet Freeman
at Hollywood Aboriginal Reserve, Yass circa 1952.
Courtesy Matilda House-Williams

The reserve was dismantled in 1959 and she was returned to her parents and Cowra. Times were not easy for the large family and Matilda was strong-willed, a trait not well received in mainstream Australian society when exhibited by an Aboriginal girl. Matilda was proud of her heritage, of her great grandfather, "Black Harry" Williams, also known as Ngoobra, of the Walgalu people, and her grandfather, Harry Williams. As far as she was concerned she "had a really wonderful father" but it was perhaps her female role models, her mother, grandmothers and aunties, who made the largest impression and that was to have pride in oneself and one's abilities. Matilda saw nothing she should be ashamed of. Her grandmother

Louise Wedge Simpson took her to Cowra infants school, because her granddaughter needed to be educated to succeed in this Australia. "She, my mother's mother, was the sassiest woman I have known." On that day the grandmother and slip of a girl who walked with her were turned away. Her grandmother did not understand so she took Matilda to the Salvation Army and asked if they would let her granddaughter enrol. It was pointed out that the Salvation Army was not a public school. "We did not know any different." The grandmother who had watched her own culture destroyed just knew Matilda needed to be educated. Matilda was finally accepted to Cowra public school but the experience was not entirely productive, the fundamental beliefs of educators of the day meant the system failed those who needed it most. Matilda says only that "Cowra was a racist town, as all towns were ... and still are. How many Aboriginal faces do you see in the Country Women's Association, or town councils?". Clearly some memories are indelibly marked and Matilda knows she speaks of more than just her own experience.

> I was sent home all the time because they said I had lice
> in my hair. I didn't and it was sad for my parents because
> I didn't. We would stop at the cattleyards all day and
> when school got out we would then go home to spare
> our parents the embarrassment. I would go to my aunty's
> and ask her to check my hair. If Mum treated my hair,
> just in case, she would put metholated spirits mixed with
> vinegar and kerosene through my hair. Can you imagine
> that running through your scalp, and she would be doing
> it with a smoke in her mouth [laugh] and I didn't have
> lice anyways. Sometimes we wouldn't even go to school.
> We would just go to the sale yards and stay with the
> sheep and cattle all day rather than be sent home again
> for lice we didn't have and upset our parents. None of

the non-Aboriginal children were ever sent home for that. We were treated as unclean.

Matilda recalls another instance of bitter disappointment to her as a young girl. Matilda liked athletics and she was good at it. In grade six she was having a good day at the school athletics championship. She won every race she entered. Another pupil had come second in every event. She said to Matilda "'Can I please win just something?'. I said 'I am in the broad jump next, see how you go there'. Matilda won that event also. The next day Matilda went to school assembly in great anticipation. Her parents would be so delighted when she returned this day with the best all-round athlete trophy. "I couldn't believe it they gave it to the one who kept coming second to me." The best athlete trophy went to a non-Aboriginal pupil.

> I was so dejected, rejected and didn't really want to go home to tell my parents I did not win the trophy. That was my first real taste of racism in sport.

Such a disappointment left its mark and the indignation bubbled to the surface. Matilda removed copper from the school bubblers and sold it to the scrap iron merchants. The family ate better for a few days.

Matilda became increasingly rebellious, rarely backed down and refused to defer to white authority. Matilda found herself bundled off to the infamous Parramatta Girls Home. She was twelve and she had crossed the white mission manager once too often.

> I was reported time and time [again] to the manager for being a rough kid, and also – in my life – I had been sexually assaulted. The manager thought that the best thing to do with girls like myself was being sent away.[1]

Her parents, Doug and Pearl, were powerless to intervene. The manager threatened them with the removal of all their children. Matilda was taken by the police and thrown into jail where she was left for nearly a week before being sent to Parramatta. Matilda reflects:

> I guess that's where the stolen generations came in for other kids too. But for me, I wasn't stolen, I was just sent ... I was uncontrollable, so I had to go away.

Matilda knew she was a survivor, but there were moments of doubt.

Parramatta Girls Home was a respectable name for an institution which was anything but respectable. It was a prison. Thousands of girls between twelve and eighteen were sent to "Parramatta" because they were deemed "in moral danger". This was open to interpretation. They may have been truly criminal; they may have been guilty of truancy; but they may also have been guilty of being high-spirited and less inclined to fit the mould society deemed theirs. Some came from dysfunctional families; commonly they came from poor families. Many would spend their teenage years there. Matilda House spent 15 months at "Parramatta". By the 1960s sentences were usually six to nine months.[2] The girls were addressed by their numbers not their names. "I was 47" Matilda remembers all too clearly. The first period was spent in isolation, no visitors, no one to speak to, no showers.

> They let you out for um, a shower, to go to the toilet. And sometimes, you know, you just can't hold on ... it was very bad.

It was bad enough for white inmates, but for an Aboriginal such confinement was worse, not being able to see the blueness of the sky, feel the dirt beneath your feet and the wind on your face. This introduction was to make girls aware of the consequences of non-conformity. When released to the company of other girls surveillance was constant, the threat of punishment for the least infringement unwavering. Domestic duties, particularly scrubbing floors, were endless. Solitary confinement was a regular feature of "Parramatta" life. A girl would remain alone, barefoot, dressed in a hessian smock and fed only bread and water. It was enough to break even Matilda's spirit – almost:

> I learnt very quickly ... learnt very, very, quickly to toe the line because if you didn't, if you didn't do that you would end up back where, in a little cell where you wouldn't be able to see anybody, detention for a week or a couple of weeks, and um, not much food to eat, and all your letters would be kept from you.[3]

Sexual and psychological abuse and emotional neglect were commonplace. On arrival a girl was subjected to a physical examination to determine if she was a virgin. Those who were would invariably not remain so. Some guards took advantage of the situation and were far more criminal than those they were responsible for. Girls were told not to bother informing anyone of abuse because they were already "bad" and no one would believe them.[4]

Matilda was kept going by the letters her father wrote. It was "just so beautiful to get a letter from him, mind you my father wrote to me all the time". The spark would return and she would find herself again in trouble, like the time she tried to tell a cooking class teacher how to make gravy, "you know blackfella gravy, chuck everything in it". She had already had difficulty with the cooking teacher.

She was very, very, English and she used to teach us how
to make gooseberry pie, gooseberry! I had never seen a
f.... gooseberry in my life.

Matilda was left to stand for a day outside the manager's office, to
rue the likely consequences of her candour, knowing she was "going
to cop it". The most common punishment:

was to be hit with a whole bunch of keys over the head,
you know, or the shoulders. And I'm talking about keys,
big bunches of them ... I'd never been belted before in my
life, before Parramatta.

On this occasion she was sent to polish the hall floor. It was large this
floor:

probably as big as the mural hall at Parliament House. I
had to do that all by myself, so I was up for quite a long
time polishing.

When the guards weren't looking a couple of other girls quietly
joined in. That is the only comforting memory, the friendships born
out of adversity.

She missed her family tremendously and it was one of the reasons
she was forever getting into trouble. It was hard for them to come so
far to visit her. Only once did her father receive permission from the
mission manager to make the long trek. And that was so he could tell
his daughter her grandfather had died. It was difficult to keep the fury
in check.

I had these little black marks against me for the entire
time I was there because I was always against the grain,

and seeing some of the atrocities that happened [at "Parramatta"].

If you survived "Parramatta" the nightmare and the stigma remained. Matilda still feels the sense of shame attached to being a "Parramatta girl". Recollection of that 15 months of misery, what this proud Ngambri woman still refers to as a "terrible" time, can still reduce her to:

a crying fool, always trying to forget, but you can't. I feel like it's travelled with me. And whenever something happened, I felt 'Oh God – it's probably because I went to Parramatta' – it has travelled with me and it will travel with me until the day I die.[5]

"Welcome to Country" Parliament House 2008,
with Prime Minister Kevin Rudd and Minister Jenny Macklin.
Courtesy Matilda House-Williams

It travelled with her, on 12 February 2008, when she stood in Parliament House. She was too intent on the occasion, on her speech, to realise she had truly defied her past, she had triumphed over "Parramatta".

The Australian Prime Minister answered her "Welcome to Country" with the comment:

> It's taken 41 parliaments to get here ... We can be a bit slow sometimes, but we got here. When it comes to parliaments of the future, this will become part and parcel of the fabric of our celebration of Australia in all of its unity and all of its diversity.

The following day the first action of the second sitting day of the 42nd Parliament of Australia was "the apology". The House of Representatives chamber and Great Hall were filled to capacity. In the roped-off section for distinguished visitors off to the Speaker's right, sat four previous Australian Prime Ministers: Gough Whitlam, Malcolm Fraser, Bob Hawke and Paul Keating. The nation's previous PM, John Howard, was not present. Unusually the public galleries held a great many black faces, faces weathered by time and emotion. Their eyes were not dry long. Nor were those of millions of Australians who listened to this historic speech. Prime Minister Rudd solemnly commenced:

> Today we honour the Indigenous peoples of this land, the oldest continuing cultures in human history. We reflect on their past mistreatment. We reflect in particular on the mistreatment of those who were Stolen Generations – this blemished chapter in our nation's history. The time has now come for the nation to turn a new page in Australia's history by righting the wrongs of the past and so moving forward with confidence to the future. We apologise

for the laws and policies of successive Parliaments and governments that have inflicted profound grief, suffering and loss on these our fellow Australians. We apologise especially for the removal of Aboriginal and Torres Strait Islander children from their families, their communities and their country. For the pain, suffering and hurt of these Stolen Generations, their descendants and for their families left behind, we say sorry. To the mothers and the fathers, the brothers and the sisters, for the breaking up of families and communities, we say sorry. And for the indignity and degradation thus inflicted on a proud people and a proud culture, we say sorry. We the Parliament of Australia respectfully request that this apology be received in the spirit in which it is offered as part of the healing of the nation. For the future we take heart; resolving that this new page in the history of our great continent can now be written. We today take this first step by acknowledging the past and laying claim to a future that embraces all Australians. A future where this Parliament resolves that the injustices of the past must never, never happen again. A future where we harness the determination of all Australians, Indigenous and Non-Indigenous, to close the gap that lies between us in life expectancy, educational achievement and economic opportunity. A future where we embrace the possibility of new solutions to enduring problems where old approaches have failed. A future based on mutual respect, mutual resolve and mutual responsibility. A future where all Australians, whatever their origins, are truly equal partners, with equal opportunities and with an equal stake in shaping the next chapter in the history of this great country, Australia.[6]

At 9.28pm Mr Rudd finished the 360-word address. It had taken 220 years and just four minutes and three seconds to apologise for the "profound grief, suffering and loss" inflicted on the Indigenous people. There was a standing and sustained ovation. All MPs stood except for the Liberal MP Chris Pearce. Liberal MPs Wilson Tuckey, Alby Schultz, Don Randall and Sophie Mirabella chose not to be present. In the public galleries and Great Hall people rose to their feet and looked to the Indigenous Australians who represented the "stolen generations" and the applause was prolonged. On the lawns of Parliament House the thousands assembled cheered, and Australian and Aboriginal flags filled the sky. Faces were streaked with tears but most wore smiles. The Prime Minister spoke for them when he said that the time was long overdue to remove a "stain from the soul of Australia".

> The time has come, well and truly come ... for all Australians, those who are Indigenous and those who are not to come together, truly reconcile and together build a truly great nation.

It was hoped the apology would usher in a new era of reconciliation between Indigenous and Non-Indigenous Australia. It was a statement of regret more than ten years after the story of "the stolen generations" had appeared in the Bringing Them Home report. Opposition Leader Brendan Nelson rose and offered his party's response. He apologised for the removal of Aboriginal children but also highlighted the previous Liberal Government's Northern Territory's Aboriginal intervention policy and the possible need to remove more Aboriginal children from their families. He admitted the horrors rendered by previous governments and their agencies upon the Indigenous people, yet indicated this was due to the best intentions:

We formally offer an apology to those Aboriginal people forcibly removed from their families through the first seven decades of the 20th century. In doing so, we reach from within ourselves to our past, those whose lives connect us to it and in deep understanding of its importance to our future. We will be at our best today – and every day – if we pause to place ourselves in the shoes of others, imbued with the imaginative capacity to see this issue through their eyes with decency and respect. This chapter in our nation's history is emblematic of much of the relationship between Indigenous and Non-Indigenous Australians from the arrival of the First Fleet in 1788. It is one of two cultures; one ancient, proud and celebrating its deep bond with this land for some 50,000 years. The other, no less proud, arrived here with little more than visionary hope deeply rooted in gritty determination to build an Australian nation; not only for its early settlers and Indigenous peoples, but those who would increasingly come from all parts of the world. Whether Australian by birth or immigration, each one of us has a duty to understand and respect what has been done in our name. In most cases we do so with great pride, but occasionally shame ... We cannot from the comfort of the 21st century begin to imagine what they overcame – Indigenous and non-Indigenous – to give us what we have and make us who we are. We do know though that language, disease, ignorance, good intentions, basic human prejudices, and a cultural and technological chasm combined to deliver a harshness exceeded only by the land over which each sought to prevail ... Our generation does not own these actions, nor should it feel guilt for what was done in many, but not all cases, with the best of intentions. But in saying we are sorry – and deeply so – we remind ourselves that each generation lives in ignorance of the long term consequences of its decisions and actions. Even when motivated by inherent humanity and decency to reach out to the dispossessed in extreme adversity, our actions can have unintended outcomes. As such, many decent Australians are hurt by accusations of theft in relation to their good intentions. Theirs was a mesh of values enshrined in God, King and Country and the belief in something greater than yourself. Neglectful indifference to all they achieved while seeing their actions in the separations only, through the values of our comfortable, modern Australia, will be to diminish ourselves.[7]

Australians considered the words spoken. The debate caused division in the "big house" and in smaller houses throughout the nation. "The apology" divided families and friends.

It is the Australia Day long weekend 2009 and the sun is golden as it drops below the horizon. Artist Margaret Hadfield-Zorgdrager has just finished painting Matilda House for the Archibald Art Prize. The painting is amazing. It has Matilda looking defiant and majestic in the full length possum skin coat she wore at the "Welcome to Country" ceremony which opened the 2008 Parliament. Matilda is relaxed now. She loved the painting, particularly her favourite grass trees and her totem the eagle soaring above. That is where it needs to be she tells us it must be higher than her head, the spirit and the eagle. Margaret has painted the soft tones of Lake George in the background, the grass, the sky – no water there in 2009. Of course Matilda and the Ngambri people know it as Weereewaa.

Artist Margaret Hadfield (Zorgdrager) and Matilda
Photograph by Kathryn Spurling

Discussion is about the day we are supposedly here to celebrate. What is it we celebrate on 26 January? Is it really "Australia Day" or is it "Invasion Day"? Can we justify "Australia Day" to commemorate 1788 when a fleet of English ships arrived in Botany Bay to start a colony? Perhaps 1 January 1901 has a more correct claim for a celebration of nationalism because it was 1901 that the colonies became the Commonwealth of Australia?

British settlers swept aside millions of Indigenous people as they painted the map of the world pink. In other lands settled by the British treaties were made with original inhabitants. In Australia there was no such treaty attempt, just dispossession. Resistance was met with violent retaliation. It is believed that in 1788 there were between 750,000 and one million Aborigines. By 1911 that population had diminished to 31,000.[8] The white moral proprietorship of the land and accompanying treatment of the Indigenous population was mostly based on belief of destiny and righteousness – conquer, expand and subjugate the "weaker" by the "stronger" in the name of racial superiority. Based on social Darwinism its basis lay in a biological interpretation which was then strengthened by governance. Missions like that which my grandmother supported played a large role in the colonisation of Australia. Missionaries may have checked some behavioural excesses but they also condemned the Aboriginal belief system and lifestyle. Their zeal to assimilate Indigenous Australians further separated Aboriginals from their quintessence.

Elements of paternalism compounded the myopic view of those in charge of "Aboriginal Affairs". Aboriginal Protection Acts were passed by all Australian states by 1912. These permitted the removal and institutionalisation of Aboriginal children. Institutionalised life and the life in "white service" were bleak. By 1937 it was decided "full blood" or "tribal" Aborigines "were destined to become extinct".[9] 1939 legislation meant Aboriginal children were placed under the Child Welfare Act – different legislation, same separation and dispossession. It was a dark and gloomy labyrinth from which escape was rare. Legislation empowered authorities to remove children from their families and the removal of families from reserves. Wives were removed from their husbands and husbands from their wives. Indigenous Australians were sent hundreds of miles away from their tribal country. At the core of Aboriginal life was the strong extended family network and their dogged determination to remain one with their land, but in the late 1940s Australian officialdom was not listening. In 1951 Australia was embarrassed by the United Nations affirmation insisting on unity of the human species and the cessation of the use of race as a category. The Australian Government was left no option but to remove words like "Aboriginal" and "half caste" from legislation so in 1953 Indigenous Australians became "wards". The new term which emerged over the next period of time was "assimilation"; it meant the same, nothing had really changed and the outlook was still bleak.

Attempts to "assimilate" Aboriginal Australians were accelerated. This was not entirely due to racism but part of a national social programme which encompassed the whole population. Australia became increasingly conservative following World War II. The family unit of breadwinner husband and suburban wife and children dominated and those in authority believed unfailingly that it was fundamental to the prosperity of the country. Of course this was "white" and middle class. Aborigines were seen as being lesser beings and there was no real thought that they would rise to being better than that. The best that could be done was that they could be tamed and domesticated. Children forced into service in white homes were deprived of their Aboriginal identity. Realising they were not "white" they struggled to comprehend who they were.

Australia had become a Commonwealth in 1901. The following year the vote was given to Australian women, at least white Australian women. It would be 60 more years before the Australian Constitution was altered to allow Indigenous Australians to vote in federal elections. Matilda remembers: "My hero was Jessie Street, she tried so hard to get rights for Indigenous people". States still classified "natives" as "wards of the state" in 1962 which made them ineligible to vote in state elections. Not until 1965 did the last state, Queensland, repeal legislation which prevented this most important civil liberty. In 1971 the Liberal Party nominated Neville Bonner to fill their vacant seat in the Senate. He was the first Aborigine to sit in any Australian parliament. Following the election of a new Labor Government the following year, a wave of reform began to alter the welfare and affairs of Aboriginal and Torres Strait Islanders. It was long overdue and Australia finally began to admit the horrors committed.

The dates, legislation and opinions from another culture impacted dramatically on Indigenous Australians like Matilda House. She was living the history and struggling to limit its affect on her family and her people. Matilda considers herself one of the lucky ones insofar as she was not one of the "stolen generations", although growing up she knew those who were. Surviving life in white Australia was never easy particularly if you were someone like

Matilda. "I was always against the grain, I knew when things were right and when things were wrong." Having survived "Parramatta" she was put into service, working for a white family as a domestic. She was "kept" and given a small salary.

> It was hard work, there were five or six kids. I had to make sure they were looked after and everyone was fed. I was the cook for the shearers as well.

Matilda paused:

> You know there is no sense dwelling on those sort of things. At the end of the day it made me into what I am today I suppose.

Another pause and then with a laugh: "a mongrel". Life during the 1960s was downright difficult. For mainstream Australian society these were the boom years, and Australia the land of milk and honey. But not for Indigenous Australians. Matilda toiled in market gardens and did seasonal fruit picking in Young, "hard labour, I can assure you". Matilda doesn't dwell on the bad, she likes to look at the positive but her reticence bears its own message.

Her inborn sense of justice continued to be frustrated by the dominant culture of her land and blatant discrimination. Things were slow to improve but Matilda was encouraged by actions being taken by Indigenous groups throughout the country. In the Northern Territory in 1966 Aboriginal Gurindji stockmen from Wave Hill Station began a protracted campaign against station owner British beef baron Lord Vesty for better pay and conditions. Their cause spread and grew into a fight for land rights. Injustices were brought to light on the lawns of Old Parliament House as Indigenous Australians established their "tent embassy".

Matilda was struggling with domestic duties, with the care of her four children, the responsibility for her younger brothers and sisters as well as the care of her aging father. She would have it no other way. But the spirit was still there and her voice was being heard. By the mid 1970s she had established Aboriginal Legal Services in the Canberra region. She began to work as a social worker with the Department of Aboriginal Affairs. By the 1980s and 1990s there were more triumphs.

This Ngambri elder would never forget her excitement on 3 June 1992 when the High Court delivered the landmark "Mabo" decision, which rewrote the common law of the nation by accepting that the country's Indigenous people had possession of land before colonisation. The "Mabo" case dealt with the Murray Islands in the eastern part of the Torres Strait. The Meriam people, led by Eddie Koiki Mabo, challenged the terra nullius doctrine which declared that when Captain Cook "discovered" Australia in 1788 it was an empty and uncivilised land. Following the "Mabo" decision Aboriginal land councils throughout Australia lobbied for legislation to protect native title that had survived 200 years of colonisation. Argument was made for Aboriginal people whose native title had long since extinguished. It was a year of emotive debate as the pastoral and mining industries argued for the "Mabo" decision to be overturned. In December 1993, Matilda House stood on the steps of the High Court of Australia while judges within gave a positive ruling on native title. The Native Title Act then passed through the Federal Parliament making the "Mabo" decision law and native title claims possible. Matilda returned to those High Court steps and danced with "Gladys my Wik sister following the Wik decision". The Wik people of Cape York in Queensland claimed native title could coexist with current pastoral leases. The court agreed. Pastoralists had an exclusive right to pasture but not exclusive possession of the land. The Wik decision recognised native title rights on pastoral leases, leases which covered 42 per cent of the

Australian land mass. It was one more important step. Gradually, ever so slowly, governments began to lean towards mechanisms which allowed some degree of Indigenous self-determination. At times it seemed like there were more steps backward than forward. Then there would be another victory and, no matter how small, it was enough to keep Matilda going, the fire within burning. Her extended family depended on her, her people needed her, and Matilda would never shirk those responsibilities. In 2006 she was named the Australian Capital Territory's (ACT) Citizen of the Year for "her contribution to the ACT community, especially indigenous affairs".

Matilda found it personally rewarding to look back on all those small issues, small triumphs, the building blocks which benefited more than herself. Not that the triumphs were not accompanied in almost equal amounts by dissonance.

No matter how hard you work and you get up there to wherever 'there' is, you are open to criticism. There is a lot of jealousy whatever life you are in and what good you have done in the past does not get acknowledged. Because I speak my own mind some people are intimidated.

The critics are not confined to white Australia. Whilst Matilda was pleased to see an invigorated Indigenous presence on the wider Australian stage she believed there are some who lack an understanding of how it was. She had seen too many real atrocities in her time not to firmly believe an understanding of history was a prerequisite to an understanding of now. Too many of those who "dole out the criticism", too many of those "who rant and rave these days", truly comprehend how life was before getting the hard-fought for mechanisms of support that now exist.

A lot of good things are happening but there are a lot of disgruntled people around saying 'this government isn't doing things for us right'; but years ago they said the same things and them days there really were no structures in place. Canberra, the Federal Government, was not in charge.

A classic instance of this occurred at the Aboriginal tent embassy. The "embassy" has been controversial for many. White Australians mistakenly see Indigenous Australians as one group. Indigenous Australians see more than 600 different lingual groups, groups which also involve different clans. A "mob" arrived from interstate to squat at the embassy. They were on land traditionally seen as Ngambri. There has been confusion over the true name of this land – Ngunnawal or Ngambri. Matilda explained that the former is a language and Ngambri is the name of the people. The confusion is directly attributed to Dr Norman Barnett Tindale. Tindale collected and collated data relating to tribal boundaries. He wished to prove that Indigenous Australians were linked by culture, language and kinship. His research culminated in the 1974 map and catalogue, Aboriginal tribes of Australia, their terrain, environmental controls, distribution, limits, and proper names. This was widely accepted in academic Australia. But it seems he got it wrong, "he called a lot of places after the languages". Matilda paused for a moment before adding with the characteristic chuckle:

He was an entomologist, this guy was a moth catcher and here he was parading himself around saying where Aboriginal people's country was. Aboriginal people should take a stand if they want to find out who they really are and no one should tell them how to go about

it or do it. I am not a Tindale black gin, I am a proud
Ngambri woman.

It is 28 September 2010 and the decorative mosaic forecourt of
Parliament House is crowded. Matilda House-Williams is conducting
a smoking ceremony to welcome the 43rd Federal Parliament. This
day lacked some of the pomp and ceremony witnessed with the
opening of the 42nd Australian Parliament when Matilda conducted
the first "Welcome to Country". In 2010 the election campaign had
been particularly bitter and resulted in the first hung parliament in
70 years, but it was perhaps a more democratic parliament which
emerged – with the Labor Government achieving majority with the
support of three independents and a member of the Australian Greens;
and Australia's first elected woman Prime Minister, Julia Gillard. The
sound of Indigenous music heralded Matilda's approach. During the
first smoking ceremony under parliament's standing orders, Matilda
invited parliamentarians to walk through the smoke of the smouldering
fire: "Please move forward and get a cleansing. It helps". Matilda
acknowledged the newly elected member for Hasluck, Western
Australia, Ken Wyatt, the first Aboriginal elected to the House of
Representatives. Matilda had seen so much in her life, lived through
so much of her nation's history as an Indigenous Australian. Perhaps
she had a premonition as to what would unfold, what was unfolding,
as she said what she believed to be paramount:

> The hope of a united, reconciled nation, the oldest living
> culture joined with the many diverse cultures of a modern,
> successful Australia.

The ensuing years would result in little unity, within the parliament,
within the governing party, within the Aboriginal community. Within
16 months Matilda would speak out against Indigenous Australians

who threatened not only unity but who threatened the physical safety of Prime Minister Julia Gillard and the Leader of the Opposition, Tony Abbott.

On Australia Day 2012 an ugly scene erupted at a restaurant adjacent to the Aboriginal tent embassy on the foreground of old Parliament House. The Prime Minister and Leader of the Opposition were at the Australia Day celebration, some Indigenous Australians were commemorating the 40th anniversary of the Aboriginal tent embassy, a few hundred metres away. It was a poor planning to conduct a major Australia Day affair in such proximity. The more volatile tent embassy supporters moved to the restaurant to protest the presence of the Australian opposition leader who earlier that day had suggested that the need for a tent embassy was over. The situation escalated and resulted in the hasty extraction of Julia Gillard and Tony Abbott by security. Whilst it was a minority who displayed unnecessary aggressive behaviour some within the media inflamed the situation by publishing front-page headlines such as: "Sorry Day" over a photograph of the PM being whisked into her car, and the sub-heading: "Fury as PM attacked by her countrymen on Australia Day".[10]

This tent embassy is on the land of her ancestors and Ngambri elder Matilda expressed her concerns. Protesters had shown disrespect to local elders by failing to share their concerns and grievances.

> If you've got no respect for your elders, why would you have any respect for anything else. They're always talking about respectability, protocols and leadership. But that went out the window.

Forty years ago she had paid her respects to those first Aboriginals: Michael Anderson, Billy Craigie, Tony Coorey and Bertie Williams, "heroes" Matilda calls them, who erected an umbrella outside

Parliament House, who "planted themselves beneath it" and refused to leave until land rights were addressed. Matilda believed that that while visiting Indigenous people had a right to visit the Aboriginal tent embassy, "to have their say, to stand up and fight for Aboriginal communities" she was weary of those who continued "to curse and complain" but who willingly accepted government fortnightly pension payments. Matilda condemned the burning of the Australian flag.

> It defeats progress; you're not a hero for burning the Australian flag. How many Aboriginal men and women went to war and fought under the flag?

Matilda reiterated that those with little appreciation of Aboriginal protest and history – individuals who had little or no first-hand familiarity with what had gone before – were endangering hard-won progress and threatening unity between Indigenous and Non-Indigenous Australians.

> All them young people who brought their families with them, how do you think they'll feel when they have to go back to where they come from and the racism starts then?

Matilda felt what occurred on Australian Day 2012 had undermined the integrity of the tent embassy. She also now questioned the relevance of the tent embassy in its present form. Matilda wanted the embassy to play a more educational role – to provide the community with proper information about the Aboriginal protest movement and their struggle for recognition. The tent embassy should offer a "proper understanding of protocols and the proper understanding of our identity", because currently, "buses will pull up and sometimes people get told the wrong story".

The word "unity" remains at the forefront of our discussion in autumn 2013 as Matilda repeats her concerns. Australia has moved forward with the recognition of the rights of the first Australians such as policies of self-determination, land rights, native title and the stolen generations apology. The Ngambri elder believes some within the Aboriginal community are pushing too hard, they are wrongly focussed on individual advancement rather than what is best for their people; everything should be about the family and the community.

> Nobody's united these days. We worked so hard and have become so powerful in our own ways, but you get the do-gooder middle- class blacks and you get the down and outers. Even top academic Aborigines they're doing their jobs but I don't see them out in the communities doing anything, Government-funded meetings are the only time you will see them out there and them days are gone, we are not going forward united and happy.

Photograph by Margaret Hadfield (Zorgdrager)

At 30 June 2011, the estimated Australian Indigenous population was 575,552. There continues to be a clear relationship between the social inequalities experienced by Indigenous people and their current health status. According to the report, Overview of Australian *Indigenous health status, 2011*:

> This social disadvantage, directly related to dispossession and characterised by poverty and powerlessness, is reflected in measures of education, employment, and income.[11]

Matilda House knows well how precarious Indigenous welfare is, how much more is urgently needed to improve the health of her people. Matilda is struggling with diabetes. Diabetes is a major problem within the Australian population but more than three times more common among Indigenous than non-Indigenous Australians – particularly type two – and Aboriginals are also liable to suffer from diabetes at younger ages. Other problems disturb her: substance abuse, deaths in custody and her "heart aches" with the teenage suicides.

Matilda pauses on this autumn day in 2013 and as the shadows lengthen outside she continues our conversation, accentuating how important it is for Aboriginal elders to support and encourage younger generations to stay at school so they can avail themselves of opportunities not opened to previous generations that "many Aboriginal kids have, a lot more must". Most Australian Capital Territory residents are unlikely to experience the emotions which accompany having a relative locked up in the Alexander Maconochie Centre, but commonly one fifth of male prisoners jailed are Aboriginal though the Aboriginal community makes up less than 2 per cent of the territory's population.[12] The imprisonment of Indigenous Australians living in the ACT is thirteen times higher than the general population. Roughly 14 per cent of those doing hard time identify themselves as

Aboriginal and Torres Strait Islander. It is 23 years since the findings of the Royal Commission into Aboriginal Deaths in Custody was released yet the number of incarcerated Aboriginals continues to rise. Matilda is angered by the lack of progress in reducing the number of her people incarcerated. The Aboriginal experience needs to be considered more in the court and sentencing processes and Matilda believes more money needs to be spent on alcohol and drug education and rehabilitation programmes. There is a failure on the part of government on "how that money is being spent, those things could be run better". It is this which the Ngambri elder believes is the crux of the lack of progress – this, and a misunderstanding surrounding the diversity within Aboriginal Australia.

> Governments still treat you the same … it will never be where white people think it should be because you are dealing with Aboriginal people from many cultures with different laws. As soon as white people understand that we will get somewhere. White people still set the agenda for Aboriginal people. While governments and councils set the agenda for Aboriginal people you will have blacks running around cursing and cussing and then they will say 'we give you everything and you still can't make good of it'. There needs to be better reconciliation.

The time for unruly loud protest has gone but governments have become bogged down in red tape and paper. Matilda says there is too much talk, too many committees, too many enquiries and too many reports. Aboriginal rates of infant mortality, disease, incarceration and unemployment remain too high, yet too much money is spent on consultants, on committee members; too many improvements have been delayed because they are stuck in committee for what seems forever. Aboriginal assistance needs to be much more "pro-active"

Prior to 1967 the Australian Constitution specifically excluded Aboriginal and Torres Strait Islander people from recognition and forbade the Commonwealth from making laws regarding "the Aboriginal race in any state". Thankfully the 1967 referendum removed this exclusion. In 2010 the Australian Government began an investigative process to amend the Australian Constitution, to remove racist provisions and acknowledge the relationship Aboriginal and Torres Strait Islanders have with our country. A 22 member panel produced a 300 page report recommending a referendum to amend the Constitution. It concluded that sections 25 and 51 be removed and a new section 51A recognise that the continent and its islands now known as Australia "were first occupied by Aboriginal and Torres Strait Islander peoples". It would acknowledge that there was a continuing relationship between Aboriginal and Torres Strait Islander peoples and "their traditional lands and waters", and respect given to "the continuing cultures, languages and heritage of Aboriginal and Torres Strait Islander peoples".[13] The report also recommended that the Constitution acknowledge "the need to secure the advancement of Aboriginal and Torres Strait Islander peoples". A new section 116A would prohibit the Commonwealth, states or territories from creating laws that discriminated on the grounds of race, colour, ethnic or national origin, although this amendment would not preclude laws and measures to overcome disadvantage or "ameliorating the effects of past discrimination, or protecting the cultures, languages or heritage of any group". A new 127A section would provide for the recognition that Aboriginal and Torres Strait Islander languages were "the original Australian languages, a part of our national heritage".[14] On 13 February 2013 the Australian Parliament voted in favour of the Act of Recognition which committed Australia to amending the Constitution at the next election by way of a referendum.

Amending the Australian Constitution has not been easy, with only eight successful referendums of the 44 held. In 1999 an attempt to insert a preamble into the Constitution to recognise Aboriginal and Torres Strait Islanders failed in every state. Matilda House is cautious. Whilst she agrees in principle she is concerned Australia is not yet ready for such progressive amendments. Matilda hopes she is proven wrong but is not confident the referendum will be successful, "we are not united and more time is needed to build support". Should the referendum not pass this elder feels there could be adverse repercussions.

I take Matilda back to the opening of Parliament in 2008 and ask if that was a life's highlight. She quickly enlightens me:

> No, the highlight of my life was having four beautiful kids and grandkids, being an auntie to all my beautiful nieces and nephews, and being a big sister. Anyways the opening of Parliament was something that was for all Aboriginal and Torres Strait Islanders.

Yes, she did get nervous standing waiting in the wings as her son Paul preceded her playing the didgeridoo. And then:

> I just felt the most marvellous feeling that you could ever have of triumph. I thought what the hell am I doing standing here? You know all the things that happened to me, all the terrible times ago which flashed through my mind and I was thinking I just can't believe this and then of course all that terrible stuff went right away because I didn't want any of those thoughts spoiling that day. Of course I had very fond thoughts of my parents and grandparents who would have been very proud of me as well as my aunties. If only; but in my heart in a spiritual way my ancestors were there for me.

Matilda felt their presence, the presence of her ancestors, of the ancestors of so many Indigenous Australians and savoured that sensation. "For the first time in Australia, they the original landowners were truly recognised."

The Ngambri elder takes her responsibilities seriously and some days the phone does not stop. Matilda encourages advocacy, she must extinguish disagreements and clarify misunderstandings, promote reconciliation rather than alienation – all with a confidence borne from truly knowing who she is and being comfortable with that. Her immediate family and the extended family of her people is the essence of this life. Matilda gestures to the photo which takes pride of place in her home – of a grandson lost. Matilda has twelve grandchildren and "two and a half great grandchildren", but continues to mourn this grandson who died seven years ago. Her hope for family is:

> I want them to come together as well, some families are torn apart. I want to see families come together like they were years ago without interference, that is what I am hoping for everybody. Being the matriarch I have always advocated the best or what I thought was the best for my family, but you stumble, you fall, you know … I just want the grandchildren to know they are always loved and no matter what happens in the past I did the best to make a better life for them.

"Welcome to Country" has been a confronting chapter to write and this had nothing to do with the person I interviewed. I visit an acquaintance and the television is on. There is a quiz programme, some bloke could win a million dollars if he gets all the questions right. A question is asked: "When did all women in Australia receive the right to vote in Commonwealth elections?" I pray the correct answer, 1962, is given, but that date is not even listed in the four choices. The contestant falters. The compere triumphantly tells the bloke in the opposite seat the correct answer is 1902. I then recall my question to Matilda: "How can things change?" "Through education" was the rapid response. She continued:

Look at you; if you still had the attitude your grandmother had you would not be here talking to me – education. And you keep on fighting. I say to myself 'they may win the war but I will win a few battles'.

The Ngambri elder is correct but one cannot evade another question: doesn't the war need to be over?

www.wwf.org *and* **www.amnesty.org.au**

---

1.   Stateline (Cbr), ABC, 28 January 2009.

2.   *The Australian*, 19 March 2007.

3.   Stateline (Cbr), ABC, 28 January 2009.

4.   *Sydney Morning Herald*, 14 October 2003.

5.   Stateline (Cbr), ABC, 28 January 2009.

6.   *http://australia.gov.au/about-australia/our-country/our-people/apology-to-australias-indigenous-peoples*

7.   *Sydney Morning Herald*, 13 February 2008.

8.   Moses, A.Dirk. "Genocide and Settler Society in Australian History", in Moses, A.Dirk (ed) *Genocide and Settler Society: Frontier Violence and Stolen Indigenous Children in Australian History*, New York, 2004, p.18.

9.   Moses, p.219.

10. *Herald Sun*, 27 January 2012.

11. Thomson N, MacRae A, Brankovich J, Burns J, Catto M, Gray C, Levitan L, Maling C, Potter C, Ride K , Stumpers S, Urquhart B (2012). Overview of Australian Indigenous Health Status, 2011. Retrieved [access date] from *http://www.healthinfonet.ecu.edu.au/health-facts/overviews*

12. 5183 Aboriginal and Torres Strait Islanders live in the ACT though one in three were under fifteen years of age.

13. Papers on Parliament No. 57, "Constitutional Recognition of Indigenous Australia" February 2012, *www.aph.gov.au*

14. ibid.

50

Helen Reddy

"The phrase 'I am strong, I am invincible, I am woman' just kept going over and over in my head."

Helen Reddy did not realise the significance of the words she scribbled down. She had strongly believed from a very early age that "women were not getting a fair go"; she felt there was the need for a song which resonated with women, which expressed the frustration nursed by many women in 1973. Her lyrics and that song were a massive hit, with Helen Reddy becoming the first Australian to have a No.1 hit in the United States and win a Grammy award. She added fuel to the fire when in her acceptance speech she thanked God "Because She is responsible for everything". The United Nations chose "I am Woman" as the anthem for International Women's Year 1975. Some would say those words, that song, changed people's lives.

It is 2008 and Helen Reddy sits in her sun-drenched unit. Over her shoulder lies Sydney Harbour at its most splendid. She fits perfectly in this scene, at home in Australia's largest city; at ease in the company of the ghosts of generations of kin folk, descended from one who sailed into this sparkling magnificent harbour with the first fleet in 1788. As with the layers of those generations Helen Reddy has many layers, she defies simple one dimensional definition; she continues to evolve and heaven help anyone who attempts to define her by her past. Anyone who wishes to restrict Helen Reddy to the 1960s and 1970s, to not honour who she is in the 21st century is in for a testing time, as I was to discover.

I was confident, I had researched exhaustively. I had consumed Helen's memoir *The Woman I Am*[1]. I had re-familiarised myself with the music and now the melodies and lyrics of: "I am Woman", "I Don't

Know How To Love Him", "You and Me Against the World", "Angie Baby", "Ruby Red Dress", "Crazy Love" and "I Can't Say Goodbye to You". They clutter my brain, playing over and over, returning me to an era I wasn't entirely sure I wished to revisit. The 1960s and 1970s were enlightening but highlighted a scary, deep misogyny. And I was already digressing. I travel to the 13th floor; that should have been another warning – that the subject of my chapter would be unconcerned to live on the thirteenth floor. When I walked into that sun-drenched harbourside unit I quickly realised that I was not the only one who had little desire to revisit a life already lived and that I was not prepared at all.

Helen Reddy was born in Melbourne on 25 October 1941 to Stella Lamond and Max Reddy. Her country was at war and these were precarious times. Within months Australians would realise the gravity of the situation as the Japanese shadow rapidly lengthened southwards and the comfortable lifestyle enjoyed for so long was under threat. Being born into such a perilous period in Australian history could be reason enough for a person to be restless and have a predisposition to living in the present. Helen's parents were entertainers, busy in vaudeville. For much of her impressionable years they lived out of boxes, constantly unsettled, constantly moving from show to show around the country. This was certainly reason enough to be restless. It was not that she felt unloved but soon she realised that sleeping on the top of your father's stage trunk was not something most children did. She absorbed the term "them and us". "Us" was show people, "them" was everyone else and "they could never understand 'our' world". First memories include a typical toddler demand for attention referred to by some as "obstinacy" and "tenacity" by others. It was quickly evident from the earliest age this girl would not back down from a battle.

I continue blithely on my way, seeking insights, confirmation of my research, and realising I am going to have to weave more than I anticipated into the story. It is not that Helen is being difficult, she is warm and friendly. There is a smile in the corners of her mouth and a twinkle in her eyes but the voice I hear is mostly my own. Max Reddy joined the war effort as a sergeant in the Entertainment Unit and was sent to New Guinea. Helen has memories of him in uniform. Most Australians seemed to be in uniform, most of the men were overseas. It was left to the women of Australia to adjust to unfamiliar roles and not only keep the home fires burning but the nation running. This was an era of unprecedented women power for women, not that Helen Reddy was of an age to fully appreciate that, but she quickly became aware of the strong female role models who filled her world – like her paternal grandmother and her Aunty Nell. Nanna Reddy offered the unconditional love only a grandmother could and she showed great strength of character. Like so many of her generation of the "weaker sex" she kept the family and household going through the Depression and two wars. Warm and self-sacrificing, she represented an age group of women with few options and pleasures.

Aunty Nell was the eldest sister of Max Reddy and was also named Helen. It was not only because of the name that an affinity was immediate. "Nell and baby Helen bonded from the word go, and were as close as mother and child. Actually they were closer than Stella and Helen" recalled Toni Lamond.[2] The older Helen was part of the cohort of women who became victims of world events and family duties. The Australian male population was decimated in a war which was supposed to end all wars. Per head of population only New Zealand suffered more casualties than Australia amongst the Allies in World War I. One consequence was a generation and a half of Australian women with poor marriage prospects in an era when women were expected to marry. There was also the expectation that the eldest daughter became carer and companion to a mother who commonly outlived her husband. It was a prison of sorts which came with the social label of "spinster". "Spinster" was a distinctly female term and conjured up someone with little personal freedom and happiness, women who would never have the opportunity to discover who they truly were or what they were capable of. The companion male label of "bachelor" was defined in an entirely different way. But if "spinsters" or "maiden aunts" were victims and sad people, Helen's Aunty Nell defied such characterisation and it was this which would leave the most lasting impression on her niece. Nell accepted the care of her mother. She was pivotal in keeping the family together, but she also maintained a successful career as a secretary. It would take a little more time before Helen transcended her typical youthful self-absorbed needs and she could truly appreciate her mother's life struggle. In 2008 Helen articulates the regret:

> My mother was very beaten down emotionally but she
> kept going. I look back ... wouldn't we all like to look
> back with the knowledge we have now. I was insensitive
> to her as a female.

Stella Lamond was a divorcee with a seven year old daughter, Toni, when such was frowned upon. It made little difference to a besotted Max Reddy and he married the lady. Three years later along came Helen. From this melting pot of women and Australian culture Helen Reddy would evolve into the woman she became.

In her earliest years Helen spent minimal time in the company of children and consequently believed herself to be a "small powerless adult rather than a child". In 1946 she made her entertainment debut. Max and Stella were appearing at Perth's Tivoli Theatre. In a pretty peach-coloured, smocked dress, the Reddy five-year-old, looking three, sang a song about babies. She was such a huge success she became a regular on the show. The precocious youngster thrived on the attention and was bitten by the showbiz bug. But even at this age Helen was bothered by a comedy emphasis which degraded women, what she would many years later articulate as "sexist" and "the exploitation of women".

The post-World War II years were popularly depicted as a wonderful time but for many they were repressive. During the war Australian women were yanked abruptly from family duties and shoved into entirely new and demanding domains. They donned uniforms to assume duties with the nation's defence forces for the first time. They dressed in boiler suits, took up tools and joined factory assembly lines. They entered occupations previously ordained as too tough, too dirty, too masculine, and they excelled. They gained good incomes, huge responsibilities, and their confidence levels soared. Following the war social diversity was nullified. An Australian culture wedded to conservative gender roles shunted women folk back into homes. The language changed, femininity was re-accentuated – the stiletto and frilly dresses replaced boiler suits. The wartime media depiction of uniformed and "Rosie the Riveter" womanhood was obliterated. In its place appeared the dichotomy of woman as the seductress Marilyn Monroe type, and the smiling cake-baking wife and mother. For some women the transformation was acceptable, but others struggled. The younger generations who had witnessed the freedom of diversity and spread their wings grappled with the curtailment, but their society, their culture, was overpowering. They harboured a restlessness and resentment which would manifest itself later in the minds and voices of their daughters.

There was little accent on academia in the Lamond-Reddy showbiz household. Both Stella and Max had left school at age twelve, but with the law now mandating that children attend school between six and fourteen there was no alternative but to have Helen halt her life on the road. Aunt Nell recommended Melbourne's Tintern Church of England Girls Grammar School and so it was that in February 1948 Helen's life took a turn for what she later realised was for the better. For the first time there would be routine, a "traditional value system", and the much appreciated opportunity to gain a solid academic foundation. There were advantages to being educated in an all-girl school. You were encouraged to do well, to be your own person. Helen says: "You weren't inhibited by the boys that was the main thing for me, because if there was a boy in the room I wouldn't have opened my mouth". She learnt quickly and books became her escape from a home life accentuated by parents who lost themselves in alcohol and argument. Max Reddy, like so many uniformed heroes who survived the war, found surviving peace emotionally challenging. Its routine, its banality, proved no substitute for the life lived on the edge, and a disappointment.

I continue to tread heavily through Helen Reddy's life, offering quotes for further comment, seeking confirmation. As we have learnt to dismiss much of what journalists choose to write I quickly deduce that published "facts" about Helen leave much to be desired. Helen adds: "I have read in a book that I am 5ft 8inches, have red hair and green eyes". Clearly there is no red hair and green eyes, can we at least get the height right?. "I have shrunk. At the height of my loveliness I was 5ft 3 ¾ inches." The conversation swerves to that perennial concern of women, weight, or at least the pre-occupation our society has with overweight women and the guilt that people of our sex are made to feel. Helen is scathing of the diet industry, of their use of the word "lose". "Our brains are hard wired to succeed and the diet industry knows this and that is why they use the word 'lose'." Helen prefers the word "light", the term "I am lighter". We empathise about chocolate. Helen admits to being a chocoholic:

> I know I am because I use what we refer to in psychology as 'addictive logic'. If someone gives me a box of chocolates I eat them as quickly as I can so they won't be around to tempt me.

Helen has studied psychology and is a clinical hypnotherapist but I was hoping to get to that later. Then with a chuckle she adds:

> I can't give the chocolates away because they have been given to me in friendship so I just have to eat the lot.

This is quickly followed by the question "Can we discuss Hillary Clinton and the American political process?". There are so many layers to Helen Reddy and I am struggling to put them in the correct order as historians are chronically prone to do. Again I wonder how I will form a chapter from where the interview is taking me, given my subject wishes to discuss the "now" more than the "then".

The word "alcohol" takes pre-eminence and clearly jangles a nerve. The Lamond-Reddy parents were not unusual in this regard. Australian culture never appeared to condemn those who imbibed freely; indeed much of Australian culture encouraged it, glorified it. But the children of those who sought freedom from their demons and life's shortcomings through drink suffered emotionally and Helen freely admits that alcohol dominated her family life.

In the pre-television days wireless was popular. Radio work was the Reddy household bread and butter although the stage may have been the preferred medium. From a very young age Helen was surrounded by actors, many of whom were American. They seemed so confident and sophisticated and this perception was further encouraged through visits to cinemas where Hollywood reigned supreme. Musical extravaganzas dominated the movies and it all seemed so very glamorous and important. Helen dreamed of going to America. She had showbiz in her blood and the indoctrination was ongoing. Helen's first piano lesson came at age nine. She had a natural flair and quickly picked up popular music tunes, at least when well away from her teacher and the only acceptable teaching genre, classical. Her mother was her first singing coach. Stella emphasised the uniqueness of the human voice and how powerful this wonderful instrument was as a social and cultural purveyor. It was a message absorbed but partly lost on someone very young. The power of lyrics would in time be put to the test and, yes, Stella Lamond was right.

Australia was again influenced by other nations to commit to another conflict deemed necessary for the freedom of mankind. This time it was democracy versus communism. With the outbreak of hostilities in Korea, Max Reddy returned to uniform and the Entertainment Unit. He formed a versatile six-person troupe which included Stella and they travelled to Korea and Japan to entertain troops. Helen moved in with Nanna Reddy and Aunty Nell.

It may have been because she was the daughter of entertainers who seemed never happier than when they were performing away from home that Helen sought a fundamental prop. To fill the void left by a dysfunctional family life she turned to religion. "I was fanatical … My dream was to become a missionary." By the time she was eleven she had thought better of that ambition. Intelligence and free thinking did not sit well with the rigid teaching of the church and Helen realised she was, after all, "an atheist". Helen laughs: "I was told 'if you are a missionary you won't be able to wear lipstick' and that was the end of that". But a particular incident had confused and reassured her in her quest for understanding. In school assembly one day around the time the hymn was sung Helen fainted. With absolute clarity she observed herself lying on the floor below. It was eerie, but calming too. When she regained consciousness she knew she dared not tell anyone lest they think her crazy. She could not discuss this out-of-body experience yet. It nonetheless left her with "no fear of death, nor doubt of eternal life" and questions she would explore later in life.

After six fulfilling and wonderfully settled years at Tintern, Helen needed to change schools. Tintern moved to a new campus further away from Nanna Reddy's home so the decision was made for Helen to become a pupil at Stratherne Presbyterian Girls School in the Melbourne suburb of Hawthorn. The initial jolt was softened by the fact that Stratherne had musical appreciation and drama included in its curriculum. Helen was delighted and also began tap and ballet classes on Saturday mornings. She never really had any ambition other than to enter the family business nor any doubt that she had the talent and perseverance to succeed. And she would get to the United States because if she made it in the US she would be an international star.

Then came a bump in the road – it was called puberty. Most young women struggled to understand the subtle and not so subtle physiological and psychological processes which ambushed them and left them wondering why their elders regarded it a "blossoming" when menstruation felt more like a "curse". For Helen too it was a little confusing initially. No longer could she sound cute singing about babies because her voice had altered. No longer was the sound the pure falsetto of a child; the sound was now deeper, even sultry. But radio was marvellous and mysterious, a case of sights not seen, of voices never matching the faces imagined, which meant the "sexy French maid" in a popular programme was in fact a 12-year-old schoolgirl.

Nanna Reddy died in May 1955. She had been a pillar of stability in her granddaughter's life. Being home alone after school was not considered a viable option for the teenager particularly after she was spied in the back alley kissing a local lad. So Helen became a boarder at Stratherne. It was not a happy experience. The chasm between life at a private Protestant girls school and life in showbiz was ever widening and Helen was getting restless.

These were exciting times in Australia. In 1956 the Olympic Games were held in Melbourne and the pride of the "land down under" was on show. Australian athletes were normally handicapped by lengthy travel and competing out of season in Olympics forever held in the northern hemisphere. Now they could finally be part of the most important of sporting events at home. And they excelled. It was impossible not to be enthralled by super athletes like Dawn Fraser and Betty Cuthbert, those referred to as Australia's "Golden Girls". Helen was delighted to have dinner with Dawn Fraser just before the 2004 Athens Olympics and believes there is a strong connection between athletes and entertainers and why they are glorified in modern society. These are after all professions "in which someone goes to work in order to play". Impetus generated by overseas Olympic interest brought television. The small black and white sets which gradually monopolised family time throughout the country had huge ramifications for the entertainment business and Helen's future. She just didn't know that yet.

At 15 she was finished with school and was accompanying her parents as they toured the nation's east coast cities and towns. Puberty still had a hold on the body, mind and heart. Her sister Toni Lamond was married to Frank Sheldon. They had a fifteen-month-old son, Tony, whom Helen adored. Her sister seemed to have it all, a career as an entertainer, a husband and baby. It seemed ideal – perhaps family life did not have to be dysfunctional. Women's magazines, the channel through which acceptable mores were siphoned, depicted the ideal in a very seductive manner. The message was all consuming: a woman could only find absolute satisfaction if she married and had children. The suburban plot with the house and white picket fence, the Hills Hoist in the backyard, a loving and good provider husband, and babies, were the only true path to fulfilment. Given her own upbringing Helen wanted desperately to believe this was true.

Helen was soon an official member of her parents "Follies" show, part of the "Follies Lovelies" troupe of dancing girls. She also filled in for just about any absent cast member and gained wonderful all encompassing showbiz training. At the time the teenager viewed it more as exploitation and desperately wanted out from under her parents' vigilance. The first opportunity arose with a job with a band performing at the well-regarded Chevron Hotel in Melbourne. Only in her wildest dreams could Helen imagine being a solo act. It was ambitious enough to believe she could make a living performing at nightclubs and cabarets. Helen had no desire to compete with other family members for entertainment gigs. She just knew she wanted to sing, she needed to sing.

Whilst touring with her parents and the "Follies" Helen had unresolved and disconcerting health problems. Her fevers and un-wellness disappeared as mysteriously as they appeared. But in 1959 Helen was hospitalised. She was very ill and surgeons removed an abscessed kidney. For a 17-year-old it was frightening but this teenager refused to be reduced to "victim". She intended to improve her voice and sing. And Max helped in his own inimitable manner. She couldn't work for six months and was then asked to sing on a television programme. There may have been a slight hesitation, then Max spoke of the daughter of his best mate, also a singer. "I just hope you will sing as well as ..." he started to say. His daughter indignantly interrupted: "I'm better than she is" and Max said "you are going to be alright". He knew all along exactly what he needed to say. "He was tremendous" remembers Helen with a smile.

In Australia in the first 50 years of the 20th century, women in the entertainment industry struggled from a social misconception. Unless you had a voice like Dame Nellie Melba, unless you sang opera, your voice, your craft, was awarded a somewhat dubious status and only marginally better support. Few women singers became household names. Radio enhanced opportunities but it was television which offered so much more. The popularity of Hollywood musicals flowed into the smaller screen. Variety programmes like the very popular Sing *Along With Mitch* (Miller) and *The Ed Sullivan Show* were platforms from which many a musical career was launched. And whether it was due to a different culture or simply the capacity and power of American support, Australian female vocalists found their careers assisted greatly by patronage from the US. Diana Trask was a performer Helen admired. Trask's career was given much deserved impetus by Frank Sinatra. Helen's career too received a boost when in December 1959 she was selected by the multi-talented American, Sammy Davis Jnr, as his opening act at the Melbourne Stadium. As television flourished in Australia home-grown popular music programmes like Bandstand meant new artists could not only be heard but seen.

"Max, Helen, Stella, Tony Sheldon and Toni Lamond.
Courtesy of Toni Lamond

But these were still the early days of television and the 18-year-old Helen Reddy needed to put in more really hard yards to be noticed. She decided to move to Sydney which offered greater live performance opportunities. Unlike Victoria (Vic) there were nearly a thousand clubs in New South Wales (NSW) supported by the Australian predilection for poker machines and flowing alcohol. In today's world of affordable and easy mobility and with technical support from internet and mobile phones, moving from Melbourne to Sydney is easy. In 1960 such an undertaking was a daunting major adventure. Helen had no family or friends and minimal logistic support: "I was being driven by determination and blind faith". She arrived in June and her first job was with the ABC, singing a duet with Peggy Mortimer. She realised she needed to break into the club scene to make a living. Agents did not represent entertainers, they represented clubs, so it meant a lot of shoe leather trudging from one office to another hoping the smile and enthusiasm and then perhaps the voice would make an impact. For a female vocalist it also helped if you were attractive. Without a car it was hard on the shoes. When the inevitable holes in the soles occurred Helen lined the shoes with cardboard. It was tough. She had envisioned glamour but found instead the money "was lousy" and the atmosphere was worse. Club patrons more intent on drinking, talking and gambling made for poor audiences. She believed in herself and in her talent and gradually she earned herself work in better clubs but it was still only subsistence and her dream of going to America seemed no closer. She became distracted by another dream, one which would prove much more elusive. Helen wanted more than anything to believe what her culture assured her would lead to complete fulfilment, her rightful place in domestic bliss. In the early sixties women were encouraged to marry early and have their babies before they turned 30, "while their eggs were still fresh".

Seven days into 1961, Helen married – the bride was 19 and the groom, Kenneth Weate, was 33 and it was a mismatch in more than age. Helen believed she had finally escaped her parents' legal jurisdiction but women had virtually no autonomy and she was now under the legal jurisdiction of her husband. Helen believed she had escaped a home life dominated by alcohol only to find the domestic bliss she dreamt of was dominated by the same. In the future she would realise it was inevitable, she would be able to make sense of it and articulate the why, but not now. Alcoholism had dominated generations of her family. She was bound to become involved with an alcoholic because she was "an enabler". "An enabler is a co-alcoholic … someone who kind of props the other up" Helen would understand later. In 1961 the dream shattered and marriage "turned out to be a lonely experience".

By 1962 she was back in Melbourne and pregnant. She needed to move out of her husband's flat when he became abusive.

> Once was enough … I'd seen my mother put up with that
> nonsense for years and I was not going to tolerate it.

She moved back in with Aunty Nell and there she stayed for the following year and a half. Traci was born in January 1963 and it was love at first sight. As soon as she was strong enough Helen returned to work singing at a hotel at which Max was doing comedy work. There was also work doing radio advertisements. Aunty Nell, ever dependable, proved a wonderful babysitter. It was a period of badly needed stability and consolidation, and Helen's belief and determination reasserted themselves. By the time Traci was walking Helen was restless again and knew she needed to follow the all pervading dream to succeed as a singer, and that still meant getting to the US.

The 1960s was an era of unheralded middle class prosperity, technological advancement and consumerism. Not only were television sets increasingly affordable but so too were transistor radios and better quality record players. A sound that emerged from a cellar in Liverpool reverberated around the world as The Beatles, and the flood gates opened. The baby boomer generation – youthful, and with disposable cash in their pockets – now dominated the music world. More and more popular music was needed as the market proved insatiable. New opportunities were opening and Helen realised she needed to move back to Sydney. With the Morris Minor her father had given her as a 21st birthday present loaded to bursting and with 16-month-old Traci strapped in a car seat next to her she headed north.

Over the ensuing months work was slow and in frustration Helen entered a talent competition being run by *Bandstand*. *Bandstand*'s popularity was huge. It dominated teenage viewing and a sizeable chunk of an older viewing public reluctant to admit they tuned in. Helen figured she had little to lose; at worst she would be seen and heard on *Bandstand*. First prize was a trip to the United States of America (USA) and a record contract opportunity. Second prize was an Australian recording contract. She needed to break into the big time music scene now, not only because this was her destiny but because she was supporting a child and at 23 she was already almost ancient. None of this seemed to help much with the nerves and the desperate search for the right songs and an engaging look. For six months Helen endured and now she was even more ancient, she had turned 24. But for six months she arose each morning, looked in the mirror and said: "Helen Reddy you are going to win that contest". In December 1965 she and twelve others out of an original 1,358 contestants, met in the Grand Final. Bedecked in a long white flowing gown, with three sets of false eye lashes weighing heavily on her lids and the big hair of the era enhanced with white flowers, she launched into her well rehearsed Petula Clark song Strangers and Lovers.

She rang her mother first and Stella's reaction said it all. Helen has a theory about parents' unfulfilled dreams, how they consciously or subconsciously carry over to their children – perhaps even later generations. "Sometimes one's heart simply feels what the other's heart has yearned for". The talented Stella Lamond had been offered the opportunity to go to America but circumstances had intervened. The regret of what might have been remained. Now her talented daughter was going for her. Helen says: "It's still one of the highlights of my life" – her Mum's reaction, and winning the competition.

Winning and going to the USA were indeed exciting. In April 1966 intercontinental travel was long, very long, and very expensive. Much of her prize money was needed to purchase a ticket for Traci. So with a three-year-old, two suitcases, a small amount of cash, enthusiasm and a liberal amount of trepidation, Helen tearfully kissed her parents and Aunty Nell goodbye, and set off for America. She had never lost sight of the dream of going to the United States and becoming an internationally acclaimed singer. Helen would need to cling tightly to that dream because she and the belief would be sorely tested.

The journey to New York seemed to go on for days and days, which of course it did in 1966. It was about as far around the globe as you could go before you started home again and that has never changed. It was also as removed in style and manner from Melbourne as anything could be. But encouragement came when she first turned on the television in her New York hotel room. She was greeted by the clear and lovely voice of Lana Cantrell appearing on Johnny Carson's *The Tonight Show*. It was a wonderful omen, another Aussie girl succeeding and blazing the trail for others. Helen's optimism was abundant when she marched in to the offices of *Mercury Records* to launch her recording career. She was out again in record time without even a hint of a contract.

> Absolutely nothing happened. Somebody from the sales department took me to lunch and said, 'Have a nice time while you're here in New York, dear. Don't forget to call us and say goodbye before you go back to Australia.' And that was that. There was no recording contract, there was no recording, there was nothing.

When Helen left Australia "I was not planning to come back" at least until her career was established. Now she was stranded in America with a toddler, very little money and no prospects. She assessed her bleak situation. The ambition still burnt brightly deep inside. "I always had a strong feeling that I was here for a purpose." Call it inspiration, determination, an almost unwavering belief in yourself and your destiny – where does it come from? Helen does not know the answer to that question but "when we confront our fears head on they usually disappear". The determination meant she would stay in America. She felt very strongly that "that was where I needed to be. I didn't feel that I had a future in Australian show business". There could be no turning back – she would become a singer known in the US and in the rest of the world. Had Helen known it would be five hard long years before her name would go up in lights, she may well have used the return ticket in her purse. That is the nature of dreams – they seem so fresh and attainable, always just a little way in the future.

Mercury Records did not even play Helen's tape sent from Australia by Bandstand. They were unimpressed when a female vocalist arrived. This was the era of boy bands and female vocalists were not the flavour of the decade. The Beatles, the Beach Boys, the Rolling Stones, the Doors, Jefferson Airplane, the Jackson Five, Creedence Clearwater Revival, the Byrds, Gary Puckett and the Union Gap, the Monkees, Steppenwolf, Tommy James and the Shondells, the Rascals, the Delfonics, Deep Purple, the Temptations, Cream and the Moody Blues – these artists saturated the charts. One all-female group resisted the complete domination but only just – the Supremes. Men ran radio stations and almost exclusively were the programmers and announcers. "They would say 'We are already playing a female record' – A Female Record!" There was not a lot of out-of-the box thinking: "A lot of people in this world don't want to make a decision but we are given free will for a reason" is Helen's appraisal.

Without a green card to work in the United States Helen immediately faced a dilemma. She needed to find work and quickly, she had a daughter to house and feed. She decided to sing for their supper in Canada and return as often as she could to the US to keep doing the rounds of the agents until someone finally gave her a break. It was hard knowing you had the talent, you had the determination. Why didn't others recognise what was so obvious? "I just never understood why it was so invisible to others."

That first 18 months were brutal, moving back and forth to wherever she could sing. One of the first places she worked was the *Three Rivers Inn* in Syracuse, New York. She was the opening act and there were twelve people in the audience. She played at some state fairs but couldn't afford an accompanist so she bought a guitar. She didn't know how to play the guitar so she would stand up on stage singing and moving her hands as if she did. Too few people were listening anyway. Traci was growing into an independent little girl and her life was just as unsettled as Helen's first years had been; there seemed no real alternative. Helen finally decided to make contact with an Australian journalist based in New York. Being so determined to stand on her own feet she had put it off, but the confidence was beginning to wane. Surrounded by Americans with their own language and customs Helen needed a friend and it would be good to have one who spoke Australian. Lillian Roxon was the breath of fresh air Helen needed and although the women were dissimilar in many ways Lillian "became my muse and my best friend". Lillian had a lot of contacts and some influence. She believed in Helen and life seemed brighter until the letter arrived from Australia.

The handwriting was her mother's but the contents concerned her sister. Helen's brother-in-law, Frank Sheldon, had committed suicide. It was a shock, her sister Toni's family seemed so ideal. With the blackness came the self-examination. She missed her family, she was barely making ends meet, and the work was unfulfilling. At her last nightclub she had an audience of one. She was almost 25. And then she met "him". Helen was still wary of men and marriage, but this bloke was amenable. "I hate booze" and he "was a non-drinker". The next man in her life needed to have a compatible career but not too compatible – "please not an actor" – preferably someone on the other side of the floodlights; he worked for an entertainment agency. He was attentive, unthreatened by this strong-willed Aussie girl and it took little time before Traci was calling him "Daddy". He was only 22 and still living with his mother in the Bronx. There were some warning signs but it was too easy to ignore them. In 1968 Helen married Jeff Wald and life and career entered a loving and lovely phase.

By spring that year the family was living in Chicago and Helen was singing in a revue. Some things were slow to change. Another female hired to share the stage had no experience, no talent, just "enormous breasts". Male comic accent of the period was very much "tit jokes". The other "performer" quickly realised she couldn't sing or act or dance and disappeared. "She took her breasts with her", recalls Helen and she smiles, "we are more than our breasts". Society was entering a troubled and disruptive era. The war in Vietnam was unsettling, creating dissension. Youth was defying a military draft. The voices of women and black Americans could no longer be stifled. The foundations of the status quo were beginning to quiver. These were particularly turbulent times in America. Martin Luther King was assassinated. Robert Kennedy, presidential candidate and brother of an assassinated president, was shot dead. Society's vulnerabilities were ever more visible.

Helen was a willing advocate for change, for a new order which offered more opportunity and equality. From her earliest years she had "deeply resented the domination and exploitation of women". Helen's own entertainment experience fuelled her contempt for some males, those who belittled women.

> Women have always been objectified in showbiz. I'd be
> the opening act for a comic and as I was leaving the stage

he'd say, 'Yeah, take your clothes off and wait for me in the dressing room, I'll be right there'.

The rising tide of the feminist movement re-ignited Helen's indignation, and she was comforted by the knowledge that she was not alone. Helen had strong philosophies concerning the strength not weakness of women. She believed that if women united they had "the power to make the planet a safer place". During the Depression and too many wars women proved their abilities and resilience. Changed social values and priorities would mean a better place for most.

With the dawn of another decade Helen was in California but the opportunities were still not coming. So many auditions, so many rejections; she still apparently "did not have the 'look'". Her inability to get work was as puzzling as it was depressing. To clear her mind and enhance her confidence she returned to school. She studied psychology at the University of California. There were questions she wanted answered, like the out-of-body experience she had at age eleven, and a couple of psychic experiences she had witnessed since. As her confidence and knowledge improved she began to write about the battle to survive; she wanted to "give other women hope". Helen Reddy continued to evolve.

The winds of change which had begun to sweep through society also blew through the corridors of recording studios. The era of the boy bands was disappearing and the market was demanding greater diversity. From protest singers like Bob Dylan to artists like James Taylor and Carole King, there was finally an open stage for soloists. In 1971 Helen gained guest appearances on *Make Your Own Kind of Music* and *The Virginia Graham Show* and more importantly she was welcomed on the hugely important *The Tonight Show*. It had been five long years in the wilderness since she had so optimistically watched Lana Cantrell on the same programme. Helen made the most of the opportunity. She was spotted by a producer from *Capitol Records* and given a contract for one 45 rpm single. It was 1972 and just two songs would decide if Helen's star would rise or not.

It was agony choosing the songs and it was agony listening to the finished "A" side song, the main song. "My nervousness permeated the track – and 'I Believe in Music' sounded more like 'I believe in terror'." This was not going well. This was so very important, she had waited so long and tried so hard and she looked to have failed miserably. Helen and the producers listened to the "B" side of the record even though it was accepted wisdom few radio stations listened to side "B". The voice was nervous and plaintive but it fitted the song "I Don't Know How to Love Him", from the hit musical *Jesus Christ Superstar*, superbly. The sides were hastily switched and the record released. The clear, strong if plaintive tones of an unknown vocalist from Melbourne took off over US airwaves and Helen hit the charts. By mid 1972 it had reached No.13. It happened so quickly *Capitol Records* was under-prepared. They rushed to have Helen sign another contract and begin work on an album.

In her very first singing lessons Stella Lamond had taught her daughter the uniqueness of the human voice and how powerful this wonderful instrument was as a social and cultural purveyor. It was a lesson Helen had learnt well. She had approved of the social protest songs which highlighted the sixties and their lyrics calling for social change. She thought of Stella, of Nanna Reddy, of Aunty Nell, of the generations of strong women from whom she had come, and Helen knew she wanted to write lyrics which celebrated them and her own evolution. But Oh! the tyranny of the blank page. Then the words: "I am strong, I am invincible, I am woman", and then, nothing. It is said that writing is 10 per cent inspiration and 90 per cent perspiration. There was a lot of perspiration in finding those next lyrics:

I am Woman, hear me roar
In numbers too big to ignore

And I know too much to go back and pretend.
'Cause I've heard it all before
And I've been down there on the floor
And no one's ever gonna keep me down again.

There needed to be a chorus, more perspiration, before the words formed.

Oh Yes I am wise
But it's wisdom born of pain.
Yes I've paid the price
But look how much I gained.
If I have to, I can do anything.
I am strong, I am invincible, I am woman.

The next passage formed slowly and proudly.

You can bend but never break me
'Cause it only serves to make me
More determined to achieve my final goal.
And I come back even stronger
Not a novice any longer
'Cause you deepened the conviction in my soul.

The words were strong but her attempts at melody failed to embrace and enhance. Aussie musician Ray Burton offered a better score. Recording bureaucrats were not renowned for bravery and suggested to Helen that on her first LP she record the current top songs. Helen had been waiting way too long for this day to adhere to the conservative suggestions of the establishment. She went with her gut, with that belief in herself which propelled her, with her innate sense of self. And the album was hugely successful.

People speak of "overnight success" which normally brings a smile to those referred to in such a way. So many years of blood, sweat and tears go into being an overnight success. The distinctive voice, look, manner, and talent just needed a wider audience to hear, see, and appreciate, but attaining that opportunity was elusive and plain hard. Jeff Wald became Helen's full-time manager. It seemed a wonderful opportunity for the couple, for the marriage. Helen had complete confidence in his business acumen and she was delighted to be able to give herself fully to the music. Life was good and for a while it just kept getting better, mostly.

In the first months of 1972 the woman who had a little tentatively ventured across the Pacific in 1966 flew to Europe three times. On an Amsterdam-to-London leg of the third trip an exhausted and pregnant Helen began to haemorrhage. Upon landing she was hastily taken to a medical centre and a doctor recommended an immediate Dilation and Curettage (D&C). Helen refused and an ambulance spirited her to St Mary's Hospital where tests revealed the baby was fine. Helen needed rest.

Women in the Western World during the 1960s and early 1970s had realised injustice was endemic. They began to mobilise and question more. Betty Friedan's 1963 book *The Feminine Mystique* gave voice to their disquiet and unhappiness. Germaine Greer's 1970 book *The Female Eunuch* shocked but resonated. And then Gloria Steinem co-founded the magazine MS to reflect women as they had never been seen before. As Steinem said: "The first problem for all of us, men and women, is not to learn but to unlearn". She then added: "The truth will set you free. But first, it will piss you off". The voices and questions became more forceful. Why did women lose their jobs when they were pregnant? Why did they earn so much less than their male peers for the same work? Why did they lose permanent work status when they married? Why did employment advertisements list in newspapers under gender? Why did those same newspapers have a separate "Women's Page" buried deep behind the world and local news? Why would banks not give women mortgages or credit cards even if they earned good incomes? Why did any autonomy disappear when they married? Why could they not apply for a passport – indeed anything – without the written consent of their husband? Why had the United Nations General Assembly yet to adopt a convention on the elimination of discrimination against women? Why were women legally and socially second class citizens?

Stage and film writers were picking up on "I Am Woman" and *Capitol Records* decided to rerelease the song as a single. Helen needed to add another verse:

> I am woman watch me grow
> See me standing toe to toe
> As I spread my lovin' arms across the land.
> But I'm still an embryo
> With a long, long, way to go
> Until I make my brother understand.

The chorus flowed freely again and she believed these proud words echoed the thoughts of so many. A more upbeat score was written. Helen was asked repeatedly to sing the song during television appearances but radio station owners and Disc Jockeys (DJs) were men who took exception to this "women's libbers" song. It was the pressure from female listeners requesting the song that ensured its success. Members of the status quo would have liked to have dismissed Helen as less than she was, to mark her as the enemy, even as a social deviant, but given her pregnancy that wasn't possible. Helen's laugh is deep when she recalls the cry "she's a feminist, she's a lesbian, she can't get a man" but "they couldn't say that about me, somebody had gotten to me". Three of Helen's singles made it into the top 40 chart. I am Woman did the same and kept going. It was Helen's first No.1

and the first for *Capitol Records* in five years.

Rarely does a song leave such a mark on society. Betty Friedan had founded the National Organization for Women (NOW). The NOW annual convention was a gala entertainment affair in Washington DC in 1973. As the evening concluded "I Am Woman" was played. Friedan recalled how suddenly:

> Women got out of their seats and started dancing around the hotel ballroom and joining hands in a circle that got larger and larger until maybe a thousand of us were dancing and singing, 'I am strong, I am invincible, I am woman'. It was a spontaneous, beautiful expression of the exhilaration we all felt in those years, women really moving as women.

The lights were blinking Helen's name ever more brightly and the work flowed. She recorded a third album on which the lead track was "I Am Woman". Her heavy programme continued throughout her second pregnancy although, in keeping with the conservatism of the day, she was filmed from above the baby bump. She even applied for a credit card arguing that she was the main money earner in her family. The bank finally conceded and Helen Reddy became one of the first women in the USA to be given a credit card in her own name.

The same week in December that "I Am Woman" listed No.1 in the US music charts Helen gave birth to Jordan. Choosing which event was the most glorious elicits the response: "The overwhelming joy that comes with the birth of a much wanted child far outweighed any career triumphs". When Traci was born ten years earlier Helen was unknown, unemployed and fairly impoverished. Now she was almost famous and had almost made her first million dollars. But "the love was the same".

Helen appeared on *The Bobby Darin Show*. Many American celebrities had television programmes and during 1973 the Australian performed on *The Carol Burnett Show* and on *The Flip Wilson Show* three times. Between 1970 and 1981 Helen appeared on *The Tonight Show starring Johnny Carson* and *The Best of Johnny Carson* no fewer than fifteen times. She was invariably asked to sing "I Am Woman" but she was particularly proud of that song. It sold over a million copies. In February 1973 Helen walked onto the stage of the Grand Ole Opry, the iconic home of country music in Nashville, Tennessee. Few edifices are as symbolically American as the Opry and in 1973 the Opry was the venue for the *15th Annual Grammy Awards* ceremony. The American music industry could be parochial and conservative yet this year the award Best Female Vocalist (Pop) went to someone from the Southern Hemisphere, from a country few in the audience or the wider nation could place accurately on a map. Helen Reddy had indeed made history; she was the first Australian so honoured. It was gutsy and well earned and Helen's acceptance speech was equally gutsy and spirited. To an audience who believed this was "God's own Country" Helen thanked God "because **She** makes everything possible". Later Helen would expand: "'God' is no more a woman or man because 'God' is not He Who is, but That Which is". I ask a dumb question: "What was it like to win?" Helen patiently replies, "winning is always great". She received some nasty mail after the acceptance speech. The strange thing about the religiously righteous is that they can act in a less than Christian manner. One of the less nasty letters asked: "If you think God is a woman then **she** and the Virgin Mary must be lesbians, is that what you believe?". Helen didn't bother answering that letter.

Traci, Helen and Jordan

Life picked up more speed. Helen's albums *I Don't Know How to Love Him, Helen Reddy, and I am Woman*, were joined by another in 1973, *Long Hard Climb*. For eight weeks NBC broadcast *The Helen Reddy Show*. Helen was proud of the show for many reasons. She was the first to have a black director and a female producer. There were women in the crew. Guest artists were inspiring and inspired, well known and those grateful for the opportunity to be seen and heard on prime time television: the Pointer Sisters, Cheech and Chong, the Eagles and Jim Croce (shortly before he was killed), Chuck Berry, Gladys Knight and the Pips, the Temptations and the great BB King. No Australian television network chose to air *The Helen Reddy Show*.

Helen thanked God
"because She makes everything possible".
Courtesy of Helen Reddy

I used to joke that this [Australia] was the only English speaking country in the world I couldn't earn a living in and I would never have moved back here if I had not been ready to retire. I mean I love it here.

But back then! She only had three top songs in Australia and around a dozen in the US "Top 40" charts.

It was wonderful being in such a creative time and place although it was challenging to understand the fickle nature of the music business. Helen was asked to record "Delta Dawn". She was a little reluctant given Tanya Tucker had recently recorded the song and Bette Midler intended to. Tucker's version became a "Top 10" country hit. Helen's "Delta Dawn" was released in the summer of 1973 two days before Bette Midler's album-cut version. It was Helen's recording that eclipsed the others, scaling the charts with breathtaking speed. It went to No.1 on the US pop charts and was as successful in other countries, including her own.

The public was not easy to understand and the success of "Ruby Red Dress" was another surprise. Helen disliked its simplicity because she sang the phrase "leave me alone" 43 times. Helen was happier to sing "You and Me Against the World". It depicted an earlier period in her life when she and Traci arrived in a foreign unwelcoming land. It was particularly poignant given her daughter's voice started and finished the recording. The song went to No.9 on the US charts. "Angie Baby" shot to No.1 on the US charts. The lyrics were somewhat cryptic and fans derived a variety of interpretations which Helen found amusing. She never has told their true meaning. The music was spreading across borders and oceans and Helen's popularity was soaring. In another of life's cruel checks and balances Helen received news that her mother had died on 5 July 1973.

At times like this the distance across the Pacific seemed so terribly vast. Helen had a great deal of time to reflect as she flew to Hawaii and then on to Sydney before she could board another aircraft for Melbourne. It was winter and the Victorian capital was fogged in. The plane landed at a disused airport well north of the city. The trip was going on forever and Helen needed to get home for the funeral, already delayed for her arrival. The chill of winter seeped into the East Melbourne church, into the bodies and hearts of those assembled to farewell Stella Lamond. She was a versatile performer who had lived to entertain, and entertained until she died. To some of her fans who gathered outside to pay their respects she was known as Molly Wilson on the popular television series *Bellbird*. Others remembered her appearances in television's *Homicide,* some there had watched her on the stage or listened over wireless waves. She was only 64.

Regret is inevitable with the death of a parent. There never seemed to be enough time, the right time, the correct conversation, and too few opportunities. In truth there never would be. Before she flew back to the US Helen visited her father who was in hospital suffering from dementia. She wasn't sure he would recognise her but was so very grateful that he did. In the visitors lounge, accompanied on the piano by a friend, Helen sang for her father. She would be back in November for an Australian tour, it was sad that Stella would not see her perform. Neither would Max Reddy, Stella's death was to be kept from him but it wasn't and Max died ten weeks after his wife. Helen made the long sad trip south again for the funeral of the man she fondly remembers as "a genuine character". Between the deaths of her parents was the death of her friend Lillian Roxon on 10 August. Roxon wrote Australia's first *Rock Encyclopedia* published in 1969. Her voice was distinctive, pithy and provocative, and her programme *Lillian Roxon's Diskotique* was syndicated to 250 radio stations across the US by 1971. She heralded the women's movement and Germaine Greer dedicated *The Female Eunuch* to her. Roxon believed in Helen when she needed it and wrote in *New York Sunday News* that Helen in "I Am Woman" "gives you the most amazing insight into the way a woman thinks and feels". Lillian was only 41. 1973 was the worst and best year of Helen's life.

In November she returned to Australia for a concert tour. Its success was only marred by some unenthusiastic press, something she had contended with before and would again. For Helen the highlight was singing at the Melbourne Stadium with her beloved Aunty Nell sitting in the front row. Nell was frail and unwell with the final stages of cancer, but she was there to see her niece as successful an international vocalist as she always believed she would be. Nell had always been Helen's "rock and my safe haven, the lighthouse in the stormy sea". She was "a very ethical and moral person, she was my moral compass". The older Helen Reddy died just weeks later leaving the woman who had been more a daughter than a niece "bereft".

The show needed to go on. There was no time to mourn. The music business and the public were demanding. You were only as famous as your last appearance or song and the personal needed to be submerged beneath the professional. But it hurt that she was "denied the normal grieving process" – four deaths in seven months; four of the most influential people in her life. She looked to her husband but he wasn't there, the "future had become scary and unpredictable; the present was almost unbearable". Jeff Wald's mood swings and verbal abuse worsened. He was a non-drinker but the behaviour pattern was similar. She thought it might be stress but she was under more stress, she didn't understand and it was getting worse. Helen sought solace in a new interest, genealogy. Without her parents and Nell to delineate her place in the world anymore she became intent on following the ancestral trail. It took her to Tasmania and Norfolk Island, back to 1788. Helen looked to those who defined her now, Traci and Jordan. She also found refuge in her work and gained inspiration from others of her profession. She sympathised with Frank Sinatra about the

At the height of show biz

hostile Australian press and in return Frank said "if anyone ever hits you, call me".

Helen's star was still ascending and the next years were as exciting as they were creatively rewarding. Her recording of "Keep on Singing" rose to No.15 in the US charts; "Emotion" went to No. 22; "Bluebird" was No. 35; "Ain't No Way To Treat a Lady" pushed higher to No. 8; "Somewhere in the Night" and "I Can't Hear You No More" both made it into the "Top 20" as did her revival of Cilla Black's "You're My World". "The Happy Girls" was listed in the "Top 10" as was "Ready or Not", "Make Love To Me" and "Let Me Be Your Woman". Helen's final "Top 20" hit would come in 1981 with the song "I Can't Say Goodbye to You". While she had three US No.1 hit songs, she managed seven US No.1 hits in the adult contemporary charts. She toured with a full chorus of backing singers and dancers to standing room only audiences. Her album output was prolific. Between 1974 and 1981 she released the albums *Love Song for Jeffrey; Free and Easy; No Way to Treat a Lady; Helen Reddy's Greatest Hits; Music, Music; Ear Candy; Pete's Dragon* (soundtrack)*; We'll Sing in the Sunshine; Live in London; Take What You Find* and *Play Me Out.*

The second part of the 1970s was incredibly busy and perhaps 1975 was the busiest of years. It certainly contained so many high points. The United Nations declared 1975 International Women's Year. The song Helen wrote after she fixated on the words "I am strong, I am invincible", "I Am Woman", was chosen by the UN as the official song. It was a huge tribute. It was the ideal time for Helen to embark on a world tour. She began the European stage in

With Helen Reddy Show guest star Jane Fonda

the Netherlands. The Dutch surprised her with a reddish violet tulip named in her honour. Her tour was greeted favourably by the media wherever she went, until she arrived in Australia.

There is a strange delight on the part of the Australian press to turn on those who moved to the front of stage; to effect a reduction of fame and favour to something they exalt as egalitarianism and "the tall poppy syndrome". The media purvey the belief that Australians love Australians to beat the rest in the world but the heroes and "sheroes" need to remain accessible and humble. For those Australians who do excel it is a juggling act. To excel requires an almost overpowering competitiveness. The reality is that you must believe you are superior before you are; you must believe without reservation that you can do better than others, before you do. In Australian culture you just have to publicly submerge what drives you, particularly a few decades ago – and particularly if "I Am Woman". There was disharmony between Helen and the Australian press: "The Murdoch press was particularly vicious". Like many in the public eye she believed the Australian press intense and combative. They appeared to enjoy crossing the line to provoke. And she had done the unforgiveable: she had become an American citizen. Helen had been living in the US for almost a decade, she was married to an American, her son was born in the US and she thought it unlikely she would return to live in Australia.

When dual citizenship was introduced she would again hold an Australian passport but not in 1975. The Australian media was also notoriously conservative. Helen was a determined lady whose song was the anthem for the burgeoning women's movement. Furthermore Helen's opening act on tour was a man she was as fond of as she was impressed by his talent. Eventually Australians would embrace him as "the boy from Oz" but then "the Australian press turned on him and was merciless in its homophobia". Peter Allen was reduced to tears by their vindictiveness.

Peter Allen was not the only Australian singer Helen encouraged. She was instrumental in furthering the career of a youthful blonde singer whose voice and manner were beginning to make an impact in the US. Helen persuaded Olivia Newton-John to move from Britain to the US. Then at a party at Helen's Californian home Olivia was introduced to producer Allen Carr. Carr decided she was ideal for the role of Sandy in his film adaption of the musical *Grease*. When Helen hosted the variety show *The Midnight Special* she shared the stage with Australian brothers who sang three-part tight harmonies and whose voices blended perfectly. Their names were Barry, Robin and Maurice, better known as the Bee Gees.

The cinematic musical extravaganzas Helen grew up loving had disappeared from the box office but she was still intrigued to be asked to star in a film. She admittedly harboured some visions of greasepaint and glamour. The greasepaint or rather make-up was there but the glamour was completely lacking. The 1974 film was *Airport '75* and Helen was a "flying, singing nun or, if you prefer, a singing, flying nun". Having ventured through an adolescent religious stage when she wished to be a missionary, for Helen the nun habit was an interesting experience:

> Portraying a nun certainly gives one a different perspective
> on life. At times while in my habit, I felt quite different
> than usual. It was a special feeling.

It would also be grounds for the nickname the media delighted in calling her. Given the adversarial nature of the Australian media the nickname could well have been worse than "the singing nun". The disaster film starred Charlton Heston and had an entirely impossible plot. A 747 suffers a mid-air collision with a small plane. The pilot, co-pilot and flight engineer are effectively wiped out and a stewardess takes control of the aircraft until another pilot can be lowered from a helicopter through the very, very, large hole in the cockpit. The passengers, except the nun, seemed prone to histrionics. Years later when the suggestion of making a spoof was explored by Hollywood, Helen commented "I'd thought the original was a spoof". The film made two listings: *The Fifty Worst Films of All Time* and *The 100 Most Enjoyably Bad Movies Ever Made*. But there were highlights for the Australian. The legendary actress Gloria Swanson appeared as a passenger, an aging alcoholic actress. She wrote her own dialogue in this her first film in 22 years. She agreed to appear because it was a film "I could take my grandchildren to see, something exciting and contemporary without senseless violence". Another highlight was that "the singing nun" performance earned Helen a *Golden Globe* nomination in the category of Most Promising Newcomer – Female. Helen unfortunately lost to Susan Flannery for her performance in *The Towering Inferno*, yet another disaster movie.

Her next film role came in 1975. Disney's *Pete's Dragon* was set in New England in the early 20th century. Pete was a nine- year-old orphan who ran away from brutal adoptive parents. The dragon was Elliott, his only friend. Helen played Nora, the daughter of a lighthouse keeper in the severely tongue-challenging seaboard town of Passamaquoddy, Maine. And no there wasn't much glamour here either. She and her father "Lampie" offer shelter and love to Pete. Reflecting real life, where difference frightens closed minded people, the townsfolk were not accommodating of a mostly jolly green dragon, particularly one which had the ability to become invisible when he chose. And of course there was also a particularly nasty character. As should be the case with children's stories, good triumphed over evil and love triumphed over all. Helen sang "Candle on the Water" in front of the lantern room windows of the lighthouse. For Helen the highlight was to share the screen with her film father, the celebrated Mickey Rooney with whom she sang "I Saw a Dragon" and "Brazzle Dazzle Day". Other stars of the film included the accomplished Red Buttons and Shelley Winters. It was with the versatile Winters Helen sang "Bill of Sale". The film became a children's cinematic classic, nominated for two music Academy Awards including Helen's solo song "Candle on the Water" for Best Original Song. There were also six Academy of Science Fiction, Fantasy and Horror Awards nominations including Best Actress – Fantasy (Helen Reddy), and a Golden Globe nomination for Best Original Score. A synopsis of the film described the character of Nora as a "passionate, out-spoken woman". Perhaps fiction did reflect life. Stella and Max would have been proud and would likely have agreed.

Helen was not enamoured with making movies. It seemed an agonisingly inefficient use of valuable time, invariably sitting around an entire day for a scene which may take three minutes. "I found film work to be boring." She preferred the power of people, the way she could stand on a stage and simply sing. If the chemistry was right that night it was as if, some singers said, "God walked into the room". When you stood in the light and the faces beamed back at you and lifted you to your best that was intense. In one such example the night didn't actually start out well. It was 1975, the venue was the New York State Fair and it was pouring with rain. Helen stood a little gingerly on a rubber mat under strict instructions not to touch the microphone lest her performance was electrifying in a different way. The guys with the electric guitars looked reasonably nervous. When Helen reached the lyric in "Bluebird" "we're out in the rain" the crowd roared.

A very concentrated time in the spotlight involved starring in Las Vegas. For seven nights a week she was giving two shows a night at the *MGM Grand*. So as not to disturb the day-to-day routine for Traci and Jordan, Helen commuted every night – Los Angeles to Las Vegas and back – by private jet. She would leave after an early dinner with the children and return after the midnight to 2am show. Sleep and sustenance came when they could. When reviews began to mention a lack of energy she admitted that this routine, and the emotions of the previous year, were taking their toll. She had lost a lot of weight but found successive doctors unhelpful. One doctor put her on placebos and told her husband Helen needed to see a psychiatrist because "she thinks there is something wrong with her". It was a relief when she met a female physician who took her symptoms seriously: sweats, fatigue, dizziness, low blood pressure, craving salt, weight loss and darkening skin. After tests it was confirmed that Helen was neither deluded nor hysterical, she had the potentially fatal Addison's Disease. The disease, which affects about one in 40,000 people in Australia, is a chronic ailment caused by the failure of the adrenal glands to produce two hormones: cortisol and aldosterone. Without these the body cannot control its metabolism and blood pressure or retain water and salt and left untreated, it eventually causes death. It is incurable but can be managed by daily cortisone medication. After a massive dose of cortisone she "felt well again for the first time in years". And again Helen Reddy made the conscious decision not to become a victim. "Sometimes I think I get through life by ignoring things. I pretend I don't have it." But the daily cortisone reminds her.

He was kinda cute, a little small admittedly. Unfortunately there was a very jealous girlfriend menacingly closeby. Oh, and he was green. Helen was smitten with Kermit the Frog and Kermit sat on her lap for a duet "You and Me Against the World". The recording of episode 313 of *The Muppet Show* was fun in 1978. She had been in a movie with a disappearing green animated dragon but nothing was quite like appearing with the strangest group of entertainers she had ever shared a stage with. Fortunately Miss Piggy did not have time to take exception to Helen's duet with Kermit because she was too busy dressing up as Marie Antoinette and singing "Stayin' Alive" with a group of French Revolution era pigs. Helen sang "Blue" backed by a very weird looking bunch of musicians. The resident Electric Mayhem band had a particularly crazy drummer called Animal. After she returned to her Muppets dressing room Animal and the Swedish Chef burst through the door to raucously serenade her with "Happy Birthday". When Helen explained it was not her birthday they broke into "Jingle Bells". The show was going from bad to worse, which is the way Muppet stage productions usually progressed. The new janitor Beauregard proved incompetent and used axle grease to clean the stage floor which caused Fozzie Bear to slip during a dance routine. Beauregard was ordered to put down some sand, but not dunes of the stuff. Helen's final number needed to be altered to an Arab desert number, "We'll Sing in the Sunshine", in which she danced with Sopwith the Camel. Sopwith's hooves looked remarkably like human feet. In the Australian's honour the Muppet gang gave their rendition of "Tie Me Kangaroo Down Sport". It was pretty bad. You have to love showbiz. It was a bright professional spot when Helen's private life was deteriorating.

From Kermit to Queen Elizabeth II professional life was a whirl.

There was another high professional episode–one about as different from *the Muppet Show* as you could possibly imagine. The year was 1980 and Helen flew from London to Sydney to sing in a Royal Command performance. That was a little back to front but the Queen and Prince Philip were visiting the southern Commonwealth. London had been on high alert and it is highly likely any Royal Command performance would have been cancelled because Helen's show at the Royal Albert Hall nearly was. As Helen prepared to leave her London hotel for the Albert Hall the city's Metropolitan Police Commissioner made an announcement. He recommended anyone going to the Helen Reddy concert stay at home. The international vocalist was surprised and puzzled but determined "the show must go on". During one song Helen wondered if the percussionist wasn't "playing really hard". It was gunfire from the Iranian Embassy next door. The SAS was undertaking an assault to overpower six armed dissidents who had been holding nineteen hostages for five days. The SAS assault was staged from the Albert Hall roof. Amid machine gun fire, detonating grenades, screams and shattering glass next door Helen truly proved a product of her professional upbringing and the show did go on. Five dissidents and one hostage were killed. This obviously was not the high point of May 1980, but appearing with a stellar cast on the Sydney Opera House stage in front of the royals was. They were some of the brightest of Australian talent: John Farnham, Olivia Newton-John, Julie Anthony, Paul Hogan, Peter Allen singing his new arrangement "I Still Call Australia Home", members of the Sydney Dance Company and the Australian Ballet – and Helen Reddy singing "I Am Your Child" for the country from which she had evolved.

Helen had provided *Capitol Records* with some great chart-storming songs, celebrity and income, but their relationship finished in less positive circumstances. Helen moved to MCA. Two albums were produced and some songs made the Asian and European charts, but not the US charts. *Play Me Out* in 1981 was not a particularly successful album. The song "I Can't Say Goodbye to You" made it to No.43 in the UK and No.88 in the US. Her voice echoed the theme song "Never Say Goodbye" from the John Belushi romantic comedy film *Continental Divide* but Helen wondered if, after five high velocity years, the music public needed a rest; she knew she did. Jeff Wald's verbal abuse and fluctuating moods finally pushed Helen to breaking point. He had promised to give up cocaine and other substance abuse. Yet she continued to find blood and nose cartilage adhering to bedding. They had tried counselling. Helen did the twelve-step programme with Al-Anon, a group of family and friends dealing with alcoholics and addicts. Nothing worked. Wald had multiple addictions and had been up on two recent weapons charges. Helen also realised that she had inadvertently been subsidising his addictions because her success had made them very wealthy. Traci was safely ensconced in university away from home. Helen knew she must take Jordan and leave the family home; "the marriage was not salvageable".

She was not dealing with a normal human but one under the influence of very destructive substances. The divorce was bitter and the custody battle over Jordan horrendous. Helen was shocked not only by the vindictiveness but also by the strength of the old boy network. The fortune she had made was no more. Through addiction, whim, poor business judgement or whatever, her husband/manager, to whom she had entrusted all their financial affairs, had ensured that there was nothing left. There was less than nothing. She thought their home was paid for – it wasn't. Taxes were unpaid. She had believed there was no debt but that is all there was, and a lot of debt. The bankers, accountants, housekeeper and other staff answered to him and had kept her completely in the dark. Even the local pharmacist refused to supply her with her life-sustaining cortisone because the bill was unpaid.

Her personal life was horrific and her career looked to be going the same way as Wald badmouthed her throughout the industry. Doors closed. Favourable comment and critique reversed. She was openly criticised as lacking "musical versatility". One reporter wrote: "The strident, acerbic edge that served her well on 'I Am Woman' is not always useful". Another wrote of her "technically accomplished voice" but also her "inability to transmit the tenderer emotions of pop music". He believed she was "fine on fire and ice, but hearts and flowers seem alternately to baffle and annoy her". Helen tried to remain unperturbed. She believed she would always sing. But these were very perturbing times. Performance contracts ceased. A television sitcom developed for her was dropped. Friends simply disappeared. MCA stopped promoting her newest album *Imagination*. The printed media was not interested in the new compilation, preferring instead headlines like "Hollywood's Dirtiest Divorce". Truth was the first casualty of this salacious celebrity-chasing media which had forsaken serious journalism. It was suggested that Helen "flaunted with a gaudy lifestyle of mansions, limousines, jewelry and speedboats". Producer Julia Phillips wrote that by the time Helen and Jeff Wald finalised their acrimonious divorce in 1982 they "had blown most of the $40 million they had made". According to Helen "it was more like 24 million and it wasn't they who had blown it". But then the public only heard the Phillips version. When Helen sang "I am Woman" at the 1981 Miss World contest some feminists were critical. Helen responded with criticism of her own: "Let them step forward and pay my rent and I'll stay home. What I'm doing is advertising a product I wouldn't use".[3] The Helen Reddy star on the Hollywood Walk of Fame was being trampled on by many unsympathetic feet. How fickle is fame.

Musically the 1970s had been diverse, even a group from Sweden with the acronym of "ABBA" captured the imagination of the general public and gave rise to the popularity of what promoters were calling "World Music". Globalisation went a step further enabling the 1980s to give birth to the "charity record". Dozens of artists sang to raise consciousness and money through songs like "We Are the World" and "Do They Know It's Christmas?" Movie blockbusters launched many 80s popular music chart stoppers like "Eye of the Tiger" from *Rocky* and "Flashdance ... What a Feeling" from *Flashdance*. The baby boomers were embracing many genres and further technical advances within the music industry offered more than ever before. But it was always youth who monopolised pop music and believed their music embraced rebellion and anti-establishment fury like no other. Theirs was now grunge music, heavy metal, and they anointed a new queen and king in the form of Madonna and Michael Jackson. Helen's music was being squeezed out of an increasingly diverse, competitive and flashy market.

She was referred to as, "the female Frank Sinatra", "the queen of housewife rock and roll" and "the hip Julie Andrews". The latter reference may have been apt as in 1981 she sang the theme song "Little Boys" for the Blake Edwards comedy *The Man who Loved Women* starring Burt Reynolds and Julie Andrews. Clearly Blake Edwards had decided that Helen's vocal tone was more appropriate, more "hip", than that of his wife Julie Andrews. But Helen's audience was aging. They continued to prove loyal; they liked her music, felt comfortable with her voice and her style. They were not in the "Top 40" singles market but they still listened to music, her music, yet her recording company seemed to have written off this audience and Helen Reddy.

1980 had been a good year professionally. It had started with an appearance at the *52nd Academy Awards*. In a slinky, split-to-the-thigh white dress she had perched on a piano stool next to Dudley Moore as they presented the theme song of another Blake Edwards film, *10* – the Henry Mancini song "It's Easy to Say", which was nominated for Best Original Song. She appeared on television in *The Tim Conway Show* and took on the persona of Elinor Green on the very popular *The Love Boat*. In 1981 she was on Top of the Pops and The Tonight Show. In 1982 she appeared in *I Love Liberty*. Her only other appearance on the small box was as a character named Suzi Swann in *Fantasy Island*. In 1983 she performed at the *25th Grammy Awards*. The next appearance was as herself in a 1985 episode of *The Jeffersons*. The only other appearance during the decade was in the 1987 film *The Disorderlies*. Helen played a "happy socialite" which could not have been further from the truth as she was neither. Helen does not recall the 1980s with pleasure.

The doors began to close at the beginning of the decade and things would never be the same again. Financially ruined, more than ever she had to make a living but her newest album was not being promoted. Music videos dominated the promotion medium and MCA was not promoting. Helen looked to someone she knew was there for her, her daughter. Traci was graduating with honours from University of Southern California Film School. With a bank loan, some help from classmates and a bucket load of enthusiasm, Traci produced an imaginative music video for her mother's new album *Imagination*. Helen ceased her relationship with MCA. But like the lyrics of one of her most popular songs Helen believed she needed to "keep on singing, don't stop singing ... you're going to make a lot of people happy when they come to hear you play".

Personal happiness was fleeting. One of the songs on the *Imagination* album was "Looks Like Love". Helen wanted to believe. Another of her well-known songs included the lyrics "who knows why we choose when we choose the ones we love". The year after her divorce from Jeff Wald Helen married for a third time. The groom was drummer Milton Ruth. She was still beguiled by the "forever after" ideal but it would prove as elusive as the end of a rainbow. Helen is reluctant to discuss private issues; she didn't even mention the names of her husbands in her memoir. Today she disarms me with:

> They have already had their fifteen minutes ... the first
> one was alcohol, the second one was drugs, the third one
> had issues.

I stumble over my next question with that unexpected retort and her laughter is followed by "let's face it I was never going to find anyone as wonderful as me". More laughter and then some philosophy:

> Things happen when they are supposed to happen. I
> am very grateful I have learnt something from every
> experience. I am very good at adapting.

The third marriage was not a match made in Heaven and officially ended in 1995. I decide one of Helen's most popular songs, one written by Harriet Schock, is fitting:

> I guess it was yourself you were involved with
> I would have sworn it was me
> I might have found out sooner if
> You'd only let me close enough to see

That ain't no way to treat a lady

No way to treat your baby

Your woman your friend

That ain't no way to treat a lady, no way

But maybe it's a way for us to end

I was only bein' a picture

With all the colours I know

While you were busy looking into

Wide blue mirrors and lovin' the show

That ain't no way to treat a lady

No way to treat your baby

Your woman your friend

That ain't no way to treat a lady, no way

But maybe it's a way for us to end

There's a funny kind of consolation

Keepin' me sane

And I'd really like to share it

Crawl on deep in my brain

And see the times you never felt me

Lovin' you or needin' you

So leavin' you now

You still won't know how to feel the pain

I was lookin' out for my happiness

While you were looking within

And before you know your own reflection

Always starts to tire you, it's happened again

That ain't no way to treat a lady

No way to treat your baby

Your woman your friend

That ain't no way to treat a lady, no way

But maybe it's a way for us to end

As a solo concert artist, Helen had played Carnegie Hall and the Lincoln Center in New York, as well as the Royal Albert Hall and the Palladium in London. Helen was the first western female performer invited to sing in the People's Republic of China. She had dined on her 35th birthday with the Prince of Wales and danced in the White House with the President of the United States. A true Renaissance woman, she continued to evolve; she needed to. The male world appeared to have locked hands and was attempting to shut her down. It took seventeen years to pay off the debts left at the end of her second marriage.

Helen had started at age five on the stage and so she would return to her roots. She had turned down offers to be in theatre over the years but she felt the time was now right. There was the pressure of one week rehearsal, one week play, but there was also the comforting backstage smell which had never changed over the years when so much else had. "It's a mix of sweat and dust and makeup, but it was home ... I loved it." Over the next years Helen starred in productions of *Anything Goes, Call Me Madam* and *The Mystery of Edwin Drood*. A fan of English composer and playwright Willy Russell, she became an interpreter of his work, appearing on Broadway and in the London's West End in the hit musical *Blood Brothers* and Russell's one-woman play *Shirley Valentine* in Toronto.

Helen won rave reviews for her theatrical work. Theatre offered the "last bastion of camaraderie and equality in the entertainment world" but she still saw herself as a singer; she still wanted to sing, she still needed to sing and she wasn't going to let the bastards stop her. Her creativity was somewhat stymied because the audience wanted her to sing those hit songs yet again, but those songs felt like well-worn clothes – not fashionable, but warm, familiar and comfortable. It was also funny that she had been around so long she was almost fashionable again, she was almost "retro chic". That song "I Am Woman" was the one so often requested, it had never disappeared and was unlikely to do so. It continued to pop up in movies like *High School High* (1996) and *My Best Friend's Wedding* (1997), and in television series from *The Simpsons* (1993) to *Cold Case* (2006). Nonetheless the industry had changed. Now you needed corporate sponsorship to be able to afford to do a concert tour. Promoters and middle men finished up wealthier than the artist. Instead of 10-piece orchestras, dancers and back-up singers Helen now travelled with four musicians who could also do back-up vocals, and a technician.

The decade 1990 to 2000 – between stage, guest appearances, concerts and recordings – was busy and professionally gratifying. Helen appeared in 1998 as herself on US television's *Intimate Portrait* in an episode on her friend Olivia Newton-John. There were guest appearances in *Voices that Care* (1991), *The First 100 Years: A Celebration of American Movies* (1995) and *The Rosie O'Donnell Show* (1997). In 2000 she played a character named Danielle Marsh in the very popular television series *Diagnosis Murder* opposite Dick Van Dyke. In 1990 Helen released her album *Feel So Young*. To those who purchased it the Reddy voice seemed ever more mellow. Her 1998 album *Center Stage* was a perfect meld of Helen's distinctive sound with Broadway songs she had claimed as her own. *HELEN REDDY: The Best Christmas Ever* came out in 2001. Many compilations followed including *The Woman I am: Definitive Collection* in 2006 which offered 23 of the songs she had made famous.

Helen was producing her own albums. She wanted more control over the creative, artistic level and harsh life lessons had taught her she needed to have legal ownership of production and merchandising. But recordings were quite secondary to her real day job, or rather her night job. She saw herself firstly as a performing artist and that is how:

> I earn my living ... I work 'live'. I do about eight or nine shows a month, one nighters here, there or wherever.

There were many concerts in the decade, all around the world, like the one given in the plush Maile Ballroom in the *Kahala Mandarin Oriental Hotel*, Hawaii on 17 May 1999 – so many countries, cities and hotels. In 1999 she recorded the song "Breezin' Along With the Breeze" with her sister Toni Lamond for Toni's compact disc (CD) *Still a Gypsy*. It was the first time the sisters had recorded together. The CD title seemed appropriate, as was the song about two sisters riding the open country in a convertible. It would have amused Max and Stella. Never one to shy away from social issues Helen came to Sydney to headline the Gay and Lesbian Mardi Gras concert "Celebration of the Female Voice".

In her "spare" time Helen served for three years as a Commissioner of Parks and Recreation for California. As with film, Helen did not do well with the long-drawn-out process, with a lot of time spent and so little to show for it. She found that from the time a piece of land was donated to the state until it was opened to the public there was a minimum of six years. Environmental impact studies and geological surveys were required and Native Americans needed to ensure there were no burial sites on the land. Not only did this mean current commissioners were dealing with something their predecessors commenced, but in a three-year term or two terms, you were unlikely to see the result of your own instigated enquiry. Helen appraises her part in the whole committee system with characteristic honesty:

> I don't do well on committees and that was a nine-person committee. It takes nine people to say 'yes'. You go and find nine people who can agree. So nothing got done and after three years I decided, 'I am wasting my time here'.

On New Year's Eve 2000 Helen considered her life. As the darkness gave light to the first day of 2001 she knew she wished to retire from show business. It was nearly 55 years since she had walked on a stage and sang a song about babies. She had indeed succeeded as an internationally acclaimed singer and sold around fifteen million albums and ten million singles. "One of the reasons I retired was to get rid of the 70's pop star label." She could never figure out why she had been labelled "Queen of Pop" because "I thought I was singing jazz and the blues". And the truth now was "I was tired and I was bored". Her sister Toni Lamond used to say that Helen was in the music business, which was very different to show business. Helen takes it a step further:

> Some live to entertain, I entertained to live. Most of the people I know in show business, that's their life ... if they can die on stage they would be happy. It was my livelihood not my life.

By 2002 Helen was retired. She had prided herself on avoiding the boxes society would prefer you fitted neatly into. She had lived her life on pretty much her own terms and now she was restless again. Disenchanted with the United States political process, namely the Florida fiasco which saw Al Gore robbed of the presidency, Helen realised she could no longer call America home. It would be a wrench insofar as both Traci and Jordan would continue to live there, and another she had lost her heart to, her granddaughter Lily. The domestic bliss and the white picket fence had eluded Helen but it had materialised for her daughter. Traci married her primary school sweetheart and in 2008 they had been married 24 years. And as one would expect when dealing with a Reddy life there was a fun and interesting twist. Traci had married Lucas, the son of actor Peter Donat and a lady with the unusual stage name of Miss Michael Learned. (The family of the latter decided after five daughters the next child would be named Michael no matter what.) Those of us old enough to remember the television series *The Waltons* remember well the mother of all the children played by the actress Miss Michael Learned. For all their dramas the *Waltons* epitomised the ideal of a close and loving family complete with white picket fence. Life can be very ironic. As for Lily, Helen smiles:

> I'm passionately in love with my granddaughter and I tell you when that little girl puts her arms around my neck and says, 'I love you, Nanna, You're my friend' I'm toast.

So Helen moved to Norfolk Island, buying the 40-acre farm owned by her First Fleet ancestor and the place where her great, great, great grandmother had been born. It felt right and it was a beautiful place. Helen continued to evolve. There was a new career. A lifelong interest in metaphysics had led to psychology and parapsychology studies. Helen returned to school and attained a degree in clinical hypnotherapy at age 60. Helen had a need to "give back by helping people". Hypnotherapy assists in resolving people's phobias with past-life regressions. This means you must be completely at ease with the concept of reincarnation. Helen is and likens life to a glass of beer with a thick collar on top; hypnotherapy is like a straw that goes all the way to the bottom. She offers another observation:

> So many of us feel guilt after a loved one has passed and think 'I should have said this' or 'I should have done that'. Reincarnation means that in reality, nothing is every truly left unsaid or undone. Life is eternal, and other opportunities will be given to right all wrongs.

Why can't we remember these past lives? "Conscious awareness of past lives would also clutter our minds with too much info and emotional baggage." Helen has come across a lot of former lives in patients. Her work is not rewarded with money. "I have been wealthy, I have been poor; money plays a small role in my life now", accentuated with a dismissive wave of the hand. Patients "have to give an equal amount of time to someone in need".

Helen found her trips across the sea from Norfolk Island to Australia increased in frequency due to demand as a hypnotherapist and as a motivational speaker. She decided to call Sydney home and return to the Norfolk Island farm as often as she could. She had concerns about a return to Australia. She had spent most of her life living away from the country of her birth although a strong bond continued to reside deep inside. She had always felt:

> Australian in a lot of ways ... I have a value system shaped by my years in Australia ... values about honesty and truth and not a lot of the BS that goes on.

But she had also felt "a tremendous amount of rejection", not from fellow Australians but from the Australian media. Her ill feeling towards the Australian media remains blatantly visible. Helen believes the media continues to manipulate. It is irresponsible with its emphasis on bleak and bad news, "miracles happen every day". She is disparaging about a conservative monopolised media which continues to preach the status quo and push gender demarcation and women as "virgins or whores".

Others realised that there may have been some "rejection". Helen was welcomed on many radio and television programmes. In 2002 *This is Your Life* featured Helen Reddy. In 2006 she was inducted into the Australian Recording Industry Association (ARIA) Hall of Fame. It was a grand affair. Vanessa Amorosi sang "I am Woman" and Helen was delighted, "I hope she records it, because I think she sings it much better than I did". That song and what it stood for, the evolution of women, is no less important today than before. That song and the woman who wrote it continued to be important. A British indie pop band called the Trembling Blue Stars wrote a song in her honour. "Helen Reddy" appeared on their 2005 album *Seven Autumn Flowers*. More importantly "I am Woman" was added to the US high school modern history curriculum text books. That gave Helen great satisfaction. She remembered when she first sang the song in Los Angeles, at the Troubadour. *The Los Angeles Times* newspaper reviewer was, Helen candidly believed, "tone deaf, couldn't play an instrument, they were usually the people who get that job". He wrote a scathing critique, he said:

> I couldn't be taken seriously as a rock artist because rock dealt with serious issues and "I am Woman" was a sociological insignificant pop song. What he was really saying was women don't deal with substance issues.

Jordan, now a writer in the US, told his mother he wanted to take out a full-page advertisement in *The Los Angeles Times* with the US Education Department announcement and a copy of that 1972 critique. "I said darling don't spend the money, you and I know it's all right."

I attempt to lead Helen into discussion on modern music. She doesn't wish to generalise or sound too much like a member of the "older" generation but she is disappointed just the same. We discuss the protest music which brought baby boomers into the streets. That was motivated in part by the Vietnam War and the draft. There is no longer a draft but there are still issues, and different wars. Helen believes she is no longer the one to tackle them, a different generation of singers and musicians need to make their music relevant to the times. But she can't completely ignore that it appears a little like "our generation marched in the streets, this generation drives to the mall". For Helen, who has spent most of her life "fighting for women to be treated with dignity and respect", the musical accent on "material girl" and "material things", encouraged by the status quo, bothers her as does "the sexualisation of little girls which accompanies it". Why is it that pubescent girls' clothing "got skimpier, male clothing got baggier? And, what about rap which is "anti-women".

Some years ago Helen was invited to be a judge on an Australian television programme compiling the "best rock and roll singers". "They had already chosen the ten 'best' and there wasn't one female artist so I declined". By chance in 2008 I had just received an advertising brochure for a large music chain, which includes the "top albums of all time". I go down the list – no woman vocalist in the top ten; nor top 20; nor top 30. Finally a female name, Carole King, and her album Tapestry at No. 33. She is the only woman mentioned in the top 50. It seems things are slow to change. Helen would like to see women's evolutionary theme continued by younger female musicians.

Is it because they think the war is over and we won? They talk about a post-feminist world. In America 35 years ago we were making 59 cents for every dollar a man made. We now make 77 cents. I calculate that is a half a cent per year. At that rate we will achieve parity with men in another 46 years. That's not winning and it won't be in my lifetime.

Photograph Jennifer Burton-Douglas

The hours in the sun-drenched Sydney unit have disappeared so quickly. The bird noises outside have increased in volume and I am reminded of an Australian saying "Music to Australian ears the drone of a blow fly and the caw of crows". Helen leaves water out for the crows on her balcony and they clearly like her for it. I am on my last page, still trying to put dates and issues in order. Helen wishes to talk about her visit to Israel and the plight of the Palestinians. She has had a lifelong interest in religion, all religions. To lighten the conversation she smiles "I married a Protestant, a Catholic and a Jew; I have been very ecumenical in my marriage habits". More serious now Helen wants to lend me a book which disturbed her. It is the story of the rise of the most powerful mercenary army in the world and one which the US is utilising, at home and overseas. She needs to travel to and within the US reasonably frequently and she is concerned by that travel:

> You virtually need a passport to take a domestic flight and
> to be treated like an inmate in a correctional institution
> and for what? Because we were lied to?

I give up with the order and questions regarding a life already lived. Helen shifts into a much more articulate gear. She is widely read, has a world-wide network of friends. "I tell my friends be very careful what you tell me because I will never forget." Most importantly this woman is interested and intrigued by the present and the future. She proclaims she is at an age when she grunts when she gets in or out of a chair but also "we cannot stop the aging process but we can stop getting old". Helen is still an American voter and has an educated and keen interest in the process taking place in 2008. She feels strongly about the biased media treatment accorded Hillary Clinton, as nothing less than shameful.

> I have long thought a black man would be President before a woman. Americans are going to show the world they are not racist, however the sexism is so overt. Sexism is so deeply embedded.

Helen was upset that early in 2008 the media chose to transmit a voter coming up to the Republican candidate and asking "How do we beat the bitch?" She draws the parallel of a voter walking up to a presidential candidate and using the "N" word in the same context: "I can't use the "N" word". Helen had just done an interview with *USA Today* and used the word "Hell". The newspaper chose to change the word to "Heck".

> I can't say 'Hell' in a newspaper but it is perfectly alright for someone to call a former first lady and two-term senator a bitch on national television. From now on I am going to call it the 'B' word.

Helen's biggest concern is the way of the world, about an economy based on unrestricted growth, on greed and unsustainable consumerism, on a technology-dependent way of life. "What is happening to the economy is just the tip of the iceberg." Helen has been an environmental activist ever since Earth Day 1970. She was well into recycling and grey water long before it became fashionable. "Start growing your own vegetables ... we already have food shortages." She is disturbed that one-third of US corn production is now going to ethanol production. Market gardens are re-appearing in urban centres like Detroit. It is encouraging but there needs to be a lot more. There is a slight American twang occasionally in the voice on certain syllables:

> We need to change the way we live, change the way we think, try to gently alert people to the fact that the way of life that they have known and expect to continue is over. It's gone and it is very necessary to go through this because we have been living an unsustainable lifestyle, we have been living a greedy existence.

Helen is involved in an organisation exploring sustainable crop diversification in third world countries and hopes – no, believes – "it will be third-world women who will save the world. They have the most to lose". She refuses to give into the disease which has plagued her for half of her life. "You're supposed to be careful", but a few years ago she went rock climbing in Brazil. No way will Helen Reddy become a victim – to disease or to a society which ordains post-menopausal women be invisible – no way.

It is difficult to believe that the years since that first interview in 2008 have flown by so fast. Helen and I have stayed in touch, my visits to her thoroughly enjoyable because Helen has a wisdom I appreciate, a feistiness I find inspiring, and a wicked dry sense of humour. Her life experiences are so extensive and her interests so diversified. She is passing through her autumn years feeling useful –

but not necessarily completely fulfilled – and seems a little restless. This is due in part to Traci, Jordan and Lily living in the United States, but also because her indomitable spirit is not yet ready, or should that be "reddy", for that seamless and graceful transition into full retirement.

In 2010 I asked Helen what had been happening and she replied in rapid-fire fashion; "Bugger all!". But of course it was not true. She had been busy with her various interests, more than most of us could handle. She has her hypnotherapy clients and was enjoying helping them overcome paranoia. And Helen did have some fun in 2010 when she undertook a small part in the US black humour film *The Perfect Host*. The role of a neighbourhood "busy body" was supposed to go to a young to middle-aged woman but the producer decided it would be fun to cast Helen. The film had a budget of just one million dollars and was shot in just seventeen days but it meant Helen received an expenses-paid trip to California, and more importantly, smelled the greasepaint yet again.

Helen had wearied of singing that song, the words, "I Am Woman", but they continued to resonate in 2012 – the 40th anniversary of when the song topped the Billboard charts. She would like to be known for many more musical creations than "that" song but believes the words within "I Am Woman" remain relevant.

I recall our discussion in Sydney during 2010 when Helen believed things were moving forward:

> I have a woman Mayor, a woman Premier, a woman Governor, a woman Prime Minister and a woman Governor-General; how good is that?

The woman NSW Premier disappeared, but during the last few years there has been a level of vitriolic against women in public positions not witnessed before; there remain too few women business executives, too few women in mainstream media. There is too much emphasis on self, on how women should look. Helen's advice to women is:

> Stop buying all those stupid magazines, you're beautiful just the way you are, you don't need to worry about the size of your boobs, the colour of your hair, or anything about yourself; you are perfect the way you are and don't buy those crappy magazines.

On a higher level Helen is concerned by the lack of activism within younger generations, particularly young women not pursuing an active interest in feminism. She was invited to speak at a women's conference, the audience largely made-up of young women. It was of concern that seminars included:

> Why can't we binge drink and have sex just like the men ...does that have anything to do with feminism on any level?

During our 2008 interview Helen had said to me:

> I love the fact that I don't care so much about things – things that were so terribly important when you're younger, they don't matter when you get older.

But in 2012 the fire still burned within, and the woman who penned the song which became an anthem for women's equality is riled by unfairness, sexual discrimination and backward steps:

> A lot of things gained during the '70s have been lost. And I think it is time to put women forward in more places.

Over the last years Helen Reddy kept telling herself and others: "I am in a very good place", and "some people live to entertain, some people entertain to live" and she was the latter. But in 2012 she gathered with friends and family to celebrate her sister's Toni's 80th birthday. Toni Lamond cajoled her into singing "Breezin' Along With The Breeze", the duet they had recorded in 1999. With emotion Toni recalled:

> She agreed, I must add with a bit of reluctance, which in hindsight I realise was fear … There were 95 people at my party, and a great many of them were crying, or smiling, and sprang to their feet at the end in a standing ovation. I heard that several guests, big names in theatre and television, had written special material, to honour my birthday. Not one of them got up! I heard later, not one of them felt they could follow our duet. We were "too hard an act to follow". They were stunned at Helen's voice, not having heard her in several years. And all through the rest of the evening they were asking her why she was in retirement? Her voice was better than ever.[4]

In October I received an email from Helen: "I am singing again and have never enjoyed it so much!". She was in California and had performed in a St Genevieve High School (Los Angeles) concert to raise funds for the arts programme. Helen had forgotten what "joy" there is in doing this sort of concert. So she agreed to "An Intimate Evening with Helen Reddy" at *Yoshi's* jazz club in San Francisco. The eyes were sparkling and the performance was the same. Helen's Facebook page lit up with hundreds of posts from fans old and young from all over the world. A combination of events, thoughts and emotions led to this and Helen's rich velvety tones were being heard again after an absence of ten years.

Helen is coming "home" to pack. She has decided to return to live in the United States. Son Jordan will manage singing engagements. She is not yet sure how this will be received by the public but she is excited and revitalised. Life just seems so much more exhilarating when it isn't set in stone. I organise another interview, in Sydney, and decide to include another inspiring woman, Geraldine Cox, because Geraldine is out from Cambodia on yet another speaking engagement. It helps that Geraldine was inspired by "I am Woman" in the 1970s, and is a Helen Reddy "fan", though the term seems quaint in the circumstances.

The interview takes off on its own course as these two great Australians enjoy each other's company and mutual admiration transpires. They share interesting lives and the same wicked sense of humour. I am again reminded of the title of the book written by Harvard Professor of History, Laurel Thatcher Ulrich, *Well-behaved Women Seldom Make History*.[5] The title evolved into a frequently used feminist saying. Although this may not be true of all women who make history, it is true here, and it is a badge both Helen and Geraldine would brandish with pride.

Kathryn, Helen and Geraldine
Photograph by Margaret Hadfield (Zorgdrager)

I struggle to keep the interview professional and on course and when I give up, Helen and Geraldine power on, asking each other questions, nodding knowingly, and chuckling at each other's responses. I have become an observer. But their discussion reflects how mature women feel and how they perceive the world in 2012. These are two intelligent, positive women, but they wonder if the world has not left them behind in some ways.

It is challenging to feel relevant in a techno world. Blackberries (the non-edible kind), notebooks (the non-paper variety), tablets (the non-talking type) iPhones, Kindles, iPads, even mobile phones dominate lives in the 21st century. Our parents in their 80s and 90s have been made to feel redundant. They are often not computer literate; they cling to bank passbooks and have never operated automatic teller machines (ATMs). They struggle in a society which does not offer face-to-face encounters, where telephone calls are answered by recorded messages or people from other countries. There is no alphabet letter in front of their generation; the world has moved too quickly, and sadly they believe they can offer little anymore. The oldest generation was once the fountain of knowledge – they offered oral history and wisdom; but now the younger generations have the internet.

Helen Reddy is of the generation who prefer books and she loves second-hand bookshops: "So many jewels you find in there". But alas, bookshops, new and second-hand, are vanishing as eBooks dominate the publishing world. Helen used to have a "fan club" and receive fan mail, now it must be Facebook and Twitter. Helen was the first Australian to win a Grammy but that was in the days of vinyl records. Then came CDs but now it is iTunes and MTV. She is considering a new album – but it is not an "album" anymore. The recording world has moved on faster than she has been able to keep up. Her son Jordan wants her to record again, but she must leave the form this takes in the modern music world to him. Music trends have changed many times since Helen Reddy performed last. Helen is of the generation when it was about "clear voices ... the voice itself was the main instrument". With the rapid rise of singers like Adele, there are signs that the music world may well have evolved so much it is coming back. Helen may even find that her voice is in fashion again.

It is January 2013 and Helen flies out for new and old horizons. She is eager and happy and perhaps just a little nervous. During that benefit concert in the latter stages of 2012: "I suddenly realised, I'm a musician again, yes, I am a musician". She is re-memorising songs of yesteryear which she realises her audiences will request – including "that" song. But more so she is looking forward to regaling audiences with "album cuts". There were so many songs which never made it onto her albums and CDs. Recording companies' stressed: "Got to have a hit". Now this is her time and she can treat audiences and herself to lesser known songs from her vast repertoire and she can finally sing more blues and jazz. Coming out of retirement Helen expected just a few singing engagements in 2013, it had been ten years and she never expected the avalanche of bookings which followed. "Gigs" in Florida, South Carolina, Virginia, New Jersey, New York State and California have filled the diary, including two in New York City at the venue with the same name as an old friend – BB King.

In many ways Helen Reddy's evolution highlights the evolution of women since 1941, though this particular lady has evolved with a little more noise, a little more flair, and a larger sense of adventure than most of us. And Helen Reddy continues to evolve; how does that song go: "I am woman hear me roar ... I am strong, I am invincible".

For information and donations:
www.addisons.org.au

1. *Reddy, Helen. The Woman I Am*, Harper Collins, 2005.

2. Lamond, Toni. Email, 28 April 2013.

3. *People*, 29 June 1981. Earlier quotes this paragraph from People, 21 March 1983 and 16 May 1983.

4. Lamond, Toni. Email, 28 April 2013.

5. Ulrich, Laurel Thatcher. *Well-Behaved Women Seldom Make History*, Knopf, 2007.

113

Geraldine Cox

"It is a pity people do not realise it is not 'things' that make you happy... I have wealth of a different kind."

It is the month before the wet season and heat and humidity shroud the upper body, a small breeze flickers through the doorway and you pray it will continue. The sound of children's laughter takes your mind away from the discomfort of the Cambodian climate. There is a throng of small bodies in Geraldine Cox's kitchen, pancake mix is energetically stirred and adult supervision ensures that the frying process is restricted to the white batter. Happy little faces fill with pancakes and sugar – more children appear. The doors are fully open not just to allow for any cooling movement of air but also for little bodies to come and go freely. The faces are cheerful and the voices clear as they echo "Hello Big Mum" and fling arms around Geraldine's neck. If she is moving they will go for the legs or waist and Geraldine is rarely still, even when seated on the orange couch in her home or in her office, the hands move constantly, there is so much to organise and it must be done now. I switch off my recorder yet again as she dashes off to make a phone call, to oversee some aspect of Sunrise life. I lose count of how many children there are the emotional greetings and moods clearly joyful as they return from the Khmer New Year week-long holiday, 2009. They want their photographs taken and then to view their images. Such a little thing results in peals of laughter and they hug you, partly for this small delight, partly to thank you for paying them the compliment of being interested, partly because they were earlier deprived of human comfort, and partly because where they are now is so much better than where they once were. The outpouring of simple raw emotion is overpowering, hearing their stories is overwhelming. At first you wonder how anyone can deal with this 24/7 and by the next day you wonder how you can leave.

The title of the Geraldine Cox 2000 autobiography is *Home is Where the Heart Is.*[1] Chapters include "Laughter and Tears", "Paradise Lost", "Paying for Love", "Fired and Fifty", "Ashes to Ashes, Dust to Dust", "Ducking, Diving, Surviving", and "Dried Tears". These promise a forthright and honest story and you are not disappointed. The titles are a warning and testament to a take-your-breath-away, warts and all, confession. Geraldine believes that had her book been released before her investiture as a Member of the Order of Australia she would not have received that honour. This may be harsh – it could well be accurate. But the truth is, no one deserves it more.

Geraldine Cox divides her life into two stages. The first is merely "BC", "before Cambodia". In "BC" there were things she was proud of and things she was not. Regardless, they were part of the journey she needed to take before she arrived in the place where she needed to be. Geraldine was proud to be the daughter of a milkman. You can understand that. There was something wonderfully honest and nurturing about those who delivered fresh milk 365 days a year. Children of today may struggle with the concept that the clink of milk bottles with coloured foil tops on the doorstep was comforting. Milk in a plastic container shoved into a supermarket trolley doesn't have the same effect. Norm Cox was one of those "salt of the earth" types – good and honest, a simple man in a simple time in a simple place. He and his sweetheart Dot married during the Depression. They worked hard and were satisfied with the small pleasures of life in suburban Adelaide. Life revolved around family. Dot was happy being a wife and mother but with the death of her third baby daughter she fell into depression. She lost part of herself and would never be the same. Geraldine came after, born in 1945. For whatever reason, Geraldine was different, unlike her sisters in manner and physical shape. She realised this from an early age. Her sisters were accepting and accepted. Unlike her sisters she was not elegantly thin, she was physically large with "tree trunk thighs". By her teens she would pretend not to care but she did, until Cambodia finally called her home.

Geraldine left school before she turned 16. In the 1960s the Australian education system reflected Australian society which was very conservative. It preferred people to remain within clearly defined stereotypes derived from British civilisation and Christian values, based on authority and paternalism. It did not accommodate difference well. The nation's education system reinforced conformity and convention and rewarded those who adhered closely to stringent scholastic parameters. Those who could not were jettisoned and branded unworthy. There was little time for original thinkers, for those who had not quite worked out what they wanted to be when they grew up, and for those who could make little sense of the why. Many struggled hard to conform, others rebelled. Geraldine was as frustrated with those who accepted their clean, clear-cut roles, as she was frustrated that she felt unable to do so. She rebelled against the system and, although she did not appreciate it at the time, against herself. And this predisposition received added incentive. Her father, who never asked more than to make an honest living by delivering milk 365 days a year and to provide a good life for his girls, was dealt a huge blow. A cartel took over his wholesale milk business and halved his income. Geraldine remembers:

He fought back, and morally he should have won his court battle. But I learned early that justice is not always on the side of the good. Dad never recovered from this blow ... he turned his suffering in on himself.[2]

Norm Cox had smoked most of his life. He developed asthma and then lung cancer. The family watched helplessly as the man who had always been so strong and active shrank before their eyes, his bitterness and disappointment helping to propel him towards death.

Geraldine did not understand society and it failed to understand her. Her behaviour became wilful and promiscuous. "Sex discovered me when I was 15." In the 1960s "good girls" were those who remained virgins until taken to their marriage bed. She later admitted her behaviour at that time was probably "delinquent". She also knew she wanted "none of this fate bullshit. I was going to be the mistress of my own destiny". Over the ensuing decade the men she would take into her life would not be members of the status quo, good Anglo-Saxon Aussie boys. Her family was always hoping for a "Bruce, Roger or Barry", even a "Bazza". Instead there was Miroslav the Yugoslav, Yakob the Israeli, Ibrahim the Turk, Meho the Lithuanian, Bruno the Hungarian, Hassan the Lebanese, Karl the German, and Andreas the Cypriot. Without realising it her choice of many "new Australians" was part of the rebellion, part of the search.

It was 1963 and Geraldine at 18 embarked on her first overseas trip. Onboard a ship headed for Europe she watched the Australian coastline disappear and "my instincts told me that it would be hard to settle for the quiet life that Adelaide had to offer".[3] But she returned when the money ran out, lived at home and worked in Adelaide as a secretary. She commenced another relationship, with Theo the Greek. About now Geraldine began to wonder whether she too could share the future preordained for good Australian girls and not so good ones. Life on the quarter acre suburban block, hanging nappies on a Hills Hoist, and answering the call "Honey I'm home" actually began to appeal. It appealed to Theo also, particularly the children bit. Geraldine did not become pregnant. She discovered she had blocked Fallopian tubes. Painful medical procedures proved useless. Her relationship broke up and, feeling broken herself, she turned her attention again to a fulfilling career, but here too there was resistance; fulfilling careers for Australian women were limited.

Geraldine was a "war baby" born at a time when women were enjoying the greatest employment opportunities. With World War II and the nation's men mostly in uniform and overseas, there was no option but to allow women to undertake employment previously closed to them. Even so a guide for the hiring of women included:

Tips on Getting More Efficiency out of Women

- Pick young married women. They usually have more of a sense of responsibility than their unmarried sisters, they're less likely to be flirtatious.
- Older women who have never contacted the public have a hard time adapting themselves and are inclined to be cantankerous and fussy. It's always well to impress upon older women the importance of friendliness and courtesy.
- General experience indicates that "husky" girls – those who are just a little on the heavy side – are more even tempered and efficient than their underweight sisters.
- Give each woman you hire a special physical examination – one covering female conditions. This step not only protects against the possibilities of lawsuit, but reveals whether the employee-to-be has any female weaknesses which would make her mentally or physically unfit for the job.
- Women make excellent workers when they have their jobs cut out for them, but they lack initiative in finding work themselves.

- You have to make some allowances for feminine psychology. A girl has more confidence and is more efficient if she can keep her hair tidied, apply fresh lipstick and wash her hands, several times a day.
- Women are often sensitive; they can't shrug off harsh words the way men do. Never ridicule a woman – it breaks her spirit and cuts her efficiency.
- Be reasonably considerate about using strong language around women. [4]

Although women proved tenacious, resilient hard workers, when the war finished and men returned, Australian women were returned to the homes and the barriers against them in the workforce were resurrected. When Geraldine Cox was searching for a "fulfilling career" the choices were still limited. Commonly women became sales assistants, nurses, typists, clerical assistants and secretaries. Geraldine was determined to find larger opportunities. She had worked for a decade and become a secretary. There had to be greater opportunities, she had to get out into the wider world, and she decided that to achieve this she must join the Commonwealth Public Service and, in particular, the Department of Foreign Affairs and Trade (DFAT).

The Commonwealth Government was the largest employer of women, but women struggled hard to gain equal rights and diversity of employment. At Federation there was little room for women in the nascent Commonwealth Public Service. As it was a "career" service, married women were not considered and were automatically excluded under the provisions of the Public Service Act of 1902. Single women could be employed but as it was expected they would soon marry they were assigned mundane duties with little opportunity for advancement. A royal commission report in 1922 cited the "physiological unsuitability" of women as justification for discouraging an increase of female workers in the Commonwealth Public Service. The commission considered the efficiency of government departments would be hampered if women were permitted to enter the 3rd Division – the main career, clerk division. They were entitled to join only as members of the 4th Division, the lowest. Things were slow to improve. When Geraldine Cox started her quest to become a Commonwealth public servant, resistance continued. This was the era of the office designated "typing pool" where women could be found in great numbers, each sitting behind a typewriter, contending with the seemingly endless flow of letters and reports from male clerks. In a 1963 report to the Director for DFAT, the possibility of women being appointed to senior positions within the department had been addressed. It discussed "Women Trade Commissioners" and found: "Even after some deliberation it is difficult to find reasons to support the appointment of women as Trade Commissioners". The report found that a "young, attractive woman could operate with some effectiveness, in a subordinate position". It did not believe women could be trade commissioners "firstly because they could not mix nearly as freely with businessmen as men do. Most men's clubs, for instance, do not allow women members". The report conceded that women certainly were a valuable asset, but as wives.

> A man normally has his household run efficiently by his wife, who also looks after much of the entertaining. A woman trade commissioner would have all this on top of her normal work.

It was argued that single female graduates would waste any training because they would likely "marry within five years". Should any not marry then they were not likely be an asset to the government because "a spinister [sic] lady can, and very often does, turn into something of a battleaxe with the passing years. A man usually mellows". The 1963 report concluded that the appointment of a woman would "preclude us from giving practical experience to one male officer". One senior official believed that despite the best efforts of those who ran his department:

> There is no way of precluding women ... Many more applications are received from women than from men ... about one woman is appointed to every twelve men. This year one out of sixteen.[5]

His written comments concluded with an exasperated "External Affairs lacks courage to slam the door because of parliamentary opinion, pressure groups and so on".

As Geraldine posted her Foreign Affairs application the National Wage Case resulted in about 18 per cent of women in the workforce receiving equal pay. However the result meant hiring and employment justifications were tightened and increases in the Consumer Price Index (CPI), between 1975 and 1981 actually widened the gap between men's and women's rates. One most important barrier was, however, removed: women could no longer be removed from employment or lose permanent status on marriage. But marriage was not on Geraldine's mind, she wanted to live on the wild side and the Commonwealth Public Service in 1970 offered her not only an "out of Adelaide" but an "out of Australia". She threw herself into training courses to qualify herself for an overseas position as a personal secretary. In December 1970 she had talked and pleaded her way into the department. "I got into Foreign Affairs through sheer determination, telling a few tiny lies, exaggerating a little bit." Those who have met Geraldine know that she could pretty much talk anyone into anything, she laughs and admits that she has seen "people cross the road to avoid me". The department didn't really know what was about to hit them.

The milkman's daughter was thrilled that she was finally moving in what she believed to be her life's true direction. She was 25 and thought she had it all figured out. Geographic mobility was still not part of modern day living but this was a period when the Commonwealth was endeavouring to expand Canberra as the centre of government. Clusters of young single public servants congregated in government hostels like Gowrie and the more notorious Reid House. Geraldine welcomed leaving home but some could not cope with moving away from family and friends networks and home cities; "depression and suicide were often the result" recalls Geraldine of the early 1970s in Canberra. Geraldine could fully understand being depressed by hostel life. She was billeted in Lawley House, "I've seen better jails in my time". Life was stark so she lost little time in moving into a town house with two other girls. There wasn't a great deal to do in the nation's capital if you were not married. It was very much a case of forming social networks and partying. And party they did. At least her flatmates did. Geraldine again seemed on a different page, ahead of the rest. To a degree it was "been there done that". She was more intent on improving her position within Foreign Affairs.

It wasn't all clear sailing, the Commonwealth Public Service was a conservative place and this could never be said about Geraldine.

"I was regarded in the grey world of the public service as
a tad too colourful ... I was definitely the only woman in
the department flaunting false eyelashes."

This was 1971 and although Geraldine did not realise it she had been ready for the 1970s during the 1960s.

She preferred long boots and dresses to the ankles rather than miniskirts. This she believed was necessary due those "tree-trunk thighs". Regardless, her supervisor believed her dress "too modern". Geraldine wore a miniskirt one day to please her supervisor and was never questioned again about wearing long skirts. Geraldine, being Geraldine, refused to make any other concessions. She was always willing to engage in relationships with the opposite sex but this was a public service town and the favoured public service young man was very northern European. "They all looked the same, sounded the same, dressed the same, said the same things and did the same jobs." Geraldine was unimpressed and then she met Slobodan the Serbian bar waiter. If not wearing miniskirts was not enough to stunt her progress in Canberra's public service world, having a Serbian lover certainly did not open doors. Of course Geraldine had no desire to enter those doors anyway and was delighted when she was assigned an overseas secretary's position in Cambodia.

Cambodia was deemed a hardship posting but Geraldine was thrilled. Finally she was leaving Australia, out of the norm, off on an amazing adventure, and flying first class. The milkman's daughter had made the big time. Her confidence took a little dint when she arrived in Phnom Penh to hear the airport had been rocket bombed by the Vietnamese and that embassy car drivers needed to check under their cars for explosive devices. Soldiers congregated in the streets; many "had hand grenades attached to their belts. Ammunition belts criss-crossed their chests like evil necklaces",[6] and they swaggered along with AK47s and M16 rifles. It suddenly dawned on Geraldine that she had arrived in a country "well and truly at war" and that "a person could get killed here". Cambodia had historically suffered upheaval and attack particularly from its sworn enemies Vietnam and Thailand – too many invaders, too many wars. The French had pronounced Cambodia a protectorate in 1864 and the colonisation was not always benevolent. French authorities crowned Prince Norodom Sihanouk King in 1941 but he refused to be a puppet king. By 1953 he had won freedom from the colonising yoke for his country and in 1954

Cambodian neutrality was recognised by the Geneva Convention on Indochina. The neutrality was sustained in the early part of the Vietnam War until Sihanouk declined United States aid and influence. By 1966 Vietnamese communists established supply lines along Cambodia's borders. By 1967 the United States Government sanctioned military raids on the supply lines and Cambodia was being drawn further and further into a war in which it had no real friends. In 1969 President Nixon ordered B52 bombing of areas within Cambodia where it was believed there were communist Vietnamese strongholds. Sihanouk was deposed and sought exile in China. When the girl from Adelaide arrived on a Department of Foreign Affairs posting Cambodia was under a military government led by Marshal Lon Nol, and the Vietnam War continued to rage.

Geraldine struggled to settle in, she had wanted different and exciting but this was about as different and exciting as it could get. Working for the Defence Attaché meant there was nowhere to hide when it came to the war and its deadly ramifications. She quickly realised why embassy staff invariably lost themselves in alcohol and she did her best to join them. There was the odd amusing incident, one being when she was awoken by screams and violent banging. Wondering if the North Vietnamese were mounting an attack from her bathroom, she ran towards the bedlam to find her maid beating Geraldine's mink false eye lashes to a grisly end with a broom. Geraldine attempted to explain that these were not some horrible Aussie insects. Judging by the mystified expression on the maid's face something had been lost in translation and Geraldine was down one pair of false eyelashes.

It is April 2009 and Geraldine arrives to collect me from the hotel. Phnom Penh has just had a tropical storm. The Cambodian capital is on a river, in the truest sense and any sustained downpour and the city slips underwater. Geraldine has a four wheel drive, which is just as well as many streets are knee deep in water, and she navigates where she can regardless of what signs say. This is standard practice in Phnom Penh; road rules are open to interpretation. Seat belts are not law; how could they be in a country where it is common for a family of five plus groceries to travel on a motorbike; where bodies stack into the back of utes and on the top of buses; where motorists drive with one hand on the steering wheel and one hand on the horn. I quickly learn the golden rule for a passenger is not to look. Geraldine mentions that on her last trip to Australia she barely escaped with any semblance of a driver's licence. In a couple of weeks she managed infringements for speeding, going through red lights and not wearing a seat belt. On this trip we manage no infringements and after parking on the pavement, finish up at the Foreign Correspondents' Club.

Upstairs it is all old wooden and leather armchairs, timber bar and ceiling fans. It is crowded. This place is an institution, a watering hole for English-speaking diplomats, journalists, photographers and tourists. Some come to hear English voices, some to take in the great view of the convergence of the Mekong and Tonle Sap rivers. Most come for the beer. Journalists, English-speaking expatriates, and embassy staff retreated here and to the Royal Hotel during the troubled years, consuming as much alcohol as they could to deaden their senses. The walls are full of black and white photos, images of how it was. In her first years in Cambodia Geraldine tried to ignore the poverty and human misery, the blind and maimed soldiers, the amputees lying in the streets, families starving in the streets, the screams of the women as they found husbands and fathers in the backs of the trucks which bore the mangled and bloodied bodies to the hospital. She drank heavily, "it helped shut out the despair". She partied hard.

Against this backdrop of human misery, I worked, dressed up, had my hair and nails done, attended dinner parties where leftover food was often thrown out, bought French champagne ... relaxed in the comfort and security of my apartment, listening to music and reading novels.[7]

Another diversion was waterskiing on the Mekong River even though the river was full of bloated bodies bobbing up and down. Geraldine went skiing only once – she hit a bloated human corpse.

As the rocket attacks intensified she turned up the music and had another gin and tonic. When a 6pm to 6am curfew was imposed in Phnom Penh, Geraldine and the other Australians resolved the problem by having "all night dinner parties". She spent a great deal of time with war correspondents, they were "uncomplicated" and they "drank hard and played hard. Most of them were stoned every waking hour of the day". As the war got closer Geraldine conceded she was learning what it was to be "shit-scared".[8] There was another lesson learnt, "never to waste time and energy worrying about things I couldn't change".

She had never lost the desire to have a child; "if maternal instincts were visible they would have oozed out of every pore". It was difficult to understand why she had been given such intense maternal instincts but was physically incapable of having children. It made no sense and was cruel. "No one knew of the heartache that I carried with me always."[9] In the 1970s Australian society deemed single mothers incapable and unworthy of raising children and unmarried pregnant women were routinely sent off to unwed mothers homes until they delivered babies who were then placed with couples deemed capable and worthy of children. Geraldine was caught on the other side of this social sanction, being a single woman she was not entitled to adopt a child. She looked to quell some of her intense feelings by offering time to a Cambodian orphanage and quickly fell in love with the children who ran to her and clung to every part of her body; "they were starved of love, of human touch". Conditions at the orphanage were awful but as overwhelming as it was, this quickly became the most anticipated part of her week. After mothering many Geraldine decided to explore the possibilities of adopting one of these discarded children.

Finally the much awaited phone call came, an abandoned six-month-old baby girl had been brought to the orphanage. "You've never seen eighty kilos of flesh move as fast as I did that day."[10] As soon as Geraldine set eyes on the malnourished baby it was love at first sight and she took baby No. 63 home with her that afternoon, "I was in heaven." She immersed herself in her new role of mother and the baby quickly put on weight under her care. As the paperwork to adopt ground slowly through international channels baby No. 63 transformed into Lisa Devi Cox. Geraldine took her daughter to an American doctor and her world wobbled violently when he asked "why would you want to adopt a cerebral palsy baby?". She listened in horror as he listed the medical problems he found. Lisa's heart was on the wrong side, she was profoundly deaf and was unlikely ever to speak. Her baby had epilepsy, diabetes and was probably autistic. Lisa was not seven months, more likely 18 months – her afflictions were incurable and would worsen. He strongly advised Geraldine to return the baby to the orphanage. Geraldine did not agree, this was her daughter and she preferred to believe there was medical treatment somewhere in this world which would cure Lisa. There were many tears. The Australian Government refused Lisa's entry on medical grounds, the Cambodian Government determined Lisa to be Geraldine's responsibility. Finally after much lobbying, her own government agreed that she could return home with her daughter.

In January 1973 Geraldine and Lisa flew into Adelaide, Lisa's handicaps were multiple and pronounced, perhaps the most difficult was her autism. Geraldine hoped she could cope with the care and attention Lisa needed and she knew she would struggle with not being loved in return. She was haunted by her inability to have children and why her chosen child was so afflicted. The best medical opinions were sought and there was no good news and Geraldine was posted to the Philippines. The first morning she and Lisa were in Manila she saw staff cleaning a large pool of blood off the foyer carpet, she was again in a nation where "guns were the order of the day".[11] While Geraldine found the work at the Australian embassy engrossing, she sustained her avid interest in Cambodia and watched as the situation deteriorated. Life in Manila was comfortable but this was the period which highlighted "the worst of Imelda Marcos's excesses". Geraldine had begun to question excesses of any kind. She did not entirely fathom yet the subtle changes to her priorities and opinions caused by time in the small beleaguered nation between Vietnam and Thailand, and being the mother of a physically and mentally handicapped child. It was simply easier to pretend the questions and doubts did not exist and try to lose herself in the good life. Geraldine threw her energies into organising great dinner parties. Later she would admit how empty it all was to try "to impress people. Half the time I didn't even like the people I was trying to impress".

Lisa's condition deteriorated and her grand mal seizures increased and the search for medical "cures" became more expensive and more desperate. Her work commitment was suffering as Lisa's condition became more critical. Her own depression deepened. Finally the dark abyss beckoned and Geraldine decided she and Lisa would leave this cruel world together. She methodically planned their departure. That night she divided the stockpile of sleeping pills, lit some incense and a candle and gathered Lisa to her. As she prepared to give Lisa the medication which would end her life, her daughter smiled at her for the first time. Throwing the pills into the toilet Geraldine dissolved into tears. She had the right to take her own life but not the life of her daughter. After a long night she realised "there was nothing I couldn't bear in the future, nothing I couldn't overcome".[12] This resolution was severely tested when she admitted she could no longer offer the care her child needed. It was with deep sadness and guilt that

Geraldine agreed to place seven-year-old Lisa in full time care in Adelaide. Seven years later a couple of "angels" in the form of an Australian childless couple asked if they could foster Lisa. It was of great relief to Geraldine but the guilt endured.

Foreign Affairs advised Geraldine she was being posted to Bangkok. Lisa had left her life empty and the posting put an end to a five-year romance. In an act of defiance she coloured her hair bright red but she felt like a rudderless ship on life's ocean, her life lacked meaning and nothing much made sense, she was "in a state of emotional shock". During work hours she acted professionally, out of hours her behaviour reverted. There could have been more booze but there could not have been more sex. Geraldine sought solace in "meaningless one night stands". She didn't care and attempted to fill an emotional void by throwing herself "into the Bangkok bar scene with an abandon I had never thought I was capable of ... I picked up whomever took my fancy".[13] Only with hindsight did she realise how fortunate she was not to contract HIV or any other sexually transmitted disease, "nothing short of divine intervention". When she completely exhausted conventional avenues to adopt another child she turned to the least conventional. "I selected a series of handsome young male prostitutes to live with me one at a time for four weeks of my menstrual cycle ... and get me pregnant".[14] Each was paid a salary but as each failed he was "terminated" and she would employ another. She thought it was the last opportunity she would have to mother children. Months of this left her jaded and not pregnant. Geraldine decided too much was enough and swore she would accept her childless nature and turn her mind elsewhere. "I'm not meant in this world to be a mother, but nobody can say I didn't try everything."

Her thoughts returned to Cambodia and the friends left behind at the mercy of the Khmer Rouge. Decades later she would relate the story of a 17-year-old Cambodian boy who asked why, if space technology meant that by the 1970s satellites were powerful enough to read the print on earthly newspapers, no nation came to the help of the Cambodian people as the Khmer Rouge murdered his people. Geraldine saw first-hand the terrible consequences of the regime. In 1979 she visited a refugee camp on the Thai border and was horrified at the "wretched mass of humanity" she encountered. She tried to help but "felt desperately inadequate" in her attempts to alleviate the suffering. "The scale of the suffering was numbing." This terrible period of time left a legacy which would reverberate for generations. It affected Geraldine greatly but she had no way of knowing how it would define her future.

It was 1975 and the black-clad cadres of the Khmer Rouge swept to power in Cambodia. Cambodians, victims of the Vietnam War, thought these were their saviours. They still believed this when Khmer Rouge authorities ordered the inhabitants out of Phnom Penh. It was to be for a few days. This was the last lie the people of Cambodia believed. For nearly four years Cambodians were subjected to torture and genocide. Their country was renamed Democratic Kampuchea and under the leadership of the infamous Pol Pot the Khmer Rouge imposed an extreme form of social engineering on Cambodian society – a most radical form of agrarian communism. Contrary to most Marxist doctrine, the Khmer Rouge considered the farmers in the countryside to be the true proletariat, the true working class. The middle class was eliminated, most of those who had any education, the professionals, urban dwellers and particularly any seen as having been tainted by people of foreign governments. The Khmer Rouge considered the remaining population should work on collective farms or forced labour projects. Children were separated from their families and brainwashed to the ways of socialism. The brainwashing was the least destructive mechanism. Children, a most important instrument of the party, were given leadership in torture and execution. It was therefore fitting that a school was turned into an institution of torture and death. And while this happened the western world simply watched.

Phnom Penh's Tuol Sleng looks innocuous now on this humid April day in 2009, almost as it did when its grounds held children at play and young heads eager to learn – almost. This was the site of a primary school and a high school pre-1975. No children will grace these grounds again. Tuol Sleng in Khmer means "Hill of the Poisonous Trees" or "Strychnine Hill". This place was more commonly referred to as Security Prison 21 or S-21. The school buildings of Tuol Sleng were converted into cells and Cambodians were brought for detention, interrogation and torture. An estimated 14,000 people were brought to Tuol Sleng. Thousands of black and white photos line the walls. They are of people who have lost all hope, their expressions are empty and defeated, they are past even terror as if, after hours and hours of torture, and seeing things no one should ever witness, their imminent death is welcome. There are faces of tiny children, children not old enough to speak let alone denounce, but they too did not survive extermination. Cell walls remain stained with blood and a large glass case holds discarded clothing and shoes. There are signs requesting that visitors refrain from laughter and jovial behaviour – it is impossible to believe anyone could see or feel anything but the grimmest of emotions. Most of the people brought here were then trucked to Choeung Ek, once an orchard, and there they were killed and buried in mass graves. The 20-metre-high memorial is filled with skulls, bones and clothes – some 200,000 lay in the killing fields.

The eyes betray a deeply haunted soul and the story being told by Chum Mey chills me to the bone. He stands in front of a tiny cell in Tuol Sleng, just a couple of small brick walls, no need for doors because the heavy metal shackles that had been fastened to his ankles and one wall ensured he could not escape. Chum Mey accentuates his story, gesturing with pencil thin fingers. He pauses while the English translation is relayed, I am speechless. This tiny man who carries such an emotional load tells his story so vividly that the interpreter too struggles. Chum was no one special, just a car mechanic. The black and red regime encouraged Cambodian to turn on Cambodian, ordained it, and a colleague denounced Chum. To this day he doesn't know what he was accused of. He was dragged to Tuol Sleng, a place overpowering with the stench of death. He was met by blood splattered walls and floors and the screams of many. They beat him with "all sorts of instruments, sticks and electric shocks". They pulled out his toenails. His wife was tortured to death. Chum Mey survived because the head of Tuol Sleng heard he could paint. He was handed a picture of Pol Pot and told to draw a likeness. His depiction did not include an unsightly scar on the Khmer Rouge leader's throat. It pleased and he was told he should paint four large paintings of Pol Pot. He told them each painting would take three months and prayed the torture and killing madness would be over in one year. Tourists file past Chum with no inkling of this man's story. For this they can be forgiven, most have the glazed over expressions of those who are beyond further comprehension. This place and its collection of terrible photos and instruments of torture defy comprehension.

Chum struggles on to tell his story to anyone and everyone because people should know this history and he takes his responsibility seriously, because the Khmer Rouge murdered most of his generation. At 78 he doesn't know how much longer he will be able to continue but he is about to be called into court as a prosecution witness. It has been a long time coming, but the international justice system grinds slowly. The Extraordinary Chambers of the Courts of Cambodia (ECCC) is finally considering the guilt of Kaing Guek Eav, the first former Khmer Rouge leader to face trial. Four other leaders are in custody – five men being judged for the death of millions seems a little implausible, but Chum Mey is looking forward to his day in court.

It is estimated that between a fifth and a third of the Cambodian population, as many as 2.5 million, were murdered or allowed to starve, to purge society of capitalism, any free-market activities. Only then did unlikely allies, Vietnamese soldiers, arrive to drive out the Khmer Rouge. It is hard to believe that when my generation of Australians were jiving to the Bee Gees, having babies, and enjoying the good life, we were oblivious to the fear and death which gripped a people, mere hours away. It is impossible not to travel the full gambit of emotions, and there is anger too, that western media and governments kept us ignorant and uncaring. Geraldine believes people should visit Tuol Sleng and the Killing Fields because more than any other history the period between 1975 and 1979 defines Cambodia, defines the people and preordained her mission.

In 1979 Geraldine had still to determine this. She was busy struggling with the reality of the Cambodian situation. She was also struggling with her inadequacy to have children and adopt children. So many inadequacies and then she was given a bad assessment by the Australian Ambassador to Thailand. She had prided herself that whilst her personal life may not impress officialdom her professional standards remained impressive. It seemed now in the eyes of officialdom the personal overshadowed the professional. She was told she would return to Australia and was unlikely to be given another overseas posting. "The only pleasure left in my life was my work and travel with the Department of Foreign Affairs."[15] She pleaded and cajoled. "I grovelled, I begged. I hated myself."[16] Geraldine needed overseas allowances to cover the expense of Lisa's care and said she would accept any posting. It was music to the ears of Foreign Affairs personnel managers in Canberra because they had been unable to convince anyone to take up a post in Iran. It was 1981 and not long after the 444 day American hostage crisis.[17] There was a revolution going on but Geraldine was desperate so she agreed to board an aircraft for Tehran, vowing her behaviour would improve.

That resolution lasted until she saw how handsome the men were. Her lifestyle was opulent but repressive. She was not a Middle Eastern woman, in her late thirties and unmarried. Her predilection for the wrong sort of male companion resulted in a near fatal beating. "Iran more than sated my appetite for danger."[18] Having said that, she began to enjoy social aspects of the posting and even requested an extension. Personnel managers in Canberra were frustrated as Iran was supposed to be a punishment posting for Geraldine, yet with few volunteers, they had to agree to her request. It was 1983 when she met Mahmoud – it was 1984 when they married and late 1984 when Geraldine was posted to Washington DC. The marriage struggled under the weight of cross-culture demands. Geraldine buried herself in embassy duties but realised she was tiring of the politics of diplomatic affairs and in 1987 she resigned. She believes that on receiving her resignation the personnel managers in Foreign Affairs immediately stopped work to party. For 17 years Geraldine had enjoyed and suffered overseas service; it was time to return home.

The first jolt of reality was discovering the cost of living in Australia, the second jolt was looking for work as a 43-year-old woman. She was finally offered a position with the Chase Manhattan Bank and Mahmoud finally secured a job with IBM. Both worked long hours and what was left of the marriage shrivelled and died. "It was a relief for both of us when we finally divorced in June 1990."[19] The feelings of inadequacy returned and unsatisfied by the boring routine of business life, the feelings that she was meant to do something more, resurfaced. It was hard to make sense of it but her thoughts kept returning to Cambodia, so in November 1992 she decided to revisit the country which cast such a "mystical, magical pull" over her.

After a couple of days in Phnom Penh she flew to Siem Reap to enjoy the magnificence of Angkor Wat, a structure some referred to as the "eighth wonder of the world". The sheer magnitude of the soaring spires of Angkor Wat took her breath away as did the intricate carvings and skilled workmanship which rivalled anything in the world. "I ran my hand tenderly along the walls of exquisitely crafted bas-relief carvings. The smooth stone was cool and felt oddly familiar beneath my touch."[20] She knew she was a tourist who would return to an office job in Sydney but deep down this seemed more, it felt like a pilgrimage. Other temples and structures in the Siem Reap district seemed to speak to her: Angkor Thom, the last and most enduring capital city of the Khmer empire; its Victory Gate, making the most opinionated individual feel ridiculously insignificant as they passed between lines of huge sandstone faces – devas on the left and asuras on the right, opposing forces depicting a violent tug-of-war. At its centre was the temple now called Bayon, a multi-faceted, multi-towered temple that mixed Buddhist and Hindu iconography. The outer walls were covered in splendid carvings depicting not just warfare, even a naval battle, but also scenes of everyday life. The last temple in this unbelievable nine kilometre complex was dedicated in 1295 and the city abandoned sometime around 1609 – war, disease and corruption the causes. Out of the jungle appeared Ta Prohm. Giant silk cotton trees and strangle figs clutched tightly at carved stone, their roots coiling around bas-relief. There seemed no words which truly described Banteay Srei – citadel of women, or citadel of beauty. Consecrated in 967AD and primarily dedicated to the Hindu god Shiva, the temple was made of hard red sandstone which could be carved like wood and seemingly every piece of its lintels and pediments were exquisitely carved. It glowed red in the failing sunshine but was known as the "pink temple". Geraldine felt completely at peace and believed the serenity she felt would remain a constant.

Upon her return to the land of her birth serenity was not the dominant emotion and she struggled with increasing restlessness. Geraldine had arrived in Cambodia in 1970 at the age of 25. The product of a loving suburban household, this woman from the Adelaide foothills was shaken by the difference between life as she knew it and as Cambodians suffered it. That first experience had stayed with her but Geraldine now saw how much worse it had become. At 25 she had done her utmost to shut out the plight of Cambodians, at 47 she could shut it out no longer. She and a friend created the Australia Cambodia Foundation and by June 1993 large quantities of medical supplies, clothes, toys, books and money had been gathered. Geraldine took leave from Chase Manhattan and with her friend escorted the donations to Cambodia. The precarious nature of the country meant Geraldine entered from Thailand, her van bursting with donated goods and locally purchased food. The orphaned children were under the auspices of Princess Marie Norodom Ranariddh and while this assisted Geraldine's party's entry it did little to belay their fears of road travel in the small country. Conservative estimates were that there was a land mine buried for every member of the population of ten million. Geraldine would eventually acknowledge that "the mines would never be cleared in my lifetime" but in 1993 the seemingly endless signs displaying skull and crossbones were very unnerving.[21] Slight comfort came from the toilet roll she clutched but this too was momentary given she was not allowed to stray from the thin trail of tyre marks to put it to good use.

At last Geraldine arrived to where the children were staying following their release from a Thai refugee camp:

> I had been prepared to fight back the tears, but with all the laughter and chattering going on, and the obvious pleasure everything we had brought was giving them, it never occurred to me to cry.
> In fact I was laughing with them.[22]

It was manna from Heaven – well, a bunch of generous Aussies and a determined Geraldine anyway. Geraldine began to prepare biographies of each child, taking pictures and asking them their stories and her blood chilled as she heard tales no child should ever tell, no child should ever have lived. Families who survived the Khmer Rouge found the "liberating" Vietnamese no less cruel. Tragedy and sadness was all they had known and their country was still caught in the quagmire of war. One generation of Cambodians had been subjected to the ruthlessness of the Khmer Rouge; their children had been subjected to the ruthlessness of the Vietnamese who occupied Cambodia from 1978 until 1989.[23] These children who gathered around Geraldine for comfort had never known anything but war and brutality. By the end of the week the twenty children were calling her "Madai Thom Thom" which translated to "Big Big Mother". Although Geraldine would have settled for one "Big" she couldn't have been happier and by the end of the 14 days she realised she was addicted.

A grant of $15,000 (US) through the Chase Foundation, the philanthropic part of the Rockefeller Foundation, offered the first major infusion of cash for an orphanage and over the next five years further infusions from the foundation proved invaluable. Six months after she returned home Geraldine heard that the situation was deteriorating as Cambodia struggled with out-of-control warring splinter groups. She applied for more leave and flew again to the children. In the nine days she was in country she accepted 18 more orphans, 18 more children with horrifying stories. When Geraldine suggested that they draw pictures of their happiest and saddest memories, one ten-year-old ardently said she couldn't because she couldn't remember anything happy.

The orphanage was called "Princess Marie's Orphanage" and it was a constant in Geraldine's consciousness whilst she tried to competently undertake her day-to-day business duties at Chase Manhattan in Sydney. Although it was increasingly difficult to think of anything but Cambodia and the children, normality was numbing and comfortable. "I didn't have the guts to actually leave my life." Fate delivered the final impetus necessary – she was sacked by Chase Manhattan. She was "fired and fifty" – it was 1995 and Geraldine had run out of excuses, so she packed up her Australian life and flew to Phnom Penh. She was given a small position in the Cabinet staff of Prince Norodom Ranariddh, a son of Prince Norodom Sihanouk. When the monarchy was restored in 1993 Ranariddh had become joint prime minister with his father's rival Hun Sen. Status was to be shared equally but in September Ranariddh asserted his primacy as First Prime Minister, and Hun Sen was made Second Prime Minister.

Geraldine's weekends were spent at the orphanage owned by the prince's wife, Princess Marie and it was here she felt most nurtured, it was she who was supposed to be caring for the children, but their love gave meaning to her life. With a new stability the children began to attend school regularly though it was difficult to motivate the children to be diligent at their lessons. Their view of life was very myopic, they did not believe they would live long enough to see any benefit from education. Even if they were to survive the violence there was then the scourge of disease and too many had watched relatives and friends die of untreated malaria, tuberculosis and cancer. It was frustrating because these children and the millions of others like them could be, "with the right opportunities, potential Mozarts, Rembrandts, and even Einsteins!".[24] Gradually scholarships would be found for those children with the ability and willingness to apply themselves. The more success stories there were, the more others realised the opportunities. Another challenge was to attain overseas medical attention for severely ill children and Geraldine was learning the hard way that this invariably came with a good deal of heartache and grief. She was also learning how difficult it was to spend her time on the greater number of children for the greatest amount of good – the learning curve was steep.

There were definite advantages working personally for Prince Ranariddh, while the salary was small, accommodation was included. The prestige of her position may have been exaggerated but there was a feeling of security. Geraldine believed the First Prime Minister and his FUNCINPEC Party was the future of Cambodia; she was feeling more and more part of this little nation and her "BC" life more a distant memory. The humidity of the climate would be something she would never entirely adapt to but the customs and ways of the people were becoming more familiar, even the newspaper content. "They had recipes for bat soup, advertisements for dog restaurants, where you could eat at a discount if you BYOD (Bring Your Own Dog)."[25]

It was 4 July 1997 when Geraldine's comfort zone was again breached. She was awoken not by the usual cacophony of noises of early morning traffic and street vendors but by the lack of them. The silence was eerie. When she ventured out she was told by a journalist that Prince Ranariddh had suddenly left the country. His staff and leading party members had mostly disappeared. There had been a coup and the coalition government put into place by the United Nations in 1993 was no more. Prime Minister Hun Sen had taken power, the streets were dangerous. After a nerve wracking trip to the Cabinet offices where she found only Hun Sen soldiers, Geraldine returned to her apartment anxious. She took stock of food and water supplies, something she had first done 27 years before in this country. Again bullets pierced the Cambodian air, again it was Cambodian against Cambodian. "The sheer lunacy of it all filled me with despair".[26] The dead were left to lie in the street and the shelling and gunfire raged into another day.

Geraldine was worried about the children but the situation in Phnom Penh was extremely hazardous. This didn't stop feelings of helplessness and frustration, she believed she should be doing more, she thought; she should not be so concerned for her personal safety. "Get off your fat bum, Geraldine. Get yourself out to the orphanage" she told herself, "self-loathing consumed me ... I was a despicable coward."[27] A woman employed at the orphanage made it to Geraldine's apartment and, sobbing, told her how soldiers loyal to Hun Sen had stormed the orphanage. Armed with B40 rockets, AK47s and M16s they held guns at the children's chests and accused them of harbouring soldiers loyal to the prince, they then vandalised and looted the orphanage. The children were so terrified they slept in the open believing rockets would hit their sleeping quarters, many were so stupefied they had not spoken a word since the fighting broke out. More soldiers came and some of the children had dropped to their knees and begged them to be merciful. Geraldine's heart sank, and it was the impetus she needed.

Foreign nationals were being evacuated but Geraldine ignored advice to be on an Australian evacuation flight. "I had already abandoned one Cambodian child, I'm not about to abandon 60 more." She drove through pandemonium, past houses riddled with bullet holes, corpses littered pavements, the wounded lay bleeding in the streets, burnt-out tanks smoldered and citizen turned on citizen in the name of party allegiance.

The journey seemed to take forever but as her car finally entered the orphanage gates the children ran towards her, laughing, crying, and yelling with joy, "look! Big Mum's here! she didn't go! she loves us!". Geraldine had trouble getting the car door open and as children fell on her she burst into tears. "It was like a thunderbolt to the heart. I was even more aware that this is what I should be doing with my life." How could she leave now? "I've had some pretty euphoric moments in my life, but this was far beyond anything I'd ever experienced."[28] She knew then that she would never leave Cambodia permanently, that she would never leave these children, that for the first time in her life she was where she should be and would become "the person I was supposed to be".

More soldiers arrived in tanks and shouted: "If you don't leave we will shoot you". Geraldine lost her temper: "Does your mother know what you're doing here today?" It was almost comical, a large red-haired woman angrily shouting something absurd in English. Absurd or not the soldiers drove away. The gravity of the situation was not lost on Geraldine; "I was convinced that Hun Sen was a killer and that he was going to take this country back to communism." Again she was advised to leave by her own government and again she refused. "I feel about these children as if they are my own. It's very difficult for me to make people understand that. These are my children." This was a message echoed over ABC radio. Regular ABC hook-ups over the following days added valuable media exposure to her plight and that of the children. The orphanage was safe for the time being, precarious as that was.

Sitha was stolen from his family's rice farm when he was nine years old by Vietnamese soldiers. He was forced to walk with other children as young as seven over landmine areas up into the mountains to carry back a cache of weapons which the soldiers were too afraid to retrieve. A Cambodian child getting blown up was of no consequence for them; they would not even bury the remains. Sitha realised that for him also the same end was inevitable. He escaped and walked a couple of hundred miles into the city, asking strangers where he could find someone who would care for him. This led him to Geraldine. It was difficult to comfort so many traumatised children like Sitha. "The main care and attention they received was love, hugs, kisses and reassurance." There was no counselling available, no psychologists or psychiatrists and, had there been, "Cambodians do not discuss their inner feelings, it is not a cultural thing". Geraldine struggled on alone. "I had a fourteen-year-old boy wetting his bed." There were disciplinary problems, the children lacked motivation.

They were drawing haunting images: soldiers standing over kneeling, praying children, a gun poised on a child's chest; bloodied torsos with no heads; a bird with an arrow through its chest. Geraldine made contact with an Australian psychologist and he recommended getting the children involved in singing and dance. She found a couple of precious Cambodians, a music teacher and a dance teacher, who could return the children to their cultural heritage. So much had been lost when the Khmer Rouge purged the Cambodian people of their teachers, of their artists, of their old people, in an attempt to destroy traditional Khmer civilisation and they nearly succeeded. But here was a self admitted "overweight" Australian woman ensuring that disadvantaged children were taught Cambodian music and dance.

Australian invitations to speak about the orphanage resulted in donations and sponsors for the children Geraldine had learnt the value of publicity and admits to being "a media slut". In 1998 a television documentary team trailed her in Cambodia and this included an audience with Hun Sen. Geraldine knew she needed to bring the children to his attention to ensure their safety. He apologised for the behaviour of soldiers loyal to him and assured her the orphanage was safe. Geraldine "could have jumped over the moon". She could now accept more children and the number soon exceeded 60. Cambodian life was settling down, elections were announced and Geraldine was asked to be an international observer. On the day of the election she watched as the ballot boxes were placed behind a locked door. With typical Geraldine exuberance she borrowed a camp bed from a soldier, placed it across the door, and lay down. The villagers were told in no uncertain terms that the only way to tamper with the ballot boxes was through her, they would need to lift her and the bed out of the way first. Such a feat was clearly beyond Cambodians and Geraldine and the boxes slept well that night. The election was a clear victory for Hun Sen. Geraldine may not have been entirely happy with the result but she knew at least in her village the consensus was true.

Her mother's illness required Geraldine to return to Australia in October 1998. In the beginning she found it easy to overdose on everything from bubble bath to movies but as the novelty of life in the western world wore off, she again yearned for Cambodia and particularly the children. Her anxiety increased as television news showed new violent unrest in the streets of Phnom Penh. Geraldine busied herself in attaining a computer school for the orphanage. She realised she could not depend on the Cambodian Government to ensure a thorough education for the children. Teachers were paid very poorly when they were paid at all, subsequently their attendance was not regular and when they did appear they did so with the expectation that students would supplement their salary. The Cambodian literacy rate was less than 40 per cent, unemployment was high and crime and corruption were rife. Geraldine knew the orphanage needed to take greater responsibility for education. Whilst visiting old colleagues at Chase Manhattan Bank in Sydney she discovered Chase was updating their computers. The old computers quickly found their way to a small orphanage in Cambodia, thanks also to an Adelaide shipping company.

In 1999 Geraldine was able to return to Cambodia in time to share the first Khmer New Year in 30 years where peace prevailed. Everything seemed wonderful, the orphanage was expanding thanks largely to the generosity of small overseas companies and Australian organisations and sponsors. The lives of the children were so much improved. Prince Ranariddh was now President of the National Assembly and Cambodia was stable. Then Geraldine received a letter from Princess Marie telling her that her services were no longer required and that she should leave by August 2000, "others" would take care of the orphans. Dismayed, Geraldine sought an audience but the meeting was a one-sided tirade. The princess was unhappy that Geraldine had instigated changes and developments independently. Geraldine followed up the meeting with a letter of apology and a full report on the orphanage. The return letter reiterated that Geraldine must leave and given that the lifestyle now enjoyed by the children was beyond what the royal patron was prepared to contribute, the children should leave as well. It was clear Geraldine's current Cambodian visa would not be extended, she was dumbfounded, where were the children to go? Who would take care of them?.

After many a sleepless night Geraldine realised there was but one option, she must seek assistance from the man she had previously labeled a murderer, usurper, communist and "thoroughly evil person" and, the children needed to be party to their own destiny. An appointment was made with the Prime Minister for the children to perform classic Khmer dance and music. Geraldine told them their performance would likely settle their future and it seemed even the youngest understood because that day they performed faultlessly. Hun Sen was overwhelmed. "He watched and listened like a proud father." Hun Sen complimented Geraldine on her efforts to care for these children and how she had nurtured them as Cambodians. Unlike most non-Asian philanthropists and charities she had encouraged the children to stay true to their Khmer culture and Buddhist religion. The nation's prime minister completely surprised her by offering an old military barracks on ten hectares for 50 years for a new orphanage, his government would provide transport to move the children, staff and belongings. As Geraldine was gasping with relief the Prime Minister quietly said that should she agree to continue her work, she would be granted Cambodian citizenship. Never in Geraldine's wildest dreams could she have contemplated such an outcome, she was overjoyed, her children were overjoyed. In just days 15 trucks arrived to take them to their new home, obstacles would continue but the future was suddenly so much brighter.

The name "Australia Cambodia Foundation" was changed to "Sunrise Children's Village". "It conjured up visions of a new dawn and a fresh beginning for orphans and disadvantaged children of Cambodia." And this was a new beginning for the children and Geraldine – her work had truly begun and she was fired up and ready. There were doubters but she was determined to ignore them.

> I love it when people tell me I shouldn't, couldn't, or can't do something. That's like red rag to a bull. I love choosing challenges or projects that seem impossible and then somehow pulling them off.

That said she had learnt two very important lessons: becoming involved in Cambodian politics was not wise; being very outspoken was also unwise, she would need to continue to work on both, particularly the latter.

At this momentous time a crew was filming a documentary titled *My Khmer Heart* on the lives of Geraldine and the children, a documentary Geraldine dedicated to:

> The children who did not survive the killing fields ... it is also about confronting memories of the past, and in a small way it is the story of Cambodia.[29]

It went on to win many awards, including Best Documentary 2000 at the Hollywood Film Festival, and was selected for the Montreal World Film Festival.[30] Cable television stations screened the documentary and generated great interest around the world. Actors Danny Glover and Matt Damon selected the documentary for an American Director's Guild fundraiser. It was another triumph for the children of Sunrise and the high profile event resulted in a badly needed boost to funding because in 2000 Geraldine needed around $4,000 US a month to keep the village going and invariably she did not have it.

When Geraldine and the children first arrived at the new site it had not been de-mined. Ghurkhas arrived and impressed Geraldine as they very professionally busied themselves with their Geiger counters. "They are little tiny fellas" Geraldine smiles as she recalls watching one of the soldiers dig and dig until he nearly disappeared. Dirt continued to fly out of the hole and Geraldine called, "whatever it is if it is that far down it can't be of danger to us". The Ghurkha continued. When he was finished a B52 bomb lay ugly and menacingly at the bottom of a crater. B40 rockets and unexploded ordnance were found in the pond. They were only three and a half hours from the Vietnam border and this did little to allay the children's unease. A teenager asked Geraldine "is the fighting over now Mum?". Cambodia had never enjoyed sustained peace. Geraldine could not lie to him, she didn't know herself if the fragile peace would continue. The teenager went on to mention that where they now were was on the main road to Vietnam and if there was going to be more fighting this was the road along which the men with guns would come. There was nothing "Big Mum" could say to alleviate that fear. She did shelve the idea of buying a second hand military truck to transport the children. "It would be a constant reminder to them that they would always be in danger."

Geraldine was adamant that Sunrise would not be an institution but a home where children and their talents were nurtured and it needed to be full of fun and laughter. With war dominating the children's consciousness Geraldine strove to encourage them to believe there were other options – the boys didn't need to go to war, the girls didn't need to be the wives of soldiers. Cambodia needed a new middle class, a generation and more of professionals who would help their nation to emerge from the third world and she was not backward in declaring it was the responsibility of the western world to assist.

This small little nation has suffered more in our generation
than any other country in the world and through the hands
of western powers. I think there should be some sort
of global social conscience for this particular country.
Everybody has had their fingers in this country.[31]

Photograph by Kathryn Spurling

Sunrise Children's Village is 20 kilometres south of Phnom Penh.
The fence is high, the gates shut and a guard asks your name and
purpose. It seems an unusual entrance until you reflect. This is a
desperately poor country and the children behind the gates are the lucky
ones, security ensures that the less fortunate do not avail themselves
of what lies within. It seems harsh to an Australian. The security also
protects the children from human predators. Cambodia is a land of
extremes of deep sadness and joy, a country with a dark history but
with a reasonably optimistic future. Presently it is a land which cannot
support a social security system, in sickness and misfortune people
flounder and die with women and children particularly vulnerable.
Geraldine says "women with children and without husbands have

four choices: starve, beg, steal or become a prostitute". With heavy hearts they bring their children to Sunrise and leave them behind and these are the kind mothers who realise their children must not face the limited choices they have to face. There are more disadvantaged children than orphans at Sunrise and on holidays they return to what family they have.

I sit on Geraldine's verandah and watch them return from Khmer New Year most, are delighted, the occasional child is not. One little boy of about six, clings to Geraldine, he does not speak and his eyes are buried in her shoulder. He is always this way when he returns and Geraldine is not sure what he is exposed to when he is home. She just holds onto him until other children entice him out to play.

Photograph by
Kathryn Spurling

A woman arrives with her two daughters. They are modestly dressed but spotless and none have shoes. The mother is tiny and delicate, the little girls very small for their age. The father lost his eyes in a landmine explosion and can no longer provide for his family. This tiny woman works on a construction site, moving rocks, receiving 60 cents (US) a day. She was a good mother and brought her daughters to Sunrise. When they first arrived the little girls were taken to the food hall and each given a large bowl of food. The elder watched her younger sister tuck in vigorously and ladled some of her own food into her little sister's bowl. Geraldine then discovered that the family had never been able to afford meat.

If the high gates and wire are unwelcoming, the rest of the Sunrise Village is the opposite. The children live in boys and girls dormitories set around a courtyard. A group of giggling teenage girls are in the first dormitory I visit. The walls are covered with magazine cut-outs of what the boys undoubtedly refer to as "girl stuff" – I could be in any girl's bedroom in Australia – this one just has a lot more beds. There is lawn, trees and a central gazebo, the gazebo is set in a beautiful lotus pond, vibrant pink perfectly formed buds on a sea of green. The dining room is full of long tables and form seats, and the noise escalates as an army of happy, chattering children arrive for lunch from classes here and schools outside the gates.

Photograph by Kathryn Spurling

The kitchen is a busy place; the head cook previously worked in a refugee camp so 138 children and a dozen or so staff is easy. A new kitchen is forming on the opposite end, all stainless steel and huge bench space. Geraldine isn't sure how the cooks will adapt because they much prefer preparing meals the traditional Cambodian way, sitting on the ground.

After the post-lunch quiet period a class gathers under the office pergola, they are busy with measuring tapes and English books. There is laughter when Geraldine takes one of the tapes and puts it around her abdomen. She enjoys spending time going through school reports at night, discovering who is good at English, who is good at maths. She loves giving individual attention to each child but there is never enough time in her days or nights. She tries hard not to favour one child over another but there is always one who has a more mischievous grin and personality to match. At Sunrise the credo is to care for the physical needs of the children but that it is as important "to nourish the soul as well". The children need to believe in themselves, in their innate talents and strengths. For some this is the first positive encouragement they have ever received, some of them "have been actually thrown away in rubbish heaps and they all suffer from some degree of post-traumatic stress disorders". In the beginning a child may struggle with the pressure to succeed so it takes constant reassurance. "I just tell them, my dream is making your dream come true. But I cannot help make their dream come true without their help." Some children are troubled and are more of a problem than others. The occasional child will steal. "You would steal too if you were used to being hungry" says Geraldine, these children just need to understand there is no need to steal any more, that they will be fed and clothed, and they are safe. There is no corporal punishment, mostly it takes patience and a few incentives along the way. It may be as simple as no pocket money for a week, or no field trips or television. These are, after all, children and they too are able to modify behaviour if it means no food snack or the promise of a watch or MP3 player for excelling at school. Geraldine does fail and that always upsets her but such disappointment vanishes when she watches her young people succeed. Sunrise helps to pay for a modest wedding reception for Sunrise graduates. "Seeing my kids married is a wonderful thing." At a recent wedding she mingled with Sunrise couples in their twenties and thirties, many with their own children. "There were nine tables of Sunrise kids and their wives, 60 who had been through here" she says with obvious pride.

Teenagers are encouraged to continue their education. Once they reach the age of eighteen they move to an outreach house with same-sex others and a married couple to care for them. Those who leave at 18 have jobs found for them and a month's rent paid in advance for their new accommodation. They receive crockery, a bed, fan, table, chair, cupboard, alarm clock, some new clothes and a pushbike, to give them a head start. Those who shine have, with a great deal of help from Geraldine and sponsors, journeyed to countries like Australia on scholarships. Students on scholarships at Prince Alfred and Seymour Colleges, Adelaide, have excelled and continue to excel. Sunrise students study in and will graduate from universities such as Adelaide, Flinders, South Australia and Southern Cross universities in a diverse range of degrees such as commerce, tourism, nursing, film and arts media. A Sunrise boy has graduated from Adelaide's Le Cordon Bleu with a degree in International Hotel Management and returned to a position in Cambodia. Others follow in his footsteps, one very bright girl who came to Sunrise with five brothers and sisters, is now studying nursing at Flinders University. Her mother died of alcohol poisoning and the father ran off – she used to be a beggar.

Photograph by Kathryn Spurling

We stroll to a sewing room equipped with treadle machines where the girls are taught how to sew and make clothes for themselves and other Sunrise children. If they decide not to continue with their education at 18 they can return to their town with a sewing machine, a treadle machine because many homes are still without electricity. They are assured of some income. Boys are taught carpentry and also work with the goats, cows, chickens, ducks, fish, fruit, vegetables and herbs of the Sunrise farm. Geraldine tries hard to find Sunrise children work and has successfully started many a career in Cambodia's burgeoning tourist industry. Local businesses have learnt it is best to say yes to Geraldine, it just saves time. We move into the computer classroom where youngsters are intent on their computer screens. The supervising teacher is himself a Sunrise graduate. I shake my head and think how the lives of these children are light years away from where they began, so many Cambodian children will never touch a computer. These children come from poverty stricken households with no electricity and little food.

In 2002, through the generosity of Australian entrepreneur John Singleton, 40 Sunrise children dressed in beautiful traditional Khmer costume performed at the Adelaide Festival of Arts to sell-out crowds. "It was a resounding success" remembers a clearly proud Geraldine. It was not by coincidence that Adelaide was chosen because it was important to Geraldine to return home with her family. This truly was the trip of a lifetime for children who previously had not ventured away from their village or Sunrise. Geraldine delighted in their responses to the Australian way of life. One small child watched a dishwasher grind away for one and a half hours and, bewildered, asked Geraldine why, given that it would have taken him and her five minutes to wash the dishes. A trip to a supermarket resulted in many questions and squeals of laughter. One giggling little girl asked why toilet paper needed to be perfumed and have butterflies and flowers on it? The children were puzzled why Australians would buy tinned and packaged food with artificial colourings and flavourings when fresh food was abundant. Geraldine never fails to be surprised by their simple wisdom. When one eight-year-old asked why she wasn't eating rice, she replied "I am on a diet". "Eat less," was the response.

Now in 2009 Geraldine has decided it is time to visit Australia again with the best troupe from her Sunrise music and dance school. Where to perform? Why not the best venue in Australia! So, on 1 October 2009, 40 Sunrise children will appear on the concert hall stage of the Australian Opera House. Geraldine secured flights, accommodation, and all related costs through the generous sponsorship of several Australian companies and a Hong Kong company donated suitcases and bags. Prime Minister Hun Sen ordained that the children's passports be provided free and airport departure tax be waived. Geraldine convinced another company to donate travelling clothes. She says it is difficult to acquire sponsorship from companies, particularly multi-nationals. "They say 'but we do not do business in Cambodia'. I tell them it will just make them feel good, but this doesn't always work." It is really best to say yes to Geraldine.

There are now two Sunrise villages with a third being built for children suffering from AIDS. There will soon be over 400 orphaned and disadvantaged children being looked after by Sunrise. Prime Minister Hun Sen would like Geraldine to open a Sunrise village in every province of Cambodia. They are now good friends and he calls her "his older sister". She does not have the resources, yet. The need for funding is ongoing and Geraldine spends up to three months a year travelling and speaking at fund-raising events. She used to find it difficult to speak to a public gathering, then she realised all she had to do was tell the children's stories and there is rarely a dry eye in the house. She never wearies of talking about the children but three months is the absolute limit she can stand to be away from Sunrise. Keeping the flow of money is a constant concern and Geraldine is forever thinking of new reasons why people should give her money for the children. "I'm fundraising, I'm begging for scholarships. I'm not everybody's cup of tea. I mean, I'm loud, I'm aggressive, I'm pushy."

Some people refer to me as 'that loud, aggressive, red-haired fat lady with the silly hair do'. It doesn't matter if they don't like me as long as they give to the children.

That "silly hair-do" came when she was in a rush and couldn't find her butterfly clip. She had just had a meal of rice so grabbed a chopstick to ensure her hair remained in a bun:

I picked up the chopstick and shoved it in and thought, 'Looks pretty good' so ever since then I've been nicking chopsticks whenever I go to Chinese restaurants.

Geraldine is quick to add that she never fails to be staggered by the generosity of some people and organisations, and it is commonly the people who have least who give more. There is a 90-year-old pensioner in an Australian nursing home who has for years sent $10 towards Sunrise postage costs out of her old age pension. Small companies and organisations like Rotary and Vietnam veterans have amazed Geraldine with their involvement. She is less complimentary about large companies and the wealthy, or those she refers to openly as the "mean bastards" who promise but never deliver. "I hate it when the children are promised and then are disappointed and this happens all the time." Having said that, it is pleasing that, "more and more, bit by bit, corporations with a social conscience are beginning to come onboard".

Geraldine does wonder how much longer she can keep up the busy schedule which is her life. Her staff has expanded and are true believers in Sunrise but there is no doubt who is the driving force. In a serious moment Geraldine admits she has considered the consequences for Sunrise when she is not around. "I hope soon to begin making DVDs which can be shown when I die. I would like the children who follow after I die to know about 'Big Mum'." Geraldine's health and energy levels wain occasionally. She breaks into a grin.

> You know working at Chase I would get up on a Monday and say to myself, 'Oh another five days of this.' Now I must remind myself it is a Saturday or Sunday.

Free time is rare but she is not complaining. "When you really are a mother and you love your children you don't say to your kids 'I'll see you Monday morning'. Every day is the same, every day runs into another and I don't think about having two days off a week." In 2000 she was asked to write her story. She thought initially she would find a little cottage by the beach and do the recluse writer thing. In the end she stayed at Sunrise, usually with the chatter of children in the background, and the words flowed.

Just before her book was launched she received a Member of the Order of Australia. Geraldine was greatly honoured.

> The Order is one of the most treasured things I have. It gives one an aura of good reputation that I might not enjoy otherwise and I always have a bit of a giggle with my family and friends because the news of the award came out about six months before my book was published and I often wonder that if my book had been published would I have got the award. It was just good timing on my part. People do respect that award. A woman came up to me and said I deserved to be sainted. I suggested she let the Pope read my book first.

So many children, so much attention and love needed, but "Big Mum" revels in it. There are so many children in need, few are turned away so it is not uncommon for a family of six children to arrive.

Sunrise has accepted children with cerebral palsy and HIV, rather than break up a family. One little girl has brittle bone disease and when she is old enough she will need to agree to the amputation of both legs. It is a hard fact of Cambodian life that disabled children often do not survive, but Geraldine believes "it is good to have disabled children at the village because it teaches the children tolerance and compassion". As she says this a group of children appears from a dormitory, in their midst is a girl in a wheelchair. They push her over the bumps and when they reach the courtyard they chatter as they assist her out of the chair. I meet one of the older boys, he is going blind but handed a guitar he plays with a wonderful gentleness. Clearly it is his passion and Geraldine hopes his proficiency improves before his eyesight totally disappears.

The histories of the children are barely believable. A brother and sister arrived, their father had died of AIDS, their mother had AIDS and remaining family rejected the children because of prevailing discrimination and lack of understanding surrounding AIDS. The children were sent to an orphanage but because of their AIDS-related past they were rejected and sent to an AIDS orphanage even though they were not infected. This orphanage rejected them because the children didn't have AIDS. When they arrived at Sunrise they were deeply traumatised. The boy declared he was going to hang himself, he was 15 and had never been to school. Two years on he is in Grade Two, too far behind to catch up, but he will receive more education and at least be literate by age 18. He has taken to computers so is receiving additional training and is also working on the village farm which has helped him with his confidence.

Another family of six arrived, the eldest a boy of 15. Their mother had been stricken with cancer. "There is no pain management program here, you just lie down and suffer." Most Cambodians cannot afford medical attention or drugs.

The children nursed their mother right through to the end and they were traumatised from that, not just her death but listening to her scream the last few months of her life.

When this family of children arrived at Sunrise the eldest boy could not read or write. With the understanding of someone much more mature he realised he was now head of the family and assumed the responsibility. Geraldine has been so impressed because "through sheer willpower and hard work" he has gone to Grade Seven in two years.[32]

Photograph by Kathryn Spurling

There are a disproportionate number of boys to girls at Sunrise. Of the 138 currently at this Sunrise village, two thirds are boys – it takes little imagination to realise why. A female Cambodian official visits Geraldine and her stories are horrible. She tells of finding girls as young as seven being taught with sexual aids on how to please a man. She tells of child trafficking and describes how children of five and six are sold to begging rings on the Thailand border. Geraldine has too many unpleasant stories of her own. A boy arrived at Sunrise, he said very little, quietly observing, quietly looking over his shoulder.

For three weeks his physical needs were met and then he asked "who do I have to give a blow job to?". It is questions like this which chill Geraldine to the bone, she pretends not to be shocked, realising it is quiet reassurance over time which is needed. Shocked least of all were the other children who simply dismissed his statement in a matter-of-fact way and assured him this was something he need not consider again.

It is easy for a westerner to condemn such activities from the safety of the moral high ground, it is hard to understand how anyone can love their children and sell them, and Cambodians do love their children. By now I am suffering extreme sensory overload. I come from a country where free health care and education are taken for granted. We complain about having to wait a couple of hours in a hospital emergency centre, we complain if every suburb does not have a primary school. Australians do not have equal access to food and shelter but we do have access. An ocean and much more separates Australia from Cambodia.

At the beginning of the 2000 documentary titled *My Khmer Heart*, narrator Sir Peter Ustinov says:

> I think it is up to people to do what they can and if everybody did what they could then the world would be a lot better place in any case. But many people I think, fundamentally good people, they lack the courage to think they can make a difference. I think it needs a sort of arrogance.[33]

Geraldine has been referred to as arrogant, as autocratic, as a lot of things and she admits that in her "BC" life she wasn't one of the "good people". During her "BC" life Geraldine was not attuned to the misfortune of others, her narcissism is something she is bluntly honest about. Except for the seven years she had her daughter it was all about:

> The clothes on my back, the kind of cars and jobs my boyfriends had, first class travel, jewellery was very important to me at one stage in my life. And I was pleased with myself.

That changed when she met the children, well the "good people" bit anyway.

What you see is what you get with Geraldine – to some it is confronting but it is honest. Sitting comfortably in her home at Sunrise in the late afternoon she contemplates life. It is not the gin and tonic which results in candid comment: Geraldine is just being Geraldine.

> It is a pity people do not realise it is not things that make them happy. You can say that to people until you are blue in the face, they have to discover that themselves. I have wealth of a different kind.

Geraldine knows all too well, she did not discover it until she was 50 and is none too proud that it took her that long, and none too proud of her path to discovery. She had travelled more, seen more, done more with her life than the vast majority of her school friends. She had gone a long way for a milkman's daughter but it wasn't enough, would never be enough. Losing her job and the ability to provide for herself was the first shock.

> People say 'Oh Geraldine gave up so much, she gave up the good life, she went to Cambodia and lived in a third world country, isn't she wonderful.' The truth was that

when I got fired at 50 there were not a lot of choices open to me. I was fat and 50 in Sydney with 40 people wanting my job. It was actually a smart move on my part to create this whole new life for myself but I never realised I was going to do such a good job ... reinventing myself, finding a new path for myself.

She found lost and unloved children responded to her care. She saw the appreciation and love in their eyes. And all the time it was the children teaching her "what real happiness was all about". She refers to "open hearted love you feel flowing to you". You can see it when Geraldine arrives back at Sunrise after a month or a couple of hours, the children rush to her car and help her out, carrying anything and grabbing at her with cries of "Hello Mum". For Geraldine it is the tonic which powers her world. No matter what sort of frustrating day she has had the greeting is like "plugging myself into an electric force and the light comes on". Anyone who spends time at Sunrise can but feel it also. The children are not Geraldine's problem, they resolved her problem. "They could not be more my family than if they came from my body." Geraldine thinks it took longer than it should have for her to realise but:

It's very clear to me now why I couldn't have children, because if I had just one or two of my own children there wouldn't be the opportunity to do what I'm doing now. It's a wonderful thing, to know that you are doing what you were put on this earth to do. A lot of people live their whole lives and they never even get to know up until their dying day whether they have done what they were sent here to do. I absolutely know without a doubt that I am doing everything that I'm supposed to be doing, and loving it.

Photograph by Kathryn Spurling

We are venturing into Phnom Penh. Geraldine is to have dinner with a couple of sponsors she hopes will pay for some reconstructive surgery for one or both of two little girls with severe facial burns. With a housemother in tow to translate, Waew and Thy arrive spotlessly dressed and excited at the prospect of a trip into town at night and dinner in a restaurant. Everyday events for western children are major events for these children of Cambodia. Waew makes no attempt to cover the right side of her face which is enough to make the most hardened among us flinch. She is an extrovert, outwardly friendly and smiling – you cannot but wonder why or how. Waew was sold by her desperately poor family to a Thai begging ring and to make her more appealing as a beggar her face was burnt with acid. Five-year-old Waew was rescued and returned to her family. They sold her again. Waew would be driven to her spot near the Thai border in her rags and left there with her little tin begging cup. When she consistently failed to get the amount of money she was told to, the leader of the begging ring did not return to collect her. Waew was rescued by the Austrian Consul who found her wandering, filthy and dressed in rags, still with her tin begging cup. Under the love and care she has received at Sunrise she has blossomed, even asking Geraldine, "when I get my new ear can it be pierced so I can wear an earring?".

I am hampered on this Cambodian trip by a stress fracture in the foot and a boot and cane, more inconvenient than anything. I am walking slowly to Geraldine's car leaning on my cane but admiring the vivid colours of sunset. I feel a small hand slide around my elbow to assure me help is near. I feel the lump rising in my throat and smile down at Thy. She has combed her hair over the left side of her face which is gnarled from vicious burns. Thy's mother allegedly had an affair with someone else's husband and this resulted in a savage revenge assault with battery acid. Thy's mother died, her daughter sustained horrific burns and lost an eye and an ear. Thy speaks sparingly – the scars are more than skin deep. Still traumatised, she remains unable to believe she is entirely safe. Thy would like nothing better than to believe that and to have a new ear and eye and a slightly normal face and yet here she is trying to reassure me. I manage to hold it together until I am sitting at a restaurant table away from Thy and Waew and Geraldine's party. I begin to write but struggle to see the page through my tears.

I fly out of Cambodia in a strangely solemn mood because it is difficult to sum up the country and its people and how I feel. I have seen such extremes of happy and sad, I want to return to Australia but I don't want to leave Cambodia. Sunrise Village was an amazing experience and I know I will never be the same. I look down at a photograph, her name is Kakada; she is four, is HIV positive, and she kept wanting me to take her photo and then see the image. She was one of those children with a more mischievous grin and personality to match and she now has a much brighter future than her past. I pause to think how her "Big Mum" truly is an inspiring Australian woman.

On the first day of October 2009 the Sunrise musical group was booked to give a concert in Sydney's grand Opera House. It has been a "mad three months" and "a blur" for Geraldine as she organised this many Cambodian children, house mothers, translators, was enough, all the pre-concert media, and then there was the concert programme itself. One can only imagine what entered the children's minds as they boarded their international flight and were shown how to buckle themselves into economy class seats which for these slender juvenile bodies seemed huge. There was never a travelling public so excited with airplane food. Geraldine and other accompanying adults were kept busy ensuring all the children's, "I have to go Mum", managed to open, close, and open toilet doors far above the earth's surface. They were easy to keep sight of on the flight, not just because of their black and orange travelling clothes, not just because they tended to cling to each other and any willing carer, but because they were the passengers with large excited eyes and big grins.

The Opera House audience are warmed up by Australian entertainers volunteering their time: David Campbell, Kasey Chambers and Becky Cole, with Ray Martin acting as Master of Ceremonies. The Sunrise musical group charmed and delighted the large audience with classical Khmer song and dance and beautiful traditional costumes. It was difficult to believe that these polished young entertainers had come from such deprived backgrounds and such a short time ago. Thirteen-year-old Chorn Chan Visal walked out to centre stage and in English sang "Tell Me Why". Chorn said:

> I got panic when I was on the stage of Sydney Opera
> House, and I did not think that I can sing very well.

He actually looked supremely self-assured and his voice clearly asked a question in song about these children and his nation, which none of us could answer. There was scarcely a dry eye in the house and Chorn received a standing ovation. He made quite a few bows and waved, smiling broadly, and told Geraldine afterwards "Mum this is my future". Chorn will either be a world acclaimed entertainer or President of Cambodia – indeed whatever he chooses to be.[34]

Geraldine's life consists of highs and lows. The second half of 2010 had triumphs like the success achieved by highly motivated students studying overseas. Several children received life-saving operations. A large shipping container of much needed donated items arrived and there was the unbridled joy as the children helped unpack. But Cambodia is a land of extremes and just before the stellar 2009 Sunrise concert, storms caused terrible flooding in Siem Reap and Sunrise Angkor was not spared. For four days lower floors were underwater when the river bank collapsed. The 55 children were quickly moved to the next storey and staff waded through knee-high water with supplies. Whilst computer and office equipment were saved many of the improvements made to buildings and surrounds were submerged and a return to normalcy would take time, patience, and yes, more money.

Geraldine has stood in front of soldiers and military tanks to save Sunrise children. She freely admits she will do almost anything to ensure a healthy and happy future for the waifs who arrive traumatised at Sunrise gates. She thought she had just about seen and had to handle everything, and then in November 2009 she was diagnosed with aggressive breast cancer. In an email she describes what a shock this was.

> The only time I have ever spent in hospital was when I had my tonsils out when I was a kid and some microscopic elective surgery when I was trying to get pregnant. I never got headaches, colds or infections and considered myself pretty invincible, with the constitution of a horse with endless energy. So when the Big C struck it was a real shock and I am still getting used to not having the energy I am used to.[35]

With ongoing treatment liable to keep her away from the children for an indefinite duration she elected to have a double mastectomy. Testimony to her indomitable spirit, she quipped "some girls will do anything to lose weight!" and announced she would be back in Cambodia by December, but it wasn't that simple.

Reference to her ongoing treatment continued, however, to receive short shift, just a brief couple of words squeezed into her schedule. In late 2010:

> I was in Melbourne in July and appeared on *The Circle* programme on Channel 10 which brought in some new sponsors which is what it is all about. Then back to Adelaide for some medical checkups before flying to Fiji to make a presentation for the Howard Storage Group's annual team meeting. August had me in Malacca in Malaysia addressing the Humanitarian Affairs, UK Leadership Symposium, where more than 300 university students from all over the world gathered to talk about how they can use their degrees for the betterment of mankind.

Having had a double mastectomy meant that Geraldine would require medication for five years, three-monthly check-ups in Thailand, and yearly ones in Adelaide. She was upbeat but faced with her own mortality for the first time:

> I was forced to go through all my personal papers, letters, and photos, as I was terrified of kicking the bucket and leaving so much scandal behind me for my family to deal with![36]

Geraldine enjoyed going through the letters and photos, disposing of many: "I lived a lot of happy and exciting times all over again". She was very grateful not to require chemotherapy or radiation, and yet again was mainly concerned for the children. So many family members of Sunrise children died from cancer; they know Geraldine has it and are very worried: "I have to keep reassuring them". There were urgent plans made "addressing the issue of succession so that my Foundation can continue in the smoothest possible way without me". Geraldine emphasises yet again, it is all about the children, their welfare is primary and she will ensure even from the grave that they are loved and well-cared for. When we met up at the end of 2012 Geraldine wanted to offer a very public and heartfelt apology to women diagnosed with breast cancer. She is "ashamed" that:

> I used to read women's magazines for years and there would be a big article on some person writing about their ordeal with breast cancer and how they survived and think, 'boring, boring, boring' and turn the page and never read them. I want to apologize to all those women whose stories I thought were boring, now I am one of you.[37]

She concedes that there is a weight which comes with a life threatening disease: "It's in your mind every time when you wake up in the morning". She will continue to take the medication and have regular check-ups and: "I do a lot of creative visualisation and meditation making sure it gets out of my body". Geraldine is "confident" she will beat this disease.

I receive news that my young saviour has had cosmetic surgery. Acid burn victim, Thy, has received an eye, no longer will her hair be combed over the hole in the left-hand side of her face. Her fellow victim, the exuberant Waew, has received a new ear, and yes finally she will be able to wear that earring. Geraldine spent the week with the girls in the Hong Kong hospital where surgeon Dr Chung donated his time and others donated expenses. For the first time in public Thy smiles broadly, life has never been better or the future brighter. What does "Big Mum" say? "Love and light, there's a crack in everything – that's how the light gets in".

An added throw-away line from Geraldine on her own health is simply: "I had more medical tests in Bangkok just to check that I am as fit as I feel".[38] Mind you if you supervised 150 Sunrise children on a three-day visit to the Cambodian Sihanoukville beach you would need to be very fit and very, very, patient. There is another saying, something about "no rest for the wicked". Geraldine admits she was pretty wicked and she doesn't have much rest but that doesn't seem to be a problem.

Tara Winkler was born into a comfortable family home in Sydney's Vaucluse. In 2005 she was given the option to have an 18th birthday party or a trip overseas. She chose a trip to Asia and became transfixed by Cambodia's lost children. She volunteered at the Akira Landmine Museum which supported 20 land mine victim children. Tara began to teach the children English and also decided to volunteer at a small orphanage in Battambang. Horrified by the conditions and the plight of the severely neglected and abused children, she returned to Australia to raise funds and sponsors. In 2007 she discovered that the orphanage director was embezzling funds and abusing the children. Tara immediately returned to Cambodia, rented an old medical clinic, and escaped with 14 orphans. She never returned to her comfortable Australian lifestyle. At an age when her peers were pre-occupied with fashion and music, Tara created the Cambodian Children's Trust. Undaunted by the struggles endured by the most abused and poor, Tara, at 21, was responsible for the lives of 14, and soon many more. She was a finalist in the 2010 "Young Australian of the Year" award and the subject of an ABC *Australian Story*. By 2011 Tara Winkler was responsible for 46 children. Her trust also assists several families in the Battambang region living in abject poverty and has developed programmes for those suffering from mental and physical disabilities, and victims of landmines. Geraldine is full of admiration for Tara and what she has achieved. They have formed a unique relationship, says Geraldine, "almost like grandmother and granddaughter".[39] Sunrise now includes older Cambodian Children's Trust youth in study tours in Australia. These two Australian women have formed a special bond and friendship which will benefit hundreds of children.

As in other years Cambodian life continued to be challenging in 2010. As the flood waters recede from Sunrise Angkor in Siem Reap and damage assessed, Sunrise Phnom Penh was on the verge of being flooded by monsoonal rains. It was all hands to the pump, then pumps, when another was hastily purchased and another hired. For three days they moved water over the levees. Sunrise Phnom Penh was not damaged but cut off from the world and the children could not attend school – like children everywhere they were completely at ease with the brief unscheduled holiday. Primary school age Sunrise children receive $2 per month pocket money, high school age children receive $4. One boy was concerned that sponsors may have lost their homes in the Christmas 2010-2011 Queensland floods so the children decided to donate 50c from their month's pocket money – $59.50 was collected and sent to Queensland Flood Relief.[40]

Geraldine was trying to reduce her travel and speaking engagements but she continued not to be very good at that and 2011 was another year which whipped past in a flurry of international airports, speaking engagements and media interviews, meeting and greeting sponsors and people who might become sponsors. Geraldine just couldn't help herself because she sees her "qualities" as "never taking 'no' for answer, believing in others around me, and really believing that basically people are good". So, 2011 was yet another case of today it is Dubai, or Hanoi, or Canberra, or Adelaide, or Sydney, or Singapore, or Cairns – more than one trip to several of these cities –

and somewhere in Thailand. There was of course travel between both Sunrise villages, and a third being built at Sihanoukville. There was an updated Sunrise promotional DVD to make. There were everyday decisions, some life and death ones; so many children, so many lives.

There was the International Women's Day launch of the book *Women's Words of Wisdom, Power& Passion*, in which Geraldine was one of 50 Australian women asked to share words of wisdom. She was constantly trying to maintain life's balance. She wasn't really good at that but she tried, and truly believed the good bits far outweighed the bad because: "I am loved unconditionally by the children in my care".[41] Those who really knew Geraldine's story would nod when she advised women to leave their comfort zone and push into a wildly different and even dangerous world, but very few have Geraldine's strength to do as she has done, and even she admits she was 50 before she leapt from her comfort zone.

All the media, all the public appearances and presentations were directed to what she was all about:

> When a new child is brought to Sunrise and I see the fear, suspicion and helplessness in their eyes. This makes my heart race in an emotional way because I know it will take a lot of love and patience to make this child feel loved, safe and have hope for the future.

There are so many children, so many children in need. Sok was sold by her family to a neighbour for 200,000R ($50). From the age of six she was forced to work in the fields and she was further abused. In 2010 she became very ill and the neighbour didn't care, another neighbour volunteered to care for Sok and took her to a hospital. Sok was diagnosed as HIV-positive and close to death. The eight-year-old continued to be hospitalised with tuberculosis and anaemia and required five blood transfusions, she had leg problems, abscesses and could not walk properly. Sunrise enveloped the little girl.

Phorn is six though he is small for his age. In the photo calling for a sponsor he has a broad smile; when you read his story you wonder how he can smile, perhaps because he is now a Sunrise child. Phorn's mother died of AIDS when he was 18-months- old and he was raised by his grandmother. His father remarried but Phorn was never going to be part of the new family. His grandmother had no permanent home so she and Phorn moved day to day. They were both taken in at Sunrise 3 at Sihanoukville, the grandmother given work, and Phorn joined the other children. According to his house mother, Phorn "eats a lot" and laughs loudly when he watches cartoons on television.[42]

Geraldine admitted in 2011 "so much for trying to keep my travelling to a minimum!" and the brief reference to her health in a newsletter was: "July had me trying to recuperate from surgery at Sunrise" and later: "It was reassuring to have the green light on my medical condition from my surgeon. Phew!!!".[43] This was on a trip to Adelaide where she met with sponsors, gave another presentation, and visited with Sunrise youth doing very well at Flinders University. In November 2011 Geraldine received the Sir Edward "Weary" Dunlop Asialink Medal. The medal is awarded to a person with an outstanding record of enhancing the quality of life in Asia, one who has demonstrated humanitarian principles and who has improved Australia-Asia relations. "Weary" Dunlop is legendary within the story of Australian Japanese Prisoners of War (POW). As a POW and a surgeon he saved the lives of countless POWs during World War II. Geraldine was delighted with the award and her one regret was that her father, Norm Cox, wasn't there because he would have been so very proud.

Throughout this 2011, as in other years, from so many different parts of the world, generous souls were fundraising for Sunrise. From companies like Computershare – which was financing much of Sunrise 3 at Sihanoukville, to a girls school in Dubai which had a "funky hair day" to raise money (I believe Geraldine was not allowed to enter that competition), to crazy cyclists travelling long distances and walkers walking long distances, to fundraising lunches and dinners. One young Adelaide schoolgirl decided Geraldine was her case study of an inspiring woman. She convinced her parents to donate prizes, sold raffle tickets and donated the funds to Sunrise. Colgate, the world-renowned toiletries company, was subjected to pleas from Geraldine to donate large quantities of their products, and they did – it is best to submit to such requests because it just saves time; Geraldine is unlikely to give-up, her memory is long, and her reach, even longer.

At Sunrise Siem Reap educational opportunities have been greatly improved. Cambodian government schools commonly have no electricity, fans or computers; teachers continue to be paid as little as $20 (USD) a month and are not encouraged to be real educators. If they decide not to attend on any given day there is no substitute teacher. Sunrise children attending government school had been running the gauntlet of drug pushers and gangs to even get in the front school gate. Their school had four toilets for 2,000 students, 70–80 students in a class, with not enough books or desks. Teachers could be bribed to pass a student and reports simply stated pass or fail. Now Sunrise children were attending private school and it meant a world of difference. There were modern air-conditioned buildings, flushing modern toilets and wash basins, class sizes of 25 and each child had their own desk and books. Private school teachers are paid four times the government teacher salary and are consequently motivated to teach. Disabled Sunrise children previously not allowed to attend government schools were now attending private schools.[44]

On 1 July 2012 Geraldine was in Sydney for the judging of the Ernst & Young Entrepreneur of the Year Awards and was awarded the "social category award for South Australia". She was the only woman in a group of six Australia-wide recipients. The following month Geraldine returned to Sydney to address the International SOS Health Care Conference. In September Geraldine visited Hobart to address the National Top Tourist Parks conference. I have personally observed Geraldine completely undeterred driving up flooded Phnom Penh roads the wrong way and coping with humidity which would melt lesser individuals but in Hobart hoping to sightsee in a city she has never visited before "temperatures of 4 degrees kept me in my hotel room".[45]

Next to warmer climes in Sydney as a guest of the Montara Circle, a group dedicated to reducing child trafficking and poverty in the world. By month's end Geraldine was in Adelaide with 29 Sunrise children and staff to perform in the *OzAsia Festival*. The music group was to perform five concerts, but they sold out so quickly there was another. The performances were billed as the world premiere of *Cambodian Sun Rising.* The players presented a cultural programme depicting the history of Cambodia through seven scenes. The costumes were beautiful, the dancing, singing, acting and music magnificent – these are Sunrise kids.

In October 2012 Geraldine was in the United Arab Emirates for a series of speaking engagements and radio interviews. She was given a day in a luxury hotel, luxury indeed after spending nine days in dorms with the concert group in Adelaide just a week previously. Then it is back to various places in Australia, including Roma, Queensland and Tumby Bay, South Australia. I must admit I was having trouble keeping up just hoping that Geraldine would make it to Sydney for our scheduled interview – and she did. Trying to keep pace with inspiring women is exhausting so to complete the research on the book and the documentary I had decided to capture Geraldine and Helen Reddy in the same place at the same time. This promised to be an interesting exercise.

Helen Reddy and Geraldine Cox
Photograph by Margaret Hadfield (Zorgdrager)

I hope the 9 December 2012 interview will go well and these amazing ladies will frankly, get along. The first disarming issue is that Geraldine turns out to be a long time "fan" of Helen Reddy. There are a number of words like "wow, gosh", and an excited "aren't I lucky" when we set up the time and place. The only word I can find to describe this is "sweet", because Geraldine would never use this word to describe herself, and Geraldine is a person who leaves us normal individuals dumbstruck. Lunch is great although I wish I had my recorder on while Helen and Geraldine get to know each other. Some of the conversation cannot be repeated, some of the discussion is highly amusing. The topic of men comes up, husbands and lovers, and our much younger camerawoman's mouth falls open and her eyes widen. By the time we move into Sydney's Botanical Gardens and begin to film, Helen is referring to Geraldine as "girlfriend" and I have completely lost control of the interview.

I am by now purely an observer as Helen and Geraldine discuss the music scene, books – how they both love real books and refuse to go to eBooks – feminism and where the new generation of women fits into feminism, do they know what feminism is? A bridal party moves into the gardens for photographs, Helen says: "You'll regret it" and Geraldine concurs: "It's downhill from here darling". My professionalism has slipped badly and I have the giggles – most of the comments I cannot repeat. By now they are discussing the media, advertising, and the shortage of women in film and television and the conversation takes a serious tone. Geraldine:

> Advertising is pushed in our faces all the time, what we should have, the things we don't have and can't afford, and when I come back from Cambodia and go to shopping malls and see little old lady pensioners in there and buying things they clearly can't afford nor do they need, but it is pushed on them through the media and through advertising and we really need so little to be happy when you stop to think
> about it.

Helen: "It is true". Geraldine: "We need a clean and safe place to sleep, we need enough to eat"; Helen: "We need water". Geraldine:

> Clean drinking water and enough money for our medical care and for our children to get a good education. That's all you need; anything after that is luxury.

Helen nods approval. Geraldine believes there is too much emphasis on "work harder to get more, be bigger, increase your profits, push, push, push, drive, drive, drive". Has it not become "too depressing because there has got to be a time in your life when you have got enough stuff". Geraldine observes a simpler life in Cambodia and is intrigued that amongst her children she sees none of the conditions suffered by children of wealthier, western countries. "We buy our food in the morning and we have finished it by six o'clock at night –

we don't eat anything out of a tin, or packet, or frozen." At Sunrise there are no "asthma puffers, food allergies, diabetes … no ADD, DDDs, or whatever you call it".

Helen Reddy is now asking the questions: "Is it getting any easier so far as there are fewer children?". Geraldine considers briefly:

> Unfortunately there is always going to be a need not just through poverty and domestic violence or HIV. Extended family don't want anything to do with HIV children and they have nowhere else to go.

Is it harder to find sponsors, is the recession biting in that way?:

> There are more than 4,000 registered charities in Australia … I have lost about 2 per cent of my sponsors, these are people who have lost their jobs, some of them have come back, but it is harder to get new people onboard. My thrust in 2013 is going to be to get corporations to have staff-giving programmes, where the staff give $50 out of their salary, and the corporation matches it. It is hard attracting people to give to an orphanage set up in Cambodia so a lot of my time is educating people that Cambodia is not such a bad place.

Helen and Geraldine are discussing the demeaning, derogatory language used when discussing women, particularly women in the public eye, from our Prime Minister down. They believe it has increased and become far nastier. Geraldine confesses she is occasionally called by men of her age group: "Dearie, sweetie and even blossom. I say try Geraldine, Geraldine will do". She adds that some use less pleasant words and that doesn't bother her:

A lot of people don't like me, I am not everybody's cup of tea, I'm loud, aggressive and pushy and I can understand people saying that about me. I was on ABC's *Talking Heads* not so long ago and a girlfriend sent me an email. She had had a client lunch with bankers and one woman said: 'Did you watch *Talking Heads* last night? That fat lady with the silly red hairstyle from Cambodia, she really annoys me, she's loud, aggressive and pushy'. I wrote back: They're my attributes!' If people don't know who you are, where you are, what you are doing, and how to get money to you, how are you going to get your project off the ground?

I am thoroughly heartened to hear Geraldine conclude: "So I am going to be loud, pushy, and aggressive, to my dying day".

It is sometimes difficult for Geraldine to nominate a life highlight but there was one on 3 December 2012. It has been a long journey, nearly five years, to provide a safe haven for around 200 HIV-affected orphans, and a home base for an outreach programme to monitor another 350 children affected by the virus. Finally the third Sunrise Village, a centre costing Aus $2.5 million, was officially opened by Cambodia's President Hun Sen. Geraldine delivered her speech in native Khmer. The President then presented her with the Royal Order of Sahametrei, the highest honour awarded to foreigners.[46] The award will sit well beside her Order of Australia.

Geraldine doesn't mess around; she doesn't have time. What you see is what you get and that is so refreshing. She has no qualms about who she was in her "BC" life – a promiscuous hedonist but wishes she had discovered, and been brave enough, to become who she was meant to be, sooner. There have been many personally challenging years and Geraldine has not withered any, she has actually thrived. Geraldine Cox was an inspiring woman decades ago, and continues to be. We don't have to be looking after 400 children in Cambodia to appreciate her words of wisdom.

> One of the things that helps me survive in Cambodia – I see misery, poverty, crime, injustice, cruelty every day just driving into town and for me to survive and to be happy I have to not see the big picture. I have to just worry about the kids whose fate it is to walk through those Sunrise gates, not to see all that other stuff otherwise I would not be able to perform. I must tell myself everyday not to worry, not to waste my time and energy worrying about the things I cannot change, focus all my energy on the kids whose lives I can change, that's what keeps me going and sane.

Geraldine will be 68 in June 2013 and in February 2013 divulges that a recent medical check-up two more lumps were found, one in the stomach and "one in the reproductive area". She says she is not unduly concerned. "I am just keeping an eye on them to see that they are not getting any bigger or looking nasty". Geraldine is nonetheless a realist and writes as only Geraldine can:

> I have also decided that if I do not shake the disease that I will not submit to chemo or radiation, but will max out my credit cards, arrange pain management and do a bucket list of places I want to see and fly off into the wild blue yonder in first class.

Geraldine Cox does not mind if you think she's loud, aggressive and pushy, and has a silly red hairstyle. If you are brave enough you can call her "dearie", "sweetie", and even "blossom" – you just have to help give the neglected, abused, and poverty-stricken Cambodian children a much better future through Sunrise.

www.sunrisechildrensvillage.org

Australians can sponsor a child for $40 per month.

1. Cox, Geraldine. *Home is Where the Heart Is*, Pan Macmillan, Sydney, 2000. Book is now unavailable from booksellers but Sunrise Australian chapter has copies available. Send email to Gaynor.ziersch@scv.org.au or contact Gaynor Ziersch, Office Administrator, Australia Cambodia Foundation Inc. PO Box 1113, Unley BC, SA 5061, Australia. Ph: +61 8 8340 4230 Fax: +61 8 8340 4920

2. ibid, p.5.

3. ibid., p.4

4. *Savvy&Sage,* September/October 2007, p.16.

5. A copy of this report was handed to me by a former employee of DFAT who did not wish to be named. I have not been able to find a copy of this report in department archives housed in National Archives although the record is more than 30 years old.

6. *Home is Where the Heart Is*, p.22.

7. ibid., p.28

8. ibid., p.50

9. ibid., p.62

10. ibid., p.65.

11. ibid., p.93.

12. ibid., p.101.

13. ibid., p.105

14. ibid p.108

15. ibid., p.116.

16. ibid.

17. The Iranian hostage crisis occurred after a group of Islamist militants and students took over the American embassy in Tehran in support of the Iranian revolution against the Shah. In what was a diplomatic crisis between Iran and the United States 53 Americans were held hostage for 444 days from 4 November, 1979 to 20 January 1981. When diplomatic resolution failed the United States

military attempted a rescue operation code named "Operation Eagle Claw" on 24 April 1980. It failed with the crash of two US military aircraft and the death of eight US servicemen. The hostages were finally released with the signing of the Algiers Accords in Algeria on 19 January 1981.

18. *Home is Where the Heart Is*, p.135.

19. ibid., p.150

20. ibid., p.155.

21. ibid., p.161

22. ibid., p.164.

23. Small skirmishes between both countries commenced in 1975.

24. *Home is Where the Heart Is*, p.187

25. ibid., p.246.

26. ibid., p.261.

27. ibid., p.272.

28. ibid., p.289

29. Hosking, J and Lowe, L. *My Khmer Heart*, Direct Cinema, California, 2000.

30. Best Documentary Hollywood Film Festival 2000; Nomination Independent Spirit Awards Best Documentary; Gracie Allen Award Winner, "Best Documentary", United States 2003; Namic Cable TV Awards Winner "Best Long Form" Documentary, United States 2002; Clarion Awards Women in US Television Winner "Best Documentary" 2003.

31. Hosking and Lowe. *My Khmer Heart*.

32. In 2013 he is graduating year 12. When he arrived at Sunrise he was virtually illiterate.

33. Hosking and Lowe. *My Khmer Heart*.

34. In 2013, Chorn is 16 and currently studying at Prince Alfred College, Adelaide. His music teacher believes he will shortly be a candidate for "Australia's Got Talent".

35. Cox, G. Email, 10 February 2013.

36. ibid.

37. ibid.

38. Sunrise Children's Villages, the Australia Cambodia foundation inc., newsletter, October-December 2010, vol.10, issue 4.

39. Cox, G. Email, 29 March 2012.

40. Sunrise Children's Villages, the Australia Cambodia foundation inc., newsletter, October-December 2010, vol.10, issue 4.

41. Sunrise Children's Villages, the Australia Cambodia foundation inc., newsletter, January-March 2011, vol.11, issue 1.

42. Cox, G. ibid., 5 April 2012.

43. Sunrise Children's Villages, the Australia Cambodia foundation inc., newsletter, January-March 2011, vol.11, issue 1.

44. Sunrise Children's Villages, the Australia Cambodia foundation inc., newsletter, July-September 2011, vol.11, issue 3.

45. Sunrise Children's Villages, the Australian Cambodia Foundation inc., newsletter, July-September 2012, vol.12, issue 4.

46. ibid.

Natasha Stott Despoja

"Politics is a living, breathing, important thing.
It affects every part of our lives ... It's not just the property of
older men wearing suits."

Australia's Parliament House is an imposing building that blends well with Canberra, the nation's bush capital. As I enter the large marble dominated lobby, the effect can be almost confronting, but the architecture still seems to instil well-proportioned degrees of respect, awe, even pride. Once past the main entrance, the building is a bewildering labyrinth of offices and suites; 22 kilometres of corridors, and I hope like mad the political staffer does not lose me because there is no way I will find the exit myself; indeed, it might be the only occasion I pray to be escorted from a building by security. Parliament House office accommodation is accorded on governmental pecking order and value. The governing party takes the best; ministers and opposition ministers inhabit the largest suites of offices; the press are forever complaining about the size of their quarters; and then come the minor parties and independents. Natasha Stott Despoja knows well what it is to have your suite reduced. She has known what it was to be leader of a party; she knows what it was to be with a party that was wooed by both major parties. But this is 2008. Her suite of three offices was once crowded with advisers and staff but shortly she will leave Parliament House and staff have been encouraged to accept other employment opportunities. It has been some time since major parties visited to lobby for support. The future of her Australian Democrats is bleak.

Natasha Jessica Stott Despoja was born on 9 September 1969, the daughter of Mario Despoja, an immigrant from Croatia, and Shirley Stott, Australian-born, of English heritage. The name Jessica was that of her grandmother, the ninth and last child of this branch of the Swinfield family. As a child Jessica stayed at home to care for a mother invalided by a stroke. She died when Natasha was two, was "strong, tactful, adored by her children; with a lovely voice and quiet charm but shy". Jessica's belief in rights and fairness for women was well demonstrated in the way she raised her daughter Shirley.

> Her feminism showed in her wish for education and independence for her daughter. To eke out her war widow's pension, she worked in a factory to send my mother to university. It was only her second paid job in life.

Though working in a motor parts factory was one of the few choices offered, having a paying job gave Jessica satisfaction and also ensured a brighter future for her daughter Shirley, "an educational opportunity that provided her with a chance to dream about a future where a woman's intellect was valued and her ability to lead assumed".[1] Shirley attended a Sydney school which encouraged excellence and she chose journalism as a career. As a court reporter she "began to learn a lot more about what was done to women and how men were excused from it", and "that the gender barrier and violence fitted together like a hinged tool to control women". She also realised that, no matter how good she was at her job, "she would never get better jobs, because she wasn't a man". Following the birth of son Luke, Shirley and Mario divorced, and Shirley supported her two young children. It has been said of Shirley Stott Despoja that she was known for her "integrity and professionalism" and that:

> Throughout the course of her professional and personal life, she has insisted upon standing up for herself, complaining about injustice and corruption and speaking

out on behalf of others who didn't have her opportunities, and can't make themselves heard.[2]

Natasha speaks fondly of her mother Shirley as "a wonderful role model, she's a feisty, outspoken feminist, and very influential on my political development". Shirley Stott was 80 per cent hearing impaired and wore two hearing aids. This is not something Natasha discusses freely. It is nonetheless feasible that this caused Natasha to grow up faster than most. Shirley certainly believed this to be the case and in a 1996 interview she suggested that because she was not always "very frank about my hearing loss", Natasha developed "early social skills".[3] The admiration the daughter has for her mother is offered readily:

> She brought up two kids singlehandedly from when my brother Luke was three and I was six. I find her even more extraordinary when I face the challenge of work and two children, with a loving supportive husband and two healthy incomes. I marvel at what she achieved.

There is the slightest of hesitations before Natasha adds, "I love her politics too, I love her brain ... she is my best friend". One of her first real political events was being on her father's shoulders at a Gough Whitlam rally. It is strange how life evolved; decades later she was on a first name basis with Whitlam. Natasha remembers the dismissal of the Whitlam Government by the Governor-General in November 1975, watching it on television, absorbing her parents' outrage. Natasha remembers being taken to a "reclaim the night march" by Shirley. The acrimonious split of her parents also left an indelible impression.

We had nasty family court battles over custody, access and maintenance. It made me very conscious just how much maintenance defaulters are responsible for families living in poverty.[4]

 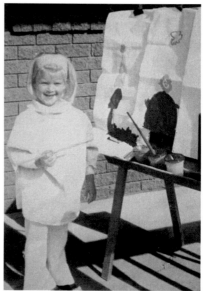

Courtesy Natasha Stott Despoja

Growing up Natasha was encouraged to have a view on issues and perhaps the strongest imprint was the importance of education. "Education was the great equaliser, education would lead to greater opportunities, in terms of health, income, democracy." Formal education alerted her to anomalies, to gender division:

Boys were encouraged to do maths and girls to consider other subjects. The boys were going to be fire-fighters, rocket scientists and other authority figures.[5]

The options and role models for girls were different. It was a volatile mixture of journalism, feminism, politics and the influence of strong women and a few men, which nurtured Natasha Stott Despoja and would continue to sustain her.

In Grade Three at primary school, Natasha declared "girls can do anything boys can do, except boys can't have babies". There was a geographic move and Natasha began to attend the Pembroke School in the Adelaide suburb of Kensington Park. The Pembroke philosophy incudes:

> We strive for excellence in tradition and innovation. We seek to prepare each student to actively participate in, and contribute to, our changing global society with leadership, wisdom and compassion, opening the door to a journey of lifelong learning.[6]

In the second half of the 1980s Pembroke introduced teddy-bear making as an extra-curriculum activity. The completed bears would be sent to charities. Natasha's interests lay in less cuddly and more hardcore areas.

She was involved in student representation at the school and her efforts resulted in the founding of South Australia's first state-wide student representative council. She entered the University of Adelaide to study for a Bachelor of Arts degree. Her interest in politics heightened: "I just loved the camaraderie of student politics, particularly all the women's groups". By 1991 she was President of the University of Adelaide Students' Association and serving as the state women's officer for the National Union of Students in South Australia. Natasha knew where her destiny lay but she had yet to affiliate herself to a party.

The Westminster form of politics Australia inherited from the United Kingdom is hinged on two major parties and their monopoly of governance. The Australian Labor Party (ALP) was Australia's oldest political party. It was formed in the 1890s and was represented in the first federal parliament elected in 1901. There had been great upheaval and splits in 1917, 1931 and 1955 which lost voter support and ensured Labor Party parliamentarians remained on the opposition benches. In the last century the ALP governed at the federal level only 28 years. In 1991, the year Natasha was President of the University of Adelaide Students' Association, and then graduated with a Bachelor of Arts degree, her nation's prime minister of eight years, Bob Hawke, was deposed by Paul Keating.

The Australian Liberal Party had also undergone periodic structural changes and debilitating splits. Originally known as the Nationalist Party and then the United Australian Party, the Liberal Party was formed by Robert Gordon Menzies in 1944. To maintain its position of power the Liberal Party governed as "the Coalition" with the other centre right party known originally as the Australian Country Party (1921–1975) and then the National Country Party of Australia.

Neither the ALP nor the Coalition seemed a good fit for Natasha, and she was uncomfortable with the same old, same old, bipolar nature of Australian politics. There needed to be a more invigorated political approach and she hoped that this might come from the Australian Democrats.

> I was like many younger Australians — quite disillusioned, a bit cynical about the major parties, disappointed and angry about the Labor Party decision to re-introduce tertiary fees.

She watched and listened and it seemed to her that the only party that had "maintained its principles as far as I was concerned" and "had stayed true to its policy of federally financed and accessible education was the Democrats".

On 24 March 1977 the charismatic former Liberal Party Minister, Don Chipp, had resigned from his party with the words:

I have become disenchanted with party politics as they are practised in this country and with the pressure groups which have an undue influence on the major political parties. The parties seem to polarise on almost every issue, sometimes seemingly just for the sake of it, and I wonder if the ordinary voter is not becoming sick and tired of the vested interests which unduly influence political parties and yearns for the emergence of a third political force, representing middle-of-the-road policies which would owe allegiance to no outside pressure group. [7]

The comment resonated through an Australian society still reeling from the 1975 dismissal of the Whitlam Government. Chipp was invited to attend a meeting of more than 3,000 disaffected voters who filled Perth Town Hall to overflowing. A resolution was passed to form a centre-line party and Don Chipp, amid resounding applause, was asked to lead. The name "Australian Democrats" was the most preferred among the 56 names suggested. In 1977 Democrat Janine Haines filled a South Australian Senate position left by retiring Steele Hall. Strangely Janine Haines was not the endorsed candidate for the 1977 federal election.

It was Don Chipp who declared at a 1980 media conference that the aim of the Australian Democrats was "to keep the bastards honest". He meant the major parties but no explanation was needed. Australians are a cynical bunch and commonly give politicians little respect but Chipp was as shrewd as he was charismatic and his comment galvanised Australians who desperately wanted change and forward thinking. The 1977 election was the first major test for the Australian Democrats. Some Australians, those with an open minded approach to their voting responsibilities and those who had wearied of the two-party monopoly, listened to what they hoped would be a fresh approach. At the 1977 federal election 9.38 per cent of the total House of Representatives vote and 11.13 per cent of the Senate vote went to the nascent party. Don Chipp (Vic) and Colin Mason (NSW) won six-year Senate terms. Sir Mark Oliphant, former Governor of South Australia, nuclear physicist and a man of distinction, voiced the hopes of many when he opened the 1980 Australian Democrats national conference. This was a party which was dedicated to preserving:

> What freedoms we still retain, and to increase them. A party in which dictatorship from the top was replaced by consensus. A party not ordered about by big business and the rich, or by union bosses. A party where a man could retain freedom of conscience and not thereby be faced with expulsion. A party to which the intelligent individual could belong without having to subscribe to a dogmatic creed. In other words, a democratic party.[8]

It was a praiseworthy doctrine – time would tell if the credo was attainable. In the 1980 election, enough Australians believed to give the Democrats 9.25 per cent of the Senate vote. The election of Janine Haines (SA), John Siddons (Vic) and Michael Macklin (Q) meant the Australian Democrats held five Senate seats from July 1981 and opportunity "to keep the bastards honest" at least in the Senate.

Janine Haines greatly impressed and influenced Natasha:

> Janine Haines came to speak to my Australian politics class and I was inspired not only because of her passion but the fact that this was a strong, capable, assertive woman in a leadership position, leading a party that was genuinely participatory and democratic, that gave ordinary people a vote and a say that was very appealing to me. Those

kind of role models you cannot underestimate I think the impact that they have on your political interest and development.

In her capacity as Women's Officer for the Students' Association of the University of Adelaide, and Women's Officer for the National Union of Students (SA), Natasha welcomed Janine Haines as a guest speaker.

> She was a trail blazer: a strong and articulate woman, she was a dynamic, clever, and witty politician and she led the way for many female politicians.

Despite her heavy schedule the leader of the Australian Democrats made time to speak and attend informal luncheons:

> To discuss politics with a group of young women interested in making a difference. She made clear her view, if we believed in changing the world for the better we had to get involved and thus began the lure of the Democrats for me.[9]

Natasha had found her political party and her political mentor. As far as the 21-year-old was concerned, the Haines campaign slogan "Give a damn" encapsulated the lady's "flair for language and her straight-talking style", a model to emulate. It was however a model the media struggled with. Acceptable and even necessary traits in a male politician were viewed differently when displayed by a woman. In 1980 Janine Haines joined the obstacle race which faced women in Australian politics, her parliamentary career over the next decade reflecting the best and worst of that world.

Although Australian women had most often been in majority within their nation's population, their place in their state and nation's houses of parliament had always been one of minority. Each step was a hard won battle. The home state of Janine Haines and Natasha Stott Despoja was the first to enfranchise non-Indigenous women, 1894. Western Australia followed in 1899, NSW in 1902, Tasmania in 1903, Queensland in 1905, and finally Victoria in 1908. Women however were not eligible to stand for election in state parliaments until 1918 (NSW and Q); 1920 (WA); 1921 (Tas) and 1923 (Vic). The exception again was South Australia which permitted women to nominate in 1894.[10]

Next door neighbour, New Zealand, became the first nation in the world to give women the right to vote in national elections, in 1893. Australian women (except Indigenous women) were enfranchised for the new Commonwealth Parliament of Australia in 1901. They were permitted to vote in the second federal election in 1903.[11] It would not be until 1943 that the first woman was elected and West Australian, Dorothy Tangney, took her seat in the Australian Senate. It would be a seat she would occupy for 25 years during which time she never stopped campaigning for equal pay. Like Tangney, Enid Lyons was a school teacher. She was also the widow of the nation's tenth Prime Minister, Joseph Lyons. In 1943 she was the first woman elected to the Australian House of Representatives and held the Tasmanian seat of Darwin for three general elections until her retirement in 1951. When she first entered parliament:

> I was fully aware of the mass of prejudice against them [Australian women in public office], and on that account was the more sensitively conscious of the burden of responsibility devolving upon me as a pioneer.[12]

She became the first woman appointed to a Cabinet position, as Vice-President of the Federal Executive Council, when the Menzies Government came to power in December 1949. Dame Enid Lyons fought for equality and was responsible for equal training allowances for men and women and welfare payments for mothers.[13]

1986 was a landmark year because Janine Haines became the first woman to lead an Australian political party when she was elected leader of the Australian Democrats. Under her leadership, support for the Democrats rose. Her party held the balance of power in the Senate and by 1990 their Senate vote had risen to 12.6 per cent. Natasha had been impressed with the Haines "passion" and that she "was a strong, capable, assertive woman in a leadership position". Australia was slow to change, and weighed down by entrenched conservatism. Australians were not too sure about passionate strong, capable, assertive women in public life, in leadership positions.

The media also struggled and painted Haines harshly as unfeminine. Political cartoonists persevered with unflattering images which relayed their own discomfort with women in power positions. Journalists asked her questions they would never dream of asking her male counterparts. They wanted to know if she provided her family with frozen dinners before she flew to Canberra? They wanted to know how her family coped without her, intending to provoke guilt on this senator's part. There was the constant emphasis on physical appearance. When a newspaper magazine did a colour feature, with Janine Haines sporting a makeover and glamorous gown, the caption read: "Sexy? Ruthless? Funny? Will the real Janine Haines please stand up?"[14]

Invariably this South Australian senator was treated no better by her male counterparts. Haines arrived early one day in 1988 for a sitting of a Senate select committee and assumed her position. The Committee Secretary, also a woman, was present. A male committee member put his head through the door and after saying, "Oh there's

nobody here", left. Haines recalled that during the sex discrimination
legislation debate:

> Brian Harradine argued that you shouldn't have equality
> of opportunity for women because what would happen
> if they got into the police force and they had to ride
> motorcycles and they dropped one of them in the middle
> of the night and they wouldn't be able to pick it up again!
> Now I'm not sure if he was worried about all those
> criminals going free or the damage that was done to the
> motorbike.

In 1990 Janine Haines left the Senate to contest the House of
Representatives South Australian seat of Kingston. The campaign
was ugly, sullied by opposition vitriolic not evidenced before, and
her opponents, regardless of political affiliation, ensured she received
no preferential votes. This was admitted in parliament in 2008 when
Senator Nick Minchin told how he was given the task of managing
the Liberal Party's Kingston campaign, the main aim of which was
"keeping Janine Haines out of the House of Representatives ... by
ensuring she came third", even if this meant Labor would retain the
seat; "she was one of the most extraordinary politicians Australia has
produced and a very capable woman".[15]

In 1995 Janine Haines was launching the career of another
Australian Democrat, Natasha Stott Despoja. Just five years later, on
20 November 2004, Janine Haines died, at age 59. Natasha would
relate what her mentor said in that 1995 speech.

> We had another Liberal MP who was worried about equal
> opportunity and used Parliament House as an example ...
> about all the terrible things that could happen, marriages
> breaking down, all sorts of things. He got particularly

Natasha with Senator Robert Bell and Senator Janine Haines
Courtesy of Natasha Stott Despoja

worried about what would happen for example if there were male and female Telecom workers working underground around a pole, or if there were male and female truck drivers trucking across the Nullarbor to Perth. At that point I got a tad testy and pointed out that, in fact, there were males and females in parliament and I hadn't noticed anything particularly untoward going on – mind you, when you look at the blokes, that's not surprising. He then went on ... he was very worried about what was likely to happen to members of parliament's marriages as a consequence of what he described as all the glamorous women using their guile to woo them in some way.

Natasha had honed her public skills scribbling newspaper articles and opinions; involved herself in community radio, and was a self-confessed "political junkie". She became a researcher/speech writer for the Leader of the Australian Democrats, Senator John Coulter, working on legislation, providing amendments and coming up with policy opened her eyes to how "lawmaking and legislation can change lives. I was pretty hooked from day one". Natasha also worked for Senator Karin Sowada from NSW. On 3 October 1993 Senator Cheryl Kernot was elected the fifth leader of the Australian Democrats and Natasha joined the Kernot staff. She now advised not only on youth, education and science policy, but also for research dealing with Indigenous affairs and women's issues.

In 1995 Senator Coulter resigned due to ill-health. The pre-selection of his replacement was hotly contested but on 29 November 1995 Natasha was appointed to the casual vacancy and departed for Canberra – and then rapidly returned to Adelaide after spending just two days in the Senate. The Keating Government had called an election on 2 March for all 148 House of Representatives seats and 76 Senate positions. Natasha was again on the election campaign: "I thought I would be the youngest ever female and shortest ever serving female".

Natasha need not have worried because within three and a half hours of the polling booths closing she had achieved the quota (14 per cent) without the need for preference distribution. "I am a bit of a drama queen ... I'm thrilled." The Democrat was delighted for her party: "The strong support for the Democrats ... shows people have 'taken out insurance' against the main parties".[16]
The electorate had authenticated her as the youngest woman to rise in the crimson Senate chamber to deliver her first speech. On 1 May 1996, and with a proud Shirley seated in the gallery above, Natasha struggled through the first nervous lines and then delivered the remainder with a frankness which disarmed fellow senators and endeared her to the majority who listened elsewhere.

> I look forward to the day when I look across this chamber
> from my seat and see such a diversity of faces – young

people, old people, different ages, men and women, and the many cultures that make up our nation, including Indigenous cultures ... When that time comes I think we will accept that neither youth nor age, any more than being male or female, black or white, is a virtue in itself, except that it deserves to be represented in a system that claims to be representative.

Natasha was gracious in her acknowledgement of John Coulter who also sat in the gallery. Coulter had been one of "Australia's most committed environmentalists" and she had been influenced by his enthusiasm. The tradition of sending parliamentarians a "chocolate bilby" at Easter became the only light-hearted response she would take to an issue that within less than a decade would monopolise public conscience and electoral habits.

Not gagged by traditional party doctrine Natasha raised issues that confronted the sensitivities of a large part of the Australian population. In rapid fire succession she called for sustainable employment, "employment creation with environmental protection" and a reform of "our constitution to reflect, to recognise, prior ownership", suggesting that "native title" could potentially go some way "towards righting institutionalised and ancient wrongs in the relations between Indigenous and non-Indigenous Australians". There was need for an "update or review of our democratic systems" to reflect "contemporary challenges"; and further discourse on Australia as a republic. Equal opportunity legislation and sex discrimination laws were all important and would change "lives for the better without dampening the fierce individualism that Australians wish to maintain". There was a noticeable stir in the chamber as Natasha spoke, heads nodded and the respect within the Senate for this new Democrat Senator from South Australia rose.

However the passion and aspirations were slightly lost on a people and a media in shock. Just days before, at 1.30pm on 28 April 1996, a mentally disturbed Martin Bryant had opened fire in a cafe at the historic Port Arthur site in Tasmania. Within a short period of time 35 were dead and a further 23 injured. Natasha struggled to put into words the gravity and horror of the massacre.

> I should say that at this time of national grief and overwhelming loss of life in Tasmania, Australians need no reminding that the first duty of government is to maintain and secure public safety. Whatever we considered the major issues to be in advance of this session, I think what happened on Sunday afternoon in Port Arthur must change our priorities. We must ensure that any legislative powers we have and all our wisdom and will are used to prevent another such massacre. I express my deepest sympathies for all those suffering personal loss as a result of that dreadful event.

It was a difficult time for Australians and Australia's youngest woman politician wanted to encourage them to enthusiastically aspire for a new society, a better society. Natasha wanted to encourage Australians to believe, particularly in their youth.

If I can speak at all for the youth of this country it is to say that we want to respect our institutions and our leaders and we want to pursue change that makes individuals free and able to pursue their hopes and dreams whatever their circumstances ... I am part of 'Generation HECS', that group of graduates who have accumulated debt for no other reason than their decision to broaden their knowledge... Education offers empowerment. It is one way that individuals can affect their own destinies. And those people who protest against disincentives to education, such as fees and loans, should not be told simply to 'get a job'. Nor should young people struggling to find work in today's workforce be told by the media, or anyone else, to 'get a haircut'.

For four years she had conducted the Democrats' Youth Poll on behalf of Senator Karin Sowada, "the only survey by a political party that gives young people a chance to express their views on a range of topics". She believed the poll painted a picture of young Australians "as a very caring generation caring about employment prospects and concerned about their families and teenage suicide levels". They demonstrated a willingness to be part of decision making processes and "determined, absolutely determined, to ensure that the environment is not further degraded". But these same young people showed "disdain for politicians and are cynical about the political process ... only 1.5 per cent of young people trust us". Natasha hoped to change perceptions and opinions so that "before I leave this place young people will no longer be unrepresented in this chamber or in the other place".

The honesty and strength of her speech should have generated respect within the Senate and among others whose seats were in the House of Representatives, but there had been feisty and sincere women before and the "glass ceiling" in state and federal parliaments had withstood shattering. The task ahead was mighty. According to one observer in 1999:

> If women are to influence the forum that is Parliament, they will need to modify 'boyo' debating tactics, focus government on conciliatory rather than confrontational processes, and challenge parliamentary traditions that are little changed from an earlier era of gentleman's clubs ... Still outnumbered by their male colleagues, they confront a culture that is heavy with male overlay, male ambience,

male preference for the way of doing things, male taste in comfort.[17]

In 1996 still only 20 per cent of federal politicians were women. Natasha had already been involved in a male-dominated contest when she beat eight male candidates for Democrat pre-selection; "I don't think I realised how ambitious I was until I had to fight for this ballot".[18] Pre-selection had been a major barrier to women entering parliament because major parties were unwilling to pre-select women in "winnable" or "safe" seats. Interviews with major party players had shown how discriminatory the process was because the ideal candidate had characteristics stereotypically found in men. A 1995 survey found:

> Qualities included criteria such as having a football career, being a good 'family man', 'tall, dark and handsome', local government experience, and a record of business and trade union work. For women, high media profiles and attractiveness were important.[19]

There needed to be a critical mass of women in Australian parliaments before life would become easier for women politicians. In 1993 newly elected MP Judi Moylan (WA) had just boarded a flight to Canberra. She moved to the locker to hang her jacket. "Two businessmen came by and said, 'Would you hang ours up luv'". The shocked Moylan took the coats and hung them up, their owners suitably embarrassed when they realised she was not the hostess.[20][21]

Following the departure of Janine Haines from the Senate Cheryl Kernot became Leader of the Australian Democrats. Very highly thought of both in and out of Parliament House, she deliberately wore bright colours, a personal demonstration within an ocean of grey suits. She would say of the men in parliamentary grey, "I don't think the men are at all serious about sharing the power". Kernot firmly believed that although the Democrats were tolerated on the margins, "particularly while you're helpful, you can't challenge the structures".[22] She was well aware of the double standards which existed, how women were judged differently.

> Where's the female version of Bob Hawke? They'd never preselect his female equivalent. Imagine a woman confessing that she had a drinking problem and weeping over her extra-marital affairs, while her faithful husband looked up at her adoringly. Susan Ryan used to drink with the boys, but they held it against her in the end.[23]

Cheryl Kernot had been motivated to enter politics, in part due to the abortion debate, how "there were two, or maybe three, women in parliament and all these men talking about abortion". It took her ten years before she was finally elected to the Senate in 1990. On her first day her husband accompanied her and parliamentary attendants kept addressing him as "Senator": "For the first six months, we got invitations for Senator and Mrs Kernot".[24] Kernot was concerned that although women had been encouraged to return to the workforce there had been no attempt to restructure the working day, nor had childcare been adequately addressed.

In 1995 Labor MP Wendy Fatin was very outspoken about her experience in the Australian Parliament, perhaps because she was not standing again, after 13 years. She was motivated to enter parliament partly because, like Cheryl Kernot, she felt uneasy with a very predominantly male parliament legislating, or not legislating, on issues directly pertaining to women and families.[25] In 1983 she was the first Western Australian woman elected to the Australian House of Representatives, in the seat of Canning. Following re-distribution, she was elected to the West Australian seat of Brand. She was being shown around Canberra's Parliament House in 1995 when her escort asked her if she wished to be address as "Mrs or Miss?". When she replied "Ms" he said "I'm sorry, we don't do that here. It's Miss or Mrs". Fatin replied, "Well, I'm sorry. Call me Ms".[26]

Wendy Fatin believed:

> When you look at the range of male politicians, some are great at it, some mediocre and some terrible. But women politicians, in order to be noticed, have to be great at it.[27]

She believed the confrontationist style of politics suited men rather than women and she believed it was not a good way to discuss issues and govern. Only when the process was altered would there be fairness on all levels. Being a woman politician had been a "lonely existence". She had found her male colleagues viewed "most things from an entirely different perspective" and tended to discuss "football, cricket and horseracing". She realised early that they "didn't really want you to talk about" those subjects so "you are just isolated from their world".[28] After 13 years in the House of Representatives, after all the equal opportunity legislation, anti-discrimination legislation, "the male culture hadn't changed" according to Fatin. "We were continuing the cultural tradition of centuries". She strongly believed it was "time for other women to carry the torch".[29]

In 1996, the year Wendy Fatin retired from political life, Natasha Stott Despoja was beginning hers. Natasha respected those who had gone before her and realised: "Men have shown over the centuries that they don't relinquish power, so it has to be taken or wrested from them". Natasha herself was once refused entry to an airport members' lounge because "she did not look like a politician" and her entry into federal politics coincided with the political and public destruction of two of the most high profile Australian women politicians, Joan Kirner and Carmen Lawrence. She appreciated there was "no sense of enduring success with women in politics in this country" and what scared her was "that there comes a point when they are stopped or cut down or forced to leave", and this included "talented, strong women like Carmen Lawrence or Joan Kirner". Being in a minor party she felt protected to a point but she had watched how strong women were subjected to "a level of media scrutiny that was outrageous. No man was ever portrayed in a similar way to Joan Kirner...".[30] The new senator from South Australia, described as an "idealist" and with the "right feminist theories", felt she knew what she was in for and time would tell if she could survive the media and the Australian Senate.

The political staffer hands me a folder cutely entitled "The Nat Pack". There is an assortment of early press clippings featuring Natasha and they demonstrated how crazy 1996 was, how insane 1997 was, and pretty much the ensuing years as well. Natasha was besieged by the media because she was so atypical. This was a house where the norm was male and the average age was 49.9.[31] Natasha was a woman; she was a member of Generation X, youthful, attractive, enthusiastic; she believed Christine Anu was the best thing that had happened to Australian music; her favourite bands were the Jesus & Mary Chain and Oasis; her preference was for Diet Coke rather than beer or red wine; she believed one should wear comfortable footwear and clothes because women's fashion and "tottering about in high heels" was not always practical or "empowering". Natasha was an outspoken free spirit, a breath of fresh air and the Senate and the press weren't really prepared for her.

The Australian media in the 1990s and ensuing decades was, and is, extremely conservative. This was also a celebrity driven era when you were a celebrity because you were in the media or featured by the media. Natasha's mother Shirley was a journalist and Natasha had toyed with the idea of pursuing the same career, and the media would figure prominently in her political life – it just would not all be gracious. *The Who* article dated 4 March 1996 was entitled "Babe in the Woods". The first paragraph read:

> At 26, South Australian Democrat Senator Natasha Stott Despoja is the youngest federal parliamentarian – and security guards and Commonwealth car drivers sometimes don't believe that the tiny, dimpled, brown-eyed blonde is who she says she is.

The article did acknowledge that beneath the "sartorial and slangy youthfulness beats the heart of a smart Democrat who believes education is a 'democratic right'". The article also quoted Cheryl Kernot as suggesting Natasha "doesn't know she's alive yet"; because it was wonderful to be enthusiastic but politics was "sheer hard work" which was relentless. "New kid in town", commenced an article in *The Bulletin* of 23–30 January 1996, the sub-heading "Stalking Canberra's corridors of power in Doc Martens, Natasha Stott Despoja is not your average senator".

The media scrambled for stories about the one they had ordained the Generation X poster girl and there seemed no end of comparison and silly headlines. An article from 1996 demonstrated what was to come:

> She's blond, she's little, she's 26, she's got a smiling mouth out of which words flow as if from a tap, except that they're all in the correct sentences, and she's recently gone from an annual salary of $20,000 to $100,000. Yes, she's the one in Doc Martens.[32]

Beneath the pretext of serious examination a February 1996 issue of *Juice* similarly got stuck on the age factor and then compounded it:

A bright satin shirt distracts the eye from a sensible business skirt and the omnipresent Docs. Her newly trimmed blonde bob frames a cheeky, fashionable pink grin.

One assumes the "pink" refers to lipstick!

Natasha believed she was prepared but the media emphasis was on the personal, on the physical, on superficiality.

Apparently footwear was going to assume an amazing importance, because at the time I just wore my Doc Martens into the chamber because that's what I wore.[33]

On a good day she could go with the flow, approach the not so serious, not so seriously. In the 1997 book *Virtuosity: Inside the Heads of 100 Prominent Australians*, she decided to take a facetious approach:

I don't know if anyone wants to be known as "good" at politics ... Politics has now fallen so far in the public's esteem I sometimes feel I should apologise to my mother for pursuing such a seemingly shameful profession.[34]

Her light-hearted list of requirements to be in politics included:

The ability to act interested during often puerile Question Time exchanges; mastering the sixty (and sometimes six) second sound bite; overcoming a fear of flying (and of who you might end up sitting next to); making long and often impromptu speeches in Parliament on what I consider to be very important issues, but it is sometimes to an empty chamber – and I know some of our listeners at home are tuned to the Parliament broadcast in order to cure insomnia.[35]

Her list of special skills included "I am mistress of the art of chocolate eating".

She wanted to enthuse about principle, about politics, about philosophy and about life, and "my shoes got the headlines, which I always thought was a bit bizarre". It was only February 1996 and already she was "starting to get a little annoyed".

> I kept getting stunned by the way that an in-depth interview on employment policies would suddenly move to my interest in Melrose Place or whether there was a partner in my life. That kind of stuff kept cropping up as the headline in the tabloids. I guess I have to adapt to that.[36]

She was dubbed "The Baby Senator" and political cartoonists delighted in drawing Natasha sucking on a dummy (pacifier). "It is actually difficult to control how you are perceived or portrayed in the mainstream media." The relationship between the press gallery and the senator would sometimes be good, sometimes frustrating – partly because she did not fit their preconceived stereotype, and partly because she spoke articulately, and because they were not as serious about getting it right as she was.

Natasha wanted to get on with the job, on legislating, on the issues that mattered, but was struggling to be taken seriously and realised this meant surviving in an alienating setting. "Parliament is a bully-boys' club driven by male egos and testosterone."[37] Leading up to the 1996 election a "Pinning Down the Pollies" event had been held in Port Noarlunga, in the marginal seat of Kingston. Natasha was clearly seen by the crowd as the only one with anything to say. Simon

Crean, the Minister for Employment, Education and Training, and the opposition spokesman on employment and training, Dr David Kemp, used the platform to hammer away at each other, or as the Democrat senator said:

> While both parties huff and puff about how important training and education is, they are notably silent on jobs creation.

She called for wages to be set that did not discriminate against teenagers. "Young people do not deserve to be paid less for equal work." This was a serious issue close to Natasha's heart but Minister Crean's retort was: "So, how old are you anyway?". Natasha continued: "Youth unemployment is the biggest election issue, but it is being put aside for the boys' bickering".

The very doors of the Senate were heavy and hard to open for the less strong senators; the air-conditioning was set for men in suits and ties. Senate seating was manufactured for large male bodies, not smaller ones. It was suggested to women elected to political office that they should wear dresses and skirts because they were more flattering. More feminine attire could result in boys' locker room and wolfish comments. But Natasha was fuelled with democracy in the truest sense and would sit in the Senate and marvel at being in this place – "What a privilege" – vowing to herself that she would take the responsibility seriously. She was determined to "keep the bastards honest" but also believed she was there "to give the bastards a few ideas". "I am daunted but excited ... But being in the chamber is the ultimate!" she told a reporter during those heady first months of 1996.[38] She would look around and think: "Gosh I am the youngest, there are very few women here" and "many of the life experiences I can't begin to relate to and vice versa", but as nerve-wracking as those first months in the Senate were it gave her a high, the chamber was "quite awesome". "When you actually walk into that chamber for the first time, it's quite overwhelming." In the Senate the 75 others were initially friendly and welcoming. She did however wonder if "they will probably never be this nice to me again", an assessment which proved somewhat accurate.

In her first speech Natasha put the Senate on notice that she would do her utmost to be taken seriously and would fight for legislation important to her, the Australian Democrats and Australians:

> Employment growth needs a healthy economy, but an economy cannot stay healthy in the long term without us making sure that we use our national assets, our environment, our saving, in a sustainable way. ... This will ensure continuing quality of life, both now and extending to all future generations of Australians.

She put up with the standard comment when the Senate was sitting late: "Isn't it past your bedtime?". She ignored the blonde jokes. She smiled away the early attempt on the part of a Queensland National Party Senator to match-make Natasha with his bachelor colleague. All this was tolerable because she wanted to legislate, to force change, and to represent those who needed her voice – and her personal mantra was "don't underestimate me".

The transition to the Senate chamber was, according to Natasha, "massive" but she was getting more comfortable with her responsibilities, and busy with being the Democrat spokesperson on science and technology, higher education, information technology, employment and youth affairs, and the responsibilities of the Attorney General. She quickly realised there was no such thing as a "typical day" in the Senate and that hours were long, very long, the pace relentless. It meant being a presence in the Senate during the day, voting, attending committee meetings, reading and researching, meeting with constituents, giving speeches and visiting schools – the responsibilities were endless and being in the parliamentary building at midnight quickly became the norm.

Others quickly realised that this Democrat Senator should indeed not be underestimated. In May 1997 Natasha accused fellow South Australian Senator, and the Liberal Government Minister for Employment, Education, Training and Youth Affairs, Amanda Vanstone, of misleading the parliament over university enrolment figures in an attempt to prove that government policy on university fees (HECS) had not deterred students. In return Vanstone made a disparaging comment about blonde Democrats. Natasha objected on grounds that the comment was inappropriate and Vanstone was forced to explain the figures better the following day.

The Australian Democrats had become a force to be reckoned with and power brokers from both major parties haunted their offices to gain legislative support. Then the party and Natasha personally received a totally unexpected jolt. On 15 October 1997 the very popular Democrat leader resigned and joined the Australian Labor Party. Kernot had forewarned no one in her former party of her intentions. Democrat Senator Lyn Allison commented, "Cheryl was one of the reasons why I joined the party ... we were all shell-shocked". Natasha concurred:

> It was a huge shock at the time, a massive shock, but I respected her right to do what she did. But I always believed she had this amazing place in Australian politics, the leader of the third party [and] arguably the most powerful woman in Australian politics ever.

Kernot had decided to pursue executive power, but she did it in a dignified manner and relinquished her Senate seat back to the

Democrats. Natasha was sad, for herself and for those who voted for a Kernot led Australian Democrats.

Labor Party polls improved dramatically while Democrat polls went the other way. The Labor Party offered Kernot a marginal seat in the House of Representatives and a media which had anointed her a darling became ferocious in their condemnation, down to the most private of issues.

> Journalists who had for years delicately avoided details of private carry-on in the lives of male MPs – serial adultery, whatever – were suddenly sounding off like prudes about just one woman.[39]

The defection caused an unprecedented and largely negative media crush. One journalist declared that "her [Kernot's] defection to Labor was sealed over coffee, and the plunger was later auctioned by the ALP for $5,000".[40] Again Australians witnessed how women were subjected to a different level of scrutiny and a double standard.

The 1998 election for the Queensland seat of Dickson was marred by murky waters. Kernot, regularly called "demo-rat", was denied preferences from most rival candidates and she won by just 171 votes. Media hostility was unrelenting: "She was portrayed in print as a has-been, a whinger and a poor performer.[41] She confirmed what women endeavouring to crack the "glass ceiling" knew:

> Ambition is regarded as a terrible thing in a woman. It's a culture thing that has lost women a lot of opportunities.[42]

In parliament too Kernot was condemned with a vehemence never before witnessed, such as the comment made in parliament on 12 March 1998 by Liberal Party backbencher Don Randall that Kernot had "the morals of an alley cat on heat". The intensity of the most public disapproval resulted in Cheryl Kernot losing her seat in 2001. In a final bid at political life in 2010 Cheryl Kernot unsuccessfully ran as an independent NSW Senate candidate.

Following the departure of Kernot, Senator Meg Heather Lees, who had assumed the Senate seat vacated by Janine Haines in 1990, was elected leader of the Australian Democrats in December 1997. Natasha Stott Despoja was elected deputy leader. Over the next couple of years there were some notable wins for the Democrats and the youngest senator – such as negotiating billions of dollars for research – but if you belonged to a minor party you were shut out from the cross benches, and it took longer to achieve change. Natasha introduced a private member's Bill, the "Genetic Privacy and Non-Discrimination Bill" in 1998 to protect genetic privacy, but neither party approved and amendments went back and forth. In 2006 the Howard Government decided to enshrine genetic privacy in law, with the same amendments Natasha had moved eight years earlier. "That's the frustration" but she still found it so "privileged and rewarding" when laws were implemented which "changed lives" for the better.

It is easy to be impressed with Natasha Stott Despoja. She is warm, engaging, articulate, witty, and passionate about causes which directly affect people. At the 1999 *Women in Uniform: Perceptions and Pathways* conference she delivered the "Clare Burton Memorial Address" and I was surprised how many mature professional women approached Natasha for an autograph, unusual behaviour for such a group. On 3 April 2000 she returned to the Australian Defence Force Academy, Canberra, to launch the book of conference proceedings[43] and undaunted, informed those crowded into the officers' mess that the themes affecting women in the military:

> Themes such as chilly climates, lack of promotion because of marriage or motherhood, the tyranny of

workplaces which are not family friendly, or the absence of support networks, the critical mass of women needed for cultural change, and the emphasis of appearance over performances are all too common barriers presented to women in professional life.

One could not fail but be impressed how easily Natasha responded to this and other audiences, showing no sign of insincerity, just genuine interest and concern. The easy rapport was proving very popular with every section of the population, and although she would have preferred to be legislating, invitations to participate in all types of social engagements were filling her diary, as were more and more media requests.

The ABC television programme *Good News Week* was a satirical news-based comedy quiz show. It featured two regular panellists and four guest panellists forming two opposing teams. Panellists needed to have a good general knowledge, a finger on the political pulse, and a quick wit. The targeted viewing market was the 18 to 39 age group. Natasha was a natural for the programme and her appearances became regular. She believed it would promote Democrat politics to the youth market. This may well have been the case but the audience turned out to be far broader than the 18 to 39-year-old age group. "It was an amazing experience, to make politics more accessible through those shows."[44] But there were always detractors – some senators would remark: "*The Good News Week* Senator. What do you know, you're just out there because you want the television coverage." Natasha felt:

> The notion that if you appeared on a light-hearted television show then somehow your IQ had dropped or that you can't be blonde and a leader because of the ditsy connotations; it was hard to be pigeonholed according to age and my

sex as opposed to being judged for my legislation or policy work of which I'm really proud. Occasionally, I have struggled to say to people: "This is what I'm about, not the mainstream media's perception".

There were opportunities to address far more serious issues and in 1998 Natasha made her first address at Canberra's National Press Club. She spoke on the topic "The Future for Young Australians", and how this did not just require a change in policies, "but a fundamental change in politics". In 1999 she returned to speak about biotechnology, "particularly, the need for a ban on human cloning and the prohibition of genetic discrimination". Speaking engagements and media appearances continued to raise awareness of Democrat policies and Natasha's profile. Two Labor Party members commented: "You've been getting too much coverage for our liking".

Democrats Leader Meg Lees lacked the warmth and people skills of the charismatic Kernot and those of her deputy, and the attention Natasha was receiving was doubtless unsettling. Over the next two years, through Lees dogged perseverance, the Democrats negotiated improvements in the Pharmaceutical Benefits Scheme (PBS) and the Environment Protection and Biodiversity Act; but the lustre had dimmed and the cracks in the party were widening. Lees was known as an unrepentant disciplinarian and had been complicit in the expulsion of eleven members of the West Australian Democrat executive in 1993 for insubordination. A former member of the Democrats' national executive, Brian Jenkins, claimed Lees had helped "decimate" the West Australian branch of the party. Jenkins was married to the former WA Democrats Senator Jean Jenkins, one of those expelled after the WA Democrats directed preferences in a state election to the Liberal Party against a national Democrat directive. Brian Jenkins let loose a public condemnation:

They are very good at getting elected in South Australia … they regarded themselves as the people who knew how to do things and the rest of us were a load of useless buggers.

Lees was unapologetic:

Some people's idea of democracy is that you keep balloting and balloting and balloting until their opinion and their choice gets up, and anyone who steps in and says, "Enough, let's get on with the business of being a political party" is then attacked.

It was a statement which proved ironic in the not too distant future.

During the 1998 election campaign the Liberal Party proposed a Goods and Services Tax (GST). The additional tax was opposed by the Labor Party, the Australian Greens and independent Senator Brian Harradine. The government needed the support of the Democrats for the Bill to pass the Senate. Publicly the Democrats argued against the tax but agreed to work with whichever party was elected. Democrat election campaign platform included the pledge that there would be "No GST on food" and Meg Lees stated that her party would oppose a GST on essential items such as medicine and fresh food. Two other party demands were for exemption for tax-free books and public transport.

Once in power the John Howard Liberal National Coalition Government lobbied the minor parties heavily for support. Within the Democrat party room there was disagreement. Natasha, imbued with the belief that education was the pathway to a better quality of life, was unhappy with GST on books. She also believed the Democrats were breaking a campaign promise to the Australian people. Perhaps indicative of a male-dominated parliament the suggestion that there should be no GST on tampons was dismissed. The leader of the Democrats pledged party support for the Bill. In the Senate Natasha and Democrat Senator Andrew Bartlett crossed the floor to vote against the tax.

> One of the hardest political decisions, crossing the floor to vote against your colleagues ... you know what is harder, it is voting for something you are not committed to or don't entirely believe in.

GST legislation was passed on 28 June 1999, gained assent on 8 July 1999 and came into operation on 1 July 2000. Few Australians would realise the impact of GST legislation because July was also the beginning of the Sydney Summer Olympic Games dubbed the "greatest Olympic Games ever".

The GST process and vote widened cracks in the Australian Democrat party. Over the next two years there was disharmony within, little love lost between the leader and her deputy, and a decline in the polls which by April 2001 was around 2 per cent indicating that there was the real possibility of at least four Democrat senators losing their seats at federal elections due later that year. Natasha had been asked earlier to stand for the leadership but declined. Michael Macklin, the Democrat Party President, telephoned. The ACT Branch had raised a petition calling for a leadership ballot. One hundred signatures of Democrats registered for more than six months was needed; if this came to fruition, would she place her name on the ballot? Natasha gathered those whose opinions she valued, in her modest old worker's cottage in North Adelaide to discuss the proposition. Natasha was not sure she was ready for what would be a very public spill, everything was happening too fast, too soon. She was concerned for the party but even if she won the ballot, could she turn around public opinion six months out from the federal election?

The petition was lodged and Natasha's name added to the ballot. She knew she was in for a battle. Meg Lees had the backing of more Democrat Senators. Lees had a staff of sixteen, Natasha just three. Harsh things were said by her opposition, particularly by Senator Andrew Murray, but Natasha would not be drawn into a personal slanging match. She refused to alter her plans to appear more moderate, one commitment being her annual participation in the Sydney Gay and Lesbian Mardi Gras on 3 March. Six weeks after the ballot was posted the result was overwhelming: 70 per cent of registered Democrat members had voted for Natasha. She replaced Lees on 6 April 2001, making her the youngest person to lead an Australian political party.

With a federal election pending, the third in eight years, Natasha hit the ground running and immediately began to turn the focus on Democrats policy. At her third address to the National Press Club, on 8 August 2001, she launched more than 30 policies on issues as broad-ranging as education, reconciliation, corporate governance, environment, tourism, innovation, science, women, small business and immigration. Natasha agreed that taxation yet again dominated political debate but unlike the two major parties the Democrats believed the emphasis should be on "where we – as a nation – should spend those funds for the greatest rewards". Elections should not be about which party offers the biggest tax cut. "The Australian Democrats today pledge we will not support any increase in the rate of the Goods and Services Tax", nor would the party support "tax cuts to the rich while the poorest are neglected", nor any tax cuts at all unless "necessary improvements are first made in education, health and environmental protection". There was concern for "the most disadvantaged Australians". Her party firmly believed "welfare reform is part of this nation's unfinished business ... One million Australians live significantly below the poverty line...", and this would be the key Democrats election platform. The address was lengthy and strong and finished with:

> The state of the nation is not determined by John Howard or Kim Beazley but by the collective efforts of every one of us.

Doggedly some journalists continued to focus on the tension between Natasha and Lees. Others continued to prefer the personal and light subjects. Natasha agreed to speak with *The Australian Women's Weekly* on the condition they would ask questions about policy. Natasha spoke of serious issues: the GST and its effect on her party, euthanasia, same-sex parenting. The magazine journalist asked questions such as "What is your favourite flower?" and "Who do you think is the sexiest man alive?".

There were vocal supporters like the 1984 Australian of the Year, Professor Lowitja O'Donoghue, who said of Natasha: "I am always inspired by her energy and commitment, her warmth and that absolute powerhouse of a brain she has". Emeritus Professor Hugh Stretton believed Natasha displayed:

> Exceptional capacity, energy, brains, homework, fast, clear speech whatever the subject's complexity and a serious intention to leave the world better than she found it.[45]

By mid-2001 the Democrats were polling around 9 per cent, demonstrating that there was a renewed interest in the party and support for its leader. But 2001 was one of the most challenging, turbulent years since the Vietnam era and Natasha needed to steer her party through an obstacle course of political opportunism, human rights infringements, and a fearful world.

On 26 August 2001 the Norwegian freighter *MV Tampa* rescued 438 refugees, predominantly Hazaras of Afghanistan, from a sinking fishing boat in international waters. The Howard Government refused the freighter permission to enter Australian waters. Australia was criticised by other nations for failing to meet the obligations under United Nations international law to distressed mariners, and a diplomatic dispute developed between Australia and Norway. When the *Tampa* entered Australian waters without permission, Prime Minister John Howard ordered Australian Special Forces to board the ship. On the night of 29 August, the Prime Minister introduced the emergency Border Protection Bill 2001, giving the government the power to remove any ship and those onboard in the territorial waters of Australia, using any "reasonable force". No civil or criminal proceedings could be taken against the Australian Government or any of its officers during this procedure, nor would asylum applications be accepted from anyone onboard the vessel. The Bill was retroactive and was to confirm Australian sovereignty to determine who would be permitted to enter.

The government then introduced the so-called "Pacific Solution" and the *Tampa* refugees were loaded onto the Royal Australian Navy (RAN) ship, HMAS *Manoora*, and taken to the small island country of Nauru. Here they and future asylum seekers would remain in detention camps until their refugee status was considered. Soon the influx of hundreds more refugees who had set sail from Indonesian shores in unseaworthy boats resulted in the establishment of detention centres in remote Australia and the Christmas Islands. International criticism of Australia increased. The crew of the *Tampa* received the Nansen Refugee Award for 2002 from the United Nations High Commissioner for Refugees (UNHCR) for their involvement in the events. The freighter's Captain, Arne Rinnan, was also named captain of the year by the shipping newspaper *Lloyds List* and the Nautical Institute in London.

Natasha opposed the legislation on behalf of the Democrats. She also found holding asylum seekers in detention camps – particularly children – for months and even years, personally abhorrent. Unfortunately it was not a belief seemingly shared by the majority of Australians, with some television news polls showing as many as 90 per cent supporting the government's actions. Any opportunity to convince the Australian people to ameliorate this attitude evaporated the following month.

On 11 September 2001 four coordinated al-Qaeda Islamist terrorist attacks were launched against the United States. On that Tuesday morning, nineteen terrorists hijacked four passenger jets in suicide attacks on targeted buildings. Two aircraft were crashed into the North and South towers of New York's World Trade Centre. Within two hours both towers collapsed and there were further casualties in surrounding buildings. A third aircraft was crashed into the US Department of Defence, the Pentagon. It is believed the target of the fourth aircraft was the US Capitol Building or the White House in Washington DC. As passengers of the fourth aircraft, United 63, in contact by mobile phone with relatives on the ground, heard of the earlier attacks, there was consensus to overcome the hijackers – the aircraft crashed near Shanksville, Pennsylvania, killing all onboard. In all 2,977 innocent people plus nineteen hijackers died as result of the 11 September attacks. Natasha lost a close friend, Andrew Knox, in the twin towers but she and her party continued to be outspoken on the course being taken by the government. Trying to return to favour with the electorate, the Australian Labor Party back-flipped on their opposition to the "Pacific Solution", leaving the Democrats and their leader isolated.

In the early afternoon of 6 October 2001, another unseaworthy wooden hull fishing boat carrying 223 asylum seekers was intercepted by HMAS *Adelaide*. Australian Government officials announced that refugees onboard the vessel, designated SIEV 4, had threatened to throw children overboard as a ploy to be rescued and taken to Australia. Natasha was one of the first to challenge the truth of this accusation and a Senate enquiry later found that the claim made by government ministers was fictitious; but not before a federal election resulted in a landside win for the Howard Government.

Despite the backlash concerning the Democrats due to GST, there had been an 80 per cent increase in Democrat membership due to Natasha's leadership. Despite polling between 2 and 3 per cent prior to the change of leader, the Democrats were now polling 9 per cent in the House of Representatives and 14 per cent in the Senate. Despite the feeling that the Democrats would lose their Senate seats, only one, NSW, was lost. Natasha was elected with the highest personal vote of any Australian senator – more than 20,000 voting for her personally below the line. 90 per cent of registered Democrats again affirmed her as leader. Roslyn Dundas was elected to the ACT legislature in 2001, the first Democrat elected to a lower house/legislative; and the following year the party won a seat in the South Australian upper house. The party had given effective responses about the budget and had taken a stance against sending the Australian Defence Force (ADF) into Iraq.

The years 2001 and 2002 had been huge and the socio-political landscape had altered dramatically. It was difficult not to occasionally make some small show of defiance towards the conservatism which reigned supreme in Australia's Parliament House such as when Prime Minister Howard banned dancing in Parliament House corridors so Natasha and several other Senators "staged a mock conga line".

Natasha is a self-confessed "girly swot" and rumour has it she was known in intimate circles as "Lisa", after the fictional character in the animated television series *The Simpsons*. The comparison is understandable as the eight-year-old Lisa is portrayed as highly intelligent and a passionate advocate for a variety of political causes including Tibetan independence. Lisa Simpson's environmentalism won her media awards and *TV Guide* ranked her 11th on their list of the "Top 50 Greatest Cartoon Characters of All Time". Whilst Natasha supported Tibetan independence, her aptitude on the baritone saxophone remains a secret. While she still wasn't winning media awards Natasha was selected as a "Global Leader of Tomorrow" by the World Economic Forum.

Natasha was her own worst critic and demanded no higher standard from others than she demanded from herself. The gruelling schedule which seemed pretty much 24/7 finally took a physical toll and a severely run down Natasha was diagnosed with glandular fever at the end of 2001. The enforced five day break gave her time to assess her life and she was not entirely comfortable with what she saw. So 2002 took a different curve, a more personal one. Working ridiculous hours Natasha had struggled with having any semblance of a private relationship. There had been the occasional romance with a journalist or two, perhaps strange given her at times strained relationship with the media; but in another way understandable because of her long standing interest in journalism. Spending 12 to 15 hour days entrenched in Parliament House pretty much reduced possible social liaisons.

Ian Smith had diametrically opposed political views to Natasha. He had been adviser to Liberal Victorian Premier, Jeff Kennett. As CEO of Gavin Anderson & Company (Australia) Ian consulted to global corporations on cross-border transactions, regulatory matters and crisis briefs. He led the Australian Government's communications strategy for the Telstra 3 and Telstra 2 share offers and a number of other government privatisations. Ian may have been a large "L" liberal but he shared Natasha's "core views about humanity", importantly about not locking up "refugees and people who seek asylum". In April 2002 Natasha announced their engagement. The news even sent the normally less than polite web page *Crikey* into a spin. Their headline was "Natasha's engaged to the dashing and loveable Ian Smith" and announced:

> Now that Natasha Stott Despoja is engaged to *Crikey's* old mate Ian Smith, the time has come to stop calling her Ah Satan (Natasha backwards) so we're open to suggestions for a new nick-name for Mrs Smith and intend to be more friendly towards Natasha in the future.[46]

The levity would be short-lived.

Despite gaining credibility within the electorate the Democrat party room remained fractured and former leader, Meg Lees, had never accepted the grassroots support for her successor, her 1993 retort: "some people's idea of democracy is that you keep balloting and balloting and balloting until their opinion and their choice gets up" clearly forgotten. Meg Lees became an increasingly vocal detractor of Natasha's ability as leader, and announced that Natasha had taken the party too far to the left; despite the party's approach to legislation remaining largely the same and the party room determining positions on most policy. The statements became more and more antagonistic as the former and incumbent leader differed on the impending privatisation of Telstra. Senator Andrew Murray continued to criticise Natasha and her deputy leader Senator Aden Ridgeway was reported as saying the party would probably have been better off retaining Senator Lees as leader. A web page popped up on the internet titled "The Unofficial Natasha Stott Despoja Web Site". The banner headline was "Natasha Stott Despoja the blonde leading the bland". It included the statement:

> The pin-up chic of the Australian Democrats ... has succeeded beyond John Howard's wildest dreams. The Democrats have not done very well since Natasha took

over the helm ... There have been a few rumblings about her leadership, but like any other politician her eye is on the main prize – superannuation!

Democrat brawling was very public and undermined Natasha's authority. She was grilled by the media and blamed for Democrat troubles. In July 2002 Meg Lees left the party, taking the Democrat seat but sitting as an independent. An independent Lees was the lifeline Prime Minister Howard needed to move his Telstra sale through the Senate. In April 2003 Meg Lees founded the Australian Progressive Alliance which she declared to be more centralist than the Australian Democrats. The electorate did not agree and Lees was not re-elected in the 2004 October federal election and left the Senate on the expiry of her term on 30 June 2005.

Although the voting members of the Australian Democrats remained resolute in their support of their leader, four of her Senate colleagues, those who had voted in favour of the GST, failed to accept the democratic principle and citizen-initiated referenda which made their party different. On 21 August 2002 they presented Natasha with a manifesto, a "ten-point reform agenda". Many of the issues, as the framers had realised, were contrary to what Natasha believed Democrat supporters desired. At 1314 the same day Natasha rose to address the Senate, her body language a mixture of disappointment, frustration, and defiance.

I am proud to belong to a member driven and democratic party. I owe a huge debt to the membership. My mantra has always been: trust the members ... In the Australian Democrats it is the members, not the party room that determine the leadership.

She explained that "in all good conscience" she could not comply with the demands made of her within the party room that day. The proposals were in no way "reasonable" as they were contrary to the Democrat constitution. Continual public criticism and negative media commentary, which focused on internal disagreement rather than legislative achievement, had also destabilised the party.

> Some commentators have mistaken my relative public silence for weak leadership – my refusal to strike back aggressively, particularly in the public domain, as weakness. But I still believe that politics can be a civil discourse, and I choose not to inflame with returned invective.

Natasha acknowledged that it had been too much to expect that a leadership change would restore internal party harmony or restore public perception that the Democrats could keep promises after "the GST debacle". She had been willing to debate issues and open the "party's processes to debate and discussion. That is why I initiated the first national strategic review of the party". Her belief in the Australian Democrats remained steadfast.

> We are a progressive party committed to human rights, to social justice and to sustainable development ... activism shapes society for the better. That is what I joined.

Unlike her predecessor who had resigned from the party, taking a Senate Democrat seat by announcing herself as an independent for the remainder of her term, Natasha was resigning as leader only. It was with justification that she said:

This must be one of the first times in history that a leader with a democratic support base – democratically elected with the support of more than 70 per cent of the members – is actually offering their seat.

Before she sat down she declared: "My pledge is to bring the party back home to the members again". Natasha would admit "it was a tough time" but was "not something I'm going to dwell on, because I've experienced incredible kindness and support ... they're the positive memories".[47]

For the Australian Democrats, this was the beginning of the end, although few, particularly Democrat senators, appreciated this at the time. For Democrat rank and file there had been significant disillusionment. They had joined a party which allowed them a greater democracy, in the very election of the party leader – 70 per cent of registered Democrats voted for Natasha's leadership and they had been disregarded. When asked to vote for the next party leader many refused to vote, some crossed out the listed candidates and wrote "Natasha Stott Despoja" on the ballot. The breach of promise on the GST left members disgruntled and now registered party members quit in droves. The general electorate regarded the feuding with little patience. To many the Democrats had become arrogant, dishonest and dysfunctional. To the uninformed, Natasha had split the party, and would forever suffer the unjust tag "Natasha Despoiler". All Natasha would add was that "it was a sad day".

The media enjoyed featuring Natasha, but its concentration on sensationalism, conservatism and exaggeration, were complicit in her resignation. This was evident in a cartoon appearing the next day which showed Natasha sucking on a dummy and wearing Doc Marten shoes, with a body pierced back and front by ten knives. Years later Natasha gave a more considered assessment.

The media I think had a field day. You know, they portrayed it almost as a catfight which was, in itself, disappointing but said a lot about the fact that there were few women in positions of power, certainly, let alone women running against each other in positions of power.

There seemed no end of challenging government issues in 2003 and 2004. Australian troops had been committed to the second Iraqi war by the Howard Government without parliamentary debate and consensus and Natasha as Democrat spokesperson on foreign affairs was outspoken. She believed the Australian people, through their elected representatives, had the right to debate such an important issue and "ensure that our troops are never deployed again to a theatre of war without the support of at least one other party".[48] A contentious but domestic battle concerned the Australian Governor-General. Dr Peter Hollingworth, appointed to the vice-regal post in 2001 by the current government, was embroiled in allegations that whilst he was Anglican Archbishop of Brisbane he failed to fully investigate child sex abuse cases. The Prime Minister refused to call for Hollingworth's resignation. Natasha had long believed the Prime Minister and the Governor-General needed to be held to account. "These two stubborn men remain in office when they make very bad judgements".[49] She had been the first leader to visit the Baxter Detention Centre and was both angry and sad that some asylum seekers had spent up to six years in detention. Natasha called for an urgent review of children in detention. "It is a soul-destroying experience even to spend a day in that detention facility, let alone six years" and she wished to emphasise how important it was for "all children to be immediately released from all detention facilities."[50] In March 2006 Natasha and her party called on the government to press the United States Government to close the Guantanamo Bay detention centre:

The blind support that we're showing for Guantanamo Bay is in breach of international standards, in breach of international humanitarian law and indeed, is breaching the human rights for one particular Australian citizen David Hicks.[51]

In August 2004 Natasha called for a review of the progress of women as measured against the Sex Discrimination Act. The gender wage gap had increased by 35 per cent under the present government.

I think that we're moving backwards and certainly the last eight years or so of the Howard Government have actually seen a regression of the status of women in nearly all aspects of society.[52]

The same month she called she reacted to the government's new law banning same-sex marriages, and the law being passed with Labor Party support. Natasha was appalled by the legislation. "This has been a shocker of a week an embarrassing, shameful, disgraceful week." She believed: "In fact, it's one of the most embarrassing weeks in this parliament."[53] Two years on, in 2006, Natasha and fellow Democrat Senator, Andrew Bartlett, introduced Australia's first same-sex marriage legislation

As 2004 drew to a close Natasha was also coping with a most significant change in her personal life. On 14 December 2004 she gave birth to Conrad Davis Stott Smith. Husband, Ian Smith, announced; "We're thrilled, it is the most wonderful day of our lives ... Natasha and Conrad are doing well." She had not had a great deal to do with babies and small children and like all mothers-to-be worried that she was not quite prepared. There had been that award-winning photograph taken by Patrick Hamilton in 2001 which went viral through media outlets, of Natasha standing very awkwardly with Senator Andrew Bartlett's four-day-old daughter – "my millisecond look of sheer terror at the thought of dropping" the baby, "needless to say, babysitting offers dropped off after that".

Being pregnant had been surprisingly a "most enjoyable emotional and physical experience" and she kept working, kept travelling, until she was 36 weeks pregnant. She even gave a keynote address at an international symposium on stem cells when she was nine months pregnant. The media continued to show its reluctance for accurate and generous reporting. One newspaper featured Natasha speaking at an education rally in Melbourne. The photo showed her standing on the back of a truck, holding a microphone with one hand and resting her other hand on her very pregnant belly. The newspaper reported she was "teetering on the back of a ute" in "high heels and a figure hugging top". Natasha was bemused and amused – she had been wearing flat comfortable shoes and "I'd love to know what's not figure-hugging when you're six or seven months pregnant!".[54] She does concede that just perhaps "I pushed myself very hard".

A fortnight before Conrad was born Natasha had fulfilled the sad duty of farewelling one of the most influential woman in her political life. She rose in parliament on 29 November 2004 to make a condolence motion regarding Janine Haines, AM. She had respected her mentor's courage, commitment, and sense of humour, qualities that others suggest she emulated. Janine Haines "has a unique place in Australian political history – or herstory ... she led the way for many female politicians". One memory Natasha offered:

> Desperate to prove the ability of the Democrats to deliver, Haines once threatened to stand in Sydney's Martin Place and progressively take off pieces of clothing as I announced legislative issues and what we had done in

the Senate that day. This is one political gem that has not influenced me.

Janine Haines had spoken of the lack of high-profile role models for young women considering politics – it seems to have been something Natasha processed well.

Natasha was quickly smitten with her new son: "I am bowled over by the absolute feeling of overpowering, unconditional love". Friends suggested that "Con rad" had been a wise choice of name given Ian was seen as the "conservative" and Natasha was the "radical" but Natasha laughed at that idea; "we weren't that clever, we just liked the name". Natasha took 11 weeks leave following the birth. There was no official maternity leave in the Australian Parliament, perhaps something to do with the norm being male and 40 something; she had to write to the President of the Senate asking permission.

Courtesy Natasha Stott Despoja

She returned to assume duties as the Democrat spokesperson for the status of women, higher education, attorney-general's, foreign affairs, republic, science, and work and family. Being a mother gave her a different perspective and yes life was a juggling act. Spending 20 weeks in Canberra meant Conrad travelled with her. "I like waking up in the same city as my boy!" she said in one interview. If she was in a committee hearing and there was tea break, "while other people had their Scotch Fingers and their tea, I'd run back to my office and feed my child".[55] She worked smarter, harder. If something important came up she would give it attention but given the choice between dinner and going back to the hotel, feeding Conrad and putting him to bed it was "a no-brainer". One amusing story she tells:

> I was in the middle of a nappy change when my staff member ran in saying "you've got to get down to the chamber straight away". I ran downstairs, stood up and was angry at the way the government undermined Senate democracy by doing a dirty deal on an education issue I cared about. I was just finishing my outraged speech when I looked down and saw poo on my dress. I thought "this is literally a crappy day in the Senate".[56]

Something which did surprise her was the shift in attitudes, how she was now perceived by political peers. The change in attitude commenced when she and Ian married and even more so when she became a mother. Her opponents thought she may have lost her edge, Natasha says the opposite was true:

> There was first of all a sense, particularly among conservative politicians, that I wasn't the same threat that I'd been. I think that some people saw me in a different

way: somehow less ambitious, less ferocious, less of a feminist, or that I was going to work less.[57]

Issues already important to her became even more important, "I think being a parent has made me an even better legislator". It was not that those without children didn't understand, it was just that everything seemed more immediate, more crucial, because it affected a new generation and the world simply had to be a better place.

Getting the work/family balance right was a constant balancing act. The parliamentary day commonly started at 7.45am and could finish around midnight. During the long sitting weeks the cot moved into the office when after-hours childcare was exhausted, and it was nice to be close to Conrad. She had rarely been absent but when she took time off when Conrad became ill, a colleague asked why she could not find someone to look after her child.

> I wondered if a male member of parliament had made
> that decision would people have said, "How good of him.
> He's such a good dad".

The double standard was evident yet again. Not only did society have very strong views about women being the nurturer, the primary carer of children, but it had been very good at instilling guilt for women to take on a "disproportionate load in family relationships". Women needed to support each other to eradicate "'mother guilt' and feelings of inadequacy". She received so much unsolicited advice that she now realised that young mothers needed to have faith in their own instincts. Always the legislator Natasha also believed this socially engendered "mother guilt" gave "institutions like governments the excuse not to act on issues like working families".

On 22 October 2006 Natasha announced she would not stand for re-election in 2007. Weeks before she had undergone emergency surgery for an ectopic pregnancy. Enforced convalescence gave her time to reflect and she decided not to extend her term beyond 30 June 2008. The polls were clear: if she ran again she would retain her place in the Senate, but Natasha had done the arithmetic and to remain for another six years would mean Conrad would be ten and she would miss important milestones. She was torn and it was one of most difficult decisions she had made. In a column appearing in *The Advertiser* in October 2006 she wrote:

> I love the cut and thrust of the parliament, the opportunity to change laws and lives for the better. I enjoy the nitty gritty of policy-making and law-making: analysing laws, drafting amendments, arguing the case as well as writing private member's bills and participating in committee work.

Yes, she would miss that.

The media had been at times critical and on occasions dismissive – now they altered. The headline of *The Canberra Times* read "Last of the Democrats?". The article was glowing: "Natasha Stott Despoja's popularity was such that she had an unparalleled ability to cut through and engage young people"; Natasha was one of only about a dozen politicians "who people could actually name".

> Natasha had attracted an audience because of her youth, gender and looks, but this was replaced by recognition that she was intelligent, articulate, and sincere. Her ability to be comfortable in most communities and surroundings endeared her to Australian voters. There was no created awkward photo opportunities drinking a beer in the public bar.[58]

The Democrats had warned that the John Howard Government could capture control of the Senate if their party was ignored, and the forecast had proved accurate. At the 1996 federal election 1,179,357 people had voted for the Democrats in the half-Senate poll – 10.8 per cent of the vote – and five senators were elected. At the peak of their power there were nine senators and they had power and influence enough "to keep the bastards honest". In the 2007 federal election only 162,975 people chose the party: 1.3 per cent of the vote. The Democrats had not won a federal seat since 2001and the last Democrat elected in Australia was Sandra Kanck, to the South Australian Parliament in early 2002.[59]

After a 31-year presence a party derided as "fairies at the bottom of the garden" – by those who hated listening to anti-nuclear, pro-environment, philosophy – but which successfully negotiated native title legislation, championed human rights, secured World Heritage listings, and countless times saved governments from themselves with amendments to Bills which enhanced the nation, was no more. Media commentators admitted too late how effective the small "l" liberal party had been. According to some the rise of the Greens was reason enough for the demise of the Democrats but the Greens, with such a limited platform, would not necessarily be seen by Australians as a worthy alternative. One newspaper headline read "Farewell to Democrats as they leave the bastards behind";[60] another "So Long, it's been good to see you".

By 2008 only four Democrat Senators remained in the great house on the hill overlooking the nation's capital. Their terms of office would conclude mid-year. Natasha gained no satisfaction that the media, political commentators, and even the major parties, finally admitted the seriousness of the demise of the Australian Democrats, a demise they had been complicit in.

I think that too late, too many of them are discovering
that a rational, sensible, hard-working group of expert
legislators sharing, or holding, the balance of power in
the upper house is a good thing.[61]

The Democrats had performed the watchdog role well, they had made
politics more accountable and more transparent, they had changed
"the living dead". The political landscape had changed forever, and
that courtyard in parliament "known to everybody as the Democrats
Courtyard"[62] would be occupied by others. The analysis of the demise
of the Australian Democrats was protracted, but perhaps the simplest
explanation offered by Senator Lyn Allison, sufficed: "we stuffed up
in various ways".

On 6 March 2008 Natasha and Ian welcomed daughter Cordelia
Jessica Stott Smith. The media release included:

This is a marvelous day. We are thrilled with the birth of
Cordelia. She is an absolute joy. Natasha is doing really
well and Conrad is excited about spending time with his
baby sister.

Mother and baby were doing well and "looking forward to celebrating
International Women's Day (IWD) together".

Natasha would write from hospital that this IWD was of "even
greater significance" because she now had a daughter. "I cannot help
but wonder what opportunities and possibilities she faces in years
ahead". Cordelia (which means "heart") was fortunate to be born in
an era and country as fortunate and as prosperous. "I wonder how
other female babies born around the globe this week will fare in
the years ahead?". The World Health Organisation believed 100 to
140 million girls and women had experienced some form of genital
mutilation. The United Nations Children's Fund (UNICEF) believed

more than 300,000 children under 18 were exploited in the more than 30 armed world-wide conflicts and that many young girls were forced to marry or have sex with male combatants. More needed to be done here and overseas to stop "direct and indirect forms of gender-based discrimination". Whilst being excited by the promise of the future, like all mothers Natasha hoped for health and happiness for her daughter, but also "for her to grow up in a truly equal society: one in which gender discrimination is a thing of the past". She hoped her daughter would use her life "to fight for opportunities for her sisters in the years to come".

What had been a juggling act now became an "extraordinary juggle". Travelling to and from Canberra with two small children was challenging.

> I'd catch the 6am flight in Adelaide, get to Canberra, go straight to my office, work through the Senate until 10.20pm and I'd stay in the building until midnight. ... Federal Parliament is a really difficult life for those people who want to be an important part of the child rearing.

Natasha returned to work immediately because her days in the Senate were numbered. She was confident she was making the right decision but there was also regret, she "had a lot of unfinished legislative policy work". There were still unrealised ambitions for Australia and Australians. There needed to be a Bill of Rights, paid maternity leave, a republic. There seemed to be a mad panic to push through the last Bills, motions, amendments and accentuate what yet needed to be done. On 22 June 2008 the *Interim Report on the Current State of Australia's Space Science and Industry Sector* was delivered. Natasha was pleased that finally this was on the Senate's agenda. She had initiated the inquiry because urgent consideration had to be given to "greater Australian activity in space science and industry".[63] There was the continuing push for paid maternity leave. The Howard Government opposed paid maternity leave and Australia had not ratified any of the International Labour Organization (ILO) conventions on maternity protection.[64] Natasha had taken a fully costed proposal to the 2001 election and introduced Australia's first and only legislation for a national paid maternity leave scheme in 2002. The Bill was examined in 2003. In 2006 Natasha would point out:

> My paid maternity leave model is unashamedly minimalist. For six and a half years I have advocated a minimum standard of 14 weeks government-funded leave at the minimum wage.

Her Bill allowed for employer top-up but did not make this compulsory as she realised many small businesses could simply not afford it, but neither did she wish to see women of childbearing age being discriminated against by business. In 2007 she had updated her legislation to reflect changes to workplace relations law. It would not be until after her departure from the Senate that maternity leave legislation (2009) would be introduced, Natasha's 2002 and 2007 Bills fundamental in the Australian Government's commitment to an 18 week scheme paid at a minimum wage. Natasha still felt this was a "half-pregnant version because it does not begin for years and it will be means tested". A generation of children had reached adulthood while her legislation had sat on the Senate notice paper "so the slow movement of this debate has been frustrating" to "the eternal shame of successive governments".

A favourite and evocative photo is of her and the late Christopher Reeve. His most amazing days as *Superman* were those in a wheelchair encouraging politicians like Natasha to force legislation on stem cells to enable scientists to cure the most crippling conditions. She initiated a Bill to progress stem cell research in Australia, in 2006 ensuring a conscience vote on the Lockhart review in federal parliament. Right To Life Australia president Margaret Tighe condemned such suggestion.

> I'd like to ask John Howard who's running the Government?
> Is he running the Government or is he allowing Senator Stott Despoja, one of the dying Democrats, to run the Government.[65]

Those last days were exciting, sad, incredibly busy, as Natasha, as usual, tried to do everything exceedingly well and was still not entirely satisfied with her own efforts.

Photograph by Jennifer Burton-Douglas

It is June 2008 when I interviewed Natasha and she is facing the end of her time in the Senate. She has been looking back as much as she is looking forward, her immediate future also is unknown, with the exception of quality time with the family.

> I am so ready for a rest and I am so open to the sheer delight of spending time at home with my children which is something I haven't done in any kind of relaxed setting.

There are photos of Conrad and Cordelia and husband, Ian Smith; occasionally there is a cot in the corner and Cordelia has just been whisked away after being breastfed. Life became harder when Conrad was born, there never seemed enough time in the day and yes the expectations, real and assumed, of being a mother and senator seemed so much higher than for parliamentarians who were also fathers. When Cordelia was born it was that much harder, according to Natasha, "the juggle is just that much more intense".

> Don't get me wrong I wouldn't change anything I have done over the last three and a half years with Conrad's upbringing. I love the fact that he is this worldly interested kid who marches around Parliament House. He goes up to Kevin Rudd and says "Hullo". He humanises the place because he talks to people and people can't resist the charms of a three and a half year old even if they can't stand me. I want to be able to drop Conrad off at school and not jump on a plane or be in Canberra when he is having his first day at school; that is just not quality of life for me.

Our conversation steers to women in parliament, and the questions: Has the political landscape for women improved since you joined the Senate? If so what do you believe was responsible for this? If not what can be done? In 1980 in the Australian Parliament there were just ten women senators and three women in the House of Representatives. By 1994 still only 13 per cent of our politicians on a federal level were women. The future looked brighter when that year the Australian Labor Party implemented quotas to guarantee 35 per cent of seats to women. The Liberal Party refused to do likewise but in March 1996 Liberal-Coalition Prime Minister, John Howard, stood on the steps of Parliament House with 27 Liberal Party women elected to the House

(17) and the Senate (10). It was a photo opportunity because this was a record for the party. But it was just a photo opportunity; four of the new women members – Ricky Johnson, Andrea West, Susan Jeanes, and Elizabeth Grace – had been given very marginal seats. They became known as "one term wonders" and by April 1998 they were no longer in the picture. Also increasing the numbers in 1996 were Labor Party members Michelle O'Byrne, Jane Gerick, Kirsten Livermore, Anna Burke, Jann McFarlane, and yes, Cheryl Kernot. The influx of women politicians in 1996 was a record, but of the 148 House of Representatives positions, only 33 were women, and of the 76 senators only 22 were women – just 20 per cent. The minor parties, least weighed down by factions and conservative tradition, took the most emancipated approach.[66] Progress had been made but there was still a very long way to go.

In 1996 the new Democrat Senator Natasha Stott Despoja had believed it was "totally inadequate" that less than a third of those elected to Australia's Parliament House were women. Australia did not compare favourably "with other Western Parliaments around the world ... the rate of progress is abysmally slow".[67] She quoted Janine Haines who believed that while it might not "necessarily make the parliament behave better ... it might bring an end to some of the political stag fights".[68] Natasha spoke enthusiastically about the possibility to "develop support networks with the women who are there, and that means across party barriers".[69] She hoped there would be more crossbench activity so that "sisters were doing it for ourselves". Traditionally women politicians from the two larger parties were loathe to taking an individual stance. With the added strength in numbers from the ranks of the Democrats and later the Greens, women politicians, at least in the Senate, decided they could consolidate on issues: from stem cell research to the removal of ministerial veto on RU486; from changing the foreign aid funding criteria to seeking to ensure transparent advertising of pregnancy counselling.[70]   It was an exciting time.

> We co-sponsored bills and held meetings, did the numbers and organised media. It was a rare but enjoyable and mostly successful example of networking among women of different parties, all driven by a commitment to issues affecting women.

The Canberra Times political commentator John Warhurst featured this gender division: "What is happening here? ... Is the prominence of these reformist women a random phenomenon?"[71] He believed this wasn't "random" but the outcome of his research had found "female MPs are decidedly more socially liberal on socio-moral issues than their male colleagues". No issue had shown this to be truer than the private members Bill instituted by four women senators, from different parties, forcing the release of the abortion drug RU486. The private member's Bill before the Senate would take control of the drug away from Health Minister, Tony Abbott. In total women from both houses voted in favour 53 to ten (84 per cent); their male colleagues voted in favour 87 to 66 (57 per cent). Warhurst agreed with the argument used by generations of women, that they should have equal representation for reasons of "justice" and "merit". In 2006 women made up 25 per cent of the House of Representatives and 36 per cent of the Senate and Australian society according to Warhurst was "poorer for it".

In the 41st Parliament of Australia (2004–07) there were 23 female senators and 38 women in the House of Representatives. In 2008 as a new government was ushered in 26.7 per cent of those elected to the House of Representatives were women and women made up 35.5 per cent of the Senate. Natasha was "optimistic, but I think that change is still too slow ... we are just starting to catch up". She was troubled by the "added scrutiny on women", especially on "how they look and whether they are married and have children". Women who may be considering a career in politics could be turned off because of how they are lampooned or portrayed by the media, and by their opponents. Too few role models added pressure as well as unrealistic expectations. Natasha could so totally speak from experience – she was an expert on pressure, on balancing the weight of her own expectation to make a difference, and on survival, though she would likely dismiss that too easily.

On Wednesday 25 June 2008 Senator Natasha Stott Despoja rose to give her valedictory speech.

> When I first set 'Doc' in this chamber on 30 November 1995 there was a lot less diversity than there is today. I said in that first speech that my aim was to bring about change, and I am proud of the modest role that my party and I have played in bringing that change.[72]

The media had fixated on the Doc Martens she wore, on the superficial, "perhaps the media needed to change as much as the diversity of the chamber". Diversity was better but it needed to progress further. Natasha hoped one day there would be young people, old people, "different ages, men and women, and the many cultures that make up our nation, including Indigenous cultures". It had been 106 years since women had been enfranchised "yet look at the numbers – women comprise less than a third of the Federal Parliament". She had "relished" her time on committees, such as the Joint Standing Committee on Foreign Affairs, Defence and Trade, and the Senate Standing Committee on Employment, Education and Training. Her belief in publicly funded and accessible education had never wavered; and it was almost impossible to believe that in 2008 with a staff of

3,500, there continued to be no childcare facilities in Parliament House.

Those who rose in the Senate to congratulate Natasha for her public service were profuse. Senator Bob Brown (Tas), Leader of the Greens, was sorry that "power" commonly went to those "who most easily climb up the ladder and can tread on the fingers and faces of other people", yet what the world needed most was "compassionate human beings who can see beyond themselves". He believed Natasha had been an "inspiration". Senator Chris Evans (WA) thanked her for making him the August entry of the calendar Natasha put out featuring senators. She had discovered he had been a member of the firefighters' union so called his entry, "Hot August Nights", with the line: "Come on, Chris, light my fire". Evans believed Natasha was probably the most publicly recognised senator, this likely "a mighty curse" as much as it was "a huge benefit". Natasha, according to Evans, had made politics "interesting, vibrant and sexy" but she "actually got to then argue serious political points". She had been subjected to the "tall poppy syndrome". Not just the media, but others "went out of their way to try and tear her down" and regretfully this is "unfortunately the case that seems to be much more prevalent as an attitude towards women in politics". Evans wished to acknowledge how "passionate and committed" Natasha was and not only was she "a serious politician who has made a huge mark" but was also "a very decent person".

Senator Nick Minchin (SA) admired her "work ethic". Not only had Natasha been "a remarkably and extraordinarily successful politician", she was, "one of the most persuasive and influential communicators we have seen". Strangely perhaps Senator Andrew Murray (WA) a fellow Democrat, but not necessarily a friend, rose to his feet to say that of all the Democrat senators leaving, he believed "Natasha will probably be the only one who will really stay on the public stage". Whilst there may have been some regret in his words on how much the media had been "fascinated with her", he believed: "Her sheer, extraordinary talents will ensure that she will march the public stage again, and I hope she does".

For Natasha there was regret as she prepared to walk out of the Senate entrance the last time – not just that she would miss the opportunity to legislate; but the entrance of the new Kevin Rudd Labor Government offered the promise of things to come, there was "momentum – political momentum". Two of the last events she attended, demonstrated how things were changing. One was the "Welcome to Country" given by Ngambri elder, Matilda House-Williams. The next was "Sorry Day", the new Prime Minister saying "sorry" in parliament to the stolen generation, to the nation's Indigenous people, on behalf of the Australian people. Natasha applauded the symbolism: "I felt that that was actually the first sense of a government heading in the right direction on Indigenous affairs". And she applauded the new prime minister's words: "His words and eloquence were a welcome contrast to years of antagonism and shame". There were Indigenous Australians with the words: "Apology Accepted" and "Thanks" on their shirts: "Such generosity of spirit outshines the weasel words of the Tuckeys and Mirabellas of this world". There remained the need for another giant step forward because while the Australian Parliament was "full of non-Indigenous decision makers ... how on earth can we get this right". Yes it felt sad: "I am leaving parliament just as a government is beginning to get it right". The passionate advocacy for social justice and human rights still burned, time would tell how she could continue the quest, for now she light-heartedly suggested: "I'll probably be one of those people who write to my local member". The "girly swot" part of her had not abated with motherhood: "I can see me now. I will be at home looking after the kids, reading legislation to get my fix".[73]

For others there was also regret, regret that Natasha and her party were no longer, because both had been more conversant with women's issues and equality than any other before. The new Kevin Rudd Government was a welcome release from the previous government but Professor Marian Sawer believed: "any good policies to undo the damage to women's equality of the Howard years were well concealed behind campaign shrubbery".[74] Political nervousness about "owning a women's policy had been extended to participation in a women's policy debate in the National Press Club". Both major parties had shown great reluctance to participate and "Senator Stott Despoja's invitation had been withdrawn, apparently at the request of the major parties". In 2007 Natasha and Green Senator Kerry Nettle had again called for legislation for government-funded paid maternity leave and only the seven Democrats and Greens voted for the motion. Professor Sawer noted:

> Both the Democrats and Greens had self-standing women's policies, of which the Democrats' offering (Women's Policy Audit, Election '07) was particularly well developed, reflecting the policy expertise of Senator Natasha Stott Despoja in this area. Unlike the major parties, both the Greens and the Democrats were committed to the return of the Office of the Status of Women to a central co-ordinating role in Prime Minister and Cabinet.[75]

Democrat senators had also raised the issue of violence against women "disproportionately", further underlying the importance of the Democrats and its former leader and the continuing need for diversification within the Australian Parliament.[76]

In 2009 Natasha delivered the keynote address at a luncheon to mark the 98th International Women's Day. 370 women intently listened as Natasha discusses how progress had been made towards equal rights, particularly in the political arena. It is encouraging that women's participation in the paid workforce had risen to more than half but:

> It is extraordinary, that in the noughties, we are still debating a women's suitability for office. Women in public life should be able to be seen as multi-faceted just like men. Our laws and workplace practices are out of step with the reality of modern work and family life. ... We still have a long way to go ... only eight out of 105 of Australia's top power brokers are women. We've also gone backwards in other areas, including the gender pay gap. Women in the workforce now experience the same gender pay gap they did in 1978. A government report in November 2009 gave the pay gap between men and women as 17 per cent.

Forever the optimist Natasha firmly believes in Australians' ability to make things better. She stills wants to see change in the houses of the Australian Parliament:

> Politics is a living, breathing, important thing. It affects every part of our lives. Hopefully younger people can see its relevance and believe they can influence and be a part of it. It's not just the property of older men wearing suits.

It is 24 September 2009 and Natasha Stott Despoja, as a panellist on the ABC programme, Q&A, is answering a question about the possible dissolution of the government. "There could be some double dissolution triggers that appear in the next couple of months, but in particular on the ETS [Emission Trading Scheme]." She looks earnestly at the audience and tells them that she is very much in favour of fixed terms. Double dissolutions are expensive and encourage "public cynicism". She would rather the government "worked with the opposition parties and got it right". Natasha continues "I think that sort of political expediency ... where you're spooking oppositions into making policy for the sake of it by protecting their political skins" is inferior to "making policy that is in the public interest". Furthermore "a double dissolution doesn't guarantee action on anything ... is that the way we want politics to function?" A government minister on Q&A defends the current "reformist agenda" of her party. Natasha shifts to another gear:

> I am waiting for the "reformist agenda" to kick in and I think we have to remember that the ETS [is] long overdue, and some of us have been talking about it, well our political parties, since at least 1983. The idea of the Coalition and the Labor Party negotiating on this particular scheme concerns me greatly. Let's not forget that these targets, piss weak targets – I'm sorry but 25% by 2020 – if this is the piece of legislation that is really going to really assist us with tackling climate change? I'm not so sure.

The audience chuckles at the "piss weak" part and applaud the statement. Other high profile individuals on the panel fail to capture the spirit of this audience as effectively as the former South Australian senator and leader of the Australian Democrats. Soon the ETS triggered enormous unrest in Parliament: extended sitting hours, heated discussion, change in the Liberal Party leadership and, yes, further talk of a possible double dissolution. Meanwhile a great many Australians struggle to comprehend how such governmental instability can develop from ETS legislation which proposed 25 per cent reduction by 2020, a target which after all is "piss weak" in light of current evidence on climate change. The days and weeks ahead would bring more turmoil into Australian politics, but for the present Natasha Stott Despoja is purely an observer.

In 2009 I interview Natasha again in Adelaide. The storm clouds cluster on the horizon turning the ocean below a darker shade of blue. Quickly the front arrives and heavy rain lashes the glass front wall of Natasha's home. She fails to notice the turbulent weather conditions perhaps because in her near 13 year career in the Australian Senate she faced many storms, far more testing than this. Natasha has had time to consider where she has been and where she is going. Clearly she misses parliamentary life, yet she doesn't. "I was so ready to have a break from that intensity." There is a pause: "I was excited to have time at home with my children". Yet the lack of power is something she clearly grapples with, not for herself, but because of her inability to help. She is no longer a senator yet the letters keep pouring in, ordinary Australians with ordinary and overwhelming problems. Natasha has no staff, she works through the post office crates of letters she struggles home with – 500 letters a week. Most recently she visited her post office and found only a few letters and smiled her relief at the postmaster before he shook his head, disappeared, and re-appeared with another crate. Former Foreign Minister Gareth Evans believed parliamentarians suffered from "relevance deprivation syndrome" and certainly the letters leave Natasha somewhat downcast: "There is so little I can do".

The home is full of the sound of children, Conrad is exuberant and Cordelia is on the floor, arms and legs moving, happily gurgling in that endearing way that babies do. When Natasha decided to give up the Senate for quality of home life, Ian also chose to reduce his travel and workload by opening an Adelaide office. He appears and whisks son and daughter upstairs. Natasha is quick to admit she misses the "camaraderie that you do develop, even across political barriers" but it has been enjoyable to have the time to become part of her local community. On the first day of a new Senate sitting in Canberra, she instead took Conrad to his first day at school: "It's a very different world".

She was warned by retired politicians to say "no" until she was rested and had time to revaluate her life. The rest bit, well she is the mother of two under school-age children. "Politics was hard", but it was "nothing compared to a good dose of full-time parenting. That can really teach you what hard work is!".[77] As for the "no" bit, to be honest, she had yet to master that. Early into her post-Senate transition Natasha received a call from a former premier of Victoria. "When Jeff Kennett phones, it's very hard to say no. He was very persuasive." The two have diametrically opposed politics, but on the issue of mental illness they agree entirely. Kennett offered Natasha a position as a director of beyondblue. She is deeply impressed with Kennett's passion for the issue. "Despite wanting to take some time off after having just left parliament, I felt very privileged to be asked, and readily accepted." She had long recognised the importance of beyondblue's work through Senate committee work and interaction with the public, and there was a very personal involvement, with Ian's brother suffering from bipolar disorder, "seriously so". "I've had dear friends who've lived with depression or killed themselves", now, "everywhere I go people want to stop me and tell me" how much beyondblue means to them".

The organisation has gone a long way in raising awareness and the profile of mental illness, while also helping to reduce the stigma associated with it. Natasha is staggered by the prevalence of anxiety disorder and depression: "I don't think there is a family in this country that is untouched". The figures she sees are scary: "One in five Australians will experience some form of depression ... A million Australians are living with depression". It is important for people to know that "women are more likely to suffer from a mental illness". Finally mental health is "on the political agenda ... long overdue", and hopefully this will result in the further resources desperately needed. "beyondblue is a wonderful and effective organisation I am proud to be associated with."

The energy levels and passion are still evident and she finds it difficult not to be involved in community work, in not-for-profit organisations like the Burnet Institute, of which she is now a director. The Burnet Institute is Australia's largest virology and communicable disease research institute, which aims to achieve better health for poor and vulnerable communities in Australia and overseas. The institute is home to around 450 medical researchers, working across six different themes of infectious diseases: maternal and child health, sexual and reproductive health, alcohol, other drugs and harm reduction, immunity, vaccines and immunisation, and the health of young people. For Natasha: "It combines my passion for science with an interest in human rights and foreign aid". Her profile continues to grow abroad.

She is a member of the Advertising Standards Board. Proud of her home state, she is on the board of the South Australian Museum. Her journalist flair is satisfied as a columnist for *The Adelaide Advertiser* and participation in various blog sites. Natasha was made an Honorary Visiting Research Fellow at her old university, the University of Adelaide, and is teaching an introduction to Australian politics course at the university with, "of all people", former Howard Foreign Minister Alexander Downer. In 2011 she was made a UNIFEM (United Nations Development for Women) ambassador. The same year she was awarded a Member of the Order of Australia "for her service to the Parliament of Australia, particularly as a Senator for South Australia, through leadership roles with the Australian Democrats, to education, and as a role model for women". Natasha was reported in *The Advertiser* as being "a little overwhelmed".[78]

Koutoula Yarce community,
Burkina Faso.

Then came another exciting contact, from former US Secretary of State, Madeleine Albright. When Madeleine Albright contacts, you certainly listen. Natasha was asked to act as a monitor for the Nigerian election. It was "an extraordinary, wonderful experience".

We get complacent in Australia about democracy and for sure we should take it for granted because it's a right, but also such a privilege when you go to a country and the people have walked from 6am to get to a polling booth at 8. Then they wait to 12.30pm to line up to vote, which may take hours, and then they stay after the vote has finished to witness the counting process. There was a nine-month pregnant woman [there]. I kept saying to her, 'Can I get you a chair, can you sit down?' in this relentless Nigerian heat.

It is another ABC Q&A and the date is 5 March 2012. According to the ABC website the studio audience is made up of 36 per cent ALP, 48 per cent Coalition, 12 per cent Greens. The only Democrat is sitting on one end of the panel. Former Coalition minister and senatorial adversary, Amanda Vanstone, sits on the other end of the panel. There are three others in between but it is the two former politicians, two of Australia's most articulate former women senators, who capture the studio and viewing public's attention

Children from the Mentao refugee camp, Burkina Faso
Photographs:
Pablo Tosco/OxfamAUS

this night. Adjudicator Tony Jones turns in Natasha's direction and says: "Let's hear from Amanda Vanstone". He quickly recovers: "Natasha ... How could I ignore you? Amanda, sorry, Natasha". As quickly Natasha responds: "It happens all the time".

The discussion concerns who should receive public accolades like, "Australian living legend", even, "Australian of the Year". "Are Australians egalitarian?" Natasha believes that whilst "we are a comparatively generous nation", the reality in Australia, is that increasingly there are "gaps in equality when it comes to income". She loses little time in suggesting that this is in part caused by "some measures during the Howard period", but also "other aspects of the workforce, labour market changes for example". The conversation turns to the mining industry. Natasha believes we have a distorted image of the industry: "Wealth creators aren't job creators". The studio audience applauds. She adds: "There is disproportionate influence from the mining sector in terms of decisions or media access". The idealist is visible and Natasha continues to have faith in "the role of the ordinary Australian ... within the democratic process".

The conversation steers towards the portrayal in the media and the language used publicly by detractors of Prime Minister Julia Gillard. Tony Jones turns: "Let's start with Natasha on this". A tweet fills the bottom of the screen: "Natasha should have been our first female PM". Natasha is unaware of this and answers that in terms of gender "there will be a day" when it is not an issue. She continues to be frustrated because of the "greater scrutiny of women who happen to be in positions of power ... There is still that double standard". Why do Australians "remark on, if not judge by, women on what they wear, their marital status, their parental status or otherwise"? The tweets are coming thick and fast: "It's a man's world; gender will always be an issue in politics". Another reads: "Still waiting for someone to bag Bob Carr for being childless".

Amanda Vanstone is asked:

> How is it OK for a politician or any man for that matter to call a female Prime Minister an atheist childless ex-Communist? If the prime minister was male and married, had no children, nor went to church, this would never come up. [Applause]. Did you have to put up with this kind of misogynist rubbish when you were in politics?

Vanstone draws breath:

> No-one was kind enough to say something to my face like that that I was able to deal with but I think a high price was paid for those remarks. ... but you would have three women sitting at a table having lunch together, the place would be full of tables of men having lunch together and some jerk would walk past and say, 'This is a sisterhood meeting?' You would think, 'you little peanut'. Look at all these... But you just can't worry about that sort of stuff. Look, we have come a long way, Nat is right, we've got a long, long way to go.

The two articulate ex-senators clearly have captured the audience and a tweet fills the bottom of the screen: "Amanda Vanstone is the bloody bees knees". Discussion turns to gay marriage, and whilst two panel members struggle to articulate their personal struggle with the issue, the former senators seem less troubled. A tweet flies across the screen suggesting one of the male panellists should cease talking: "Stop now. Your digging your hole". Natasha tries to get the conversation back on track:

I respect other people's conservative or religious or other opinions but surely we are beyond this debate. Surely as individualists ... It is time. It is absolutely time.

Loud applause ensues. Tweets are coming in fast and furious now. "Can Natasha come back please?", and: "Natasha keep the bastards honest, again please".

Jones asks Vanstone if it is an error for the Liberal Coalition leadership not to allow a conscience vote on gay marriage. "I think it was a mistake to give that away, as I understand it, by leadership fear." There is a sense of days gone by, of reformist women senators ignoring party platform, for the liberation of Australian society. Vanstone continues:

> I personally think conservatives can learn a bit from liberals here ... I think conservatives should welcome more people openly saying 'I'm going to have a life relationship with this person, we will be dependent on each other, we are going to ask things of each other instead of asking from the State'.

It is a pity that panellists cannot view the tweets because some are clever: "Let gay people marry so they can suffer like everybody else", and after a comment from Amanda Vanstone as to what is all the fuss about: "Amanda Vanstone is wasted on heterosexuality. She would make a robust and breathtaking lesbian".

Tony Jones believes it is time to get off this emotive topic, to broach another, the assimilation of migrants. He turns to Natasha and asks: "The implication is some migrant groups are practising reverse discrimination by not assimilating. What do you think?".

The answer to that question for me in a broader sense is about tolerance, and the fact that as a multicultural community of course we are going to face challenges with diversity and different cultures. It is how we respond to that [sic] is going to be the judge of who we are as a society. I think it's an incredibly exciting time to be living in Australia and South Australia in particular where you see different cultures, we look different, we're of different backgrounds, we've got different experiences.

She is concerned that "Sudanese immigrants are not getting the support and the assistance they require". One of the results then is that an enclave of unsupported people will stay together, "because they don't feel necessarily a welcome part of aspects of our society". She quickly adds: "I worry because a lot of the women are feeling isolated". Her closing comment nails several issues raised during the programme: "Governments [need] to provide the services instead of cutting them back because it might be electorally appealing." The studio crowd respond with loud applause. A final tweet sweeps across the screen: "Natasha is right. It's not the problems we face, but how we respond to them that defines us as a society".

As 2012 approaches its close, Australians, those who continue to listen, shake their heads at the vitriol in parliament and the way those in the government hammer away at each other. Natasha visits and, seated in the visitor's gallery, witnesses a "level of nastiness" she has never seen nor heard before. She is "shocked by the venom, really sad ... quite nasty". She finds it difficult to believe how adversarial politics is now and that there is no "constructive alternative":

I wanted to block the eyes and ears of the school children entering the House of Representatives galleries ... Tit-for-tat accusations, sniping interjections and gagged debates surely left everyone wanting a shower ... The ambience in Parliament House is toxic. Backbench government MPs felt morose about the prospect of losing, and some of the most talented Opposition MPs seemed obsessed with a tawdry saga that has sapped the energy and goodness out of Parliament.[79]

Natasha mourns the fact that parliament does not "set a standard that Australians can look up to and respect ... that's not happening at the moment".

Former Cabinet minister in Margaret Thatcher's British Conservative Government, and the last Governor of Hong Kong, Chris Patten, has listed what he believed to be the four key requirements for good political leadership:

1. Courage of intellectual convictions
2. Knowing when and how to make big decisions.
3. Knowing when and how to mobilise consent through skilled communication
4. Being across the details.[80]

If this is true Australians are perhaps correct in their despair and disrespect.

Courtesy Burnett Institute

It is the third week in April 2013 and we are seated in a room in the Burnett Institute in Melbourne. Natasha has just rushed in fresh from an appearance on a morning television show and she will be back for an appearance on *The Project*. Soon she will move next door for a board meeting. Her words come quickly in that animated, enthusiastic way. I get the distinct impression she is still not at all good at saying "no" particularly with regards to any social issue. She hints at the establishment of an important new organisation and the role she will undertake – clearly it is exciting and daunting at the same time.

The establishment of the Foundation to Prevent Violence against women and their children is announced in July 2013 and, the Chair is Natasha Stott Despoja AM. Federal and State funding will enable a greater focus on reducing domestic, family and sexual violence. Natasha finds the right words:

> Think of an Australia where women, girls and boys live without the threat or fear of abuse and violence, of any kind, whether in their homes or in other places. Think of living in a country in which we all speak up about these issues and as a community say we do not and cannot accept violence in the lives of anyone.[81]

A 2009 survey found that 22 per cent of Australians believed domestic violence could be excused if the perpetrator regretted what they had done. Awareness and prevention are fundamental because 89 Australian women were killed by their partners between 2008 and 2010 – one in three women have experienced physical violence and one in five Australian women experience sexual violence. Natasha writes: "The biggest risk factor for becoming a victim of sexual assault, domestic or family violence is simply being a woman."[82] For years courageous Australians have raised the issue of this violence.

Those involved in the *White Ribbon Day* had been at the forefront. This is the next step to rid Australia of "the prevalence and devastation of violence against women and children. We must begin to make a positive impact as soon as possible".[83]

There will be a federal election in September 2013 and rumour has it that Senator Nick Xenophon had asked Natasha to share a ticket with him.[84] She admits she had spoken with Xenophon but declined. It is too soon, the children are now at school but are still very young and it is nice to be regularly involved in their schooling and activities. Spending long sitting weeks in Canberra holds no appeal; neither does the current spiteful climate within the houses of parliament. People continue to tell her they don't know who to vote for without the Australian Democrats. I have heard the same comment – disillusionment with the two major parties and lack of appeal of the minor parties. Natasha does not say "never" when it comes to a return to politics and there is general consensus within her home state of South Australia that she would be re-elected should she stand.

In 2013 Natasha Stott Despoja's life is super busy and she is immersed in deeply important, compelling social issues. Wherever she travels in Australia there are still a lot of: "I remember you". It is disappointing that the memory might be because of those Doc Martens and not because of the 500 or so keynote addresses, lectures, and other speeches she gave; the 1,800 or so times she addressed the Senate; the 24 private member Bills she introduced; the 128 motions she passed; and her 108 successful amendments to government legislation. And one can only repeat what the online respondent proclaimed in June 2011:

It was a shame that Natasha was lost to politics, she was a real breath of fresh air. She was honest and said what she felt and stood for, a lot of the current ones in parliament both state and federal could not hold a candle to her. She is one of a very rare breed of politicians who had honour and stood up for her beliefs and would not bow to pressure. Well done and congratulations Natasha .[85]

www.preventviolence.org.au

1. Henningham, N. *Australian Womens Archives Project* 2008, http://www.womenaustralia.info/exhib/cal/stottdespoja.html

2. ibid.

3. *Who*, 4 March 1996.

4. *The Bulletin*, 23 – 30 January 1996.

5. *The Age*, 17 January 1997.

6. www.pembroke.sa.edu.au

7. Chipp D and Larkin J. *Don Chipp: The Third Man*, Rigby 1978, pp 179-80.

8. *Beyond our Expectations*, 1980 Conference Proceedings.

9. Australian Democrats webpage, 29 Nov 2004.

10. It would be 1921 before the first woman was elected in a State Election when Edith Cowan won a seat in Western Australia. Dame Florence Cardell-Oliver was the first woman in Australia to attain full cabinet rank, as Minister of Health in 1949 in the West Australian Government. She created the school milk scheme to ensure generations of children received a daily quota of free milk at a time when families struggled to afford good nutrition for their children. A woman of imposing appearance, she was not slow in taking a stance and during a 1941 debate became the first woman to be suspended from any Australian Parliament. Although she opposed the establishment of free birth-control clinics in 1939, in 1941 she opposed her Liberal Coalition Party Government to unsuccessfully move for the abolition of the death penalty. Millicent Preston-Stanley was the first woman elected to the NSW Legislative Assembly, in 1925. The Nationalist Party candidate for

the Eastern Suburbs was a realist. She declared "I'm not fool enough to suppose my going into the House is going to make any sweeping alteration. The heavens won't fall because a woman's skirts rustle on the sacred benches, so long the sacrosanct seats of the lords of creation". In Queensland Irene Longman won Bulimba from Labor for the Country and Progressive National Party in 1929. During her parliamentary term she campaigned for improved care for the mentally handicapped and was responsible for the appointment of the first Queensland women police officers. She and her government were swept from power in 1932 and for Queensland women candidates it would be a very long drought. Not until 1966 was the next, Vi Jordan, elected. Jordan after some argument managed to get a women's toilet in her State's Parliament House. Margaret McIntyre was the first Tasmanian woman elected to her State's Legislative Council, as an independent in the division of Cornwall. Unfortunately her career and life were cut short when she was killed in a plane crash on 2 September 1948, just six months after the election. South Australia, although forward in giving women the vote and the right to stand for political office, proved backward in actually electing them. Jessie Cooper and Joyce Steele were the first, in 1959, to both houses. Victoria, the last to enfranchise women, in 1908, and last to permit them to stand for political office, in 1923, saw Lady Millicent Peacock become the first woman to enter Victoria's Parliament in 1933, in a by-election for Allandale, following the death of her husband, the sitting member. Along the way there were other firsts. After Edith Cowan in Western Australia came May Holman elected in 1925. She would be the first Labor Party member elected anywhere in the world. Helen Sham-Ho was the first Chinese-born parliamentarian elected in Australia. She served in the NSW Parliament for just one month shy of fifteen years, from 1988 to 2003. Marion Scrymgour was the first indigenous woman to be given a ministerial post. Born and raised in the Tiwi Islands, she became the Member for Arafura in 2001 and a minister in the Northern Territory Legislative Assembly the following year. She was Deputy Chief Minister between 2007 and 2009 but in 2009 she resigned from the Labor Party over its position on support for remote Indigenous communities. Marion Scrymgour continued to sit as an independent, holding the balance of power. She rejoined the Labor party in August 2009.

11. Suffragette Vida Goldstein was the first to stand for federal elected office in 1903 but to no avail and Australia would be the last western nation to elect a woman to federal government. Was this because women candidates argued for equality of justice in marriage and divorce; the same rights to property; and equal custody of children following divorce? Gradually the women's vote began to have an effect on Australian law and Australian society. Divorce laws were made more equitable, women were permitted to practise law, women's hospitals were established, woman justices were appointed to children's courts, there were enquires into sanitation, health and housing regulations, slum clearance, and the health of children belonging to low income families.

12. Lyons, E. *Among the Carrion Crows*, Rigby, 1977, p.5

13. Not a great deal was achieved by women politicians in the Australian Parliament over the next decades. Not until 1976 was the first Australian woman appointed to a Cabinet portfolio. Dame Margaret Guilfoyle became the Minister for Social Security in the Fraser Government and would continue to serve as a Minister until 1983. The next Australian woman to hold a ministerial portfolio would be Senator Susan Ryan who was appointed Minister Assisting Prime Minister Bob Hawke on the Status of Women 1983–88, and the Minister for Education, 1984–87. Susan Ryan

and her government passed the Sex Discrimination Act 1984 and the Affirmative Action (Equal Opportunities in Employment) Act 1986.

14. Lyons, p.5.

15. *Commonwealth of Australia Senate Hansard*, 25 June 2008, p.90.

16. *The Advertiser*, 4 March 1996.

17. Henderson, A. *Getting Even: Women MPs on Life, Power and Politics*, Harper Collins, 1999, pp. 113 – 114.

18. *Vogue*, February 1996.

19. Simms, Marian. "Women and the secret garden of politics: preselection, political parties and political science", in Grieve, Norma and Burns, Alisa (eds) *Australian Women: Contemporary Feminist Thought*, 1995, Oxford University Press, p.243.

20. Henderson, p.116

21. Lorna Stone (MLA NSW 1997-1999) was appointed Chairperson of Southern Sydney Health Services. At a reception she was introduced to a man by her chief executive officer. The man ignored her, turned to the Chief Executive Officer (CEO) and asked, "Who's your chairman now?" The CEO replied that he had just been introduced. According to Lorna Stone, the man "stood back and surveyed my outline, starting at the feet. I met his gaze and when he got to my eyes ... all he said was 'Interesting'. I just smiled and said, 'Yes, isn't it'". Another NSW MLA, Gabrielle Harrison, was appointed NSW Minister for Sport 1995 – 99 and she "often ran the gauntlet of being mistaken for just another secretary". At a Cabinet meeting in a rural electorate, the ministers were filing into a meeting room when she was stopped at the door by an attendant who said "Miss, you can't go in there". When she told him she had arrived on the bus with the other ministers the attendant scoffed, "Oh yeah, me too". On another occasion a parking attendant refused to believe she was the Minister for Sport, here to open an event. He replied "Yeah, you and twenty others. Turn your car around lady". Trish White was an engineer with Defence Science and Technology (DSTO) prior to becoming a South Australian MHA. She would recall technical briefings when senior military officers would say to her "Oh, luv, I'd like mine white with two sugars". "I had a wonderful boss. I'd turn to him and say 'Yes, and you can get two blacks, one with two sugars as well'". He'd say, "Oh, straight away, Trish". It was a great way to get them all to take notice of everything I said from then on. Another South Australian parliamentarian, Carolyn Pickles, fought long and hard for a tampon dispenser in the female toilets, toilets shared with the general public. There were about seventy women working in Parliament House. It would not be until 1998 that women MPs in the South Australian House of Assembly finally "got their ground-floor loo".

22. Mitchell, S. *The Scent of Power: On the trail of women and power in Australian politics*, 1996, Harper Collins, p.10.

23. ibid, p.11.

24. ibid, p.13.

25. She was encouraged by the Women's Electoral Lobby (WEL) which was founded in 1972. Finally there was a body of women, a feminist advocacy, speaking about politics, action, and change. She joined WEL and decided to attend the WEL National Conference in Canberra. This wife and mother approached her bank for a small loan for travel and was told by the bank manager that they would not give her a loan unless her husband approved. It strengthened her resolve and Fatin joined the Labor Party.

26. Mitchell, p.225. The seat of Phillip was abolished and McHugh became the member for Grayndler.

27. ibid, p.227.

28. ibid, p.230.

29. ibid, p.232.

30. ibid, p.245.

31. *Juice*, February 1996.

32. *HQ*, March/April 1996

33. Denton, Andrew. *Enough Rope*, ABC, 21 July 2003, episode 19.

34. *Virtuosity: Inside the heads of 100 prominent Australians*, New Hobsons, Sydney, 1997, p.94.

35. ibid.

36. *HQ*, March/April 1996.

37. Vogue Australia, February 1996.

38. ibid.

39. Henderson, p.20.

40. *Sydney Morning Herald*, 21 June 2008.

41. *Sydney Morning Herald*, 28 August 2004.

42. Henderson, p.24.

43. Spurling, K and Greenhalgh, E (eds) *Women in Uniform: Perceptions and Pathways*, UNSW@ ADFA, 2000.

44. Denton, Andrew. *Enough Rope*, ABC, 21 July 2003, episode 19.

45. Stretton, H. "Leaders" in Craven, P (ed). *The Best Australian Essays*, Black Inc., 2000.

46. *Crikey*, 28 Apr 2002.

47. *ABC AM*, 23 October 2006.

48. Australian Democrats media release, 27 March 2003.

49. Australian Democrats media release 13 May 2003. Hollingsworth resigned and his commission as Governor-General was revoked as of 29 May 2003.

50. Australian Democrats media release, 19 July 2004.

51. ibid, 14 March 2006

52. ibid., 1 August 2004.

53. ibid., 14 August 2004.

54. http://www.motherinc.com.au/magazine/community/vip-mums/348-vip-mum-natasha-stott-despoja.

55. http://aussiebubblog.wordpress.com/2007/05/30/natasha-stott-despoja-talks-motherhood.

56. ibid.

57. http://www.motherinc.com.au/magazine/community/vip-mums/348-vip-mum-natasha-stott-despoja.

58. *The Canberra Times*, 28 October 2006.

59. ibid., 21 July 2008.

60. ibid.

61. *Sydney Morning Herald*, 21 June 2008.

62. ibid.

63. Australian Democrats media release, 23 June 2008.

64. Sawer, M. "Presence and the Price: Women and the 2007 Australian Federal Election", Australian Feminist Studies, Vol.23, No.56, June 2008, pp.263 – 269.

65. Australian Democrats media release, 17 August 2006.

66. Four members (8 per cent) of the ALP in the House of Reps were women; nine (32 per cent) of ALP Senators were women. Seventeen Liberal Party women (24 per cent) were within the House of Representatives and the party had ten (32 per cent) women Senators. The National Party was represented by one woman (20 per cent) in the lower house and there was also one Independent (20 per cent). There were however, four women Democrats Senators (66 per cent) and the Greens had one woman Senator (50%).

67. Mitchell, p.242.

68. *Vogue* Australia, February 1996.

69. *HQ*, March/April 1996.

70. Senator Amanda Vanstone publicly disagreed with conservatives in her own party concerning euthanasia.

71. *The Canberra Times*, 5 October 2006.

72. *Commonwealth of Australia Senate Hansard,* 25 June 2008. pp.77– 95.

73. Australian Democrats media release, 17 June 2008.

74. Sawer, M. "Presence and the Price: Women and the 2007 Australian Federal Election", *Australian Feminist Studies*, Vol.23, No.56, June 2008, pp.263 – 269.

75. ibid.

76. Sawer, M. "When women support women ... EMILY's List and the substantive representation of women in Australia" in Sawer, M. Tremblay, M. And Trimble, L. (eds) *Representing Women in Parliament: A Comparative Study*, Routledge, 2006, pp.113-119.

77. *The Age*, 23 October 2006.

78. *The Advertiser*, June 14, 2011.

79. *The Advertiser*, 28 May 2012.

80. *The Canberra Times*, 16 Oct 2010.

81. www.preventviolence.org.au

82. www.mamamia.com.au/.../natasha-stott-despoja-violence-against-women 26 July 2013.

83. www.preventviolence.org.au

84. *The Advertiser,* 28 July 2010.

85. ibid., 14 June 2011.

261

Fiona Wood

"What I do is ordinary to me, it feels normal."

An Australian poll conducted by *Reader's Digest* in June 2008 found "the most trusted Australian" to be Fiona Wood. It was the fourth time the Australia-wide survey was undertaken and the fourth time Fiona finished first – the pollsters considered that the only person who could "knock her off the top is Mother Teresa, and she is dead".[1] Fiona thought it all a bit of a mystery, she believed she was just "ordinary". Clearly she was not, in the minds of Australians and clearly the Bali bombings of 12 October 2002 events which catapulted her unwillingly into the limelight – were anything but ordinary. They changed life for Australians as much as they changed life for the Perth doctor.

On a bright Perth October afternoon in 2008, the day I first interviewed Fiona Wood within the outer University of Western Australia precincts. Students sat at external restaurant tables oblivious to traffic, their clothes were comfortable and they eagerly shared information and indulged in academic exchange. It was an interesting mix of people sharing the food and sunshine; professionals monopolised the inside air conditioned comfort. Fiona Wood is at ease in eclectic surrounds, although relaxed with prime ministers or students, she perhaps prefers the latter. Fiona has observed her own six children during their teenage years, years marked by curiosity, absolute resolve, indecision, the full array of emotions – and found each so different, but always interesting. Fiona failed to notice as heads turned in her direction as she moved towards my table. Her immediate warmth was disarming and she appeared amazingly unburdened by the many titles she bore: Director of the West Australian Burns Service, plastic surgeon to both Royal Perth and Princess Margaret hospitals, co-founder and Director of Avita Medical, Winthrop Professor with the School of Surgery at the University of Western Australia and Director of the McComb Research Foundation. Little did I realise how far in distance, time and diversity this and future conversations would be – and how much I would learn about skin.

The north of England and a cluster of mining villages may appear unlikely origins for one who was named Australian of the Year 2005 and the most trustworthy Australian 2005–08. The grime and harshness of environment which enveloped villages like Upton, Frickley and Hemsworth were testing for all those who went down in the coal mines and the families who prayed they would come home again. It was 1 February 1958 when Fiona Melanie Wood was born into such a Yorkshire household. She was the first daughter and third child of Elsie and Geoff Wood. Her first childhood memory is of her sister Nicola coming home from hospital; Fiona was four. Another is of sitting on her father's shoulders listening to the loud ardent voice of union leader Arthur Scargill addressing miners. President of the Yorkshire region of the National Union of Miners, Scargill was viewed by unionists as honest, hard-working and genuinely ncerned for their welfare, but to Fiona, the child of a miner, he was plain long-winded.

A youthful Fiona Wood
Courtesy Fiona Wood

It may sound a cliché but Fiona's parents inspired her to be as good as she could be. "I was just extraordinarily lucky to have the parents that I had." They taught her there was something worth nurturing in everyone. Accepting this gave added strength to move forward. Such sanguine advice would be useful in the years ahead and especially across the world and in a new century. Her father was an intelligent man condemned to a miner's lot at a very early age because of economic hardship. Geoff Wood won a scholarship to grammar school but needed to contribute to the family income. He relished playing soccer for Nottingham Forest, but after breaking a leg could no longer play high grade soccer and found himself in the blackness of the pit. Fiona remembers his mood changes, the difference in her father on work days and non-work days: "he was significantly grumpier" on the days he trudged off to the mine; "it was hell on Earth". "He hated crawling around in the black dirt that he'd done since he was 13 years of age" which left him in no frame of mind for such a fate to happen to his children. Consequently Geoff Wood felt "very strongly" that "we had to explore our potential with respect to sport and education, to give us a choice in life". One of his sayings was "you never win a race on your last performance". It was one Fiona clearly took to heart as she did her parents' concept of developing potential so "that we got up in the morning and enjoyed what we did".

Elsie Wood was an achiever, a "go-getter". Nothing was too much, too difficult, or insurmountable. "My mother's great line was, 'Grasp the nettle with two hands girl, because if you don't somebody else will'". In Ackworth there was a private school run by the Quakers. Fiona was impressed by their "ethereal" uniform, "Harry Potter" cloaks. To the then 13-year-old the students looked "so happy". Ackworth School had been founded in 1779 by John Fothergill. Unaware of the cost of private education Fiona decided she would like to go to this school which looked so enchanting. Elsie

Wood applied for a job as a matron at the school and then took one as a physical education teacher. Her mum had "sorted it" and Fiona joined Ackworth School as a "staff child". It was this combination of hard work ethic and never accepting anything as impossible attitude, which was the making of Fiona Wood.

Mining villages could surprise outsiders with their strong sense of community and intellectual curiosity. It fostered a fascination with knowledge and the resolution of problems through greater learning and investigation. Ackworth School encouraged these. "There has to be a clear disciplinary framework and our expectations are high", reads the school guide. Fiona flourished. She realises how fortunate she was to "have the level of education that I did, it was fantastic". In 1974–75 she was Head Girl. Ackworth School never stopped watching the Head Girl. The school web page included:

> we have constantly been impressed by the achievements
> of this extraordinary young lady and we are very honoured
> to count her among our Old Scholars.

On 15 June 2008 Fiona returned to Yorkshire to address the school community. The theme of her lecture was motivation. "Achieve your best – everyone can make a difference", Fiona told those who packed the Fothergill Theatre to capacity. According to the principal the Australian delivered her message with "energy and passion". She was:

> Thought-provoking, invigorating and inspirational. It
> should motivate the next generation of Ackworth students
> to a life of endeavour and of service, in the best Ackworth
> tradition: 'Non sibi sed omnibus – not for oneself, but
> each for the good of all'.

The Religious Society of Friends, also known as Quakers, began in England in the 17th century and expanded throughout the world, especially to the Americas and Africa. Members believed their faith did not fit the religious dogma and hierarchical structures of the traditional Christian religions. A Quaker could develop individual religious beliefs arising from personal revelations and conscience. Whilst some "Friends" believed theirs to be a Christian movement others considered themselves to be agnostic, atheist, realist, universalist, post-Christian and nontheist. Others identified themselves as followers of Buddhism or Islam.

Whilst divergent beliefs developed in different continents the central Quaker concept is "Inner Light". God is everyone, the spirit is "within" regardless of whether an individual seeks mediation through a minister, pastor, or through the sacraments. Isaac Penington, the son of the Lord Mayor of London, who became a Quaker, wrote in 1670: "It is not enough to hear of Christ, or read of Christ, but this is the thing -- to feel him my root, my life, my foundation".[2] Quakers were intent on casting aside superficial differences and focusing on the spiritual elements which connected all people. Quakerism was group oriented rather than focused on the individual. Platforms of belief or "testimonies" were expressions of "spirituality in action". Whilst these altered as society evolved, fundamental were those of peace, equality, integrity and simplicity. The Quaker movement proved influential and forward thinking. In America it played a role in the abolition of slavery. From early in its evolution Quakerism acknowledged the equal rights of women and promoted education.

It was a perfect fit for the teenage Fiona Wood. Her earlier education had not been particularly attuned to her needs, to where she was mentally. "I felt distinctly that I was the odd one out. I tried very hard to fit in but I couldn't." She concedes that "today I would have been considered a bit hyperactive" but utilised this hyperactivity in a positive way. "I was hungry to learn." For others Fiona concedes this hunger may have made her "a right royal pain in the neck always asking why? why? why?". During her time at Ackworth School she would observe and learn: "when you're 13 to 16 you absorb the different things around you and learn from them and work out where you fit in this whole jigsaw". Fiona would sit in class "concentrate fiercely and say 'I'm only going to listen to this once'". Clearly the accent on education, equality, the group, and nurturing others left their mark. "It was a pivotal time in my life because I was able to achieve more than if I'd stayed in the Comprehensive School System that did not go past GCE level."

In 2008 Fiona Wood does not define herself as religious, but should she adopt a religion "I would likely become a Quaker". Over a cup of coffee she deliberated thoughtfully on just why she was of such interest in her adopted country. The caffeine hit was weak because she might need to operate later that afternoon; evenness of mood and decision-making processes are a prerequisite.

> What I do is ordinary to me, it feels normal. Working hard, to the best of your ability, is just what everyone should do.

Fiona was raised to believe "it was normal to work, not normal not to work". She can't specifically remember being "taught how to work".

> Some think 'I can do this on the minimum' and I am of the mindset that I work to make it better.

She worked hard to make her grades better at Ackworth School. She does remember failing one examination and being devastated. Looking for sympathy she told her father "Oh Dad, I just got unlucky". Geoff

Wood was not about to commiserate. "Well, Fiona, you know, the harder you work, the luckier you get."

By the time the teenager was considering her future direction of study her community was witnessing turbulent times. Arthur Scargill's rhetoric which bored her as a child, was becoming louder as he attempted to safeguard the livelihoods of miners like her father. Unemployment in England by 1972 was climbing rapidly. The British Government inflated the economy in an unsuccessful attempt to reduce unemployment. Next it attempted to rein in an increasingly militant trade union movement by introducing a new Industrial Relations Act. Under this Act striking dockworkers were imprisoned. This inflamed public opinion when English workers were struggling with galloping inflation and unemployment.

The government's desperate confrontational approach continued and there was a face-off with the National Union of Mineworkers. Under the direction of Scargill, miners employed the tactic of flying pickets in 1974. It resulted in the nation's industry being reduced to working three-day weeks in an attempt to conserve energy. While some immediate concessions were achieved for miners and their families it was the beginning of the end for mining communities. They "never recovered" Fiona recalls of the period. Mines were closed and "unemployment soared". It was crisis time for politics also. The resulting breakdown of domestic consensus led to the downfall of the Conservative Government led by Prime Minister Edward Heath. Geoff and Elsie Wood had both served for a short time with the Royal Air Force and consequently travelled. Although their community was breaking apart they offered awareness to their four children that there was a "much bigger world out there and that it was there for us to explore if we chose to do so".

Fiona favoured majoring in mathematics and physics at Cambridge University but her "mum and brothers knew better and opened my mind to medicine". Her brother David thought her first preference "far too nerdy" and believed his sister too gregarious for such a career. Her mother saw medicine as a career which would make her "financially independent of the male". Fiona was taken to London for a weekend. By the time the weekend was over she agreed with them. By 1975 Fiona was in St Thomas' Hospital Medical School in London. One of the most prestigious of medical schools, it had been founded around 1550 and was part of St Thomas' Hospital which had begun to accept the infirm in 1173.[3]

There was a long tradition of restricted entry of women to medical schools throughout the world. In 1872 one Harvard Medical School professor, Dr Edward Clark, warned that should women participate in medical studies they would suffer catastrophic physical consequences, "monstrous brains and puny bodies; abnormally active cerebration and abnormally weak digestion; flowing thought and constipated bowels".[4] A colleague, Horatio Storer, announced that women were ill suited to become doctors because of menstruation which caused "temporary insanity".[5] Elizabeth Blackwell overcame this temporary insanity in 1849 to be the first woman awarded a medical degree in the United States. It took longer, till 1870, before Frances Hoggan became the first British woman to receive a doctorate in medicine. And longer still before Constance Stone became the first Australian woman to be registered as a doctor in 1890.

Valiant women doctors began to establish medical schools of their own during the 1800s as a way of circumventing the discrimination. These schools thrived and the male medical hierarchy, like Harvard professors Clarke and Storer, became alarmed. Warnings concerning women's fragility of body and mind increased and now they were accompanied by accusations concerning the erosion of medical standards. It became time to "professionalise" medicine by way of the Abraham Flexner Report under the aegis of the prestigious Carnegie Foundation.

The study to examine medical education concluded in 1910 and called for higher admission and graduation standards; and the adherence to stricter teaching and research protocols. On the back of the Flexner Report half of the 155 medical schools in the US closed between 1910 and 1935. Only large well-established institutions were capable of maintaining the standards now required and therefore to qualify for government funding. These institutions had long resisted the entry of women students. Small medical schools, many specifically set up to enable women to become doctors, did not survive this move to "professionalise medicine". Neither did US medical schools set up to educate African Americans. Flexner was not a medical doctor but a secondary school teacher who believed:

> Any strong demand for women physicians or any strong ungratified desire on the part of women to enter the profession ... is lacking .[6]

Women's participation in the medical professions was now severely impeded by law and practice. By 1914, only 4 per cent of US medical students were women.

Little would change until the passage of equal opportunity legislation during the early 1970s. Gradually medical schools around the world were forced to dismantle the barriers to women applicants. Since 1970, the number of American women physicians rose from 9.7 per cent to 32.4 per cent in 2010.[7] In the UK, prior to the 1970s, between 20 and 25 per cent of medical students were women. Interestingly under nationalised British medicine, the rise in women physicians has been more spectacular. By 2010, 55 per cent of those accepted as medical students were women and it is predicted that women doctors will outnumber men by 2017; women in general practice are expected to outnumber men by 2015.[8]

When Fiona Wood commenced her medical studies at London's prestigious St Thomas' Medical School in 1975 the walls and corridors were layered in tradition – which meant change sat uneasily. Fiona was one of only 12 women students. She noticed the little things, like the shortage of toilets for women. Harder to ignore were the individuals who, "didn't consider it appropriate that I would pursue a surgical career". She decided on day one she was going to pursue surgery as a speciality. An initial anatomy procedure on a cadaver was a dissection of a forearm. Fiona failed to notice how many of her 60 strong first-year class fainted around her because she was so intent on the surgery and:

> Blown away by how exquisite we all are on the inside. It
> is just phenomenal how everything fits together and how
> it all makes sense and how the hand moved.

That first morning she was only one of three left standing at the dissection table and she "was hooked". Fiona decided this was "where it's at ... if a surgeon puts this back together then this is where I want to be".

The training of women as surgeons was historically contentious. There was a military connection to early surgery. Given the nature of wars and battles and the ongoing debate surrounding women and combat, it was, and is, deemed no place for women. It was a spurious argument considering the very long tradition of women nursing wounded warriors close to the front lines. There was the argument surrounding the size of early surgical instruments and women's physical ability. It was the same argument used to restrict women from other male dominated careers – the one that women were physically, mentally and most definitely emotionally inferior to men. Surgery was prestigious. Only the best medical graduates were considered for a surgical internship. Women were hampered not by individual ability but because they were women. In the UK in 2011 only 8.7 per cent of surgeons were women; 30 plus years earlier the statistic was even worse.[9] Fiona Wood was determined to become a surgeon. She was not about to be thwarted by the opinions of the less enlightened who said "oh, girls don't do that". "I didn't consider it appropriate that they should tell me that" – that women were not suited to be surgeons. She chose to ignore the negativity, ignore those who doubted her commitment and ability. When she couldn't ignore them her standard retort was "well, I'm really good at needlework so look out". It soon became apparent that negative comments were having no effect; Fiona intended to stay and intended to do well.

Fiona began to undertake additional research. "It was a very, very exciting time, when people were just starting to re-plant hands, thumbs, digits." It was an amazing period in medical science and for Fiona "it was a really defining time, because I'd already made my decision in life that I was at med. school, I was a surgeon, this is just a matter of where or when and how to move forward". As Fiona progressed through the different surgical levels she realised that surgery could not be a purely technical craft, it was more – it had to be more. "I realised really very early on that you may be the surgeon, but the surgeon in isolation is relatively useless." She began to find that one surgical specialty was of particular interest.

East Grinstead, England, was home to the Guinea Pig Club, a quaint name for a place where badly burnt World War II men were treated with elementary reconstructive surgery by Archibald McIndoe. "Burns injuries are so completely devastating." Fiona's focus began to turn to regeneration and rehabilitation rather than repair. Burns was a most challenging area because it encapsulated so many areas of medicine, so many different processes.

> Burns was a really interesting mix of that initial resuscitation, keeping the person alive, with the demands

in the intensive care environment and understanding pain measures and the stress responses.

One phase merged with another, it was holistic care, complete medical attention of the patient and Fiona realised that "to actually bring all that together was the ultimate challenge".

Her enthusiasm had no bounds and this seemed to irritate the Professor of Surgery. Admittedly she was forever "at his elbow". "He couldn't get rid of me, he couldn't shake me off however hard he tried." When Fiona applied for her first position she discovered the professor had written on her report that she "shouldn't be a surgeon". It was fortunate the interviewer was not an admirer of this particular professor and found the comments amusing. Fiona was struggling to digest the information and possibly her own indignation, when she was offered a position in spite of, or because of, the remarks scrawled on her report. Slights would never deter her, they just further ignited her determination. "I'd gotten my first step on the ladder and wasn't going to lose my grip." The next step was demanding. It was not unusual to work for 14 days, sometimes 12 days and seven nights. But you didn't "whinge" because surgical specialities were "hotly contested". There was someone else waiting in the queue ready for you to fail. "It is a powerful job. It is also stressful." There was the added pressure of being a member "of the weaker sex". Overcoming tradition is always challenging but:

It never occurred to me that there was an alternative. I learnt early on that a person's negative attitude was their own and they could keep it.

During her training Fiona met another surgeon whom she decided she fancied rather a lot. His name was Tony Kierath. An Australian, from the west of the continent, he was a quiet determined man who made it clear he intended to return home as soon as he could.

It was non-negotiable. He said you marry me, we live in Perth, I had known him three weeks so it seemed reasonable.

She and Tony married 13 months after they met. Fiona graduated in 1981. She and Tony had two children, Tom and Jess, when they arrived in Australia in 1987. Western Australia was so very different. She was used to the grey of a normal English day and the muted soft colours of the landscape.

Coming from the frozen north when it's grey one day and grey the next and dark the next day ... Is there a sun?

In Perth the light was strong and bright, the colours vibrant. "My first impression of Australia was how sunny it was." Indeed the first morning after the evening arrival she was excited by the broad blue sky. As Europeans have a tendency to do Fiona wanted to leap out into the sunshine. It was 5am when Fiona urged Tony to "wake up we're going for a walk 'cos the sun is shining". Her sleepy husband, with typical Australian bluntness, assured her the sun would very likely shine for the next 365 days of the year so there was no hurry. Fiona quickly adapted. "I love the lifestyle and am very pleased I chose to move here." Many childhood holidays had been spent on a windswept pebbly beach lashed by the North Sea. Now Fiona gloried in Aussie white sandy beaches. The hurry part, greeting each new day with great enthusiasm at around 5am, is just part of Fiona Wood.

The mobile phone makes its presence known several times during our 2008 conversation. Each time Fiona apologised and I assured her it is fine. There is a patient to be operated on, schedules need readjusting. I felt guilty that I was delaying her with what appeared to me as banal enquiry. During research I had come upon a standard day's schedule in the life of this Australian of the Year; normally days started at 5am and ended at around midnight. I only got as far as midday in the schedule before I felt I needed a good lie down. I had this vision of a particular television advertisement. My subject was the battery bunny with the happy demeanour and endless energy and I was the bunny on substandard batteries left a long, very long way behind.

The discussion came around to sport and exercise and clearly one of us had been exercising a lot and the other needed to exercise more. Fiona loved to run, enjoyed athletics, planned to become a champion 400 metres runner. She was fast enough to be dubbed "The Frickley Flyer". She soon realised 400m elitism was not going to happen because she was just 5ft 2inches (157 cm). "These people with longer legs kept going past me, it was most disconcerting", she said with a grin. We discussed basketball. Fiona divulged that she was made captain of her school basketball team because she never gave up. Visions of that supercharged bunny returned and my memories of basketball games when small players were a real pest. You could hold the ball out of their reach but they never went away and they complicated your game no end. Yes, a school-age Fiona would have been one of those.

Sport played a huge role in the socialisation of Fiona Wood.

> If you want to get better, you try harder. If you want to improve you practise ... It's not rocket science, but you learn an awful lot from sport and certainly I did in the early days.

It is a lesson she has passed on to her own children. "My kids are all very active, they're all very involved kids." In 2008 the Kierath children, Tom, Jessica, Daniel, Joe, Jack, and Evie, who ranged in ages from 14 to 22, had learnt the lesson well. All six had represented Western Australia in a host of sports: athletics, triathlon, trampolining and modern pentathlon. She just figured she was "very lucky" to be their mum. Tom and Joe took up triathlon around 2003 and Fiona purchased a bicycle to keep them company. They sort of left mum behind but Fiona continued to ride – loved it. Her bike was sacrosanct; it was "the one thing that no-one else touches or uses". She rises at 5am to go on a 30km ride from the family home in City Beach along the Swan River and back again. "It clears my head and wakes me up." Either that or she walks along the beach.

The daily schedule continues with the same energetic commitment. Breakfast is followed by getting family members to places they need to be. There was not quite the same amount of rushing around after the older offspring were licensed to drive. Fiona likes to start the working day at Royal Perth or Princess Margaret Hospitals. It helps to be a skilful multi-tasker. Her days would exhaust most mere mortals but seemingly invigorate her. Appointments are juggled with rounds, meetings, surgery, fundraising, media, teaching, lectures and speaking engagements. At one presentation she showed a slide of a man juggling chainsaws while standing in a ring of fire and confided "there comes a point where you drop one of the chainsaws and it gets really messy!".

Whilst I seriously doubted that Fiona Wood had dropped too many chainsaws it must always have been difficult to juggle the sensation of guilt. Women, mothers, have been long conditioned to burden guilt. There is never enough time in the day to divide yourself up sufficiently to truly believe you have been the best daughter, wife, mother and professional. High achievers are never completely satisfied and by her own admission Fiona firmly believes:

Doing any less than your best is just not good enough in
my book and relaxing into mediocrity helps nobody…
how can we do anything but our best.

She admitted to reflection on her life's balance. Would she have been
more productive as a surgeon had she not had children, had she not
had six children? Would she have been, and be, a better mum if there
were no research projects? She worried about missing events in her
children's lives although she could remember apologising to one
teenage child and his reaction was "get over it Mum". Being flexible
is not always easy, it took "lots of juggling which is tiring". It is hard
to make the compromises you make without compromising yourself
or those around you.

The children dilemma sorted itself out very early on. When she
held her first baby "I was hooked; I thought I'm going to have a
whole heap of these". Fiona laughed when she told the story of giving
birth to her first baby. "I took a marking pen, the type used to mark
an operation site and put a cross on his foot." This was to ensure
everyone knew Tom "was mine". Perhaps it was just as well the other
new mums in the hospital did not think of such delineation. She and
Tony decided that given they were both going to be busy surgeons
the children would need each other so it was essential to have a few.
Fiona was one of four, Tony one of five so "it had to be six". Whilst
delighting in the large family Fiona acknowledges it was not always
easy. "I was trained to be a surgeon but not to be a parent." She
is plainly proud of the six individuals who are her children and the
balance has been possible thanks to Tony and lots of assistance from
others who people her world. In the end "I am what I am" – no one
could accuse her of not getting the maximum out of every second.

Fiona finished her plastic surgery training to become the first
woman plastic surgeon in Australia. She realised she needed to become
more familiar with Australian geography when she was informed by

hospital staff that she had a patient coming in from Kununurra, "so I wait – I wasn't the sharpest tool in the shed". She finally asked when the patient might arrive and the answer was: "tonight, tomorrow, if we are lucky". Australia was rather bigger and locations rather more remote than England.

The memory of those first English burns patients continued to motivate her, indeed incense her. "We needed something radical to actually cover these large areas." Fiona was bothered by how burns were traditionally treated. There had to be something smarter than traditional split-thickness skin grafting. It was back to the credo she had been imbued with as a child, the environment she had come from and the mindset of "always trying to get it better". Improvements had to be made. Scarring had a profound effect on a patient's psyche, on their quality of life. There were too many unanswered questions, too little data on long-term consequences of burns. About 75 per cent of the scarring from burns remained permanent if the skin was not grafted in ten days. It wasn't so much about the appearance of the scar as it was about how the scar impeded movement and function.

Fiona freely admits she could speak about skin all day. Those who worked with her knew this and she jokes that when she began to speak of the gecko her registrars ran for cover. I learnt that skin is really "an organ". That if you lose only 15 per cent of the surface area of your skin (about equivalent to almost a leg) you are in for a battle because your body response will affect all the organs. Apparently humans shed around 18kg of skin cells in a lifetime. I was not entirely comfortable with that particular piece of information. The power of regeneration is a marvel and that is when the subject of lizards comes up and the question "if a gecko can do it why can't we?"

In 1990 the first patient treated in Western Australia with culture skin was a 56-year-old woman with burns to 75 per cent of her body. Fiona was registrar and she realised the ordeal that was ahead, for the patient and for the doctors. It was a fight against time, a fight against infection, the urgent need to close open wounds as wave after wave of infection assaulted the body. Every piece of skin needed to be sealed urgently, a desperate battle. Fiona was in her car when she heard on the radio that specialists in Melbourne had grown skin sheets and she made a beeline for the closest phone. The Victorians were moved by how desperate the West Australian registrar sounded and agreed to help. Fiona took the last bit of healthy skin from her patient and sent it by urgent flight across state borders. The skin was grown into sheets. The culture process seemed to take forever before the layers of skin arrived back in Perth. Fiona's team worked all night to "put all the skin sheets on and three weeks later she was completely healed". The patient was finally out of intensive care and transferred to the burns unit. It was a triumph, a couple of weeks later the patient was walking down a hospital corridor and dropped dead.

Clearly the case resonated strongly because in 2008 Fiona remembered it was a Friday when the patient died. A fungal infection to the heart was the cause of death but Fiona knew the burn wounds had been exposed way too long. "Because of her ... within weeks I finished my training as a registrar, on Friday 19 January 1991, and on Monday I became the Director of the Burns Unit." Fiona was only 32 but the recent experience had made her even more determined and she thought "I am going to make a difference". Her motivation had come from "severe suffering, a tragedy"; if only the skin had been grown more quickly, applied sooner, the woman may have lived. From this point in Fiona's life "skin became an obsession".

In October 1992 high school science teacher Mark Mulder was admitted with 90 per cent of his body burnt in a petrol fire. With his 80kg frame quickly swelling to 130kg he was not expected to live. It was a race against time because there was not enough skin left for a graft. Fiona took a two centimetre piece and sent it to the Victorian laboratory hoping it was enough – it was. It was a turning point for patient and doctor and Fiona would say "if I never did anything else saving that life was worth it". Mulder would say "God saved my life through Fiona".[10] As rewarding as this was Fiona decided she could no longer wait for others to improve the technology. Burns victims should not only be saved but should not be condemned to a life of pressure bandages and the side effects of scarring. She simply had to find more hours in the day and when that proved impossible, she worked nights.

Fiona vowed to "make the quality of the scar worth the pain of survival". She borrowed laboratory space from scientist Dr Marie Shorter to experiment, to improvise, and to work at finding a better treatment. They were growing sheets of skin: "We were skin grafters ... but that didn't make sense. There are no blood vessels in epidermis." It took a lot of hours and a lot of nights. Her efforts were enhanced when Shorter became intrigued. She had some experience in cell culture. She too was driven and became infected with Fiona's drive and enthusiasm. The two women made a powerful duo, the doctor the supreme optimist, the scientist more cautious but equally determined. Fiona had begun with the traditional method of growing skin cells into sheets of epidermis, the surface layer of the skin. "There's a lot of problems with that. It takes a long time, it's fragile, it's difficult to use." Now she wondered why they could not harvest cells when they were more active, during the preceding stage. It was one step forward, one back, small increments, but all so important and in themselves inspiring the surgeon and scientist to go further, try harder. Fiona remembered the journey well. She learnt a lot along the way, the most important being:

> Life is not a mountain you climb. You are never going to get to the top and say 'flag on' back to the beach ... we have to keep working.

This surgeon believed utterly that life was sometimes frustrating, sometimes rewarding, but overall life was an enriching journey. Having said that she admitted the journey to scarless healing had taken rather longer than she anticipated:

> 20 years ago I didn't have any concept that this would take the effort it has taken to make the small progress that we have. I thought we'd crack it and I'd be on the beach by now; fat chance.

The burns and skin obsession sometimes had a more direct effect on her children than she intended. Fiona would sometimes take a young son into the laboratory with her to check on results. She received a request to go to his school from his Year One teacher. "For his art project he'd built a skin incubator out of cardboard." Another story she told with humour was when she was entering the kitchen one morning to see a cup of coffee spilling down the front of her six-year-old. She grabbed him in a half nelson and bundled him rapidly into a cold shower. His loud cries of protest caused Tony to appear with the information that the kettle had not even been put on this morning, the coffee was last night's and was cold; "I was in overdrive".

By 1993 Fiona and Marie Shorter had established Western Australia's first skin culture unit at Princess Margaret Hospital for Children. This unit also serviced the Royal Perth Hospital which was the state's premier trauma referral centre. They then became intent on taking the technology still further. And they did. The doctor and the scientist became pioneers in the field. It was 1993 when their tissue engineering began its novel and revolutionary main stage entry. They successfully utilised the cells during the most active period, while they were growing. The cells were nurtured in a tissue culture flask and when harvested while active the cells had a preponderance to connect, migrate, divide and spread over the wound. Whereas previous techniques of skin culturing took 21 days to produce enough cells to cover major burns, now it could be done in five. They then needed to work out how the cells could be directly applied to the wound. "We should be able to spray this on", commented Fiona. The team went to the chemist and collected everything that sprayed. Fiona was amused that years later she would open a conference for aerosols in medicine. "If only I'd known you guys existed" she told them, "it would have made life so much easier".

Making it happen in the laboratory was burdened and complicated so the duo decided the essential elements of the tissue developing laboratory should be moved to the operating theatre. Skin the size of a 20 cent piece was harvested from an undamaged part of the body and placed in a kit with the enzyme so that the process began while Fiona operated and prepared the burn. Instead of grafting, the healthy skin cells were sprayed straight onto the wound. The capacity of the human body to treat itself, to regenerate and repair was enhanced so the rapid spray-on process changed the balance, accelerated the healing process and optimised scar quality.

As with every giant leap the media oversimplified and beat up the story. Cynics quickly surfaced. Some declared spray-on skin had limitations, that it was not effective with deep burns. Others declared it too expensive, others simply muttered. Enthusiasm, optimism and innovation invariably struggle in the Land Down Under, at least in the beginning. Whilst conceding it was expensive Fiona knew it was in the long run half as expensive as a standard skin graft. There was the no small matter of less scarring and the improved physical and psychological welfare of the patient. Fiona was fully aware that spray-on skin was only part of the journey, another step towards her "holy grail" of scarless woundless healing. Fiona had little desire to engage those who preferred the negative as reduced positive energy and energy and time were precious in the Wood world. "Maybe I'm naive. I know I'm a rabid optimist." Whilst clearly she finds the "energy of ego" disturbing, because it commonly does not translate into "energy of progress", she challenged the doubters with "well, fine, give us something that works better. Then come and talk to me". Naive or not Fiona believed competition could be harnessed.

> I want to connect with people that are positive ... it does not matter which one of us solves this problem, what matters is that we solve the problem.

As she had when told in 1975 that women could or should not be surgeons, Fiona ignored the negativity and continued to perfect a faster, better system for the treatment of burns.

By January 1999 she had founded the McComb Foundation to advance research and the development of new skin culture technologies. The name was in honour of plastic surgeon Harold McComb, who was a pivotal person in Fiona's career, and who taught her "never to be satisfied with the result and always strive for excellence". The same year a custom-built skin culture laboratory, evolved as Clinical Cell Culture (C3). The process known as Cellspray, "a cultured epithelial autograft suspension", was born. C3 established laboratories in Technology Park, in the Perth suburb of Bentley, and construction commenced on a dedicated skin culture laboratory in 2000. The company's first investor came in a very tall frame, Australian Olympic basketball player Luc Longley. He had returned home after playing in the United States and was introduced to Fiona. Fellow Australian Olympic basketballer Andrew Vlahov was another early investor. The commercialism did not sit well with Fiona, "the idea of a company was a really alien concept", but the motivation for C3 was not personal gain. C3 royalties to the McComb Foundation meant a financial basis for the future of the research. Rather than wait for government funding the company could ensure further research and conform to that Wood credo of "making it better" sooner rather than later.

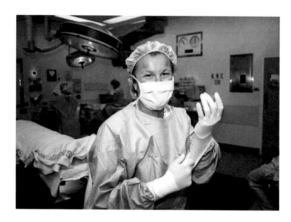

Courtesy of UWA.edu.au

By 2001 Cellspray was commercially available and C3 was floated publicly in 2002. This information would normally pass under the public radar as few Australians knew or cared about Cellspray or C3, or about a Yorkshire born doctor with an obsession for skin and an amazing surgical aptitude with burns. That would change within a year when Australians would be wrenched into the horror of mass trauma and the Yorkshire born doctor, would become one of the most recognisable figures in her adopted country.

There are defining moments in history, in everyone's life. For an individual there are births and deaths. The same can be said for that which is larger than us because history is people. For members of certain generations defining moments were when war was declared and when peace finally came. Those alive in the 1960s would probably say how their activities abruptly stopped when told: President John F Kennedy and Martin Luther King were shot; how the Vietnam War divided their nation. We realise the emphasis of our media is not without fault, that we are conditioned to accept events in the western world as being more significant than elsewhere but the day which would become known as simply "9/11" was significant in every sense.

We watched, transfixed by images of large commercial airliners tearing into New York's twin towers and Washington DC Pentagon buildings on 11 September 2001; by pain and anguish and death as two of the tallest buildings in the United States shifted and crumbled to their foundations. We imagined ourselves numbed to the death of others but we weren't. We struggled to distinguish live-to-air fact from "reality" television because blanket coverage amplified the disaster and we wondered if the very sky was falling. The orchestra of fear struck up and as hard as we tried we could not ignore its discordance. When the dust settled slightly it was a little easier to put things into perspective or to try, but the world had changed, and would never be the same. But for Australians the tyranny of distance was like a warm embrace. Hidden away in the lower extremity of the southern hemisphere we could pretend that this happened to "them" and not "us". Then it happened; 21st century chaos touched "us" too.

It was just after 11pm on 12 October 2002, not late for the revellers in the very popular *Paddy's Bar* in Kuta on the Indonesian island of Bali. It was noisy with music, chatter and laughter, the dance floor crowded with people intent on enjoying themselves. These revellers were from many nations, but the Australian drawl was omnipresent. For many Australians Bali epitomised a holiday paradise, it was "overseas" but not too far from home. It didn't cost a fortune to get to Bali and the value of Australian currency ensured one could holiday day and night. There were many Aussie groups here this bright happy night at *Paddy's*, and just over the road at the *Sari Club*, notably members of Western Australia's Kingsley Football Club and members of Sydney Coogee Dolphins Football Club.[11] Then on this October evening their world imploded. A bomb hidden in a backpack worn by a suicide bomber exploded inside *Paddy's Bar*.

Approximately ten to 15 seconds later a much more powerful bomb, close to 1000kg, concealed in a white Mitsubishi van, was detonated by remote control outside the *Sari Club*. The violent explosion ripped a one-metre-deep crater, and shattered windows throughout the town. A third bomb exploded outside the American consulate. This bomb, packed with excrement, was intended as an insult and only one person was slightly injured. The first two bombs were intended to inflict maximum human bloodshed.

Fiona's phone rang on the Sunday morning after the Bali bombing. By chance Fiona's senior registrar was holidaying in Bali. News was relayed about the chaos and carnage; about the hundreds of badly injured, the badly burnt. Fiona rang the hospital's Executive Director, and Director of Clinical Services, saying "I think we've got a problem". It was a gut instinct because she assumed that being the closest major hospital Royal Perth Hospital was about to receive an influx of seriously injured patients: "I didn't know how many there would be but we knew it was going to be double figures".

Bali medical facilities were overwhelmed. The Indonesians were stunned. They accepted an offer from the Australian Government for the worst injured to be emergency air-lifted to Australia. Royal Australian Air Force aircraft flew to Bali and returned bearing the wounded of several nations. Fiona believed "having the triage in Darwin proved to be very positive and effective". There was no burns unit in Darwin so after initial stabilisation the planes flew on.

Peter Hughes was in *Paddy's Bar*. The first blast blew him backwards and he suffered shrapnel wounds. He came to and saw two women covered in flames – he carried them into the street suffering burns to 60 per cent of his own body. Interviewed in a Bali hospital he was swollen but almost cheerful. It was this same news that alerted Fiona to how bad the situation was. She was actually at a wedding when she saw Peter on a television screen:

I was on the phone to Canberra and I remember seeing Peter Hughes on TV and he's there, quite humbly, telling everyone that he has 50 per cent burns and he's OK and there are people worse off than him. And I'm telling them in Canberra that if you don't get him out of there pretty soon he will not be OK, he will be dead.[12]

Flown to Australia Hughes remembered the fight and the pain.

When I woke up, I just couldn't believe it. I just thought, 'no human being should go through this' and I screamed and cried.[13]

The most severely injured began to arrive at Royal Perth Hospital in the early hours of the next morning. A lasting memory for Fiona was "the relief on their faces as they arrived at Royal Perth" and the appreciation in their rasping voices before they were intubated. Fiona remembers too her second impression, as the dressings and sheets were removed she thought "we've got a little bit of work to do". The hospital burns unit was full before the flights began arriving from Bali. Fiona had been involved with the development of a hospital and industry disaster plan for such an emergency and this was put into action. She always insisted "the value of teamwork can never be underestimated". All the burns unit personnel hoped the director's strategy would never be put to the test but its benefits were quickly obvious. The flow of burns patients continued, too many needed urgent attention. Assistance was needed from burns units in other Australian hospitals. It was hard admitting you could not treat everyone but on that first day Royal Perth Hospital burns unit dealt "with 20 per cent of our annual workload". Half the burns patients came to Perth, 28 patients suffering from between 2 and 92 per cent total body surface area burns and delayed shock and with already potentially deadly infections. The unit had never seen such a case load before but Fiona accentuated that they "treat everyone of those 28 patients as an individual".

It was a situation she and her unit had been training for and "when you're involved in it and actually active in doing things it's a very motivating situation", but the situation was grim. Fiona and her team had never faced so many shockingly burnt people, furthermore these patients suffered from blast injuries and this meant a sharp learning curve. They came off aircraft but could not communicate properly, medical staff realised they could not hear because of perforated ear drums. It was initially assumed that lung damage was due to smoke inhalation, but it was due to blast injury; "muscles were striped white and pink" because of the shock wave. It made the decision to amputate limbs even harder because it appeared part could be salvaged, but this wasn't the case. Fiona and her team were powered along by the realisation that their actions would greatly affect the lives of these individuals caught unwittingly in something so much larger than themselves. There was the really positive feeling of being part of a well drilled and talented team. Fiona believed:

> It was a real privilege to be leader of the burns team – it is
> on a daily basis, but even more so at that period of time.

Initial decisions about which patients went straight to theatre for cleaning and debriding (where damaged and dead tissue was removed) and which were rushed into the Intensive Care Unit (ICU) for ventilation and support, were crucial. Speed was of paramount importance and Fiona needed to assess each patient quickly. "It's the fluids, airway, circulation and the escharotomy." An escharotomy is when a surgical incision is made to stop the burnt, swelling skin becoming so tight that it restricts breathing and stops blood flow;

because if blood is not maintained amputation is the only option. Escharotomies are, according to Fiona, when:

> We cut around the chest like a Roman chest plate so it loosens the skin and the patient can actually breathe. It's very distressing not being able to breathe. So it was my job to decide who needs an escharotomy and who needs it quick.[14]

During mere seconds of inactivity, there may have been the faintest of doubts concerning her own ability, her team's ability, to give the 100 per cent every patient deserved. The major surgical procedures took place from Wednesday 16 October until Sunday 20 October. The injured skin layers had to be removed without delay and new skin had to be cultured swiftly and introduced to the wounds. Speed was imperative to stave off infection. The pace was frantic and Fiona knew "we were in there for the long haul". She and her people needed to come back each day, and the next, and the next. A roster ensured each member slept, ate and saw their family briefly. "We were able to sustain this, not through a sprint but it was a marathon." It is stifling during burns procedures. The operating theatre temperature needs to be kept at between 34 and 36 degrees to protect the patient from heat loss and excessive bleeding. Some members of the medical staff were better at withstanding the atmosphere than others.

For five days it was mainly a team of 60 doctors and nurses drawn from five hospitals who operated 30 times between Wednesday and Sunday. At one point the treatment team numbered 150 and included 12 surgeons working in four operating theatres. Fiona forgot where she had left her clothes. She shook this off because she would simply stay in scrubs for a week, or more. It was all about speed. If a wound healed in ten days it reduced the scarring risk to 4 per cent. Bali patients were treated in accordance with routine practice at Royal

Perth Hotel and received the spray-on skincell suspension developed by a pair of determined women and commercialised by C3 in 1999.

The urgency of the disaster, and the desperate need to repair wounds, meant cells were sprayed onto patients in addition to traditional skin grafts in the operating theatre. The aim was to give the opportunity for rapid wound closure with better colour match. As Fiona argued, nothing could beat using the body as a tissue culture environment because the body knows how to heal better. Not even the latest technology could save all. Jodie O'Shea, age 29, died on the Tuesday. Tracy Thomas, a 41-year-old, died late that Sunday night after three operations – the longest lasting 12 hours in an attempt to save the Perth woman who had burns to 60 per cent of her body. Fiona knew they had tried their hardest, that "the injuries were beyond what was technically possible"[15] but that never made it easier. There were times she would walk out of theatre and could not avoid the tears. After that first week many facial burns were healing well, swelling was decreasing enough so that patients were recognisable.

In 2012 Royal Perth Hospital Nursing Director Carmel McCormack would consider that first frantic week.

> I remember at one stage I turned around and there were all these surgeons who had worked here over the years saying, "Where do you want us Fiona?" And plastic surgeons from around town came in to help as well. Fiona would say, "OK, you, you and you in theatre four, you over there". She'd have a whiteboard up and talk them through it saying, "This is what I want you to do". And they'd do it. Then she'd pop from theatre to theatre telling everyone what to do. I've known her for 30 years, since she was a training registrar, but she really did pull it off that week. I'm mindful of all the others involved, too, but it was Fiona who brought it all together.

Australians were shocked, angry and disbelieving that anyone's beliefs could persuade them to commit such crimes against humanity. Political parties, police forces, intelligence agencies and academics debated international relations and shortcomings and due process. It was given fancy names like "Dissimilar Warfare". Many tried to attribute blame. The massive media coverage enhanced the fear by showing the relative inability of governments to protect its citizens from determined fanatics. In February 2003 two men found guilty of the bombings confessed to being members of Jemaah Islamiah, which was believed to be affiliated with al-Qaeda. They declared that the 88 Australians who were killed were targeted because of their nation's involvement in East Timor's independence and support for the United States. Apparently the other 114 killed, including 38 Indonesians, were guilty by association, so too the hundreds injured. The rhetoric meant little to victims, their families and those who tried desperately to save them.

Days, or was it weeks, into October 2002 Fiona was still powering along. Royal Perth Hospital Chief Executive Glyn Palmer recommended she take a little time out, go visit the family, sleep in her own bed.

> Fiona would go on forever. She'd turn around to me and
> tell me to mind my own business. It's my responsibility
> to say "it's time to take a breather".

His burns unit director begrudgingly went home. On entering the house Fiona noticed lots of casserole dishes she did not recognise. In her absence the Wood household had been eating well. The kids were pretty pleased. She was tired, feeling guilty for not being home, guilty for being home. Her reaction was one of embarrassment. She rang one of those who had delivered food to say thanks but that the kids were really capable of looking after themselves. A voice came back at her. "What makes you so selfish? What makes it such that you can't accept help?". Fiona was initially stunned. The voice continued to explain that everyone felt they wanted, needed, to help. Fiona could operate, others could cook a meal. "I learnt a lot about myself that day. I learnt it was not a failure to accept help." It was really easier to let the adrenalin continue. When you stopped you realised how tired you really were. When you stopped normal life appeared surreal. When you stopped there was time to think of what you had seen. It was better to continue and the emergency did not finish after the first week, or the second, or the third. Secondary surgeries were needed to alleviate suffering, to continue the battle, to do everything you could. The emotional fallout would need to wait another week.

The Hanleys considered themselves a regular Aussie family. Renae and Simone were more than sisters; they were great mates and went on one of those holidays of a lifetime, to Bali. Their parents hoped they would thoroughly enjoy the overseas trip but, parents being parents, couldn't help saying "be careful" and think "stay safe". It did not matter how old your children were, they were always your kids and you never stopped worrying about them. Danny Hanley was biased like most dads, his daughters were beautiful. Thirty-year-old Renae was more of an extrovert than her sister. She was married to Jason and had a small son, Noah. Renae probably felt a little anxious when she agreed to accompany her sister and a couple of girlfriends from Sydney's Sutherland Shire to Bali, but it was only going to be a quick trip. Simone was the quieter of the two sisters and had the nickname "Snowball" because of her blond hair. The few days in the idyllic tropical Bali went quickly and all too soon the last night of the holiday was there.

The sisters and Francoise Dehran decided to enjoy a last drink at the *Sari Club*. The remainder of the group returned to the hotel. How fickle fate is, what a difference a split second decision can make. The terrible explosion engulfed the club and instead of boarding a plane for home the girlfriends searched the 15 hospitals in the Kuta and Denpasar district for their missing mates. Total confusion reigned. They couldn't find Renae but found Simone shortly before she was flown to Royal Perth Hospital – she was severely burnt. On Simone's arrival Fiona Wood assessed her condition.

> My initial impression was that survival would be an extraordinarily difficult thing to achieve, we had to do absolutely everything we possibly could to give that opportunity for survival.

The Hanleys kept a vigil at the hospital, and still there was no word on Renae. As the days came and went it was difficult to retain an optimistic outlook and then came the dreadful news – Renae's body had been identified. At Royal Perth Hospital her sister's battle continued. The burns team struggled to keep her alive as the infection in her organs increased. According to Maryjane Hanley, Fiona decided drastic measures was called for and donor skin grafts might be a final option – a procedure Fiona had not undertaken since 1992. Simone's father and brother volunteered to have skin stripped from their backs but when Simone suffered a respiratory infection Fiona cancelled the surgery. Fiona refused to give up and the following day, 9 December, she decided to proceed. The surgery would have to take place in Simone's room because she could not be moved. Unfortunately by now Simone was not responding and she died, 58 days after that terrible night in Bali. Simone was 28. According to the leader of the burns unit:

> I can feel the anguish. When the mother looks at me and says "I've lost a daughter. Please don't lose this daughter of mine". When a mother says "My husband died six

weeks ago, this is my only son". There is nothing I can say to ease the pain. But you can feel a little of it.

She knew all the members of her team felt the pain but for the family "it's infinitely worse".

The families would never completely recover. For the medical staff who tended the Bali victims there was also an ongoing healing process. Fiona endeavours to assure.

> I had the easy part out of the Bali tragedy. I didn't have to look for family or friends in the rubble. My job was to work with positive people and that was a privilege.

Nonetheless even those who believed themselves hardened professionals were surprised. A chance meeting, an incident, would mean "it floods back". "You close your eyes at night and they are there with you" Fiona admits.

> Bali is just like one huge episode that you can't forget, nor should you … I remember those people and I remember them well because everything we learnt means we do better tomorrow.

A nurse working with the burns surgeon handed her a piece written by George Bernard Shaw. It moved Fiona but also inspired her and continues to do so.

A Splendid Torch

This is the true joy in life, the being used for a purpose recognized by yourself as a mighty one; the being a force of nature instead of a feverish, selfish little clod of

ailments and grievances complaining that the world will
not devote itself to making you happy.
I am of the opinion that my life belongs to the whole
community, and as long as I live it is my privilege to do
for it whatever I can.
I want to be thoroughly used up when I die, for the harder
I work the more I live. I rejoice in life for its own sake.
Life is no "brief candle" for me. It is a sort of splendid
torch which I have got hold of for the moment, and I want
to make it burn as brightly as possible before handing it
on to future generations.[16]

Bali robbed Australians of their innocence, that carefree attitude we prided ourselves on and displayed at home and overseas. It is uncertain if Fiona is speaking for herself, her team or Australians generally when she says:

> We didn't lose optimism, certainly we lost innocence in
> that period of time but we can put it in a framework that
> protects us.

There had been so much focus within the burns unit. There was so much constructive focus in the wider community. Additional equipment arrived, local businesses made unrequested deliveries of all sorts of goods and services in an attempt to help out, to do something. Red Cross centres around the nation were besieged by volunteers. On a normal day the NSW blood service would take 200 pledges. In two days following the Bali bombing 5500 volunteered blood. In Perth on the first Monday 3000 wished to donate blood. It seemed disappointing that a tragedy was needed to bring people together.

Fiona stood back at the end of the three weeks, when only four of the 28 patients remained in hospital. As tired as she was, she could see the positives and the basic good in people even if the question remained: "why is it that we only see so much positive energy in response to such a profound negative?" A colleague made a bold statement. He commented that they were unlikely to live through such an event like this again and he had felt privileged to do so. It was a constructive comment even if it seemed not quite right to admit to a sense of achievement because you and your team had functioned so expertly amid the most awful suffering. Yes, it was hard to feel pride at the expense of others but nonetheless there had been success – lives had been saved even if others were lost. Fiona is philosophical. "Why can't we actually lift our game?" "Why", she wonders, can't all Australians "just give that bit more" every day? It shouldn't take a catastrophe before Australians come together and work just that much harder.

Anthony Svilicich was the last Bali bomb victim to leave Royal Perth Hospital. He arrived with burns to 64 per cent of his body and spent 44 days in a coma and four weeks undergoing surgery and rehabilitation. It was a pleasing result for the director of the burns unit who begrudgingly conceded she may have "made a significant difference". Svilicich was more forthright: "She's a pretty amazing woman. She saved a lot of people's lives ... including my own. In my mind she's a superwoman".[17] When an eerie quiet finally settled Fiona felt soulful and empty. She needed some down time but admitted she was not good at that, but there were always the kids and they had a habit of levelling her world. She tells the story of how she can return home after a sustained period at hospital with her staff acting instantly on her directions to find a child's bag she had asked to be moved still where it was a week earlier. It was good to realise she was after all "normal".

Fiona is asked frequently how she copes with what she sees. She needs to convince herself that "any given day is my best", then the emotion becomes proactive and positive to ensure that she can make her "best better". It is not a question she is comfortable with. "It can be very, very hard." "Sometimes the only place to go is around the corner and have a good cry." Focus needs to be on the fact that she is doing something to help:

> The feeling of helping someone is like no other feeling on earth. How can you stop when you know these people need you to keep trying?.

Fiona sees suffering every day and that encourages further efforts to reduce future suffering. In that suffering there is inspiration. "I think people are astonishing." She is amazed with how an individual can take so much and continue – "it is a mystery to me". Where does that strength come from? It motivates the surgeon to "work damned hard to make sure that even if the person doesn't survive you can learn". The Bali bombings left her with the belief deep in her gut that out of the horror there had to be a global sharing of knowledge. A national burns plan agreement was put in place with Australian and New Zealand colleagues and work continues with collaborations around the world.

Less than a fortnight after Fiona shared a lovely Perth afternoon with me and pondered over a coffee just what it was about her "ordinary" self which impressed Australians so, the Bali bombers were shot. On 9 November 2008, Amrozi, Imam Samudra and Mukhlas were executed by firing squad. For some relatives of the 88 Australians who were killed on 12 October 2002, it had been a long six years and this meant closure. Maria Kotronakis, who lost two sisters and two cousins, was "over the moon".[18] Erik de Haart, a member of the Coogee Dolphins Football Club in Sydney and a survivor of the Bali bombings, remembered his nine fellow members who did not survive and believed:

> For us and for the Dolphin families it is never going to end, no matter what happened in Indonesia last night and no matter what is going to happen in the future.[19]

Former Adelaide Magistrate Brian Deegan, whose son Josh died in the explosion, was concerned: "I have a sense of trepidation as to what might happen as a result of this".[20] The Australian Government announced it would lead a new global campaign calling for a moratorium on capital punishment.

Fiona Wood admits she is obsessive, passionate, and probably even "mad". She prides herself on her honesty and that "what you see is what you get". You "get" this on a first meeting. She would probably be happy that this is the first impression, that she appears down-to-earth, unashamedly "normal", warm and quick to find the humour in situations. She has a fondness for inspirational phrases, particularly those of Ghandi and Nelson Mandela. "Inspiration in my mind is something that motivates you to go further." One saying she uses when referring to grit showed by many of her burns patients comes from Winston Churchill: "if you're going through hell, it's a smart thing to keep going". The "mad" burns surgeon and the scientist were awarded the Australian Technology Achievement Award in 2005 for their pioneering work on skin repair. Prior to that award Fiona Wood was singled out for the highest award her adopted land could award, Australian of the Year, and that was very hard to get her head around.

On the eve of Australia Day 2005 she wasn't all that comfortable with talking in public, particularly talking about herself. She had always left that to others she felt were better at it; "it wasn't part of my work". Operating theatres and laboratories were her domain and treating the physical. When she was named West Australian of 2004 she was surprised. When she was named Australian of the Year 2005 she was amazed. She didn't think she was "good enough" and argued "whoa, I wasn't comfortable with that; I'm not a famous kind of person". Given that the Australian of the Year 2004 had been another West Australian, another physician named Fiona – Professor Fiona Stanley – this Fiona sat relaxed on a warm Canberra evening in the shadow of two parliament houses.

> To follow after Fiona – two Fionas and two doctors winning just wasn't an option and when I looked at the contribution and amazing work of the other finalists I was sitting very comfortably at the back thinking I would be clapping someone else.

Yes, that "ordinary" thing was showing again. The representative from WA was "completely overwhelmed" when her name was announced by Prime Minister John Howard. With typical dry humour she tells of starting to climb the stairs to accept the award when a member of the Australian Day Council asked her "you are Australian aren't you?"; Fiona smiled and replied "does that matter?" When the official blanched she replied she was but was also proudly from Yorkshire. "There aren't many places where you can say that, honouring your past and striving for your future."

This incredibly capable professional needed to fit more into her almost manic schedule. The award was just one more important thing to juggle and she had "always been able to keep a fair number of balls in the air at one time". She realised it would further intrude on family time so she cornered her children. They were pretty proud of their mother and their reaction to her earnest question was "yeah whatever, get on with it".

Sydney Morning Herald

The kids were the easier audience because she knew she needed to push herself where she had never been comfortable before. Being in the public eye did not come naturally and now she had to connect with people and that was slightly scary. As usual Fiona faced it with typical head-on tenacity, no personal discomfort considered.

Characteristically she decided to take her new responsibility seriously, merely representing her country wasn't good enough. Believing the award "wasn't just about me ... it was about the whole community", she decided this was a tremendous opportunity to encourage people to believe in themselves and in each other. Hers would be a message of empowerment. Australians needed to be congratulated on who they were. They needed to realise their individual value and the individual value of others.

> Every one of us is unique and special, every one of us has
> a gift, a gift we should share; if we don't it's worthless ...
> How often do we do less than our best? How often do we
> challenge those around us to be their best?

She loves the diversity she sees in Australian society.

> We should really embrace it, not just tolerate it. Let's take the next step, let's embrace that difference, be it religious or colour or whatever. Embrace the difference and learn from it.

Her upbringing and schooling were shining ever so brightly. There was another message she wanted to spread, a more cautious message. Australians needed to take responsibility for themselves, their education, their wellbeing, their choices. It was not someone else's fault. This was particularly true for health. "Go for a walk for half an hour a day and you'll live longer." The health system is struggling to bear the weight and responsibility and that is just not sustainable.

Fiona adjusted her priorities. Her focus was now on her work, her family, and speaking to complete strangers. She had not figured out the "why?" quite yet but believed it was her duty if it helped just one person. "If I didn't do it I would be selfish, I don't understand the why but this has been put in my way for some reason." She found it strange and "disconcerting" particularly as she continued to believe she was "ordinary". She muses that she probably gave around 600 talks during 2005, and countless since. Not bad for someone who previously was "insular" and "lacked engagement" with others.

It has been a rewarding journey. People have been nice. "There's an awful lot of positive energy. There's a lot of people trying their best." Particularly enjoyable is speaking to young people and watching them engage. She had always told her own children that if someone at school was being horrible they should smile and now tells her larger youth audience to choose their company carefully. "I learnt early on that a person's negative attitude was their own, not mine, and they could keep it." There's no point in taking on other people's negative energy; "walk on by and find some positive energy to connect with".

The best response is to say "I am out of here, you can stay here and talk to yourself if you like but I am gone". She asks schoolchildren, when did it become "cool to be negative to someone?" She adds with a chuckle:

> I don't get that. Negative energy is far more powerful
> than positive energy? I don't understand that, maybe I am
> an alien, an alien life form.

I seriously doubt Fiona Wood is an "alien life form". Certainly she is known for futuristic scenarios, some of which make her Registrars "roll their eyes and go 'here she goes again'". This is when the discussion becomes one about *Stars Wars* and Luke Skywalker, in particular Skywalker getting his hand chopped off.

> They put on a fantastic mechanical prosthesis, the likes
> of which we will have one day. The technology is there,
> it's just the cost.

Apparently myo-technology needs some refining before it is not just a stormtrooper but a human who, when blasted to "smithereens", will be put into a "bacta tank and regenerates". She really wouldn't mind being put out of a job. In a lighter moment she came up with a wonderful scenario. The burns unit of the future looks a little like a large car wash. The patient is placed in the tube-like device and proceeds into the "wash". The first phase identifies the affected areas. During the second phase the burnt skin is removed. During the final phase the new skin cells are sprayed on. The patient pops out of the end of the "wash" regenerated.

It comes as no surprise to know Fiona is optimistic and enthusiastic about the future. She loves moving forward, embracing the wonders of science and technology. It can be a little frustrating trying to get others to keep up but she needs others to help with the giant jigsaw of life.

> I haven't the intellectual capacity or the time or energy to actually manufacture all the pieces of the jigsaw but I know where I can find them. I see amazing science being done.

Fiona has the vision to see how the different pieces should and could, fit, and loves to convince others to work with her.

> I think "whoa, can we work together? Because that is one of the pieces of the jigsaw; I can see that it will fit and I can see I can help you with maybe a little bit of yours but you can help me with mine".

It excites her to believe "we can make a difference".

The technology of the present interrupts the conversation again, the "dink" of a text message. It is a little pleasing to hear Fiona mutter that she is exasperatingly slow at texting – it seems some things are universal for those over 40. The patient she has been trying to get into an operating theatre today has been scheduled for tomorrow. Modern technology can be wonderful and annoying – as in March 2007 when news was rapidly transmitted that more damaged and burnt Australians needed her in Indonesia. She was bundled onto an aircraft only to pass in the night an aircraft bearing the patient who needed her most, flying in the opposite direction.

It was late in the evening of 7 March 2007 when Garuda Indonesian flight GA200 was ten miles from the Yogyakarta airport on the Indonesian island of Java. Among the 140 onboard were ten

Australians including a group of diplomats and journalists and RAAF and Australian Federal Police (AFP) personnel bound up with the visit of the Australian Foreign Affairs Minister Alexander Downer. The Boeing 737 was well above the normal approach height. The pilot took the aircraft down steeply in an attempt to reach the runway and the airspeed increased dramatically, in excess of the wing flaps approach and double the normal landing speed. In the cockpit alarm systems emitted their shrill warnings but the pilots chose to ignore and not to go around again. In the main cabin RAAF personnel looked at each other and agreed the plane was coming in far too fast and would not make the runway. Nor did it. As passengers braced themselves for the impact the 737 slammed into and then off the end of the tarmac and hurtled out of control across a road. The landing was so hard the jet's nose wheel snapped off. As the damaged aircraft bounced through an embankment and culvert, the right wing snapped free causing fuel to stream along the fuselage. By the time the main part of the plane skidded to a stop in a rice paddy it was 300 metres from the airfield. In an instant it burst into flames, trapping those sitting in the front right-hand section. Passengers struggled through smoke in a frantic attempt to reach emergency exits. With dreadful urgency they fell into the rice paddy. Rescue vehicles could not reach the wreck. As rescue workers approached on foot the 737 exploded. Further explosions engulfed the passenger cabin preventing the rescue of survivors.

Twenty-one passengers were killed. Those sitting in the business class section bore the brunt of the fire and these included five Australians. Elizabeth O'Neill, 37, spokeswoman for the Australian Ambassador in Indonesia, had received the Order of Australia Medal for her work in the aftermath of the 2002 Bali bombings and was a member of the crisis team after the Australian Embassy in Jakarta was bombed. She was married with a nine-month-old daughter, Lucinda. AFP agents Brice Steele, 37, and Mark Scott, 41, were leaders in their fields. Steele, at 19, had been the youngest to graduate from the AFP academy in 1990. He was fluent in Cantonese and Mandarin and in 2007 was an AFP Commander and the regional counter terrorism expert. Scott was the leader of the AFP's Jakarta-based regional engagement team. Allison Sudradjat, 41, was head of AusAID in Indonesia. She had spent 18 years with AusAID with missions in Papua New Guinea and Indonesia. Jakarta-based *Australian Financial Review* journalist Morgan Mellish, 36, was actually booked on another airline because the Garuda flight was full. At the last moment O'Neill found a spare embassy ticket. Again those left behind pondered on the fickleness of fate.

Many of the survivors suffered serious burns and other injuries. Cynthia Banham was a journalist with the gift for turning a phrase. Fiona flew back to Perth overnight and went straight to the hospital. She operated on Cynthia for eight hours and emerged to say her patient remained in a "very severe condition" with burns to more than 50 per cent of her body, broken bones and other injures. There was further surgery over the following days. On 12 March the medical team was forced to amputate one of Cynthia's legs at the thigh and the other below the knee to save her life. Four months later she finally left hospital. Those months had been unbelievably difficult. The long road to rehabilitation would continue but the journalist who had run marathons amazed doctors with her courage and progress.

It is easy to philosophise in an attempt to explain the nature of life and reality. Fiona finds it fascinating. "I see the uniqueness in people, everybody has a gift to give". She sees the worst of life but she also sees the best in life and admits to being amused when people get worked up by the unimportant.

> I see things that are so much more significant and if you can deal with the significant then everything else is trivial.

She is inspired by the tenacity and resilience of patients. It is nonetheless perplexing when some patients with relatively minor burns do not survive and others with extensive burns do. Each individual is different. In some there is "something in their spirit. Some people are just not ready to die yet and they come back for more". The Australian of the Year 2005 wishes she could work out what it is and bottle it – "here we have Lazarus, take eight times a day!" I ask a question I ought not ask. Does there come a point when she wonders if a life is worth saving; a feeling in the gut that the injury is so overwhelming it is difficult to know where to start? My question receives the treatment it deserves:

> I don't make that choice, we do everything we can and then the choice is made for us. If we give 100 per cent and they don't survive we have done all we should have. If we give 80 per cent and they survive they survive at 20 per cent less than they should have. Where there is life it is all or nothing.

In 2006 Fiona Wood was awarded the Order of Australia for her work with the victims of Bali. In 2005 the National Trust added Fiona to Australia's "Living National Treasures" list. She and 14 others were selected by popular vote to replace the fifteen original 100 "Living Treasures" who had died since 1997. This was a little disconcerting. Fiona was honoured to be "living" and "chosen" but accolades like this sometimes seem to have a "been there done that" shade, and she is certainly not happy with this. "I feel like saying 'I'm not finished yet!'"

> I believe to a point I've made a difference to a significant number of situations, certainly. But it's not enough.

> There's an awful lot more difference to be made out there,
> and there's an awful lot more work to do.

There can be no resting on laurels. "I don't want to stop asking questions. The answer's got to be in there somewhere." And even if the answer is found there is always another problem, another step. "I haven't started yet, gosh I have so much work to do." The quest for the scarless burn is still not complete. C3 now has headquarters in the United Kingdom and the research and work goes on. In excess of 40 countries have approval to use ReCell technology now commercialised by Avita Medical.

Another aspect engages her attention. The fierce determination which distinguished her as a student is visible as she discusses the impact of the brain to injury. The structural levels of the nervous system and brain and their different responses to injury now intrigue a great deal. Fiona first published in 1986 on the impact of surgery on the nervous system but another obsession took hold, the small matter of skin.

> I have over twenty years of seeing how people heal in a
> holistic way and I want the opportunity to join the dots.

Now she wants to know more, particularly about "the neurological drive to injury and regeneration to improve the quality of the clinical outcome". Of course understanding that would "lead to the ability to effect change to the drivers to repair, and the implementation of care" and the burns surgeon can't wait to see that.

The Australian Medical Association described Fiona Wood as:

> A person of rare talent. She is someone who manages
> to achieve superhuman results in her personal and
> professional life yet remain down to earth. She constantly

pushes the boundaries and is prepared to commit herself and her own resources to making a real difference.[21]

Living Treasurers Committee chair, Michael Ball, believed Fiona was "deemed to have added lasting attributes to our culture and heritage". The Australia Day Council noted her "passionate dedication and unfailingly positive attitude".[22] True to her own upbringing and Ackworth School socialisation she is convinced "my life belongs to the whole community, and as long as I live it is my privilege to do for it whatever I can". The interview comes to an end and Fiona has decided she has just enough time to pick up trays of mangoes to take to hospital trauma unit personnel. They looked after one of her sons recently following a "spectacular prang on his bike". Fiona Wood leaves, still convinced she is pretty "ordinary" and "normal". I am convinced of the opposite. Images of Mother Teresa and the pink battery bunny come to mind. I prefer the latter and I am sure Fiona would be much more comfortable with that also.

My next meeting with Fiona Wood occurred during National Science Week in August 2011. Fiona Wood has a busy few days; she is giving a presentation on "Burns Survival in the Mass Casualty Situation", another on "The Quest for Scarless Healing" and another on "The Highs and Lows of a Successful Research Career". She is also doing two lunches and at Questacon she is joining a make-up specialist in a discussion about the cause and treatment of burns. I wonder why science appears to scare a lot of people and leave them squeamish. I did mention to Fiona in our first interview that I wasn't good with the "icky bits". She roared with laughter and said: "Why are you interviewing me then?".

My research made avoiding the "icky bits" impossible but here I was on a cold August night sitting in a CSIRO lecture theatre listening, and watching, a presentation on "burns survival in the mass casualty situation". I already knew that Fiona and the make-up specialist had

made a good many parents queasy at Questacon that afternoon – the
large audience of children loved it!

Photographs by Margaret Hadfield (Zorgdrager)

Fiona speaks of the urgency of the response to and management of
burns, reiterating: "I do nothing in isolation, I am just very privileged
to be the team leader". She explains how skin helps control the body's
temperature, so when a large portion of the skin is injured, you lose
body heat. This increases your risk of hypothermia – the body loses
heat faster than it can produce heat, causing a dangerously low body
temperature. Burn injuries induce a state of immunosuppression
that predisposes burn patients to infectious complications, so speed
is paramount. She had been involved in at least 14 mass causality
events, different events, with different patterns of injuries and burns.
Prior to the 1999 Sydney Olympics Fiona attended a symposium
on disaster planning when the Minister for Health gave a 45 minute
presentation and he "did not mention burns once". Fiona put up her
hand and said:

> Excuse me, what if there is an explosion in Sydney, there
> are only nine beds in Westmead [Hospital], 14 in Concord
> [Hospital], 12 children's beds in Westmead [Hospital],
> that's the most we have across the country?

She argued for a dedicated burns unit and staff, because it was not the sort of thing that a trauma team could manage and because the collateral damage continues for days and weeks with the struggle to seal the skin before infections takes over. Australia has a large mining industry, particularly in Western Australia, and off-shore oil rigs and too many bushfires. At that time "terrorism was on the bottom of the page, not in the same font". It was largely due to Fiona and like minds that Australia acquired its co-ordinated disaster plan and this would be vital when terrorism moved to the largest font.

The disaster response team must always be fully prepared: "you need to plan, you need to think about what you are going to do". Fiona teaches registrars to visualise what they are going to do before the patient arrives, think about their options, make sure they articulate all the equipment they need so it is in the room before they start. "There is absolutely no substitute for prior planning – planning is key." And it does not end there because Fiona then asks:

> How can we learn from today's experience so that we can be better tomorrow not because today's bad but we must think about how we can get better and go forward.

It is not just the burns service staff who need to be involved; all Australians need to be educated, every Australian should have first-aid instruction. "We have fire drills, we know what to do – trust me you don't."

> Every Australian should know if you cool a burn for 20 minutes within an hour of injury, between 15 and 18 degrees clean cool running water – you will have reduced that burn by 80 per cent; clean cool cloths if no running water.

This sort of primary intervention reduces the necessity for surgery and drastically reduces burns treatment and scaring. Every intervention influences the quality of life – it was "good solid science".

We were well into Fiona's presentation and burns photos when I noticed the young woman beside me fidgeting and turning pale. She then muttered indecipherably at the man next to her. Clearly she was there to please him, and clearly she would never allow him to forget her sacrifice for as long as they were a couple. Fiona as ever enthusiastically powered on, and the woman intently studied the pattern of her shoes. I have to admit I was feeling pretty good by this stage, I had not said "yuk" once nor looked away. Fiona had taught me not to be afraid of the unknown, and the "icky bits" – though I still did not understand the "good solid science" and thank goodness for the humanities.

The Bali attack rocked Australia to the core. It was painfully clear that the memory of Bali and its victims still resonates with those who gathered to mark the tenth anniversary, and those who doubtless shed tears in the privacy of their Australian homes. Ten years seems a long time yet for those whose lives changed forever when bombs were triggered in *Paddy's Bar* and the *Sari Club*. The legacy of that day had been omnipresent. For Australians it was one of those defining events, terrorism was on the doorstep.

At the Bali memorial in October 2012 Australian Prime Minister, Julia Gillard, commented that with the deaths of 202 people, including 88 Australians, we witnessed:

> the worst and the best in human life. The worst: this shocking murder of innocent people by fanatics motivated by hate and trying to spread that hate to all. And the best: the courage and compassion of so many ordinary people caught up in this extraordinary event.

More than 300 people attended the tenth commemorative service in the Great Hall at Parliament House, including 70 victim relatives. Governor-General Quentin Bryce led the service and spoke of "futures cut short, potential snatched away in a heartbeat, lives shattered". Fiona Wood then addressed the audience.

> Australians, today is the day to look into your heart, to look into your heart and find in it the love and human energy, the strength and human energy to face such horror and keep going, knowing there is a bright future ahead when we have seen so many beautiful smiles snuffed away.

Her voice was unsteady as she continued, to say that we must work to make tomorrow a better day, she had felt privileged to be able to help those who came back, in the largest peacetime emergency evacuation of Australians. Survivors and relatives rose to place flowers on the newly created national memorial wreath. The wreath would later be placed in the Parliament House Bali memorial gardens.

Two months later it is a beautiful Canberra summer day in early December 2012, but according to the Mayan calendar the world is about to end this very week, assuming you believe in such doomsday predictions. With the end of the world nigh it is wonderful to be in the company of a very positive force. Dr Fiona Wood continues to believe in the importance of staying engaged, embracing life and maintaining a healthy sense of humour. Our conversation briefly touches on politics and the media. Fiona does not know how our elected parliamentarians can continue to operate in such a negative space, "there is something wrong with our political system". Nor is it the end of the world that Fiona is no longer Australia's most trusted person. Neurosurgeon Dr Charlie Teo now carries that mantle. Fiona laughs and says she rang Charlie Teo and told him "if it had to be someone I am glad it was you Charlie". She admires his positive attitude and his skill. "If something goes wrong with my head I want Charlie to operate." Fiona Wood is in second place on that list of 99 names but remains the most trusted woman.[23]

Fiona would prefer to discuss arriving to speak at a recent leadership conference to find that the other presenter was Victoria Cross winner Corporal Benjamin "Ben" Roberts-Smith. Initially Fiona thought what an odd couple they made:

> The dichotomy between the two of us was, I was keeping people alive and he wasn't, and that was his core business.

But Fiona was open to a different discourse and quickly became impressed:

> He is someone who puts himself on the line day in day out and articulated it in way with compassion and humility and clear intelligence, which made it very human and very engaging.

She chuckles at the memory of organisers attempting to photograph their presenters together. Ben Roberts-Smith is 191cm, and Fiona Wood is 157cm "on a good day" – camera lenses were simply incapable of overcoming such a disparity.

Corporal Roberts-Smith had been the target of some tactless media comment and although Fiona believes he handled this with decorum, Roberts-Smith later took leave from the Australian army for an indefinite period. Public interest and ensuing demands had proven difficult. This is something Fiona completely understands because she too faces what she refers to as a "tsunami" of media interest, and had struggled to find a balance between private, supporting the public and "doing what I do".

Before Bali she worked in virtual anonymity. Even whilst fundraising for burns research Fiona was "really fastidious" about not being named in media releases reading "the plastic surgeon said". Fiona laughs at this attempt to conceal as she was the only woman plastic surgeon, and Director of the West Australian Burns Service. Nonetheless she was working in a profession which had a level of hostility towards using publicity to gain favour, an environment "where we needed to raise money" but she needed to remain personally "under the radar". With Bali all that changed and Fiona remained beneath the radar no more. She considers and admits it caught her totally unprepared. When Perth Hospital Public Relations media staff suggested she speak to the press Fiona's immediate reaction was a shade hostile.

> I made the mistake of saying something I shouldn't, I said "let's face it I have never seen anything in the newspaper that I have known anything about that is accurate". I realised that criticism without engagement is negative, a black hole, so don't go there.

It was also very obvious that Fiona was team leader and that "the concept of keeping me as the phantom, the ghost that walked, was not going to happen". Press conferences were held twice a day in the aftermath of the Bali bombings with the last, sadly, when the last Australian victim died. Fiona had been way out of her comfort zone but she was impressed. Nonetheless:

> I thought that was it, I thought back to life as normal, how stupid was I, back to work, how naïve was I.

Anonymity was gone and Australians were feeling vulnerable, they needed a hero. Fiona did not meet the younger Australian who nominated her for Australian of the Year until after she won the title in 2005. The balancing act became just that much harder. "I do say no to 75 per cent of the requests I receive." She says yes if the timing is convenient, and "Oh, that's interesting, or I'd like to contribute", and most importantly if "it may engage and inspire school children to do science". But there is always a "but" – "I actually have a job which is time intensive". She worried about the perception that she was out for publicity, but in true Fiona fashion remarks that she decided this was the belief of "a small number of people who have that negative energy … the black hole energy".

> I found the hardest thing was the personal spotlight and I tried really hard to deflect it because it is everybody else's story; but I realised that the story could be useful to someone. I have never been comfortable with it, it is the most difficult thing for me personally and I always say, "I have done nothing in isolation, being a team leader is a privilege". So for me if I can share something which is useful it's wrong of me not to. I'm in this position because of an awful lot of people and I have to work hard to justify that capacity to work, I just have to keep going and deliver.

Fiona is still uncomfortable with agreeing to change the name of the burns research foundation from "McComb" to the "Fiona Wood Foundation" so clearly the Quaker ethos remains pre-eminent. Fiona agrees that her life philosophy is a combination of environment and genetics – the "to work is to live" from her parents and that Quaker ethos "not for oneself but for others". Though she admits she really doesn't behave "Quakerly by a long way" sometimes.

Our conversation returns to the subject of her conference presentation with Corporal Ben Roberts-Smith, VC – leadership. She believes she leads differently from some of her male counterparts. The essential ingredient should always be respect.

> I'm a big softie … you need to treat everyone with respect and consideration to get your message across … at some point you have to engage in a level of bluntness which you're not entirely comfortable with and I've found as a woman in my field that if you go straight in with that blunt 'That's not good enough' it's not a conducive environment to then teach and then progress. If you go in with 'Have you thought about? Have you finished? Have you considered?' then that opens doors to facilitate a better outcome for the patient and that's what I'm interested in.

Fiona believes some may see this hesitation as unnecessary, even weak leadership, but it is different leadership, she believes nothing can be gained by her loudly exclaiming: "OH GOODNESS GRACIOUS, YOU DID WHAT?" That, is "counterproductive". She likes to believe everyone gets up in the morning to do "the best they can and maybe that's naïve of me but that is something I will hold onto". Egos can get in the way of productivity, "I'm not interested in your ego I'm interested in how we move forward". Egos can also cause a breakdown in the best course of action.

> Sometimes you can lose sight of when you should hand over, or should hand on, or should ask for advice – sometimes you should realise that this is as far as your experience or knowledge base, or energy at the time goes. Because you're exhausted, you have kind of overthought about it, you just need to take a step back and say "Hey what do you think about this?".

Women tend to do this more easily than men, they find it easier to step back and consider, and relinquish authority. She laughs and says that her approach: "Dare I say it, [is] more girlie". And is that wrong?

Seriously injured patients help Fiona to maintain her own equilibrium and that of the six Kierath children, now aged 18 to 26. They adjusted to having a notorious mother a long time ago, and at the end of the day she is just "Mum". A mother's pride is evident and Fiona continues to be intrigued if not charmed by how different her children are, due to how the genes are expressed, their place in the family and those knocks and nudges along the way.

> The greatest achievement in my life is my kids. Both my husband and I have been strong on the fact that they are first.... that's our personal philosophy and if that's not obvious to everyone else then it doesn't matter.

The guilt thing? Her loudest critics were other women. "The guilt is something you mature out of but it takes a while."

It has been challenging keeping up with these young adults, but really interesting. The oldest, Tom and Jess, seemed closest to following the path of their parents. They both enjoyed science and made high school "Tournament of minds" teams. Tom pursued science and engineering at university. Jess is studying medicine. The Kierath offspring were encouraged to see education as a tool and access university for the knowledge they needed. Dan studied business strategy, Joe is studying sports marketing and working in a similar area. Jack spent 2012 with the Australian Army at the Australian Defence Force Academy. Evie is the youngest. She won the World U19 Women's Individual Trampoline Championship in Birmingham England in 2011. Fiona had seen quite a few Australian flags raised and anthems played, but none so grand as when Evie stood with that gold medal around her neck.

Fortunately the Mayan calendar was wrong; the world didn't end as 2012 finishes. Fiona Wood is in a good place because there are exciting changes on the immediate horizon. From March 2013 she has a medical practitioner fellowship, the first time she will be funded to do her own research. Fifty per cent of her clinical life will be done by someone she has trained, which relieves her to work "with a level of head space and practical hands on time". There will be scans of the brains of patients through the whole period of injury and recovery because she needs to understand the background information.

> We have some tiny pieces of the jigsaw, we know there are changes, we don't know the significance of those changes.

Fiona knows there is a body image patterned on the surface of our brain related to the density of the nerves: "It is quite a distorted pattern but recognisable as a body shape". She knows that "if I am burnt on my right hand the nerves on my left hand will be affected" and desperately wants to know how better to understand how the brain pattern changes over time. This will then allow for "opportunities to innovate and change therapies". Fiona continues to believe in the holistic approach and hopes this research will not just assist burns patients but "right across the board in all sorts of healing". She grins and adds "I am a dreamer, maybe one day!" Fiona returns to Perth with seven weeks to "clear the decks" so "she can hit the deck running" and that is pretty much the way Fiona approaches life in general.

When I first interviewed Fiona Wood in October 2008 I felt a sloth as I noted down her daily routine. I had visions of a pink battery bunny which just kept on going, and going. That vision returns. On 1 February 2013 Fiona will be 55 – don't believe *Wikipedia*; one of her sons did and missed her birthday, much to the merriment of his sibling. I am almost heartened by Fiona's good humoured comment:

I feel my age now and again – I have to curb the enthusiasm now and again, head and body disconnect, my head thinks I can still do it but my body says "hang on a minute this is far enough".

However on the previous weekend she completed the bike leg of an ironman event, 180 kilometres. Her time was 5hrs 38 mins and I am sure she is trying to make me feel better when she adds with that laugh that she got off her bike with "cramps burning my legs, thinking 'okay been there, done that, got the t-shirt, I'm not doing this again'". She has decided she can no longer allow for the training commitment for such a feat so she will just commit to half ironman events, 90 kilometres!

Fiona Wood's ambition is that she leaves this world feeling "thoroughly used up". This is no lament because, borrowing from Bernard Shaw, she believes, "the harder I work the more I live". Flattery does not sit well with the former "Frickley Flyer" so it's only to myself that I say "the harder Fiona Wood works the more others live".

www.fionawoodfoundation.com

1. *Herald Sun*, 19 June 2008.
2. www.quakers.org.au "Religious Society of Friends" and "History of the Quakers".
3. In 1900 the school became aligned with Kings College, London.
4. Wynn, R. "Saints and Sinners: Women and the Practice of Medicine Throughout the Ages", *Jama: the Journal of the American Medical Association*, 2 February 2000.

5. ibid.

6. Hiatt, M D and Stockton, C G. "The Impact of the Flexner Report on the Fate of Medical Schools in North America after 1909", *Journal of American Physicians and Surgeons*, vol.8 no.2, Summer 2003. See also, Flexner A. Medical Education in the United States and Canada, New York, NY, Carnegie Foundation for the Advancement of Teaching, 1910.

7. "Despite Growing Number of Female Doctors and Lawyers, Women's Pay Still Lags Behind", www.thinkprogress, 5 December 2012.

8. Mail online, 30 November 2011. In 2003, 65 per cent of the UK medical graduates were women. In Moore, A. "Why aren't there more female surgeons in the UK? The Foundation Years, Elsevier, vol.2, issue 2, pp.83-84.

9. http://surgicalcareers.rcseng.ac.uk/wins/statistics.

10. www.clinicalcellculture.com/one/pdf/Weekend Australian Magazine, June 2-22, 2003.

11. Six members of the Coogee Dolphins and seven of the Kingsley Football Club would be killed.

12. perthnow.com.au "Remembering Bali: Inside RPH a Doorway to Hope and Heartache", 5 October 2012.

13. Lindsay, P. *Back from the Dead*, Random House, Sydney, 2003.

14. perthnow.com.au "Remembering Bali: Inside RPH a Doorway to Hope and Heartache", 5 October 2012.

15. *The Australian*, 22 June 2002.

16. Shaw, G.B. *Man and Superman*, Penguin, 1973, p.84.

17. *7.30 Report,* ABC, 26 January 2005.

18. *The Canberra Times*, 9 November 2008.

19. ibid.

20. ibid.

21. Australian Medical Association (WA), 25 January 2005.

22. www.australianoftheyear.gov.au

23. *Reader's Digest*, Trust Poll 2012 People.

Information also from:

Thompson, P. *Talking Heads*, ABC, 14 August 2006.

Negus, G. *Tonight*, ABC, episode 9, 2 April 2003.

Denton, A. *Enough Rope,* 14 June 2004.

7.30 Report, ABC, 21/10/2002; 26/1/2005.

Science Network WA "More than skin deep: Profile of Dr Fiona Wood", 10 May 2005.

Readers Digest (Australia) "Australia's 100 Most Trusted List", 10 May 2007.

Daily Telegraph, 8 March 2007

The Age, 20 March 2007

Notebook Magazine, November 2005.

PM with Mark Colvin, ABC, 24 November 2003

ABC News Online, 11 March 2007.

321

Lauren Jackson

"It has always been an athlete's dream to be in the Olympics and now it is mine". Lauren Jackson, age 12.

The line of people awaiting the opportunity to ask for a photograph or signature runs down the length of the basketball court and disappears out the door. It is the first home game for the *Canberra Capitals* in October 2012. The game is well over and most *Caps* players and staff have departed for the change room. Lauren Jackson did not play due to injury, but it made no difference to the crowd who were just excited that she was here, and would spend the WNBL season dressed in the blue and yellow Caps jersey. It would take over an hour for those on the end of the line to reach the figure sitting behind the desk, patiently signing, offering a few words and smiling a little awkwardly for photos – she is never truly comfortable when the attention is focused entirely on her. A large number were young girls, invariably dressed in an oversized no.15 singlet, eager to meet their sporting "shero". They may not play basketball but live in a sports-mad nation though one which rarely accords sportswomen their due. For decades Lauren Jackson has been best in the world and that cannot be ignored.

Lauren Elizabeth Jackson was born on 11 May 1981 in Albury, New South Wales, to Maree and Gary. If such exist, basketball genes filled the bloodstream of the new arrival. Maree Bennie had created records of her own whilst on a basketball scholarship at Louisiana State University.[1] Maree played for Australia from 1973 to 1980 and the sport also introduced her to Gary, who played for Australia in 1975. Maree was selected again for the Australian team in 1982 but with two young children, Lauren and younger brother Ross, she was unable to make the necessary commitment. New parents are always a little bewildered by their first born, and the Jacksons wondered if all toddlers were as determined and competitive as their 14-month-old when Lauren waddled up to Maree bottle feeding newborn Ross and declared in no uncertain terms that it was "my bottle" and she wanted it back, now! Before his daughter was four Gary was so impressed with Lauren's hand-eye co-ordination and running speed he confidently predicted, "she will represent Australia"[2] – he just wasn't sure in which sport.

Basketball remained the major Jackson interest and the family spent a lot of time at Albury stadiums. As a small child Lauren would make a nest of discarded tracksuits, curl up and go to sleep. Another strong female role model was Maree's mother, Irene, who cut one of her daughter's Australian tracksuits down to fit Lauren – call it intuition or premonition. She believed there would be another generation wearing the green and gold. Lauren started playing basketball at age five. Encouraged by her parents to try other sports she played tennis, competed in "Little Athletics" and swam, but basketball emerged as the sport of preference. Maree was coaching the Albury representative U12 squad and her daughter earned a place in the team at age nine. Then the team won their district championship.

Lauren was definitely strong willed. "If she wanted something, she would go out and get it, she wouldn't give up," remembers Maree,[3] but more was needed. Lauren was around 12 or 13 when Maree and Gary realised their daughter had truly separated from the crowd. Physically Lauren had a growth spurt which meant the teasing at school intensified, she was long and thin and called "chicken legs"; but the quiet, dogged determination was increasingly evident also. Others also were observing the development. Head Coach of the Australian Institute of Sport (AIS) women's basketball programme Phil Brown:

> I first observed Lauren playing basketball when she was
> just 13 years of age. Even at that tender age, it was fairly

obvious that she would have a great future in the game. Lauren was already 6'2"-6'3" – tall, thin and rangy, but moved remarkably well around a basketball court for such a tall young athlete. She had an incredible "nose for the ball", exceptional hand-eye co-ordination, and used her length and great hands very effectively to rebound and score, primarily around the basket.[4]

Lauren was chosen to attend an Australian U20 team training camp. She was initially full of misgivings; she was shy, only 14 and she had an injured thigh. The phone rang one evening at the Jackson home. Maree fully expected it to be Lauren saying she wanted to come home from the camp. It was Lauren, she had made the Australian U20 team – Maree burnt the dinner.

Lauren had realised basketball was her destiny; more than that it was her passion. Education merely became a requirement. Murray High School was enjoyable and a particular English teacher a great motivator, but by Year 10 Lauren wouldn't participate in peer discussion concerning years 11 and 12. "I used to say I won't be here, I will be off to the AIS on a scholarship."[5] In the beginning this elicited disbelief, but not for long.

The AIS in 1996 was daunting for the 15-year-old. It was a "huge adjustment" moving away from the familiar surroundings of provincial Albury to the Australian capital Canberra, away from the family who tethered her world. Lauren cried a lot those first few weeks. The shy, gangly country teenager needed to dig deep; tenacity and strong will were required in abundance. After playing part-time basketball in Albury, she had entered the eat, breathe, serious training, Women's National Basketball League (WNBL) competition world of basketball. No longer the carefree lifestyle surrounded by family and friends; no longer local club basketball and two practices a week. At the AIS it was practice two or three times per day all year and around

60 games a year. Coach Phil Brown was an expert not only in the technicalities of the game but also convincing teenage girls of their potential – but he realised how challenging the lifestyle change was.

> The young athlete goes through an adaptation process from a girl playing the game of basketball to a young woman playing the sport of basketball in a high performance elite developmental programme.[6]

He saw enormous potential in Lauren but there was only so much support and encouragement the AIS could give; the rest was up to her.

In the rarified world Lauren now occupied she needed to grow up fast, perhaps too fast. Everything was moving incredibly quickly, there was little time to stop and smell the flowers, to stop and be a regular teen – indeed she knew little of the word "regular". The non-stop AIS world was interwoven with Year 11 and 12 studies at Lake Ginninderra College and at just 16 she not only won a silver medal with the Australian Junior World Championship team but was named in the senior Australian women's team, the *Opals*. It was scary and wonderful at the same time, playing alongside such basketball luminaries as Michele Timms and Robyn Maher, role models whose "best attributes" she quietly tried to absorb, athletes she "wanted to be a match for". They were generous with their encouragement but she was very young. Marian Stewart was manager of the *Opals*. She remembers when the Australian team was visiting a United States training camp in Colorado. The Australians gathered in a hotel room discussing the day with Michele Timms who had arrived from playing with the *Phoenix Mercury*. Lauren was quiet and then confided:

> Maz I have to ring my brother, I have to tell him I am in the same room as Michele Timms. She was just an

over-awed kid then and look who she is today – the best
female basketballer in the world.[7]

In 1997 16-year-old Lauren was named the WNBL Rookie of the
Year.

At the AIS the focus was on multi-skilling, developing all-round
basketball skills in tall post players – passing, dribbling and shooting
skills – so they could be effective in the low post area as well as playing
away from the basket. The AIS offered the strongest of foundations
but it was up to the individual athlete to accept, and adopt, the hard
work ethic necessary to endure and succeed. Also crucial to success
was the burning hunger, the all-consuming resolve to work harder,
the insatiable need to be better. By 1998 Phil Brown realised Lauren
had it all, the physical and mental traits needed to succeed. In 2008
Lauren would say the AIS years were possibly "the best years of my
life" but ten years earlier she was living at full throttle and just trying
to keep up.

Being chosen for the *Opals* team to travel to Germany for the
1998 FIBA (International Basketball Federation – *Fédération
Internationale de Basket-ball*) Women's World Championships was
thrilling. It was an incredible experience for a 17-year-old from the
Murray River heartland; it was also a huge test of character. Lauren
was the youngest ever to pull on the Australian uniform. She was in
an Opals team whose members were between six and 22 years older
and much the same in international competition experience. The
FIBA World Basketball Championship for Women had been founded
in 1953, three years after the first men's event. The first "Worlds" was
held in Chile, and by 1967 the quadrennial cycle was established,
while after 1983 the scheduling was altered so the championship
would be held in even-numbered non-Olympic years. Only 16
countries could qualify to compete. The United States and the Soviet
Union dominated until 1994 when, in a surprising final, Brazil beat

China. Australia's best results were fourth place in 1979 and 1994; in 1998 they hoped to do better.

This was basketball at its very best, at its toughest, no quarter given or expected. Players representing their nations try just that much harder, dig just that much deeper, play with just that much more assertiveness. They look to exploit the weakest link on any opposition team, and the new kid on the block was likely to be a soft target. There was much for Lauren to learn from the gifted Australian coach Tom Maher, from her more experienced teammates and from watching the best in the world and, she was a good student of her chosen craft. When she came off the bench she did so with flair and scored a point a minute. The opposition quickly realised this new Aussie kid was no pushover; not only did she exhibit basketball maturity beyond her years but the girl showed "mongrel" tendencies, mental toughness and aggressiveness. The United States beat Russia 71–65 in the final, Australia took the bronze medal by beating Brazil 72–67.

Her first "Worlds" further inflamed the passion, and the return to the AIS after the heady days of top international competition was almost a letdown. It was back to perfecting the basics, drill after drill, same old, same old, but it was the AIS basics which formed the foundation of the Jackson game. This AIS skill set, according to Phil Brown, enabled Lauren to develop:

> incredible versatility in her game that few players with her size possess anywhere around the world. She can post up the smaller or weaker defender close to the basket and score on them, or she can take the bigger slower defender out beyond the three point arc and use her quickness or shooting range to score from there. Lauren's proficiency rating is amazing and second to none in the world![8]

There was the occasional teenage wobble in the busy AIS days – every teenager is entitled to the occasional wobble. During 1999 the AIS team travelled to Perth for another WNBL game. It was an important game, it was late in the season and head to head both teams had one win each. Phil Brown had tried to drill into the girls how important this game was because potentially it could determine who would be minor premiers and subsequently host a major semi-final. He admittedly was reasonably worked up about this big game given the AIS team was broaching new standards. He counted heads on the team bus and Lauren was missing. Minutes ticked by painfully and Lauren did not appear. Her coach's patience was wearing a little thin so he sent a player up to Lauren's hotel room. More minutes passed and time was getting critical "by this stage I have steam coming out of my ears!"[9] Lauren had fallen asleep and was not dressed or packed. She came stumbling down dragging her gear. "I cannot believe what I am seeing. We play in an hour" recalls "Brownie". Not wishing to upset the rest of the team he struggled to maintain his demeanour but took Lauren aside and said "we'd better win this game!!" Lauren scored 25 points that day, pulled down 14 rebounds, and the AIS team did win.

The AIS team was a work in progress, used to being on or near the bottom of the WNBL ladder. It may have been a case of strength breeding strength or perhaps it was a unique group, but the AIS class of 1998 - 99 was the best the institute had seen. Athletes Penny Taylor, Belinda Snell, Suzy Batkovic, Kristen Veal and Lauren Jackson blossomed; they were mates and they believed in one another. The competitiveness between them as athletes pushed each to better form, higher skills. The AIS team was included in the WNBL purely for the competition so the teenagers could learn from their elders, from their betters. But this AIS team had other plans and then coach Brown voiced what they had all been thinking – "we can win this thing". The unthinkable was in fact feasible. This band of talented young basketballers achieved what no one thought possible and the AIS class of 1998–99 won the WNBL Championship.

For Lauren winning the WNBL championship meant more than winning the WNBL Most Valuable Player (MVP) award. That's how it was and continues to be for Lauren – she takes more pleasure in the team winning. It is gratifying to know she has played as well as she can but this is primarily a team sport and teammates mean a lot; they are family and being part of that family is most important. As a consequence for her changing teams would forever be unsettling because it deviates from the primary principles of family and loyalty. She had graduated from the Australian education system, she had graduated from the AIS basketball programme, but it was now time to move on. Teammates, confidants – the AIS family – was breaking up and scattering far and wide; a new chapter beckoned but it did not feel all good. Lauren was comfortable in Canberra, her first home away from home, and she was therefore particularly open to a professional offer from the local WNBL team the *Canberra Capitals*. Several members of the *Caps* were earlier AIS graduates and Lauren knew she would enjoy playing with Australian Atlanta Olympian Shelly Gorman-Sandie. The transition was made less painful when AIS teammate Kristen Veal joined the Canberra-based team. Over the ensuing seasons the understanding between Lauren and Kristen, between guard and forward, would be a highlight and help propel the *Caps* up the WNBL ladder. When Lauren joined the *Caps* they were bottom of the competition. Teams which Lauren joins have a habit of starting on the bottom and finishing on top and in 1999–2000 the *Canberra Capitals* won the WNBL title – and Lauren Jackson was named WNBL MVP.

The year 2000 marked another milestone for Lauren and basketball; the Olympic Games were in Sydney. Not since 1956 had Australia hosted the Olympic Games and the nation was determined to show the world that Australians could put on "the best games yet".

Basketball was first contested at the Olympics by men in 1936 and by women in 1976. In the early years Australia's women's basketball teams struggled to reach Olympic standard and did not qualify for the 1976 Montreal or the 1980 Moscow games. The first breakthrough came in 1984 when the team not only qualified but finished in fifth place. Further success in Seoul in 1988 saw the Opals lift to finish fourth. The bubble burst when the team failed to qualify for the 1992 Barcelona games. The following years saw a huge resurgence in the sport, more funding, improved coaching, and the first AIS graduates were bolstering the quality ranks. The Opals took a huge leap and won the bronze medal in Atlanta in 1996. In 2000 the Opals were determined that on the home court they would aspire for better than bronze. Of the 1996 bronze medal team eight returned in 2000. [10]

In 1994 a 12-year-old Lauren had written:

> It has always been an athlete's dream to be in the Olympics and now it is mine. The year 2000 Olympics is six years away and I have six years to show everyone what I am made of, not a bag of wuss like everyone calls me.[11]

The dream came true in 2000 but like so many dreams the reality was not as glorious. There was enormous pressure brought to bear on Lauren by the Australian media. Before every Olympics the media waxes lyrical on how many gold medals Australia is going to win, on how individual athletes will raise the nation single-handedly to greatness. The media says it reflects society, what Australians feel, but more commonly than not this is a misconception. In 2000 the media exceeded even its own usual hype. It was hard for an unworldly teenager to discern fact from fiction, hype from commonsense. Lauren felt the pressure. Prior to the Olympics she played poorly and her confidence took a bump.

There are athletes who thrive in big time events, who appear to step out of themselves to another level. During the 2000 Sydney Games Lauren was the key to the Australian offence and defence, averaging 15.9 points and 8.4 rebounds. The *Opals* fought with great spirit and courage and for the first time in Olympic history they made it to the final. The bad part was that they now had to play the United States. Riding on tremendous crowd support there were times when it looked possible that this group of never-say-die women would conquer the colossus of women's basketball, but it wasn't to be. The silver medal was an incredible result and the massive crowd rose to applaud almost as one. The 19-year-old made 20 points and brought down 13 rebounds that final. One publication in singing her praises believed "she will be the target of American professional clubs in the near future". Assistant Australian Coach Carrie Graf believed:

> That gold medal game was a defining moment … She kicked the American team's butt and showed the world how good she was. That's when I realised, "Oh, this kid can dominate the world."[12]

Australian Head Coach Tom Maher referred to Lauren as:

> A once-in-a-lifetime player … I've never seen anyone like her, for her age, for what she can do … never seen anyone in Australia or overseas, not close.[13]

For Lauren, the Olympics had gone past in pretty much a blur.

The next step, to the United States' Women's National Basketball Association (WNBA), was big, huge. Maree encouraged her somewhat reluctant daughter to make the leap. "After the Olympics I was so set on not playing in the WNBA," but Lauren realised deep down her mum was right and she needed the WNBA for her development as a player. The rationale was fine, but for the young Australian putting the theory into practice was fairly terrifying – the USA was a long way from Albury. Lauren threw her name in the hat and was named 2001 WNBA No.1 draft choice – an extraordinary achievement for a foreign player. The fair-minded WNBA system allows the lowest ranked team first choice of player so Lauren was picked up by the *Seattle Storm*. In 2000 the *Storm* finished its first WNBA season with six wins and 26 losses. It was a very young franchise desperately trying to make its way in the rough and tumble world of big-time basketball and the girl from the land down under was desperately trying to do the same. It was a perfect union and would prove an enduring and wonderful partnership.

Seattle is a picturesque city tenaciously clinging to the misty hillsides of Washington State overlooking a picturesque harbour dotted with islands. On a clear day the skyline is dominated by the towering Mt Rainer, making the city feel small as cities go, not too overpowering for girl from country Australia. Washington State was just across the Pacific from Australia so the tyranny of distance was nowhere near as bad as it could have been had the team been in New York or another east coast franchise. This was all good but that first year was still really challenging. "I hated it, I didn't feel comfortable, socially I needed to step out of myself and make friends."[14] This was hard for a shy teenager in a foreign country; Lauren was homesick and it felt alien surrounded by Americans in a strange land. These people didn't even drive on the same side of the road.

Ill at ease in social situations Lauren only ever felt comfortable when her alter ego was in charge, the take-no-prisoners tough character who emerged whenever she stepped onto the basketball court. But this character too was being severely tested. Used to dominating on Australian courts she needed to prove herself all over again and in the best competition in the world. The WNBA was a full-on, tough, physical contest, which constantly tested her determination. But as the saying goes "when the going gets tough, the tough get going" and Lauren Jackson was no quitter. She steadfastly stuck with the resolve that she could and would get better, that basketball was her destiny – it was still her passion. Battling among America's best the body took a beating, that's how it is for tall post players and Lauren was thin, underweight and the muscles had yet to catch up with the bones and joints. She missed a couple of games because of an injured shoulder and was concussed during another. She still finished the season with an average of 15.2 points per game and 6.7 rebounds; was the top *Storm* player in scoring, blocked shots, steals and rebounds; was named reserve with the Western Conference WNBA All Star game; and was runner up in the WNBA Rookie of the Year. By the end of the 2001 season the *Storm* had 10 wins and 22 losses and both the team and the Australian had earned some hard-fought respect.

It was a habit, one ultimately hard to break, to come home in the WNBA off season to play the WNBL Australian season and it was good to return to the relaxed familiar lifestyle of Canberra, to the company of mates who played with the *Canberra Capitals*. Her constant reply to questions about her success is: "I owe so much to great coaches and great teammates". *Caps* coach Carrie Graf was, according to Lauren, also "passionate about basketball" and for the next several years Graf was instrumental in Lauren's development.

> There's only one pace for Graffster, she just goes which is awesome, it's just great … she leads people and she's a great communicator … we've got a really good friendship and I've grown up playing under her … as a coach I can learn from her.[15]

The admiration is mutual particularly when it comes to loyalty. Graf believes Lauren is so "loyal to her country" and "to her friends". Graf had also been Assistant Australian Coach of the medal winning

Olympic teams in 1996 and 2000 and she, Lauren and the "great teammates" excelled when the *Capitals* beat the *Sydney Panthers* in the 2001 - 02 WNBL grand final. Lauren averaged 24 points and 11.8 rebounds for Canberra during the season. The following season the Sydney team changed its name to the *Sydney Flames*. It made no difference and the *Caps* beat them in the grand final to become the 2002–03 WNBL Champions. Along the way the individual records tumbled as fast as awards were handed out to No.15.

2002 was a big year, yet another big year, because Lauren was again called on to represent her country, first in a series against Japan and later in another FIBA World Championship. *The Opals* made it "three-zip" against Japan in Tokyo on the first Sunday of May, crushing the opposition 113–63. The Japanese were ranked in the world's top 12 but they were no match for the height and talent of the Australians. Lauren was in magnificent form in the final game, scoring 31 points and bringing down ten rebounds. It was then onto yet another plane, to Seattle for the commencement of the WNBA season.

In 2002 the *Seattle Storm* was again permitted the No.1 WNBA draft choice and selected a two-time All American guard out of Connecticut named Sue Bird. There was also a new Assistant Coach who spoke perfect Australian, Carrie Graf. It soon became clear that the *Storm* would lose early preference in the next year's WNBA draft because the team finished the season with seventeen wins and fifteen losses and made the Western Conference playoffs. Although then beaten by the *Los Angeles Sparks* it was a huge step up for the *Storm*. Awkward to begin with it soon became apparent that the playing partnership between Sue Bird and Lauren was something special, and the crowds in the home court, *KeyArena*, increased. The two would soon become "best mates" off the court:

Sue is just an awesome person, really genuine, really down to earth. She is a very cool girl whom I am glad to know.

Lauren registered a *Storm* franchise record with eight blocks in a game against the *Utah Starzz* and finished the season fourth in WNBA scoring.[16] Both Lauren and Sue were named in the Western Conference All Star team. For Lauren it was good to have another "star" in the Storm; it is tiring shouldering huge expectations alone, particularly when you demand nothing less from yourself.

Lauren's introduction to top international competition had been at the tender age of 17 in the 1998 FIBA World Championships held in Germany. By 2002 she had played around her native country, all over the US, in Japan, and now between 14 and 25 September she found herself playing in China, again as a member of an Australian FIBA World Championship team.[17] Australia was in Group A.[18] The final was contested between the United States and Russia with the US winning a close tussle 79–74. The battle for the bronze was not a close game and Australia beat Korea 91–63. *Opals* players were not happy; they knew they should have been playing off for the gold and silver. Next World Championships would be different. There were a few things to work on over the next two years before the Athens Olympics and the two years after that before the next "Worlds" in Brazil – weaknesses to overcome and a little communication breakdown to rectify. It was only part of the fabric which bound the *Opals* together but Lauren and the Australian coach Jan Stirling needed to understand and value each other better.

When Lauren was welcomed into the Australian senior team she was a youngster walking with the giants of her world. Head Coach was Tom Maher and his wife Robyn was one of the toughest and most committed players ever to pull on the Australian uniform. Lauren thrived under their auspices. Jan Stirling had replaced Tom Maher in

2001 and her methods were different. It was a struggle of wills. Two strong women passionate about basketball and a little wary of each other, one a coach trying to replace a dynasty and the other a player who preferred things the way they had been. Jan realised very well that "Lauren had incredible athletic talents" but more was needed. The new Head Coach brought a physiologist into the Opals structure and placed a lot more expectation on players being developed in their strength and conditioning levels:

> Lauren in the early stages was a bit blasé about that component in accepting the fact that internationally she takes a pounding and to be physically stronger was going to secure her longevity. That message probably wasn't well received by her from me in the early stages.[19]

Jan could see Lauren "struggled personally with me, she had issues with certain aspects of my coaching style as did other athletes". It made the first years as *Opals* Head Coach a huge learning curve. The landscape had changed – the relationship between elite coach and elite player was now more democratic than autocratic. Jan Stirling was not too proud to learn from Lauren that:

> Different people take criticism in different ways. I learnt how to communicate differently, to lean towards positive criticism rather than negative criticism.

Lauren needed to understand that as a coach Jan had to make decisions which best suited the widest perspective; so too the *Opals* captain. Over the ensuing years Jan Stirling watched Lauren mature in that role.

Her exceptional capacity is she genuinely loves the uniform she wears. Despite the pedestal she is on, she cares about her teammates and she wants her teammates to do well. Her approach to leadership is she wants to be a good leader. She is learning that as a leader there are times when she can't be everyone's best friend; that sometimes she has to deliver a hard tap on the shoulder and say "hey that's not what we agreed". She is learning to deliver the message to someone who is not living the *Opals* way. She is entitled to tell people that. Lauren's blossoming as a young woman has been exceptional and it has made her a better player.

When it comes to "white line fever" the Australian coach believed she could make millions if only she "could bottle what Lauren has – few athletes have what she has".

In 2003 it was a much different Lauren Jackson who arrived for the beginning of another WNBA season. *Seattle Storm* team photos from 2002 and 2003 clearly reflect the transformation. There was the new look, bleached blond hair, brighter lipstick, more weight, more muscle, more fitness, but days away from her 22nd birthday there was also an air of greater confidence and determination.

My first two years were really tough, I struggled to get through them and wasn't sure I was going to come back. I'm glad I did.[20]

It may have helped that two new *Storm* players were Australian. Sandy Brondello had represented Australia in the 1988, 1996 and 2000 Olympics and was someone Lauren admired as a person and an athlete. The other was guard Tully Bevilaqua a ferocious defender who would play quite a role in Lauren's basketball future.

It always helped to have other Aussies around so nothing was lost in translation; there was no need for patient explanation of throwaway colloquialisms. There were teammates who knew you ate *Vegemite* and *Violet Crumbles* and listened to the Whitlams.

Under the tutelage of new *Storm* Head Coach Anne Donovan Lauren moved to another level. "Anne's been the best coach for me that I could possibly ever dream of" Lauren said at the time. "She makes me work harder than anyone, yet she's a player's coach." And the Jackson-Bird court combination shifted up yet another gear, rapidly entering the "poetry in motion" hallmark. As the season moved from spring through summer to fall, Lauren's name was seldom out of WNBA discussion and those who believed they had seen it all revised this belief. Television announcers became more and more challenged to retain perspective as they attempted to describe what unfolded before their eyes. In one game Lauren scrambled for a ball and from her knees made the basket, with the announcer shouting, "Are you kidding me, that's ridiculous". A later game elicited a similar reaction:

> Are you flippin' kidding me, LJ is just playing a game that no one else has ever done this league has never seen anything like her.

As teams tried to contain her over the years, with double teams, triple teams, box and one, announcers found themselves feeling sorry for the non-*Storm* team because Lauren was:

> pretty damn good … she's opened her bag of tricks … She's got a repertoire of all kinds … you name it, Lauren Jackson can do it.

As LJ demonstrated the repertoire the announcer suggested "it doesn't matter who guards her" instead of three on one perhaps the whole team should guard Lauren, perhaps some of their fans should come on the court to help – better still "call the fire department".

Nothing contained LJ in 2003. On 7 June she became the youngest player in WNBA history to reach 1000 points. On 31 July during a game against the *Charlotte Sting* she recorded the fifth 20-20 game in WNBA history. On 6 August it was a *Storm* record with 34 points and a WNBA record of 17 field goals during a game against Los Angeles. Lauren finished the season as the *Storm*'s all-time leading scorer and rebounder. More importantly she finished first in WNBA scoring, third in WNBA blocks and fourth in WNBA rebounds.[21] Lauren Jackson was named WNBA Most Valuable Player (MVP), easily the youngest and the first non-American player to be given the award.

Being named MVP in 2003 was great. Lauren had been touched by the faith shown in her at KeyArena when fans started wearing T-shirts with the inscription "LJ for MVP". After the first home game that she heard them chant her name and MVP in the same sentence she ran into the locker room and burst into tears. "I never expected them to do that for me. They were so supportive – and all the signs and everything"; for Lauren this belief in her "was awesome". She gave MVP no further thought when the Storm failed to make the playoffs. Lauren was with her mum in Australia when the official phone call came. Maree started crying and Lauren was "so overwhelmed by her being so proud of me I got pretty upset".

Through the tears the two women were sharing a very special occasion. They are very much alike these two. Gary goes so far as to suggest mother and daughter are "the spitting image of each other".[22] They have the same sense of humour, same strength of focus, same emotional intensity. Occasionally the intensity flares into a toe-to-toe "discussion". The Jackson men, Gary and Ross, have learnt over the years when it is best to quietly withdraw. To interfere in the "discussion" results in their becoming the victims because the two Jackson women then support each other to the end. Heaven help anyone who verbally messes with "my daughter" or "my mother". It was wonderful to be able to immediately share the WNBA MVP news with Maree because Lauren freely admitted "she's been such a huge influence on my career". They then ran to tell Gary.

Like Mother like Daughter
Photographs by Kathryn Spurling

At the award ceremony Lauren admitted she was very proud to be the recipient.

> It doesn't happen to very many people, and the people it
> has have been a very prestigious group of players: Sheryl
> Swoopes, Lisa Leslie, Cynthia Cooper, Yolanda Griffith.
> It means a lot to me. It does. This is the best thing that any
> female basketball player could want in her career.

But Lauren was not entirely comfortable, that trouble with the personal spotlight thing again. Lauren wanted to help hold the WNBA championship trophy aloft, preferably in KeyArena; she figured that would feel amazing. The press were intrigued by her attitude. This MVP was humble and her cheeks hinted colour with the fuss. They referred to "her laid-back, Australian surfer attitude" and admired her "focus on the team". The following year the media would not be as generous with their praise. Lauren returned to her homeland to play with the *Canberra Capitals* during the WNBL season over the Australian summer months. As the US and Australia are at opposite ends of the earth and the Australian summer is the US winter and vice versa means Lauren can play professional basketball all year round and that is how she likes it.

> Playing basketball night in and night out, and loving it.
> I love it. Not everybody has the opportunity to do this. I
> love it. I'm just in such a lucky situation.

Sometimes she has to remind herself this is work, until she succumbs to the fatigue.

In the 2003–04 WNBL season Lauren scored 391 points, an average of 27.9.[23] She finished top of the league in points, points per game, rebounds, defensive and offensive rebounds per game, in blocks, blocks per game, in efficiency ranking, in field goals made, in free throws made, and in field goal percentage. Yet again she was WNBL MVP and again named in the WNBL All Star team. Lauren had pretty much destroyed the *Canberra Capitals* record book. They were running out of awards to give her so Lauren was presented with the keys to the Australian capital city. She was disappointed that the Caps did not win the WNBL Championship.

Lauren had been fielding offers from other parts of the world for some time but there never seemed enough time or inclination. Now she decided to play for a month with *UMMC-Ekaterinburg* in the Russian league title series before the beginning of the WNBA season.

It was not an entirely satisfying experience. Lauren was used sparingly and sometimes "subbed off" at odd times. In one important game Lauren was not sent in until the second half. She promptly scored 16 and with 40 seconds to go she was "subbed off". *Ekaterinburg* lost by one point. Not surprisingly the club was bundled out of the final series. Next stop Seattle.

The *Storm* was well into their training camp when a jet-lagged Lauren walked into the gym at the end of April 2004. According to Coach Anne Donovan the mood changed when the Australian appeared.

> Everybody couldn't wait for the drill to stop to come over and see her. There's just a calming presence for everybody to know that help is here.[24]

Some coaches may have been a little annoyed at a disruption to routine but Donovan believed Lauren's presence was entirely positive:

> There are no words for Lauren Jackson, her passion for this game. She is the MVP of this league ... Tremendous skill level, but it's what drives her that sets her apart ... It's a coach's dream to have somebody like that. It's contagious for other players. When you've got your superstar that wants to be on the floor, wants to go through drills when I'm telling her she doesn't have to practise until she feels like it that sends a message to everybody else: "It's a passion for her and it better be a passion for me".[25]

The *Storm* had finished the WNBA 2003 season in fifth place in the Western Conference with 18 wins and 16 losses – yet another franchise record. With the previous season's MVP in their starting five local interest gathered momentum with the start of the 2004 season in

May. One newspaper article stated the 23-year-old Lauren "displays enough grit, talent and grace to be called the world's best female basketball player. Maybe even the best ever".[26] The comparisons had started as soon as the photos of Lauren standing with the MVP trophy were processed. Was she as good as this player or that player? She was even described as the "female Michael Jordan". As if the clock stands still long enough for any two players to be accurately compared, as if it really matters, as if greatness should not simply be accepted and admired for what it is. Lauren was uncomfortable with such comparisons; she still didn't think she was "good".

Anne Donovan wanted very much for her gifted team to win the championship and realised much depended on LJ who she believed "keeps getting better; her desire gets greater and greater". Donovan could have said "I told you so" when Lauren scored 29 points in 26 minutes in the *Storm*'s pre-season finale and 31 points during the season opener against the *Minnesota Lynx*. Double teams against LJ became a regular feature. Only San Antonio tried a one-on-one in their first 2004 game against Lauren and she scored 27 points in that match-up so the *Silver Stars* didn't try that again. On 3 July 2004 she caused despair for the *Sacramento Monarchs* by scoring a *Storm* record of 23 points in the first half and finished with 32 and 12 rebounds. In the rematch in Sacramento on 15 July in front of a crowd of 11,275 Lauren scored the points needed to push her past 2000 for her WNBA career and become the youngest player to reach that milestone, and the second fastest. On 14 July Lauren received the ESPY Award (Excellence in Sports Performance Yearly Award presented by the American cable television network ESPN) award for "Best WNBA Player of 2004".[27] On 17 July Lauren scored a season-high 33.[28] It was a thrilling game against *Washington Mystics* which went to overtime. LJ blocked a Chamique Holdsclaw jumper, and Sue Bird ran off with the loose ball for the game-winning lay-up. It was moments like those which are remembered, plays like that which make all the training and practice worthwhile. The KeyArena crowd were on their feet for much of that game and didn't seem to want to go home after. The people recording game statistics were beginning to get writer's cramp thanks to Lauren.[29] With the Bird-Jackson duo bringing magic to the "Key" and inspiring greater things from the rest of the team the *Storm* was going from strength to strength, until they were forced to take a month-long break. This was an Olympic year and the very best players were required to join their national teams in Athens in 2004. Before Lauren could link up with the Opals she faced her first real controversy and she never saw it coming.

It had been an Australian tradition since 1996. *Black+White* magazine published a special Olympic edition featuring 35 of the nation's male and female Olympians in black and white artistic poses. While the chosen athletes posed nude it was done as a tasteful tribute. Lauren was asked to pose for the 2000 edition but decided she was too young. In 2004 she was asked again. After discussing it with her parents she agreed. Lauren was chosen for the front cover as well as six poses within the magazine pages. Athletes received no fees but had input as to which photos were included in "The Athens Dream". Overall it was a celebration that these beautiful athletic bodies were made in Australia and the nation was justifiably proud of them.

Unfortunately the tribute thing got lost in translation in the journey across the pond to a different culture. There was indignation, real or imagined and the Seattle headline read: "Nude photos of Jackson may stir up a storm of controversy". The play on words was clever but the headline stirred up the vociferous righteous who wished to impose their morality on the less conservative. Media space was given to too many of the close minded:

> Jackson's decision to pose nude is decisive for our family … and Jackson has spoiled our reason to support the *Storm*.[30]

It quickly became ridiculous when across the US even the *Washington Post* referred to "The Athens Dream" *Black+White* tribute in the same sentence as *Playboy*.[31]

Newspaper journalists previously hard pressed to explain what the initials "WNBA" stood for decided this was salacious stuff and blew it entirely out of context. One Philadelphia newspaper columnist reported: "Some believe Jackson posing nude hurts the credibility of the WNBA and female athletes in general". [32] The more officious members of the WNBA hierarchy believed "Lauren is WNBA property" and this photo shoot could only bring disrepute on the league. Lauren was not going to apologise to anyone because she believed:

> We work so hard, as athletes, on making our bodies look great and to be in the best shape that we can be. I feel really comfortable with my body and shape that I am in. I was really nervous at first, but it was conquering one of my fears. This celebrates the athletic body and how much work you put in.[33]

The printed media was having a field day; the controversy sold newspapers and that was their credo. *Black+White* magazine weren't complaining because all the free publicity generated amazing sales and the edition sold out in record time. The photos began to appear on web pages everywhere. One of the most absurd or comical depending on point of view ensured *Storm* bandaids were plastered across nipples. And so the debate raged, Americans arguing in the media, for and against. One of the more resounding messages of support appeared in the *Seattle Times*.

> Being a founding fan of the Storm and an older feminist hopefully gives me the right to comment about Lauren

Jackson's photo. I love it! Good for her! She is beautiful, she is talented, she is smart, but mostly, it's her choice. There is nothing degrading about the way she looks, definitely nothing to be ashamed of. It is an artistic photo which shows that outstanding, athletic women can also be sexy and very attractive. Thanks, Lauren, for it is a celebration that women have come a long way, baby.[34]

Lauren got trampled in the stampede. In her last game before the Olympic break she scored her lowest points of the season – just 14 – and the *Storm* lost at Houston. The Australian, like the majority of her countrymen and women, couldn't fathom the fuss:

I didn't think it would be that big of a deal. I was kind of shocked, actually. I guess I was naive in thinking that people would react differently. I should have been prepared for this, but I wasn't.[35]

It was nice to be able to remove herself from the mess and concentrate on what was really important – playing basketball in the Olympics. Lauren was never happier than when playing in the green and gold: "It's the best thing in the world. I'm Australian through and through". Perhaps if pinned down she would admit she could definitely lose the Australian bodysuit in preference to standard WNBA-style garb. The clinging bodysuit caused a media frenzy at the 1996 Atlanta Olympics and the style had been used in WNBL competition since. It cut in in all the wrong places, particularly if you were tall. But for now Lauren's focus was on playing as well as she could for Australia in the Athens Olympics. Four years earlier the Olympics had rushed past in a bit of a blur. This time there was going to be a true appreciation of the amazing occasion, this time she would savour every day.

Athens was post "9/11" and the world was a different place. Athens lacked the easy friendly atmosphere of Sydney. Maree and Gary made the trip to Greece and that was comforting. It was always good to have her parents watching from the stands and these days with so much time spent playing overseas such opportunities did not occur as often as Lauren would have liked. This Olympics Lauren was wearing the No.15, her mum's old number. Australia was in the tougher of two groups. They would need to beat Brazil, Japan, Nigeria and Russia, and host nation automatic qualifier Greece, in front of their fanatical supporters on 20 August. The *Opals* cruised into the medal rounds. They were in very good form and effortlessly trounced New Zealand in their quarter-final.[36] Next foe was Brazil. The *Opals* had already beaten the South Americans 84–66 in a preliminary round but Lauren knew the next clash would be a harder fought contest. "We're just going to go out there and give it our all and leave with no regrets." She and her teammates were quietly confident that the *Opals* would be in the Olympic final and whoever they met next was going to have a fight on their hands for the gold.

On the other side of the draw Russia and the United States progressed and would yet again face off in the other semi-final. Lauren was right about the match-up with Brazil. It was a bruising physical encounter – an unrelenting grind – before they looked up and saw the final score was 88–75 in their favour. Again Lauren was top scorer with 26 points. The *Opals* were in another Olympic final, and yet again their opposition would be the United States.[37]

The US women's team was truly impressive, one could only shake one's head and say "Wow!"[38] Not so the less famous Australians; but they were not about to be intimidated by anyone. Lauren was the first Australian to score and thanks to some great defence the USA led by only three at halftime. Penny Taylor inspired her teammates by opening the scoring in the third to tie up the score. Suzy Batkovic was having an outstanding game, forced a turnover and followed up with a tough basket over Lisa Leslie to give the Aussies their first lead of the game. Lauren and Leslie were hammering each other under the basket. No one would expect the best two players in the world to do less. Penny Taylor went on a run and Australia had a lead of four until Dawn Staley stole the lead back. Penny had the hot hands with 12 in the period but needed to be "subbed off" after her fourth foul. At three-quarter time the deficit was still only two: US 52, Australia 50.

The US women's "dream team" knew they were in a real fight. The USA's population was 293 million Australia's was just 19 million. How on earth had the "land down under" produced 12 such athletes? *Opals* point guard Kristi Harrower ensured her team remained focused. The US team needed to dig deeper but right through their bench the team was extraordinary, their skill level the best. Lauren had led the Olympic tournament in scoring coming into this game. These were WNBA professionals over whose teams Lauren had dominated. Dominating the best of the best was more difficult and they had practised hard to shut Lauren down. Lauren was hounded and would finish this game with 12 points. What they didn't know was that Lauren was ill; she was also injured and playing in pain. But she would never use that as an excuse. She continued to rebound like someone possessed and brought down 14 boards. By the fourth quarter the Australians were running on fumes. The Americans continued to retain their focus. The Australian containment "D" (defence) was pushing the Americans to shoot from the outside but they did. The US bench was such a factor and battered the *Opals* into submission. The final score was USA 74, Australia 63.

When that final buzzer went, for the Australians the initial emotional response was of loss and failure. And then the next reaction kicked in: "Bugger! We have won the silver medal". In the inevitable game autopsy Tina Thompson graciously congratulated the Australians on their effort:

Australia is an exceptional team … they have a lot of
great players. We knew it was going to be a very tough
game and it was. This was not a team to be overlooked.

Australian Coach, Jan Stirling simply said of her players:

The way these ladies conducted themselves on and off
the court, and the way they respect the game, makes them
all players that people all over the world look up to and
admire.

Of Lauren:

Her passion and desire to win with her fearless physical
combat is something special … There are very few
players who can bring to the table what she brings. Each
season, she creates a new piece of history for herself. So,
it's an open book at the moment.[39]

The final had been a truly legitimate contest. The *Opals* were getting
closer to their sport's female "dream team". The future and their
prospects for the 2006 World Championships and Beijing 2008
Olympics were looking extremely bright.

It is always hard to return to playing basketball following
something as big as the Olympics as the adrenalin rush that comes
with playing for your country is hard to describe. The intensive play
of the ten-day period totally depletes emotional and physical energy
but Lauren was back in Seattle with the *Storm* hell-bent on winning
the 2004 WNBA Championship. Heading into the August Olympic
break Seattle was second in the WNBA.[40] Then Lauren received
news that her grandmother Irene was very ill and did not hesitate to
board a plane for home. In her absence the *Storm* lost three games.

The loyalty thing is never easy. When Lauren returned to Seattle the *Storm* losing streak was snapped with an 86–67 defeat of Detroit. These were heady days. Next aim was to achieve a home-court advantage and this Seattle did.[41] Lauren Jackson finished the season as top WNBA scorer with a 20.5 point average.

On the eve of the playoffs Lauren received word that her grandmother had died. She could not return home. During the series against the *Minnesota Lynx, Storm* players agreed they would each wear a strip of black electrical tape on an upper arm to show solidarity with their Australian teammate. Lauren had trouble with focus in game one; her thoughts were elsewhere. She got into foul trouble early and was benched. In the last two quarters Lauren scored 12 and her team won 70–58. The next encounter was no less physical and Sue Bird had her nose broken. The small Australian, Tully Bevilaqua, came off the bench and provided some classic clutch play.[42] Lauren's focus was a little better next game and she top scored with 18 points as the *Storm* swept the series.[43]

Against the *Sacramento Monarchs* Lauren was sensational. In game one she appeared to see only net and scored 31 points including four three-pointers and brought down 13 rebounds. Unfortunately the *Monarchs* won on the final buzzer. Game two was at KeyArena and this game had to be won. The *Storm* dominated 66–54.[44] Seattle started game three as favourites but the *Monarchs* took a while to accept that concept. Despite surgery on her broken nose the day before Sue Bird played. Resplendent in a protective Perspex mask she set a WNBA playoffs record with 14 assists. Midway through the second half the *Storm* hit a purple patch going on a 20 to nil run and won 82–62. Lauren shot 27 and set a WNBA playoffs record with five three-pointers in one half. The *Storm* advanced to the WNBA finals for the first time.

When your love of the game is so great, when your loyalty to your country, club and teammates is so strong, you can lose sense and sensibility. You can fail to take proper care of yourself. Lauren had badly injured her right ankle during the Olympics but refused to submit to pain or admit she was hurting. Fellow *Opal* Suzy Batkovic refers to Lauren as "the toughest little cookie I know".[45] When your club makes the WNBA playoffs and then the WNBA finals you play, you just keep playing. Sue Bird and Lauren were awarded WNBA First Team honours. During the regular season Lauren scored double figures in all 31 games she played, extending this streak to 84 consecutive games – the second longest in WNBA history.[46]

From the first whistle of the WNBA final series it was clear the *Connecticut Sun* intended to aggressively stop Lauren and the first game was very physical. The *Sun* won 68–64. The next two games were at KeyArena. A sell-out crowd of 17,072 filled the "Key" to overflowing on 10 October. It is an extraordinary feeling playing in front of so many fans at home. It was close with the heart-stopping final score of 67–65 favouring the *Storm*. The rest of Seattle heard the KeyArena crowd that night or should have. Two nights later it was another sell-out crowd. Connecticut had no answer to the might of the *Storm* and to the deafening noise in KeyArena. The fans counted down the final seconds before pandemonium broke out because Seattle had won 74–60. The rest of Seattle definitely heard that.

The party began and the party was wild. Lauren finally got to help hold up the WNBA trophy not just that night but for many days after. The *Storm* had existed just five seasons and was now the fourth WNBA team to win the championship. This was the first Seattle professional sports title in 25 years and the city celebrated. On a typically cloudy Friday afternoon thousands of fans packed the Westlake Centre to cheer the players, and to hear the Governor of Washington State, Gary Locke, proclaim *Storm Week* throughout the state.

When the celebrations finally ended Lauren had no option but to admit she was hurt, really hurt, if that is what you say about a right ankle that wobbles free, seemingly only just attached between the leg and the foot. She flew back to Australia to seek medical treatment. It was no simple injury but one which required immediate reconstruction, arthroscope and posterior clearance. Lauren was told she would not be playing basketball for some months but needed to be philosophical about the surgery in the context of longevity:

> Given the level I play at and with basketball being such
> a high energy sport, injuries are an unfortunate aspect of
> my craft.

Lauren's surgery was performed at Sydney's St. Vincent's Private Hospital, by pre-eminent orthopaedic foot and ankle surgeon, Dr Martin Sullivan. There was extensive cartilage and ligament damage. Lauren had been playing for months in pain not only from the ankle but also with painful shin splints and back pain. Over the preceding months the muscle bulk in her right leg had reduced. Medical staff couldn't figure out how she had continued to play at all let alone at the highest level in her sport. The surgery was announced "successful" and after the healing process the rehabilitation would begin. 2004 had been the most emotionally and physically taxing year of Lauren's life. She had been playing non-stop basketball for nine years, since the beginning of 1996. Lauren needed time to recharge her batteries but first she needed to add the word "patience" to her vocabulary. Those who knew her best weren't entirely sure if she could. Her parents were there for her as always. Gary recalls the first 24 hours Lauren was out of hospital. In the morning Gary and Maree were woken by their mobile phone. It was Lauren in the bedroom down the hall. She wanted to give them her breakfast order. Gary was inclined to stay in bed but Maree went off to the kitchen. That's what mums did especially when their daughter was immobile. Gary knew better than to intervene in Jackson mother daughter business. Perhaps it would take a little longer before his daughter learned the word "patience".

Rehabilitation seemed to take forever, but didn't, and Lauren returned to Seattle for the start of the 2005 WNBA season. She was rejuvenated. The injury "hit me at the right time" because she now would no longer "take basketball for granted". Her passion was rekindled. There were huge expectations given the *Storm* was the reigning WNBA championship team. Players needed to work with the hype that came with the trophy. Lauren's philosophy was to go out and play "good ball" and have "fun no matter what outside forces there may be. So, I just focus on what I have to do". Also distracting were team changes. Tully Bevilaqua was playing elsewhere; so too five others. Personnel changes were always disruptive, it took a while to accept loss and to accept new faces. One new face pleased Lauren a lot – her great friend and fellow *Opal* Suzy Batkovic. Suzy and Lauren had grown up playing NSW basketball. They were members of the AIS class of 1998–99. They saw each other as "sisters" so this WNBA season promised to be a lot of fun. Of course like all sisters there "were days when they can get cranky at each other but the love is always there" says Suzy; "She is a really big hearted person, I have a lot of time for her"[47].

It would be great to just play basketball but you can't, the playing is only about 10 per cent. There is the grind of training, fitness regimes, community work, public appearances and media. The MVP title and a championship meant increased visibility. The public is demanding of their "sheroes", everyone seems to want a piece of you and some can get a little close. Sometimes it would be nice to disappear in the crowd but a floppy hat and dark sunglasses don't do it when you are 198cm. You learn to turn in on yourself a little more to become a little more guarded. Of her great friend Lauren Suzy Batkovic says:

> She is so tough, she can be going through an emotionally
> rocky period but you can't tell. Unless you were one of
> her closest friends and she discusses it with you no one

would know, the people watching from the sidelines wouldn't even know.[48]

2004 had been an emotional roller coaster and Lauren had faced derision following her appearance in *Black+White*. She was not about to give detractors the last word. During July 2005 she featured in the *Sports Illustrated Swimsuit Edition*. She then got down to the business of playing basketball as well as she could, though the next couple of seasons were marred by injury. She then started to put on weight which seemed to compound the injuries, a "catch 22" situation.

> When I was 18, 19, 20, I had the fastest metabolism. Then I hit 21 it was like plop. All that bad stuff went straight to the hips and my shoulders.

Yes, there were a few things going on in 2005, but Lauren was all business on the court. Suzy calls her "a machine, an absolute machine" and doesn't mean this in a cold robot way. There is plenty of emotion, plenty of fire in the belly, but Lauren "can shoot 30 and it is just another day in the office".[49] During the 2005 WNBA season Lauren scored 597 in 34 games and brought down 313 rebounds but the *Storm* failed to make the finals. Sue Bird and Lauren were again named in the All-WNBA First Team. And yes the WNBA season was more fun when "Loz" could hang out with Suzy Batkovic even if sometimes their behaviour regressed somewhat and involved dares and weird outfits. Heck, there just is not enough fun in the world.

In October 2005 Lauren returned to play in the 24 game WNBL season with the *Canberra Capitals*. For yet another season she was playing with old friends: Tully Bevilaqua, Kellie Abrams, Tracey Beatty, Jenny Whittle, Nat Hurst and *Caps* captain Eleanor Sharp, who was retiring at the end of the 2005–06 season. Her team intended to send "Sharpie" out in style and win the championship. Carrie Graf, coach and friend, was still as motivating as ever but before the *Caps* could take control of the competition Lauren was diagnosed with a stress fracture in her left leg. There is a lot of adjustment to be made when you are missing a quality player like Lauren. The *Caps* needed to regroup and they did and then Lauren's recuperative abilities ensured that the *Caps* had her back for the business end of the season.

On 4 February 2006 in the elimination final the *Canberra Capitals* fought back from a 12 point deficit to win 67–62. Lauren led the way with 29 points and 13 rebounds in 29 minutes. As usual she gave the credit to teammates.

> When it comes to utter determination and doing it for each other ... we're all such good mates as well which makes it even more special.

The record crowd who came to the "Palace" that night included not only the Canberra basketball stalwarts but others who had never before been to a *Caps* game. The word had got around that this would be the last chance to see Lauren play in the capital and they realised the opportunity was not to be missed. None went home disappointed.

Although she loved living and playing in Canberra Lauren knew it was time to consider other international offers. Lauren's serious basketball career had started in Canberra. She was named "ACT Sports star of the Year" three times and "ACT Female Sports star of the Year" four times. The Caps were named "ACT Team of the Year" four times. It was fitting that her WNBL career finish with the Canberra team. The Australian capital would miss her.

On 18 February 2006 the *Canberra Capitals* defeated the *Dandenong Rangers* 68–55 to win another WNBL Championship. Coach Carrie Graf had been limiting Lauren's time on the court to 20 minutes due to the pain caused by the stress fracture. This night, this grand final, Lauren leant forward to the coach and said "screw it

Graffy, play me for 40". She played in pain, was the game high scorer with 24 points and won another WNBL MVP award.

Queen Elizabeth II opened the Commonwealth Games in Melbourne on 15 march 2006. Some 4500 athletes from 71 nations would contest 16 sports until the closing ceremony on 26 March. Basketball was included in the games for the first time, but would be dropped from future Commonwealth Games. In the women's competition FIBA ranked Australia as number three in the world, New Zealand was 19, Nigeria 22, Mozambique 37, India 41, with England, Malaysia and Malta unranked. The Australians were determined to win this Commonwealth gold. Lauren told reporters:

> I think it's something about being Australian. It's pretty special to me being the first women's basketball team there and winning the gold medal – well, I'd hope we'd win the gold medal … There is a Commonwealth Games tradition and I want to be part of it.

The *Opals* preliminary competition was a lopsided affair. They defeated India 146–46. Lauren played half the game and nearly matched the entire Indian score with 41 points. The next match against Mozambique was another blow-out with the Australians winning 106–26. Lauren played half the game and was the top scorer with 23. The game against England was a slightly closer affair but never in doubt with the *Opals* winning 95–43. Lauren was the top scorer on the court with 31. In the semi-final against Nigeria, Australia easily controlled play and won 105–49. Of the 23 players on the court that day Lauren was the top rebounder (eight) and top scorer (37). On 23 March 2006 England took the bronze medal over Nigeria in a tight contest. In front of a capacity crowd the Australians took the court against the New Zealand *Tall Ferns* in the gold medal game. The game was tougher and closer than the 77–39 score indicated and a credit to hard-working defensive efforts. Lauren brought down 11 rebounds, was top scorer with 23 and said: "This is so awesome. To play in front of this crowd is something I will never forget".

The shins were still causing problems but there was too much to do, too much basketball to play to worry about them. With a gold medal in her pocket Lauren checked her diary and it went something like this: guest appearance in home town, Albury, in the south-eastern league; the Opals World Challenge with games against the US, China and Taiwan in Cairns and Canberra in April; the usual WNBA season with the *Seattle Storm* from May to August; the FIBA World Championships in Brazil in September; and then a ten-week season in South Korea. No worries – that would be easy, just as long as the shins and the rest of the body, and the emotional levels, and the motivation, kept up.

Within days of winning a Commonwealth Games gold medal Lauren was playing basketball again. The venue wasn't huge although there was a capacity crowd of around 1000. Posters with her image and her motto: "Believe in yourself and your dreams" adorned the foyer of the Albury sports stadium. Lauren stood not in an Australian green and gold bodysuit but in the blue and burgundy uniform of the *Albury Lady Bandits*. Lauren continued to value her Albury roots and had promised she would play in Albury again. This was the first game in the south-eastern Australian Basketball League competition for the new team from Albury, a team managed by Gary Jackson. It seemed the perfect opportunity. The opposing team was the *Nunawading Spectres* and one can only imagine their reaction when they noticed Lauren's name on the *Bandits* players list. It was hard to determine whether the *Spectres* were more nervous at the prospect of trying to contain Lauren or the other *Lady Bandits* at the prospect of trying to keep up with her. The crowd cheered every time she touched the ball. The *Bandits* only won by a point; they clearly needed to keep

Lauren in their line-up. Pity she had other playing commitments in three continents. She simply said "thanks Albury for letting me play here".

In April 2006 Lauren signed another three-year contract with the *Seattle Storm*. Until the end of the 2008 season she would continue to spend a most important part of her year based in Washington State. Coach Donovan recalled that when she took over as *Storm* Head Coach at the beginning of 2003 the opposition belief about Lauren was:

> Get physical with her, she loses her temper. She likes to float out on the three-point line. She doesn't like to do the work down low and is an iffy three point shooter, dangerous but not deadly.[50]

The opposition stopped saying that pretty quickly in 2003 and Lauren won MVP. The opposition were still looking for a weakness in 2006, any weakness. Lauren joined an esteemed list on 7 June 2006. She stepped to the free throw line with 7.32 seconds left in the second quarter. She was as usual focussed on making the points to help Seattle beat Chicago. The first one went up and through and the crowd stood and applauded a little louder than normal. Then Lauren realised. She bent her knees, followed through and the next free throw dropped through the net. She had become only the 11th player in WNBA history to reach 3000 career points. She was the first player to enter the league after 1999 to score 3000 points, as well as the youngest and the fastest at 162 games. Her coach believed this was just another reflection of "how special Lauren is. She is one of the best if not the best player in the league". Over her 162 WNBA games, Lauren had averaged 18.6 points per game.[51]

On 13 June 2006 Lauren joined another even more prestigious list. As part of the WNBA ten-year celebrations the ten "best and most influential players", the "All Decade Team", was named. Lauren was included, as was that little American mate of hers, Sue Bird. There was a lot more net in 2006. Lauren finished first in the WNBA in efficiency (23.7), fifth in rebounding, third in blocks, fourth in scoring and fifth in double doubles. She made her fifth WNBA All Star appearance. Not bad for someone whose injuries restricted training and hampered some play. It had been a great season individually, particularly given the shins. Unfortunately the *Storm* did not win the championship.

Lauren could recall when she needed to be cajoled into leaving her country and joining the WNBA. Now she welcomed new opportunities; now she was "comfortable going into new things". Lauren accepted an offer from Korean team *Samsung Bichumi*. The South Korean Basketball League (WKBL) season ran from the middle of December to early March and teams only played two matches a week. Lauren was coming off a couple of injury marred years and in 2006 the FIBA Women's World Cup would be contested and Australia's prospects were golden. Korea felt like the right decision and it was.

It meant three months in a completely foreign culture but she relished the opportunity. "The Korean people were totally different but so friendly." No one on her team spoke English and Lauren thought that was "fantastic"; she had always felt comfortable in her own space. For Lauren it meant "I could just concentrate on playing basketball". She was provided with a four-bedroom apartment in Seoul ten seconds walk from the training court. Yes, the weather was a little chilly, but she preferred the cold and could totally concentrate on white line fever. Lauren adjusted to the "very different refereeing" and the "quicker style of play" run by the much shorter Koreans. After the first "few low blows" from opponents Lauren adapted to the offensive flow. One US report suggested "Lauren Jackson has found a new country to terrorize".[52] The Australian broke just about every WKBL record. In one game she scored 47 points. In another her team won 96–76 and she scored 56, shattering the Korean individual scoring mark. She was truly in the zone and averaged a WKBL record of 30.2 points per game. Lauren was the unanimous choice for MVP (Foreign Player) of the WKBL. Three continents, three MVPs down, how many to go?

On the world sports stage basketball is second only to soccer. No fewer than 213 nations registered for the 2006 FIBA Women's World Championships. After qualifying games around the world, this number was reduced to just 16. The best of the best met in Brazil between 12 and 23 September 2006 and everyone knew the team to beat was the United States. After that it got a little hazy with a number of teams good enough to surprise. Australian Head Coach Jan Stirling may just be a smidgen biased but she believed "the *Opals* are fantastic". Over the last dozen or more years the Australian national team had achieved "a wonderful reputation". In 2006 the *Opals* were seen as excellent and fair sportswomen. They were also seen as being tough as nails.

The first game for the Australians was to be against Lithuania on 12 September. The Lithuanians did not make it to Ibirapuera Arena in time for the tip-off due to a cancelled flight and the game was forfeited. The *Opals* were awarded two points but they would have preferred to play for it. Next stop in this global time capsule was Senegal on 13 September. The Africans were enthusiastic but their skills not in the same class and the Australians won 95–55. The *Opal*s then played Canada. Not surprisingly Lauren attracted a lot of attention early. This left the Canadians vulnerable to the fire power of other *Opals*. Lauren shrugged off the defence, scored 23 and pulled down nine rebounds. Australia won 97–65. The four best teams from each of the four groups moved to the next stage and this victory gave Australia a top seed position in the cross-over round. On 16 September Australia moved to the next level with a win against Spain 72–68.

Just 14 hours later the *Opals* had to roll out of comfortable slumber to do it all over again. By 0820 the players were on their bus and, with a police escort, made their way to the stadium. This time it was a contest against the host nation, a big ask. There were a few butterflies flapping but Erin Phillips broke the tension when she absent-mindedly put her body suit on back to front. She is superfast but not so superfast that you see her back before her front. The game was as competitive as anticipated. The very vocal Brazilian crowd screamed every time a Brazilian hand touched the ball, and booed every refereeing decision that favoured the Australians. The lead went back and forth but at half-time the *Opals* were up by seven. Tully Bevilaqua kept a diary blog for *Basketball Australia* and her comments on the game included:

> Lauren Jackson continues to be beaten up inside but just
> her presence on the court makes the defence have to focus
> on her and frees up other players.[53]

The crowd went home disgruntled because their national team lost 82–73. Next opponent was Argentina.

It doesn't matter where you are, whatever the country, whatever the place, you can get an upset stomach. It is inconvenient at any time but when you are trying to play basketball in the world's toughest competition it is a real pain. Kristi Harrower, the team's general, was struck down on the eve of the game and immediately quarantined from the rest of the team. Tully Bevilaqua's advice was "get stuck into that *Vegemite* mate". Guard Erin Phillips was thumped in the nose early in the game and sidelined. It was beginning to be a case of last woman standing so the Australians decided to finish the match quickly before any more of their number went missing. They won 83–49, Lauren bucketed 30.

On 20 September Australia faced off against France in the first semi-final. France struggled to contain the *Opals* offence. Lauren and Penny Taylor were the main destroyers and were then rested for a bigger game the following day. After every game Lauren strapped two enormous ice packs to her lower legs to help cope with those troublesome shins. She was attracting a lot of hard physical contact in "the paint" but was determined to keep going, just keep playing and yes, to give back no less than she received. She wanted that gold for her country; for her teammates and for herself – in that order:

> As long as we get the win I really don't care. At the end of the day it is all about winning and I'm very, very excited at the prospect of gold.

On 21 September Australia faced the unenviable task of playing an improving Brazil in the first semi-final. Again they were against determined players on their home court with a stadium full of emotional and parochial Brazilians. This game was the biggest game in the lives of the women in this *Opals* team. Penny Taylor was calm enough to hit the first seven *Opals* points and finished with a very impressive 13 for the quarter – Australia 21, Brazil 21. Australia was fortunate to trail by just one point at the long break. The crowd was going berserk because Brazil appeared to have the match in control in the third quarter. "The Brazilians run on emotion and they can burn you" Jan Stirling says.

Lauren was smothered throughout the first three quarters by the defence and only had nine points. The Australian coach would say:

> They did a good job on Lauren and she was probably a bit of her own worst enemy for the first three quarters, but she showed great maturity.

To Lauren Jan Stirling said: "They have had their way with you, now it is your turn". There was no way the opposition were going to contain the Australian captain for the full 40 minutes. Lauren realised

"I tried to push too much". A lot of players might have capitulated but Loz just refocused: "I let go and just tried to play my own game and have fun". It wasn't fun for the Brazilian players or supporters. The crowd became upset and began to throw things onto the court, at the Australians. It is incredible when you can lift and your teammates lift at the same time; when you play as hard as you can because they do. It almost feels like everything is in slow motion except it is at 100 kilometres an hour. But it all clicks. Lauren believed that was the most amazing quarter of basketball she had played in. The *Opals* won 88–76.

The next semi-final, between the perennial basketball enemies Russia and the United States amazed the basketball world. Going into the match the Russians had lost three games. The US had dominated, winning every game. Almost everyone believed this semi-final was a foregone conclusion, but it wasn't. The stadium was almost silent when the stunned crowd looked to the final scoreboard. It read Russia 75, US 68.

The *Opals* found it hard to sleep that night. The incredible adrenalin rush which came with winning the semi-final against Brazil was slow to subside. Then there was the knowledge that they were to play the 2006 final the next day, and not against the country that had dominated women's basketball for a decade. As the Australians took to the floor it was almost an anti-climax. The Russians had left so much on the court the previous day their energy levels were largely expended. Unlike the Russians the Australians were fully focused not just on where they had been but where they were going. Jan Stirling believed that after the game against Brazil she didn't care who the *Opals* played because she knew the Australians would win. Her team, the ones she referred to as being "on the important side of the white line", still had fire in their bellies. As the final minutes ticked down the depleted Russians made no attempt to foul, it would have been

363

useless. As the final buzzer sounded and the scoreboard froze at 91–74; the Australians and their supporters were jubilant.

The *Opals* had taken their rightful place at the summit of women's basketball. Lauren would comment later that Australia winning the gold medal game "was amazing". Right then she was too emotional to say anything. The *Opals* were still grinning, crying and waving when they stepped up onto the dais to receive their gold medals. As usual Lauren was draped in the Australian flag. When she accepted the trophy on her nation's behalf she graciously carried it down the line of players and handed it to Jenny Whittle. Whittle had been an Opal since 1996. She was a member of the Atlanta Olympic bronze medal winning team. That team told the rest of the world that Australia had arrived and was only going to get better. They were proven right in a stadium in Sao Paulo, Brazil, ten years later.

Lauren shared the emotion of the occasion with Maree and Gary and went up into the stands to Tom and Robyn Maher. For Lauren "it was a dream come true" and the Mahers had been true believers – in Australian women's basketball, and in her. The *Opals*, their families and friends, celebrated and in Brazil that means quite a party. A slightly worse-for-wear Lauren told a television crew before she left South America: "It has been a fun two weeks; hopefully it lasts a little longer". When the triumphant team returned home, their captain led them through the Customs doors into a packed international terminal. She carried the trophy and had a grin ear to ear: "We have made our place in history" she announced. In 2006 Lauren won the Maher Medal as Australia's Female International Player of the Year. It was the fifth time she had won the award in the previous eight years.

Lauren arrived in Seattle for the beginning of the 2007 WNBA season fifteen pounds lighter, fitter, with a spring in her step and a fresh optimism: "I feel ten times better physically than I have in a long time". She still had two fractures in her left shin but was determined this was going to be a good season. In just the second game of the season she scored 31 against Phoenix. Against San Antonio on 2 June she scored 20. Against the Lynx on 9 June she scored 30 and nine rebounds. At Indiana on 13 June she brought down the 1500th rebound of her WNBA career. In the game against Houston she scored 30. In 2004 One US reporter had written:

> Watch her instinct for the basketball, her great hands, leaping ability, finishing touch, range, mobility, body control, fearlessness. Jackson is maximizing the great genetic package she got. And then there's the famous Aussie characteristic of really caring about what she's doing but acting very laid-back about it.[54]

In 2007 the WNBA was seeing how a healthier LJ could move between the three and four positions with the rebounding of a centre and the stroke of a shooting guard. At Los Angeles on 24 June she scored 35. Two days later it was 33 against Chicago. *Chicago Sky* coach Bo Overton said:

> Lauren Jackson is not a prototype, she's a freak. She's a post player with a guard's body, control and skill, who can shoot the three, drive and handle the ball. There's no one like her.[55]

Two days after that it was 30 against Houston including her 250th three-pointer. Lauren didn't care who she played, she just wanted to play.

In only one game during July 2007 did she score fewer than 20, her worst game was 19. At Phoenix on 17 July she scored 33 and was the top rebounder with 11. Against the *Washington Mystics* she scored a remarkable 47 points in an equally remarkable overtime game which the *Storm* lost by one point 96–97. The 47 tied the WNBA single game record set by Diana Taurasi in 2006. Lauren was also the top *Storm* rebounder with 14. Anne Donovan commented:

> I've never seen an individual performance like it … to go with the kind of energy and intensity and consistency that she had … I don't think I've ever seen a player play like that.[56]

By the end of the 2007 season Lauren had averaged 35 points and 10 rebounds against *Mystics*. The *Mystics* did not really like her that much.

During the next game on 27 July against the Fever, Lauren scored 27 points and ten rebounds. One play in particular would enter the basketball annals. Betty Lennox cleverly sent a behind-the-back pass to Lauren. The Australian converted the pass into a basket beyond the arc and career point number 4000. She was the youngest and fastest player to reach 4000 in WNBA history and needed 21 fewer games than all-time scoring leader Lisa Leslie. KeyArena gave her a standing ovation and a video tribute. Lauren played 31 games for the *Storm* in 2007: 1020 minutes of basketball in which she scored 739 points, 300 rebounds, 63 blocked shots, 31 steals and 40 assists. The 93 personal fouls just showed she was playing hard. Finishing the 2007 season with an average of 23.8 topped the WNBA. Lauren also finished first in rebounding with a 9.7 average and double doubles (seventeen). She was named "Player of the Week" five times. Lauren was delighted to be named "Defensive Player of the Year". She had believed defence was her weaker area; not any more. Named in her sixth All Star team she said: "I am so proud to be voted in by the fans; I am not even American".

On 6 September 2007 Lauren won her second MVP award. Only four others – Cynthia Cooper, Lisa Leslie, Sheryl Swoopes and Yolanda Griffiths – had won it twice. Her comment was that although she was grateful for the honour she would prefer to hold the WNBA Championship trophy aloft with other members of the *Storm*. Her team had failed to progress past the first round of the WNBA finals. "It's definitely bittersweet". Lauren's dad proudly announced:

> I think what she's done this year in the League she's stamped herself as not just one of the best, but the best in the world in the sport.

Perhaps Gary recalled watching his four-year-old running down the street beating all the other kids; and his prediction that she was already special and was destined for greatness. It was back to Gary, Maree and Albury that Lauren retreated for a well-deserved rest and some good old normal Aussie lifestyle.

The salary cap in the WNBA was just $98,000 (USD). Considering the many, many millions players in the men's league, the National Basketball Association (NBA) received, the sum was insignificant. A professional basketball career is finite. One needs to make money while the body holds up, while your averages are maintained; before the rookies take over and, most of all, while the passion is still there. For Lauren money is not the main reason she plays basketball:

> I play this game because I love it. I do it to please myself and when the day comes that I don't love it anymore I will walk away.

She did nonetheless need to secure her financial future. The best women players needed to follow the money and in 2007–08 it was not in the US but, somewhat ironically, Russia.

There seemed no limit to the excesses in Russia. Oligarch-owned sports teams covet the best sportswomen in the world as they emphatically vie for awards and trophies. Lauren had played briefly for *UMMC Ekaterinburg* in 2004. That club now had three *Opals* in their starting five – Penny Taylor, Kristi Harrower and Suzy Batkovic. It was the colourful Shabtai von Kalmanovic, co-owner of the *Moscow Spartak* women's team, who made an offer hard to refuse. The *Spartak* team roster sparkled with US Olympians and WNBA players. Add Lauren, not to mention talented Russians, and the line-up looked invincible. The salary was in the vicinity of a million dollars (USD) and Lauren shared a luxury five-bedroom house with friends Diana Taurasi and Sue Bird. Invariably there was a private jet available. The main attraction for Lauren was that she could continue to indulge the one true love in her life, basketball. The European competition was of the highest quality which meant she could continue to improve. *Spartak* Head Coach Natalie Hejkova believed Lauren was "the best in the world".[57] Yes Lauren was tall, athletic and talented but she was also a very "hard worker" according to Hejkova. The Australian was always the first to practice and the last to leave. Still it all seems "a bit of a fantasy" to Lauren here she was playing elite basketball for a Moscow-based team!

The Russian season is long, very long – October to May. The routine is vigorous with training sessions twice a day and there is a lot of travel, but unlike the WNBA season which consisted of 34 matches, the European league consisted of only fifteen. The goal of *Spartak* was to win everything and the star-studded team did. They won a second consecutive Russian Superleague title and were destined for another EuroLeague championship. Along the way Lauren who subjugated the low post at both ends and could shoot from anywhere, dominated yet another continent. It didn't matter much where or with whom she played; the scenario was the same. In the last week of January it was a case of "today is '!' this must be Vidnoje, Russia, I am playing the French team *Valenciennes*". The French saw her briefly as she raced up and down the court scoring 31 points, pulling down six rebounds, and blocking four of what they believed to be perfectly good shots. They had been warned that in her previous three games she scored 33, 34 and 26. They had been warned but there was nothing they could do.

In the April European Superleague semi-final against *Ekaterinburg* Lauren scored 35 and recovered 12 rebounds. *Spartak* won 78–68. The final against *Gambrinus Brno* was expected to be harder given the Czech's home court advantage and their intimidating fans. Lauren played the entire game with a painful injury – skin torn away three layers deep from the ball of the right foot. She was harassed by tough physical play after she scored 14 points in the first 15 minutes. *Spartak Moscow* defended its EuroLeague Women's with a 75–60. Lauren was named a member of the EuroLeague All Star team and All Final Four Team. She was named EuroLeague Final Four MVP. Lauren finished first in the Euroleague point per game (23.6) and three-point percentage (56.5). Lauren told the media how much she wanted to win, not just for *Spartak* but for her teammates. Four continents, four MVPs, are there any left? The seven-month European season had been exhausting and Lauren was showing its effects when she flew back into Seattle. She was tired and had lost weight. A great deal had gone on in Seattle since the start of 2008.

In 2007 the future of Seattle's WNBA team was bleak. *Storm* franchise was part of the NBA *Seattle Sonics* organization and an Oklahoma businessman had just purchased both with the intention of relocating the teams to his home state. Lauren was an outspoken critic and made it well known that her loyalty was to Seattle, her second home since selected by the *Storm* in 2001. She was not about to leave the city; "I want to stay here. The thought of not having a team here, or not being able to end my WNBA career here, is really sad". Lauren had been named WNBA MVP for the second time, and she carried more clout than she would take credit for. The man from the mid-west knew when he was beaten and agreed to sell the *Storm* to a group of four Seattle women executives (Force Ten Hoops) and the *Storm* stayed.

It came as both a surprise and a jolt to hear that Anne Donovan had resigned. She had been an important part of Lauren's WNBA life. Brian Agler was the new Head Coach. Lauren had heard good things about him. Most important to her continuing enthusiasm with the game is "having good coaches to motivate me". Her first training session felt really "different" although she "really liked" Agler who was "a teaching coach", always good. There were many player changes too. It was hard to adapt to such a degree of change rapidly and Lauren needed to find her place in this very different *Storm*.

The 2008–09 WNBA season was underway when I flew into Washington State to interview Lauren. Lauren approached with the easy loping stride of someone completely comfortable in her body and with the awareness and appreciation of every ligament and muscle that only a professional sportsperson can have. She looked tired, sleepless in Seattle; a rugged training session had stolen most of Saturday morning. It was hard to back up for training after the adrenalin charged game of the previous evening against the *San Antonio Silver Stars*. The 30 May game was never really in question after the first quarter and the final score was Seattle 78, San Antonio 57. The Australian scored the team's first ten points, 28 during the game, and was awarded "Player of the Game". Characteristically she put the victory down to the team, and additional training meshing individuals. San Antonio's coach Dan Hughes simply said "Lauren was fantastic". I asked Lauren how she kept the momentum going?. Her reply came with a slight smile: "You need to play smarter as you get older".

It is 1 June 2008 and the evening mists of Seattle are beginning to descend. With the Space Needle piercing the heavens nearby, KeyArena's doors are open and the fans pour in, eager to get to their seats. Those gathered here in their thousands represent an amazing cross section of Washington State citizenry. That's one of the interesting things about the sport of basketball all over the world, its appeal traverses age, social and racial lines. In one section a group of season ticket holders proudly wear their *Storm* shirts. Each home game this vibrant group of sisters, mothers and daughters – members of the Yakama Nation – travel two and a half hours to be present.

A group of young girls dressed in way too big *Storm* shirts and resplendent in wigs in *Storm* colours congregate as close to the team entry as the security guard will allow. He is struggling to maintain that sombre expression because the wigs have him amused. The girls don't notice because they are intently watching the tall figure in *Storm* sweats practice shooting at the far end. She is alone – always the first out, last to leave – and she likes to get just those few extra baskets before the official warm-up. She moves back towards the locker room and the little girls clutch their programmes hopefully and smile. Lauren pauses and with a couple of words signs her name and disappears. The smiles have become huge grins and the little girls giggle as they rush up to families in the stands.

The atmosphere in KeyArena needs to be witnessed to be believed. *Seattle Storm* fans are loud and fervent, loud and basketball savvy, and yes loud. The opposition is introduced to muted applause, the stadium lights are doused and amid smoke, spotlights, fanfare and cheering, *Storm* players run onto the floor. It is show business and that is what professional sport is. Lauren is very popular in Seattle not only for her basketball prowess but because of the loyalty she has shown the city. Ask any of the fans who stand and cheer – they are grateful, even if the cry "Aussie, Aussie, Aussie, Oi, Oi, Oi" sounds just a little strange with the American accent. It is all about flattening the vowels and they need to work on the nasal delivery but in this United States the chant is a compliment any way it comes.

KeyArena is jumping. Fans are beating their bright yellow blow-up clappers and the stadium reverberates. The announcer is not satisfied and shouts "I can't hear you!". On the giant screen overhead pre-recorded video features *Storm* players issuing the same chant and the noise escalates a couple more decibels. The home team is down and this is definitely not supposed to happen. The *Houston Comets* are proving slow to accept that in 2008 only the *Storm* wins in Seattle. The three-quarter buzzer sounds and players retire to their bench and listen intently to their coaches. *Storm* mascot "Doppler" is prancing around the court trying to encourage the crowd. He is a weird looking maroon orangey bronzy brown character with a Storm top, rather tubby with large eyes and what could be mistaken as one of those three-cup type wind gauges you used to see at old airfields on his head. (The more technically pedantic would refer to it as an anemometer but the crowd just think it is a weird cup thing.) You really have to feel for the person inside that outfit and wonder what he puts under "occupation" on official forms. Well the kids like him and they pour down from the stands in every direction to form a conga line behind Doppler, or what here at the "Key" is called the "Doppler train". The whistle goes and hundreds of kids scatter madly to run back into the stands. It's back to the business of tough basketball.

Some of those in KeyArena wonder why they pay for seats because they seem to spend a lot of time too nervous to sit. The fans groan at each missed field goal and there are more than the usual mutterings regarding referees as the whistles are worked overtime and stop any game flow with 53 fouls called. Houston defence has effectively shut down LJ. Whenever Lauren receives the ball she is triple teamed, but continues to get the ball away to unguarded teammates. Houston refuses to accept the inevitable and edges ahead 63–62. There are mere seconds remaining, the crowd can no longer sit, they are not sure they can look. A *Comets* shot is blocked and Lauren gathers the ball. Her best mate, point guard Sue Bird, moves rapidly towards the other end:

Once I saw Lauren with the ball, I knew we didn't have timeouts and there wasn't a lot of time on the clock. I just thought to myself, "Run!"

The Australian propels the ball down the court ahead of Bird who deftly gathers and lays it up into the basket. The roof on KeyArena appears to lift with the commotion – the *Storm* has won 64–63.

Photographs by Kathryn Spurling

There is a lot of travel involved in the WNBA, particularly for the *Storm* and the *Los Angeles Sparks*, the two teams whose home cities hug the Pacific Ocean. Air travel has become increasingly arduous in the shadow of "9/11", more time and patience needed to venture through increased security. Air travel is only glamorous to the uninitiated and WNBA players continue to fly economy class. Only four of the ten-strong Storm team are less than six feet in height and there are never enough exit row seats. According to Lauren the WNBA is "pretty intense" and while it offers "constant quality" she concedes:

It takes its toll. The WNBA is every other night. It's tough, everyone is as physical as I am if not tougher and stronger than I am.

The WNBA schedule is demanding – perhaps too demanding – typified by ten days in June 2008 when the *Storm* played five basketball games in ten days in three cities.

It is another 2008 game at home, the *Storm* versus the *Connecticut Sun*. The KeyArena crowd is getting dizzy with the lead changes. They are anxious by the end of the third with their team is down 55–50. Final score is Connecticut 74 and Seattle 67. Lauren finished top scorer with 26 points as well as seven rebounds, two blocked shots and a season-high four steals. But she isn't happy and admits it was a "really tough game" and "we didn't capitalise" on *Sun* errors.

Another day, another basketball game and in the players area the iPod ear pieces are firmly in place and the heavy metal sound of Marilyn Manson is blasting away. Lauren is getting in the zone for the game against the *Los Angeles Sparks*. For KeyArena fans it is one of the most important games on the calendar. They don't like the *Sparks*, they are brash and brassy, pretty much like the city they represent. The tussle between Lisa Leslie and LJ has gone on for years and one would expect no less from the two best "bigs" in the game. The WNBA MVP trophy is impressive but it comes with a tunic with a target on it the following season. Everyone appears to want a piece of you, to want to take you down a peg or two, to show they can match your play and you need to show you deserved that title and deserve it again. This 2008 season Lauren believes:

There have been games I have struggled.
You are going to get people coming at you. You are going to get hit. You are going to get all sorts of trouble. It is best not getting frustrated.

The KeyArena fans get their money's worth. Nine lead changes and four tied scores is the simplest set of statistics. The referee blows his whistle again at Lauren. What does he expect – she plays with a lot of emotion and occasionally it boils over in frustration with another player or an official, but mainly with herself. She gets pinged again, clamps her lips and walks away. The KeyArena crowd are disagreeing very loudly on her behalf. In the battle of the "bigs" no one noticed that a "short" Sue Bird decided to top-score for Seattle. Lauren blocked five shots. Pity about the five personal fouls that sent her to the bench before the game was done, but the *Storm* did win without her on the court. This was Lauren's last WNBA game for a month and a half.

Next Lauren is on a plane across the Pacific, another long 14 hours in the air but the time goes quicker when you are going home. Still she can't help but feel torn. Her first loyalty is to her nation so she needs to return to Australia to lead the *Opals* in two tests against Brazil on 28 and 30 July. It will be special playing in the green and gold on home soil because it seldom happens. Then it is full focus on to the Beijing Olympic Games. She just has to hope Seattle wins the five games she is going to miss because currently the *Storm* is second in the Western Conference.

The Olympic draw is out. The *Opals* are in Group A and will play Korea, Russia, Belarus, Latavia and their old foe Brazil.[58] The USA's strongest opposition is likely from home team China. The *Opals* are entitled to be disappointed with the times of their games. Australia was not required to go through Olympic qualifying because they are the reigning world champions, yet this achievement appeared not to have been taken into consideration by organisers. Programming favours nations whose prime time television rights and public are larger and Australia has a population of only 21 million. For the second Olympics in a row the *Opals* have their first game at 9am. It is pretty prestigious marching with other Australian Olympians behind your nation's flag in the opening ceremony but with a return to the Olympic village unlikely before 2am, marching is not an option. Lauren is philosophical; it is a shame but she and her team are in Beijing to represent their country and it is of primary importance to "focus on the job". The *Opals* need to win all their games to receive the best run into the final.

Before Beijing there were a couple of match-ups with Brazil. On a cold rainy 28 July night the *Opals* played Brazil in the NSW coastal town of Wollongong. Lack of publicity and the weather resulted in a small crowd, it was a shame but not unusual. Yet again the print and television media featured men's football of many codes and quality rather than one of the very few reigning world champion teams Australia can boast. Consequently too few Australians were aware of the opportunity to witness the *Opals* defeat Brazil 99–62. The *Opals* covered any disappointment with a business-like performance to ensure the green and gold was not defeated at home.

Family close, with Gary and Maree
Photographs by Jennifer Burton-Douglas

The second match-up in Sydney received only marginally better publicity and a slightly larger crowd. As the *Opals* took the court for their warm-up there was no sign of Lauren. The crowd became restless when the game commenced and the captain was nowhere to be seen. They nonetheless delighted in Australian on-court brilliance and the win, 85–62. Lauren appeared at half time having spent hours in medical waiting rooms to have her right ankle scanned – yes that right ankle again. The previous day in training she had landed awkwardly and it hurt. She did not wish to disappoint the crowd but Maree, Gary and *Opals* medical staff argued that playing in Beijing was more important. Lauren as always made light of the injury.

The *Opals* flew to China the next day to participate in the FIBA Diamond Ball competition held in Haining. The 5 August final against the United States involved play which could at the least be described as "spirited". Penny Taylor was given a very black eye and there were plenty of knocks and bumps in the most physical encounter between the two most determined teams in the world. Lauren characteristically said that's "how it is":

> Teams are going to try to beat the crap out of us because we are so good, people have to stop us somehow ... and generally that means black eyes and broken noses ... the international game is a contact sport ... people are going to get broken bones. It is always going to be a dogfight between Australia and the US because of the rivalry.[59]

The USA won, but only just 71–67. Lauren was named tournament MVP. The Australians felt good and set off for the Olympic village.

The *Opals* had never played Belarus before. They felt the nerves, that sinking sensation in the gut and the goose bumps as soon as they set foot on the court – yes this was indeed the Olympics. Suzy Batkovic took the game to the opposition early until Penny Taylor warmed up. Kristy Harrower, a 15 year *Opals* veteran, was the steadying influence. Laura Summerton would prove herself the most capable of those on the bench. Lauren was not connecting. She started to during the third quarter, top scored with 18, but she was unhappy with her 40 per cent conversion. All the *Opals* needed to be shooting in the highest percentages by the finals. The team from Belarus was beaten but not disgraced, 83–64.

On 11 August the Australians took the court against the Brazilians. On paper the competition was won if you go by the law of averages, but basketball is not that sort of game and, this was the Olympics, which adds a capricious dimension. Those who are comfortable with statistical averages were nodding their heads by half time when the Australia threatened to make it a one-sided contest but the Latin temperament could never be underestimated and by the third quarter it was a different Brazil. The Australians stopped messing around and closed down the other side 80–65.

The *Opals* received a scare against Latvia when at one stage the Europeans led by seven. Lauren had been unusually subdued in the Olympic tournament. She decided: "I've got to do something". She led her team into a higher zone. They didn't panic, they believed in each other and played great basketball to win 96–73. Penny Taylor said of the team captain: "Lauren was amazing. She kept us in it the first half and we helped her out in the second half". Lauren scored 30 which included five three-pointers, although the Australian public missed this display. Domestic television (Channel Seven) chose to neither share nor show, not even the highlights.

There were some sweaty palms among Australian spectators who watched the *Opals* physically intimidated by the Russians. The *Opals* were behind 12 points at the main break. They had received their fright and took to the court with determination in the third quarter. "When you look up at the scoreboard and see your dream slipping away, it motivates you", Lauren explained. By midway they had drawn level. They were attacking the zone and forcing the Russians to rotate more. They blew the Russian team away scoring 30 points to ten which included a pair of demoralising three-pointers from the Australian No.15. As three-quarter time sounded Aussie spectators were smiling. They could tell by the body language on the court this one was won and so it was.[60] The quiet achiever of the starting five, Belinda Snell, equal top scored with Lauren who admitted:

> for us to be good enough to get the gold medal we really have to play 40-minute games and we can't have those sorts of deficits and lapses in concentration in the first half anymore.[61]

Luck plays a huge part in sport and it was choosing not to favour the Aussies this Beijing Olympics. After 15 minutes on the court against the Czech Republic, vice captain Penny Taylor drove to the basket. Two Czech players moved to stop her progress, Penny's ankle rolled awkwardly and she crashed to the boards in great pain. The *Opals* won 79–46 but their vice captain sat forlornly on the bench with the lower half of her leg in an ice-box, with medical and coaching staff looking concerned. Their captain wasn't saying anything about the pain she was in with her right ankle but they knew.[62]

Lauren was the tournament's top scorer. Given her injury that was fairly remarkable; she had pain every time she pushed off and landed. It was hard to get into a groove and painkilling injections can do only so much. The body makes subconscious adjustments to protect the injured part. It only takes the most subtle of adjustments to throw basketball shots off the millimetre needed for them to find all net. Lauren continued to make light of the handicap, but one sound bite caught the comment "ahhhh bugger". She remained overtly confident about her team's brilliance and supported the men's team, the *Boomers*, in their game against the United States resplendent in green and gold and with Aussie transfer tattoos stuck all over. She said she would "run naked around the village like five times" if the boys won. It was a shame the *Boomers* did not win but perhaps it was good for the Jackson ankle that they didn't, given the promise of a marathon five trips around the village. Asked who would win in a game between the Australian men's and women's team she answered diplomatically "I think we shoot better than they do but I don't think we would be able to do anything inside so I think they probably would".

There was a lot of history in the semi-final between Australia and China and the Chinese players had nothing to do with it. It was attached to an Australian coach, now Chinese National Coach, who had started both the *Opals* and a gangly Albury teenager on the road to the highest echelon of women's basketball, also it included the Assistant Chinese National Coach, who a decade before had caused the same teenager to quietly ask for a phone so she could call family in Australia to tell them she was in the same room as the mighty Michelle Timms. They were now on opposition benches but the respect was still evident. Of Lauren Tom Maher once declared "God sent her to play basketball. He woke up one day and said 'basketball needs Lauren Jackson'". He also believed that Lauren was "not just the once-in-a-generation, she's the once-in-a-lifetime". Lauren said of the now Chinese National Coach:

> Tom Maher is an amazing coach. He is my favourite coach of all time. I have so much respect for him as a coach and as a person.

Tom Maher had brought the Chinese team to their first medal contention rounds in 16 years. The only problem now was that they faced the *Opals*.

The crowd was going to be a real factor. There was a group of hardy Aussie supporters, husbands and boyfriends dressed in *Opal* bodysuits and green and gold wigs who had become very popular with the Chinese. No Chinese spectator would ever dress this way but admired those brave enough to do so. Still, the arena was full to capacity, a sea of red and white. Many did not understand basketball; they were there to see their nation beat Australia. The noise was loud every time a Chinese player had the ball and every time a referee dared call against one. A dejected Penny Taylor sat on the bench. The *Opals* started cautiously and the Chinese, buoyed by local support, stayed in touch, just two down at the end of the first quarter. The crowd was silenced by Australia's suffocating defence with the Opals stealing the ball ten times, forcing 20 turnovers, out-rebounding the Chinese 56–34 and scoring at will.

The Australian headlines were sensational – "Get Physical with us and you're dead" and "We'll fight US to the death: *Opals*". Too many sports journalists concentrated on what they believed to be ill feeling between the USA's four-time Olympian Lisa Leslie and Lauren. They reported this emanated from the 2000 Olympic final when Lauren's fingers accidently dislodged a Leslie hair piece. It should have been acknowledged that this was more about competitiveness, about athleticism. Lauren was the young Australian who had wrested the WNBA MVP mantle away from Leslie and the *Opals* dared threaten US basketball supremacy. For the *Opals* there was the huge weight of expectation, their nation's and their own. They wanted the gold medal so badly they could taste it but the weight of all that expectation – and just plain bad luck – would shatter the dream.

Vice captain Penny Taylor had been icing her ankle every two hours, day and night, even moving into the corridor to sleep rather than disrupt the sleep of the teammate she roomed with. The press referred to it as a "sprained ankle". It was a lateral ligament tear. Lauren had needed a pain-killing injection before the semi-final against China. The *Opals* captain was well below her best and would return to Australia for surgery the following week. Both Penny and

Lauren were superstars, both were leaders, both were in pain, both needed medical attention and injections before they could take to the court against the US. Neither of them could play well and the *Opals* were thrown into disarray.

You need to have a fully fit team firing on all cylinders to stand a chance against the colossus of basketball – this was not the *Opals*. In the Olympic final the Australians tried, they probably tried too hard, and as the "wheels came off" they tried harder; but there was too little brilliance this day. The Americans won easily in the end, 92–65. The injured captain top-scored with 20 points and took 10 rebounds on that bad ankle. Lauren and Penny were distraught, too upset to face the media. Kristie Harrower assumed this chore and admitted that the *Opals* had played a "shocker". To lose by 27 points when you played as well as you could was one thing but this was not the case. Crippling injuries to the two best Australian women basketballers made a difficult task impossible. Never had an Australian team shed so many tears and looked so sad on receiving the silver medal.

Before she flew home Lauren was the subject of a mini scandal at least as far as the Chinese were concerned. At the closing ceremony Lauren was filmed giving a hug to Chinese NBA star Yao Ming. He is a huge national celebrity, had carried his nation's flag at the opening ceremony and, was married. He reciprocated with the friendly western style hug, but the Chinese do not hug friends in public. The laurenjackson.org.au web page all but crashed under the weight of 14,000 additional hits in the next 24 hours. YouTube quickly highlighted love song videos featuring the two. The Chinese media went crazy. The two knew each other from Basketball America. According to Lauren:

> There's one photo where I'm looking at him – not in awe;
> it was, agh, I'm so tired and a little bit drunk ... It's not a

loving look at all. None of us slept for 24 hours. It was a long month that came to a disappointing end.[63]

The love song segments featured those nude photos taken before the previous Olympics.

> Instead of being known for my basketball skills, all of these nudie shots are always the first thing you see. But the Yao Ming thing was pretty hilarious ... It crosses those cultural borders and Aussies do things differently.[64]

Yao Ming was an impressive basketball player but for Lauren such a relationship was the last thing on her mind, "that's just not my thing".

Lauren had arthroscopic surgery in Sydney within days. There was a broken bone and five bone splinters in that ankle. After a week she flew to Seattle to watch the *Storm* contest the Western Conference playoffs against Los Angeles. The first game they lost, the second game they won. The American press was not entirely sympathetic to the Australian, suggesting she should have forgone the surgery to play for Seattle; that she should have forgone the Olympics to have the surgery and then play for Seattle. In less than a year Lauren had gone from heroine to something less. She tried to explain that her first basketball loyalty was to her country but some weren't listening. The *Storm* was beaten in the final playoff. Lauren returned to Australia, her *Seattle Storm* contract finished in December and she was a free agent for the first time in her life.

On 13 October 2008 Lauren boarded yet another plane for yet another long series of flights to Moscow and the long seven-month European season. She had spent a few quiet enjoyable weeks in Australia with Maree and Gary. She faced continuing rehabilitation of that right ankle and intended to return to the basketball court as soon as she could. She still felt the disappointment of the Olympic campaign and that would affect future career decisions. Lauren had decided to play in the London 2012 Olympics. Next time she planned not to play WNBA prior to the Olympic tournament, and planned to stay injury free.

Back in 2004 the AIS Women's Head Coach Phil Brown said of Lauren that if her body held out she would be her best at 28 and 29. The same year Carrie Graf said the same. In 2008 Australian National Coach Jan Stirling believed: "Her best is yet to come. She will peak around 28 that's the scary part". Lauren turned 28 on 11 May 2009 which was great news for those she played with and dreadful news for those she didn't. Basketball remained "everything in my life". If hard pressed she admitted she didn't know where her dedication came from but continued to believe she could:

> always get better in some way. Personal satisfaction is a huge thing. I want to be as good as I possibly can be. I am definitely not satisfied with my game but I am getting there.

She was now a free agent and although there was US media speculation, Lauren would not play for a WNBA team other than the *Seattle Storm*. The first game of the 2009 season was against the *Los Angeles Sparks* and their star Candace Parker who had been named WNBA MVP the previous season. She still had a lot to learn and Lauren dominated the game with 23 points and ten rebounds. Lauren's defensive play at the other end meant Parker was restricted to ten points, four from eleven shots. Against the *San Antonio Silver Stars* Lauren shot 27 points in 28 minutes. Two nights later her hands were as hot and she knocked down 32 points including five three-pointers.

I caught up briefly with Lauren in early September 2009 in the players area beneath Seattle's KeyArena. She was pink. Everything and everybody were pink. It was the annual breast cancer fundraiser game. Lauren was carrying an injured back but was confident she could continue playing. I was pretty sure I had heard this before. The *Storm* needed to win this home game against Connecticut to cement their place in the playoffs. Lauren threw herself at every loose ball. There was a collision with the *Sun*'s Lindsay Whalen and Lauren hit the floor hard. The *Storm* won the game; they had made the playoffs. Lauren was hurt more. Scans the following day showed stress fractures in her back. Her season was over. For the second season in a row at the critical time in the WNBA season the *Seattle Storm* did not have their "big" star player, who was leading your team in points and rebounds, who posted 36 points in a game just nine days prior. For the second season in a row the *Storm* did not progress through the playoffs and of course they had to lose that contest to Los Angeles! Lauren was nonetheless named in the All WNBA First Team and the WNBA All Defensive First Team.

After the end of the WNBA season Lauren was supposed to travel to Russia but she first needed to return to the AIS in Canberra for treatment and rehabilitation. Maree and Gary had retired to the NSW south coast, within three hours of Canberra. On 2 November 2009 Shabtai von Kalmanovic, the colourful owner of *Spartak Womens Basketball* was gunned down in what was believed to be a contract killing. Lauren was shocked Shabtai had done much to further Lauren's career and boost her bank balance. She called him "Poppa". "For years he's supported me, put me under his wing. He was my safety net."[65] Lauren flew to Israel for his funeral. The future of *Spartak* remained as unresolved as his murder. For two seasons Lauren had been a large part of *Spartak* and was due to fly to Russia for her third season. Mum Maree confided that she was pleased her daughter was safely in Australia.

Lauren sat down over a bottle of wine with Carrie Graf, now the Australian *Opals* coach as well as the coach of the *Canberra Capitals*.

It was summer and the attraction of the beach, her parents' company and the Australian summer was making the decision to travel around the world to a snowy, freezing Moscow winter even harder. "What would it take for you to play here?" was the question Graf threw her way. The WNBL season was almost half over but the *Caps* and Lauren had always been a great fit. It would take $220,000. Such a figure for a sportswoman was unheard of in Australia but the ACT Government and local businesses pulled together and found the money within a fortnight. As soon as her back was healed she donned the uniform – and the WNBL had lost the bodysuits, they were back to comfortable shorts and singlet, even better. Wherever she played the crowds were huge. The ACT made her the 2010 Australia Day Ambassador.

It is 6 March 2010 and thousands have gathered at "the palace", Canberra's AIS indoor stadium. The WNBL grand final against the *Bulleen Boomers* was going to be all about defence and *Caps* coach Carrie Graff conceded: "The Jackson factor is big in every game". "Graffie" was right because Lauren had averaged 26 points in her four games. The grand final was a hard fought tough grind and for most of the game Lauren was triple teamed. The better team on the day won 75–70 and the *Capitals* became the first team to win seven WNBL championships. The basketball whirlwind continued as Lauren prepared to board yet another long haul flight across the Pacific to commence the 2010 WNBA season in the *Storm* starting five. It would likely then be a season in Europe unless the people of the ACT and their government could come up with what was necessary to bring her home for the next WNBL season.

Lauren so wanted to stay healthy during this WNBA season though she well knew the basketball would be as physical, ruthless and unrelenting as ever. During June 2010 she almost averaged a double-double, with ten plus rebounds four times. She was merciless against the opposition. At the beginning of July LJ suffered a concussion in a spiteful away game against Los Angeles. She was forced to sit out the next game before returning in an away game against Phoenix on 14 July 2010. It was a triple overtime marathon won by Seattle 111-107 and Lauren finished with the second-best effort of her WNBA career scoring 31 points and 18 rebounds. It would not be her last 30 plus game – she finished with five, a season average of 20.5 and stated, "I don't think individually I had the best season". Lauren was named the 2010 WNBA MVP, for a third time – only Americans Lisa Leslie and Sheryl Swoops had won it three times. The Australian also won the Finals MVP award, only the fourth player to win both MVP awards in one season.[66] According to LJ she won the awards "because of my teammates and people around me".[67] American fans did not entirely agree. One blogged:

> The countless times I saw an opposing player take a pass, find themselves faced with a one-on-one against LJ and just stop dead in their tracks – I loved it.[68]

One *Storm* fan believed: "She is a demigod. There are five aliens in the world of basketball – Jordan, Kobe, LeBron, Nowiski and Lauren Jackson" – the first four were male NBA legends. Another blogged: "She was just awesome in virtually every game. Her absolute intensity and grit when we were down were awesome". Lauren appreciated the praise, but the best part of the 2010 season for her, was that the *Seattle Storm* beat the *Atlanta Dream* to win the WNBA title again.

I had decided by 2010 that keeping up with Lauren Jackson was near on impossible – to be honest, I actually decided that a couple of years earlier straight after our first interview. The brief catch-ups and news via Maree and other sources did not resolve the perennial question "where on the earth is Lauren?". Not content to rest on her 2010 WNBA laurels Lauren agreed to join Sue Bird back in the Russian winter to play for *Spartak* during the 2010–11 European season. Eight games in Lauren was averaging 17.3 points and 8.4

rebounds and then came the "acute" injury to a tendon near the Achilles. Despite the discomfort Lauren attempted to continue but the body would not co-operate and she reluctantly admitted:

> I couldn't move, the swelling was very obvious and the pain was just a little bit too painful ... when your body says stop, you have to listen.

By co-incidence the WNBA had just released its 2011 season preview. At the top of the *Seattle Storm* page as the reason for the Storm's 2010 championship season was "Lauren Jackson's health". And her subsequent 20.5 points, 8.3 rebounds and 31 minutes per game averages:

> Even though she's only 29, Jackson's health is always the x-factor for Seattle because of all the basketball she's played in her career. And knowing that, (coach) Agler might have to be careful with her minutes this year so that she's plenty rested come September. That's easier said than done though, and will require the lesser-known players in the frontcourt to step up more so than usual so Jackson doesn't have to put up 20 and 10 each night for Seattle to win.[69]

Lauren was on her way home from Europe for yet more surgery and more rehabilitation.

The premature finish to her European season meant that Lauren could be in Seattle for the *Storm* training camp in May 2011 for the first time in five years. That first training session was also the most extensive play since surgery.

Today was the first 5-on-5 I've done. It was fun being out there. I was a little bit tentative at times … It felt good, though. It felt great.

In the 2011 WNBA season Lauren would play only 13 of the 34 games. During a game at the end of June Lauren was giving her usual 110 per cent against the opposing team and threw herself at the loose ball. The pain was hauntingly familiar and she knew it was bad, really bad. "I knew right away that I had torn something … I was pretty upset".[70] It was yet another surgery and yet another painful rehabilitation. She was determined not to be defeated and within four hours of surgery she was riding an exercise bike. Nonetheless it was difficult to distinguish who was the more dejected on the night of 12 July 2011, the KeyArena fans or Lauren, as she awkwardly manoeuvred towards courtside seating on a pair of crutches. Sue Bird believed not only was there the physical pain but Lauren needed to rehabilitate "through phases emotionally … She hates not being able to play". Her coach added: "She's a mentally and physically tough person".[71] Lauren said simply there was "nothing more heartbreaking than having to go through injuries like this", then added, "I can't even really explain how I feel right now". The WNBA prediction that *Storm* fortunes depended on the health of the co-captain proved accurate, the team lacked that winning cohesion no matter how many combinations they tried and failed to progress through the WNBA playoffs.[72]

In July 2011 at a grand affair in New York Lauren was named one of the top 15 players in the fifteen-year history of the WNBA and "the best, most versatile centre in the history of women's basketball".[73] American fans would have had difficulty understanding that in Lauren's hometown of Albury there was dissension surrounding the move to rename the Albury sports stadium the Lauren Jackson Sports

Centre.[74] It took ten months of debate before on 22 October 2011 Lauren was present to unveil the new signs bearing her name;

> I'm very excited but humbled. … I'm very proud to have this connection to a city I love and can represent.[75]

It is October 2011 and Lauren Jackson is standing with a basketball under her arm. The pose is casual but she is not entirely comfortable posing for artist Margaret Hadfield (Zorgdrager). That is how the off-court Lauren is – the shyness, the reticent disposition is still never far away. Margaret has decided to paint Lauren life-size for this book and an art prize entry.[76] Lauren is 198 cm and Margaret is 168 cm on a good day which requires the artist to stand on a ladder to paint on canvas the head of the Australian *Opals* captain. Margaret has watched Lauren play basketball and is trying to reconcile on canvas the two different individuals – the quiet private one and the ruthless on court persona – which is challenging. How to capture the real Lauren?. Even Lauren admits it is complicated.

Lauren was the focus of larger discussion this day in October because she has just signed a $1 million contract to play for the *Canberra Capitals* for the 2012–13, 2014–15 and 2015–16 WNBL seasons. Media reaction, sports reporter reaction is mixed. Canberra business and basketball communities had combined to secure Lauren, but the major *Canberra Times* article is tinged with disbelief bordering on indignation. Comparison is pivotal:

> The Canberra Raiders and ACT *Brumbies* high-profile players can earn upwards of $500,000 a year. But Jackson's deal puts her level with or better off than the majority of players in the *Raiders* and *Brumbies* squads.[77]

In 2009, the then ACT Chief Minister, Jon Stanthope, had needed to justify his government's decision to contribute to the sponsorship deal to have Lauren join the *Capitals* for the remainder of the WNBL season. The decision caused consternation and claims that the sponsorship was "financially reckless". Stanhope had answered:

> It's about community, it's about vibrancy, it's about supporting sport and it's about supporting women's sport. I proudly declare and stand by the decision ... to support the greatest sportswoman that this city has ever produced and I think that Australia has ever produced.[78]

Stanhope struggled with the prevailing double standards, as did many others:

> Why is it that when it's a women all of a sudden I start getting letters and snippy little comments, and "how can you justify this when there are other priorities?" I didn't receive one suggestion or negative letter or call … in relation to a half-million dollar payment to a male footballer and here we are having to justify half as much to a female sports star. At some level isn't it symptomatic of just the nature and state and reportage and support of women's sport in Australia? An undone story in terms of continuing discrimination.[79]

Two years on, at the end of 2011, the media continued to inappropriately compare the best woman basketball player and one of the highest profile sportswomen in the world, with male football players.

There was nonetheless little time for further discussion because a professional sportsperson is only as good as their last season, their last successful season and 2012 was to be yet another huge year in the life of Lauren Jackson, as was every year since she first played with the *Opals* at age 16. She was due to fly to Spain to play with *Ros Casares Valencia* in the Euroleague. This was an Olympic year and LJ would not suit up with the *Storm* until after London; before then returning to play for the *Canberra Capitals*. Lauren had battled hip injuries, Achilles tendon strains, shin splints and back problems in recent years, not to mention ankle reconstructions, but believed; "I'm really confident, I think I have [had] my run of back luck".[80]

The Euroleague involves loads of travel, loads of different countries, and a great many basketball courts. There may not be much time to be a tourist but Lauren was still getting a rush from being an international basketball player.

> Being so far away [from Australia] it makes you grow up, it makes you change, it definitely changes your perspective on the sport itself and I think I will take back better skills, basketball skills, life skills.[81]

She played 19 games but by her extraordinary standards her season was not that successful.[82] With an average of only 20 minutes on the court Lauren still managed eight 20 plus games, including 31 against her old team *Sparta*, now amalgamated with *K.M.R. Vidnoje*. Asked by a reporter if she was intimidated by playing a finals away game when the stadium was full of trumpet playing, drum banging, screaming opposition fans, she replied that she was: "probably the shyest person on the court … I'm used to it, I get booed everywhere I go". It was just another challenge, another country to dominate – and *Ros Casares Valencia* won the Euroleague.

Lauren turned 30 on 11 May 2012. She returned to Australia from Europe and as promised four years earlier, she would miss the first half of the WNBA season to concentrate on improving the chemistry within the national team she captained. The *Opals* is simply the most important part of her professional life. This was not entirely a popular decision in Seattle as the *Storm* was already struggling. Fan blogs included: "Too bad because *Opals* don't have a chance against Americans"; and another: "We can win without LJ, she and her team won't beat the Americans. Go *Storm*".[83] *Storm* Head Coach Brian Agler had a better understanding and supported Lauren's decision:

> Lauren is one of the greatest competitors I've ever coached, so I can appreciate her drive to win a gold medal.[84]

Nonetheless, Agler knew without Lauren the *Storm* was in for a bumpy pre-Olympic season because in the five years he had coached this team, it had been "35–29 without her" and with LJ "66–24. There is a drastic change when she is on the court".

The 2010 World Championships had been disappointing for the *Opals*. The competition is unforgiving, lose a match or two and you find yourself playing for fifth place. It was a long fall from winning the 2006 gold. Unfortunately the *Opals* Olympic campaign was off to another bad luck start – the Australian vice captain, Penny Taylor, suffered a season-ending injury, her Olympic dreams again in tatters. Australia needed to look to the physicality and talent of a youthful Liz Cambage to be the "go to" player. The 20-year-old 203cm Cambage had been the 2011 WNBA No.2 draft choice and after joining the *Tulsa Shock* she had matured during her 2011 rookie WNBA year.

The *Opals* had not even arrived in London before controversy emerged. As they boarded their Qantas aircraft members of the Australian men's basketball team, the *Boomers*, turned left for business class; the women's team turned right for economy. Basketball Australia had financed an upgrade for their men but not their women. The *Opals* were ranked 2nd in the world, and the Boomers were ranked 9th. The *Opals* had won silver in the last three Olympics, the Boomers reached only the quarter finals. Admittedly most of the Boomers were taller than their women counterparts but there could be no doubt that Liz Cambage, Suzy Batkovic and Lauren towered over a few. Fortunately the *Opals* were upgraded by Qantas to premier economy, but the discrimination was not lost on the Australian public. Some of the public online response made for astonishing reading. "No one really wants to watch the girls play basketball" wrote one. Clearly this blogger was unaware that all Olympic basketball sessions, male and female, were sold out well ahead of the Olympics. "The men are well known and have the ability to draw sponsorship money" wrote another, unappreciative of the classic "catch 22" anomaly. One blog which would perhaps come back to haunt was: "Show me a slam dunk, and I'll show you equality". Basketball Australia agreed their policy was discriminatory. The slam dunk fan hopefully agreed when Liz Cambage became the first woman in Olympic women's basketball to dunk, on 3 August 2012, helping her nation beat Russia 70–66.

Another case of discrimination was clearly obvious in the number of women chosen to carry the Australian flag during the Olympic opening ceremony, particularly when consideration is given the Olympic success enjoyed by the nation's women athletes. There had been only two. Sprinter Raelene Boyle led the Australian team into the Montreal Olympic stadium in 1976 and springboard diver Jenny Donnet carried the flag in the Olympic opening ceremony in Barcelona in 1992. Sprinter Denise Boyd co-carried the flag with swimmer Max Metzker into the Moscow stadium for the 1980 Olympics.

Maree and Gary Jackson were on their flight to London when cabin staff woke them with champagne and the news that their daughter was to be the first Australian woman to carry the flag in an Olympic opening ceremony in 20 years. Lauren's achievements had continued to surprise them but this was pretty special. Australia's Olympic chef de mission, Nick Green, had summoned Lauren to his office in the Olympic village. Lauren thought initially, "I was in trouble for something I'd done" but Green told her she was "an inspiring and high-achieving woman", epitomising "wonderful leadership qualities on and off the court"; she was "admired by her teammates and respected by her opponents". Green believed Lauren had "all the qualities I admire in a leader and that is the person our team needs as a captain here in London."[85] Lauren was overawed:

> I can't think of anything that would ever top this. Obviously a gold medal would be awesome, but I feel like this is something that will never happen again. This moment makes me feel like nothing's impossible.[86]

All the awards, all the MVP titles, nothing surpassed wearing national colours and carrying the Australian flag at the London Olympic Games. The wide grin stayed on Lauren's face during the very special stadium circuit in front of 90,000 and billions more watching the ceremony via television and internet link. Lauren used her tall frame to maximum advantage and waved the Australian flag very high indeed. The heady days continued when she, Maree and Gary, were introduced to Prince William and Catherine, Duchess of Cambridge. Clearly they were overwhelmed and fittingly Lauren was seen to mouth "Oh my God" when the future British king and queen moved to meet other Olympians. "I was in love with him when I was a kid. Like any young girl, you always dream of marrying the prince."

Lauren's previous three Olympics had been physical and emotional rollercoasters and London was no exception. Lauren was injured and yes once again the public was never to know – she never made excuses. Only much later would she admit "at the Olympics it was terrible" and there were more painkilling injections. For those with knowledge of her game there was an awareness in the early rounds, there was less than the usual 110 per cent vigorous play, and the shooting was uncharacteristically a smidgeon off. Lauren was content to allow other *Opals* to dominate play under the basket and less experienced *Opals* to shine. But again with no Penny Taylor and an injured captain it was never going to be enough.

There were wins against Great Britain (74–58), Brazil (67–61), Russia (70–66), and Canada (72–63). The loss to France (74–70) was costly. It steered the Opals into a quarter-final match against China. More importantly, should they win against China the Australians would meet the USA in the semi-final, instead, as they hoped, in the final. As the pressure and tempo increased the less experienced players began to struggle and their captain took an increasing responsibility, injury and all. Against China Lauren rallied, or perhaps, as she would admit, "the bitch was back". She realised to be in the medal hunt this game had to be won. With 3.46 seconds remaining on the clock she shot a jumper. She was intent on the *Opals* winning, but this basket gave her 536 points and Lauren became the top-scorer in women's Olympic Games basketball.[87] Lauren was unfazed, concerned only with the semi-final. Olympic history repeated itself and the might of the Americans could not be overcome. The final score was 83–74 but unlike the previous Olympic match between the two countries it was clear the *Opals* played to their ability, younger Australians bravely uninhibited by the biggest names in their sport. Australia was in the bronze medal game.

Russia was always a tough opponent and the pressure was immense. Lauren again ignored the pain and was ruthless under the basket, top-scoring with 25 points and lifting the *Opals* to a nine-point win. Last Olympics she had been inconsolable with a silver medal, this time:

> To be honest it feels great because winning a bronze instead
> of losing a gold medal is a different feeling. This feels

really good, I have no regrets and I know my teammates don't. I think we gave it everything we could.[88]

If you play as well as you can, leave it all on the court, that is satisfying in a way only understood by those who play the game.

Lauren needed to return to Seattle to play the remainder of the WNBA season, but she was hurt and hurt bad. "I'd made commitments to those teams, but it got to the point where I couldn't walk." As Seattle entered the playoffs Lauren couldn't get into bed without muttering "Oh my god, I've done something bad". She was "in a lot of pain", and virtually playing on one leg.[89] Lauren was left on the court in the playoffs against the *Minnesota Lynx* on 2 October for 31 minutes but scored just nine. On 30 September Seattle won at home, Lauren was on the court for 33 minutes but shot four from 17 to finish with a score of nine. Seattle lost the third match-up. Lauren played 27 minutes, shooting five from 12, scoring 12. The 2012 *Storm* season was harsh; the team won 16 but lost 18 to finish fourth in the Western Conference.

Lauren returned "down-under" and regardless of her injuries she remained optimistic.

> Hey the sun is shining, we're alive and living in this beautiful country, I really can't complain all that much. I am going to be better coming back from this [injury] and the goals I am setting for myself moving forward are to come back fitter and healthier, ready to take on the world again.[90]

This was the desire, but in professional sports the link between the imagined and reality is often tenuous. She was at least at home and could continue to draw strength from Maree and Gary. Whenever she was injured or in a bad place overseas, a phone-call and they was on the next plane. "I may have had a nervous breakdown if they had not been around."

The Canberra public was supportive and just glad she was home. The crowds at the AIS stadium were loyal but the level of stress kept building. Lauren realised her $1,000,000 contract to play three out of the next four seasons for the *Canberra Capitals* came with huge expectations. She believed she could recapture her best basketball form and would lead the *Caps* to another WNBL championship. The treatment for a tear in her abductor magnus muscle was ongoing with a great many needles – "40 injections all up, it was just a nightmare". Still the injury was not healing. The *Caps* were struggling; the team had been built around Lauren and she wasn't playing – the Canberra team was losing more games than they were winning. No one could doubt that Lauren was totally dejected as she sat glumly on the bench.

> I don't want to let anyone down again, I hate it and it's a horrible feeling – I want to be there with my teammates.[91]

As the first months of 2013 passed the crowds began to dwindle as the *Caps* hovered at the bottom of the WNBL ladder and news came that Lauren had undergone surgery – she would not play this season. The public mood altered; one newspaper column read: "Injured athletes need to be saved from themselves". The *Seattle Storm*'s decision to play Lauren Jackson under duress in its WNBA play-off campaign was selfish".[92] Basketball Canberra Chief Executive Officer, Tony Jackson, highlighted the level of frustration:

> Seattle may not have been aware of what it was dealing with either, but it was clear Jackson was in pain and in need of rest. It is highly doubtful Seattle would have played

her if it was involved in routine regular-season games. Understandably the *Canberra Capitals* are disgruntled they have been given the rough end of the pineapple and will not see a commodity sponsors have paid $333,000 a year for on court this WNBL season. ... It's been well argued and debated that cultures in other leagues around the world is win at all costs, forget about player welfare and someone else picks that up down the track. We can't allow that to be us every time.[93]

Lauren, "the commodity", was caught in the middle. "The biggest thing for me was I didn't want to disappoint anybody. I still don't".[94] Her rehabilitation continued and she announced that for the first time since she joined the *Seattle Storm* as the 2001 no.1 draft choice, she would not play in the WNBA in 2013. *Storm* pain continued when Sue Bird announced knee surgery would result in her exclusion from the 2013 team also.

Lauren wondered if it was just too hard; if the sacrifices, the juggling act, the injuries were worth it – she was physically and emotionally exhausted. Retirement entered the mind.

I've played with a broken back, broken ankles, broken fingers and toes, but I couldn't actually play, and that was the one thing where for the first time in my career I'm like, "Damn, I'm really not invincible".[95]

The incredible pace of the previous dozen years had left little time to reflect but Lauren was now considering her future. She had completed a Diploma in Business Management and had begun to study psychology through Lomonosov Moscow State University. It was difficult with her full-on basketball regime and moving constantly between continents. The intellectual direction changed and she commenced a degree in Women's Studies. While living in Canberra and moving in a wider circle of acquaintances Lauren had become aware of society's darker side. She had met women who had been abused and women touched by violence and had regretted there were not enough hours in her day to do more, she wanted to be more involved with women's refuges. Lauren agreed to be patron of the NSW Rape Crisis Centre:

> I'm passionate about promoting an awareness of the impacts sexual assault and domestic violence have on an individual and our society; it's the first step in creating change. I'm equally passionate about the services that NSWRCC provide, and I am proud to be their patron.[96]

Whilst physical rehabilitation continued in 2013 Lauren felt more settled emotionally than ever when she moved into her new Albury home. The commanding two-storey house on a hill overlooking the restful waters of Lake Hume was built to her specifications. High ceilings were the first essential and lots of glass to fully appreciate the Australian scenery close behind; she could sit on her top deck and hear nothing but nature.

> Every room I feel really happy in, I mean, there's not one place I don't want to be in this house … I'm just getting to that age where … I need to find where I'm happiest and then obviously make some roots. I needed that peace and that sort of calmness in my life.[97]

The pace had slowed and "I have loved living back in Australia and it's given me time to do other things."

On 27 February 2013 the Australian Government hosted a glittering function at Parliament House to celebrate Australia's top 100 women athletes of all time. Named the greatest was Dawn Fraser, the first of only three swimmers in Olympic history to win individual gold medals for the same event (100m freestyle) at three successive Olympics. Four-time Olympic athletics sprint gold medalist Betty Cuthbert was the second. Seven-time surfing World Champion Layne Beachley and, Margaret Court (Smith) winner of more women's major tennis titles than any other player, could not be separated for third position. The athlete chosen fifth was Lauren Jackson.[98]

In February 2013 Lauren accepted the role of Australian Womensport & Recreation Association Ambassador.

> Australia needs more strong, healthy, women and girls participating in all levels of sport and recreation and taking leadership roles in all levels of life from government, sport, schools and social groups.[99]

She also continued to be concerned with the disparity in sport: "there is a very big gap between women and men in sport especially here in Australia"; a smile appears, "and we're great".

Sport is fundamental to modern day culture. There have been comparisons made between sport and battles between armies defending geographic regions and populations. It is also a lot simpler. For a couple of hours Lauren Jackson removes people from the ordinariness of their lives and they ride with her into athletic supremacy. They return to their everyday jobs, as mundane as they may be but that amazing lay-up, that turnaround fade-away jump shot, that three-point shot that really deserved five given it was successful from just over the half way line, that look on the opposing player's face when a perfectly executed lay-up shot is abruptly ejected by the outstretched hand of No.15; are discussed and appreciated for days or more.

In February 2013 *Storm* Head Coach Brian Agler said: "Lauren is the best player in the world at her position so it will be impossible to replace her".[100] As the pain dissipated and fitness returned Lauren considered her options. "I'm running up hills … pain-free, so it's brilliant. I feel good".[101] It took a little more time but the challenges involved with elite basketball, passion for the sport and the feeling that it could be "fun" again, began to motivate. There was the knowledge that the *Opals* would play New Zealand's *Tall Ferns* in Canberra on 18 August 2013 to qualify for the 2014 FIBA World Championships in Turkey. Loyalty to the green and gold proved yet again paramount – Lauren was back[102].

www.nswrapecrisis.com.au

1. In 1977 she averaged 27.7 points and 16.4 rebounds.
2. Interview Maree and Gary Jackson, June 2008.
3. ibid.
4. Brown, P. Email, 10 July 2008.
5. Jackson, L. Interview, May 2008.
6. Brown, P. Email, 10 July 2008.
7. Stewart, M. Interview, July 2008.
8. Brown, P. Email, 10 July 2008.
9. ibid.

10. Michele Timms (Capt), Rachael Sporn (VC), Carla Boyd, Sandy Brondello, Trish Fallon, Michelle Griffiths, Shelley Sandie and Jenny Whittle. There were four new members in the team: Kristi Harrower, Jo Hill, Annie La Fleur and Lauren Jackson.

11. *60 Minutes*, Channel 9, "Hoop-la", 28 September 2003.

12. *Sport Monthly*, ABC, January 2003, "The weight of the world".

13. ibid.

14. Jackson, L. Interview, 1 June 2008.

15. *Stateline Canberra*, ABC, 11 November 2005.

16. 17.2 per game and third in blocked shots (2.89).

17. Along with Trish Fallon, Jenny Whittle, Michele Brogan, Allison Tranquilli and Sandy Brondello. For her AIS classmates Penny Taylor and Suzy Batkovic as well as Hollie Grima, Laura Summerton and Jae Kingi this was their first Worlds.

18. With Japan, Argentina and Spain. Other qualifiers were Lithuania, Yugoslavia, Senegal, Chinese Taipei, Russia, Tunisia, France, Cuba, Yugoslavia, and the US. China, being the host nation, qualified automatically.

19. Stirling, J. Interview, July 2008.

20. www.sports.espn.go.com/wnba/columns/storyid=1844323 "From Down Under to Seattle ... Jackson rules", 22 July 2004.

21. (21.2ppg), blocks (1.94bpg) and rebounds (9.3rpg).

22. Interview Maree and Gary Jackson, June 2008.

23. Her field goal percentage was 50 per cent. She managed 19 assists, 25 steals and pulled down 193 rebounds in the short season.

24. www.wnba.com/storm/news/Jackson_Sleepless_But_In_Seattle

25. ibid.

26. *The Seattle Times*, 30 June 2004.

27. She would receive the award in 2005 and 2008 also.

28. Which included 11of 17 from the field.

29. She finished July with an average of 22.3 points per game.

30. *The Seattle Times*, 20 June 2004.

31. *The Washington Post*, 29 July 2004.

32. *Delco Time*s, 3 July 2004.

33. www.espn.go.com/wnba/storyid=1824568&src=desktop, 22 July 2004, "WNBA Mag issue features athletes competing in Athens".

34. *The Seattle Times*, 24 June 2004.

35. ibid.

36. Final score was 94–55. Lauren scored 28 points.

37. USA beat Russia 66–62.

38. Players included Dawn Staley, Sheryl Swoopes, Lisa Leslie, Tamika Catchings, Tina Thompson, Shannon Johnson, Ruth Riley, Diana Taurasi, Yolanda Griffith, Swin Cash and Sue Bird

39. Lauren finished the Olympic tournament with the average of 15.9 points and 8.4 rebounds,

40. With 17 wins and 8 losses.

41. Seattle won at Indiana 76–70 with Lauren top scoring with 20. At home against the Mercury Lauren scored 25 of the *Storm's* 73–58 win.

42. Tully scored nine points, grabbed five rebounds and made four assists.

43. Score was 64–54. The *Sacramento Monarchs* beat Los Angeles to advance to the Western Conference Finals and give the *Storm* home-court advantage.

44. Lauren scored 23 and grabbed nine rebounds

45. Batkovic, S. Interview, July 2008.

46. She finished third in blocks, 62 in all; third in three point field goal percentage 42.5; seventh in field goal percentage and tenth in rebounding.

47. Batkovic, S. Interview, July 2008.

48. ibid.

49. There was one game of 31 against Sacramento on 3 July. There were eleven games of 20 or more.

50. www.espn.go.com/wnba/columns/story, 22 July 2004, "From Down Under in Seattle".

51. She had scored double-figures in 150, topped the 20 point mark 67 times and hit at least 30 points on eight occasions, including her career-high 35 points at Phoenix on 25 May.

52. *Seattle Storm*, News, 13 March 2007, "Jackson Breaking Records in Korea".

53. www.basketball.net.au

54. www.espn.go.com/wnba/storyid=1844323, 22 July 2004, "From Down Under to Seattle".

55. *Sports Illustrated*, 23 July 2007.

56. www.wnba.com/storm/news/jackson070726, 26 July 2007, "Jackson Making History, More Concerned With Wins".

57. *7.30 Report*, ABC, "Aussie globetrotter heads for Beijing", 29 April 2008.

58. The United States has arguably an easier competition with New Zealand, Mali, Spain and the Czech Republic.

59. www.abc.net.au/olympics/2008/sports/basketball/media "First Cut: Jackson ready to 'focus on the Olympics'".

60. The winning score was 75–55.

61. *The Sydney Morning Herald*, 17 August 2008.

62. Opals defence caused their opposition to turn over the ball nineteen times. Lauren could be rested for much of the game but with just 25 minutes on the court she was still the match top scorer with seventeen points and the top rebounder with 12.

63. *The Seattle Times*, 26 September 2008.

64. ibid.

65. *The Daily Telegraph*, 21 January 2010.

66. She averaged 31 minutes per game, with a field goal percentage of 46.2 per cent, and a three point field goal percentage of 34.6 per cent. She had a free throw shooting percentage of 91.0 per cent. She made 220 field goals, ranking sixth in the league, and ranked fifth in the league with 476 field goal attempts. She attempted 156 three point field goals this season, ranking eighth in the league. She had a player efficiency of 27.9, ranking first in the league in this category this season.

67. www.wnba.com/features/preview2011_storm, "2010 in Review: Lauren Jackson".

68. ibid.

69. www.wnba.com/features/preview2011_storm

70. ibid.

71. ibid.

72. Lauren averaged 24.9 minutes per game. Her field goal percentage was 39.6 per cent, her three point field goal percentage was 31.1 per cent and free throw shooting percentage was 88.4 per cent.

73. www.wnba.com/features/preview2011_storm

74. *The Border Mail*, 14 December 2010, "Jackson stadium quest hits trouble".

75. www.laurenjacksonsportscentre.com.au/about/lauren_jackson. Lauren Jackson Sports Centre.

76. It would be a finalist in the *Portia Geach Memorial Art Prize*

77. *The Canberra Times*, 13 October 2011, "LJ signs on for Caps – at $330,000 a season".

78. *ABC news online*, 27 November 2009, "Jackson payment justified: Stanhope".

79. ibid.

80. ibid.

81. youtube, "Ros Casares Valencia feature on Trans World Sport".

82. 8.7 points, 3.1 rebounds, 0.9 assists per game.

83. www.wnba.com/storm/news/jackson.

84. www.StormBasketball.com 27 April 2011

85. *Grandstand*, ABC, 27 July 2012.

86. Sydney Morning Herald, 27 July 2013, "Grin and bear it, Lauren: Jackson to carry flag at Olympics opening ceremony".

87. Held by Brazilian Janeth Arcain.

88. *Sydney Morning Herald*, 12 August 2012, "Opals stand tall after gutsy bronze".

89. *The Canberra Times* 14 Dec 2012.

90. *Grandstand*, ABC, 3 November 2012.

91. *The Canberra Times*, 19 January 2013.

92. *The Canberra Times*, 12 Jan 2013.

93. ibid.

94. *The Canberra Times*, 8 Feb 2013.

95. *The Canberra Times*, 27 March 2013.

96. www.nswrapecrisis.com.au

97. *The Border Mail*, 5 March 2013.

98. First twenty-five in order: Dawn Fraser, Betty Cuthbert, Layne Beachley & Margaret Court, Lauren Jackson, Heather McKay, Rochelle Hawkes, Shirley Strickland, Anna Meares, Cathy Freeman, Karrie Webb, Liz Ellis, Elizabeth Kosmala, Belinda Clark, Louise Sauvage, Julie Murray, Shane Gould, Susie O'Neill, Evonne Goolagong, Sharelle McMahon, Betty Wilson, Marjorie Jackson-Nelson, Cheryl Salisbury, Sally Pearson, Alyson Annan.

99. www.australianwomensport.com.au

100. www.wnba.com/news/lauren_jackson-will not play 2013

101. *The Canberra Times*, 27 March 2013.

102. Unfortunately *Canberra Capitals* administration proved either negligent or arrogant or both and although Lauren offered to play the 2013/2014 WNBL season it is not to be.

Conclusion

When I embarked on this journey in 2008 I believed this book would be completed within a couple of years. I did not appreciate how challenging it would be to keep pace with six very different amazing women from very diverse spheres, nor how the twists and turns of their lives would reflect those of our world. Completing it in 2013 did, however, allow not only a more in-depth examination of the lives of Matilda House-Williams, Helen Reddy, Geraldine Cox, Natasha Stott Despoja, Fiona Wood and Lauren Jackson, but also a consideration of how much the lives of Australian women had evolved in five years and whether or not they had achieved equality in all aspects of Australian life.

Fundamental to equality in society is economics, because this in turn can lead to independence, education, opportunity and status. An article from *The Bulletin* of 8 February 1969, discussing the approaching test case on women's pay, commenced with the words: "I sometimes think most women have missed the point. It is their status which is important, not their salaries." Only 25 per cent, or 1,207,400 Australian women, were employed outside the home in 1968. In the United States and the United Kingdom however, 40 per cent of women and in "many European countries" 50 per cent, had jobs. The *Bulletin* journalist felt it necessary to mention how important it was for an Australian woman to finish at 3.30pm so "she will be home in time for the children, and … at 6.30 there will be a husband to feed". But that was 1968; one would think that in Australia 40 odd years on women's battle for equal salaries and status would be achieved?

Australia ratified the UN *Convention on the Elimination of All Forms of Discrimination against Women 1979* (CEDAW) in 1983. Under the terms Australia was required to take "all appropriate measures" and legislate to ensure the advancement of women; to guarantee human rights and equality with men. The *Sex Discrimination Act 1984* forced Australia to be more pro-active and the *Equal Employment Opportunity for Women Act 1986* did much the same. In 1999 language seemed to be the most important issue and the term "affirmative action" was removed, but the objectives remained the same:

    a. to promote the principle that employment for women should be dealt with on the basis of merit; and

    b. to promote, amongst employers, the elimination of discrimination against, and the provision of equal opportunity for, women in relation to employment matters; and

    c. to foster workplace consultation between employers and employees on issues concerning equal opportunity for women in relation to employment.

The 2008 study *Equal Employment for Women in the Workplace* revealed that within the corridors of corporate Australia "the myth of the male breadwinner" still lurked and was one of the underlying reasons why female executives were paid less than men. Female chief financial officers and chief operating officers earned 50 per cent less than men in the same positions within ASX 200 companies. It appeared that both government and business still believed:

She's a woman, eventually she is going to be having kids, maybe she is not going to be moving through career advancement as quickly as a man.[1]

The study *Census of Women in Leadership* the same year offered more disconcerting international comparison. Among Australia's top 200 companies there were only four women chairs and six women chief executive officers and just 8.3 per cent of board directors were women. Only 49 per cent of Australia's top companies had at least one woman on their board whereas in the USA it was 88 per cent and in the UK 76 per cent. New Zealand, Canada and South Africa all ranked higher than Australia. The percentage of women executive managers had actually gone backwards – dropping to 10.7 per cent from 12 per cent – and the number in the next level down dropped from 7.4 per cent to 5.9 per cent. Researchers were very concerned by "old-fashioned discrimination, rigid patterns and a lack of female mentors and role models for women failing to break through". The study predicted that women would remain marginalised while the employment world remained inflexible and structured to suit men and old boy networks. Leadership and management styles needed to alter before women with greater skills and qualifications became less reluctant to push themselves forward.[2] Another government report stated:

> Women are under-represented, under-paid and prevented from advancing in greater numbers to the most senior levels of leadership. This represents a huge waste of talent.[3]

However that was in 2008 and surely over the next five years progress would surely be made?.

The wording was changed again when *Equal Employment Opportunity for Women Act* was updated in 2012. It was specified that there should not be any discrimination on grounds of marital status, pregnancy or potential pregnancy, or breastfeeding or family responsibilities, nor indirect discrimination.[4] A few more clauses were added as was the word "men" but the reality was heartbreaking for anyone who had hoped for real progress.

The 2012 Census on *Women in Leadership* reported that more than 60 per cent of Australia's ASX 200 listed companies still did not have any women in their senior management ranks and women made up less than 10 per cent of executive key management personnel positions. There were only 12 female chief executives in the ASX 500. Just 9.2 per cent of ASX 500 board memberships were held by women and women occupied only 13 chair positions. Smaller and mid-tier entities were also falling short and company focus continued to be "on running the business and less on culture". Former Business Council of Australia chief Graham Bradley described the situation as an embarrassment; progress had been at "glacial pace".[5] At the current rate of increase it would take at least another 30 years to reach even the 40 per cent target – not parity.

When it came to women in leadership in 2012 Australia continued to lag behind many other western nations: 16 per cent of board directors in the United States were women (compared with 12.3 per cent in Australia); in South Africa 5.3 per cent of board chairs were women (compared with 3.0 per cent in Australia), and in Canada 6.1 per cent of CEOs were women (compared with 3.5 per cent in Australia). By 2012 women Commonwealth public servants comprised 57 per cent, but as the pyramid of promotion progressed their promotion opportunities diminished.[6]   The implementation of quotas looked to be imperative as employers continued to demonstrate significant reluctance to increase opportunities for women employees.[7] According to the Australian Bureau of Statistics:

> Women in Australia have more employment opportunities and are more educated than ever before, however gender equality at senior levels in the workplace has yet to be achieved. In senior leadership positions, men outnumber women across the public and private sectors, as well as in the upper and lower houses of federal parliament ...

Despite aspirations for more women in senior leadership roles, progress over the last 10 years has been slow. While in 2011 – 12 women represented close to half of the labour force at 46 per cent, and 45 per cent of professionals, women remain under-represented at senior levels within both the private and public sector.

Education is generally believed to be a prerequisite to advancement and security and in Australia women were distinguishing themselves. Nonetheless this did not equate into higher salaries or even the same. Across the developed world in 2011, 46 per cent of women and 31 per cent of men by age 34 would complete a university degree. Australia with just 1.6 per cent of the world's university graduates ranked tenth; but came sixth for women university graduates with 56 per cent.[8] That year a NSW study revealed that 72 per cent of girls completed year 12 compared with only 63 per cent of boys, and girls continually outperformed boys at Higher School Certificate level.[9] The 2012 *GradStats Report* conducted by Graduate Careers Australia showed however, that median full-time employment starting salaries for male graduates was $55,000 (up from $52,000 in 2011), compared to $50,000 for women (no change from 2011). The current graduate gender pay gap across all occupations was 9.1 per cent with the most pronounced being in architecture and building (17 per cent, $9,000 difference), and the least in law – but still a 7.8 per cent or $4,300 difference.[10]

Nationally by 2012 there was a 17.4 per cent salary disparity ($13,026 pa) between men and women in general employment. The state with the largest differential was Western Australia with 25.8 per cent and then Queensland with 21.4 per cent, suggesting that the mining boom was a boom for male workers. Women who did manage a career in mining earned around $35,000 a year less. The ACT with an emphasis on white collar professions boasted the least disparity but this was still 12 per cent. Whilst the physicality involved with the mining industry occupations could account for salary disparity, another example of pay inequality was the very non-physical financial/banking sector. The National Australia Bank boasted that in 2012 its "gender pay gap" had decreased from 37 per cent in 2007–08 to 29 per cent; the financial/banking sector gender pay gap in 2012 averaged 31 per cent.[11]

Regardless of the change to the wording of successive wage equity and discrimination legislation, they remained mere words. The Australian workplace was still modeled on a previous age, resisted change and greater flexibility for individuals, couples, and the modern family. In the first half of 2012 the Australian Attorney-General Mark Dreyfus, announced:

> There was significant anecdotal evidence that women were being demoted, sacked or having their roles or hours unfavourably restructured while on parental leave or on return from leave.[12]

Women continued to fight for equality in wages and promotion and continued to be considered less – because they were women.

The 1968 *Bulletin* article had suggested that women should not be intent on gaining parity in salaries because status was more important. The *Weekend Australian* 23–24 March 2013 published a "Top 50" list of Australia's most influential people. Prime Minister Julia Gillard was first. Gina Rinehart (Hancock Prospecting) managed to edge out the Australian cricket captain, Michael Clarke, for 11th place. The next women in the list were No. 26 Gail Kelly (Westpac Bank chief), No. 32 Catherine Livingstone (Telstra chair), No. 45 ABC 7.30 host Leigh Sales, and the only other woman on the list was Peta Credlin, Opposition Leader Tony Abbott's chief of staff coming in at No. 49. Women made up 10 per cent of the most influential people in Australia. It would appear 45 years on equity in "salaries" and "status" were yet to be achieved.

The "glass ceiling" is the term often applied to women being unable to progress from middle to senior management, and inequality is due to unconscious bias towards age, gender and race. Unconscious bias cannot be measured but is imbued in a culture, embedded in a society. This book features projected images and editorial emphasis in the media because the role of the media in all forms is pivotal. Not only does media offer a window into the culture of the nation but the media has the power to manipulate and tell the story the media, and vested interests, want to safeguard the status quo. The globalisation of the media and the internet ensures that a particular emphasis is instantly transported to Australia and it is one which has increasingly subjugated women.

On 6 May 2011 the New York published orthodox Jewish paper *Di Tzeitung* published a photo of the US White House situation room and President Obama surrounded by key advisors monitoring the US raid which resulted in the killing of Osama bin Laden. The newspaper chose to digitally delete the image of US Secretary of State, Hillary Clinton, and the Director for Counterterrorism in the Executive Office of the President, Audrey Tomason. The newspaper defended this decision with the comment that it did not publish images of women. *Grazia* an Italian fashion magazine airbrushed, or as Helen Reddy referred to it as "virtual liposuction", the Duchess of Cambridge's already tiny waistline on its May 2011 cover.

On 10 April 2012 World Youth AIDS Ambassador, Ashley Judd, launched an internet paper titled "The Conversation" – about women's bodies and how women were commonly defined by how they looked by the media. As an actor she admitted that the media had promoted her career but had been equally antagonistic. She had struggled to retain her "power, my self-esteem" and her "autonomy". To preserve these she desisted from reading and listening to any media about herself because it was so destructive. Unfortunately media coverage of the most recent event she attended was impossible to ignore and it was:

> pointedly nasty, gendered and misogynistic and embodies what all girls and women in our culture endure every day, in ways both outrageous and subtle. The assault on our body image, the hyper-sexualization of girls and women and subsequent degradation of our sexuality, as we walk through the decades, and the general incessant objectification ... Patriarchy is a system in which both women and men participate. It privileges, inter alia, the interest of boys and men over bodily integrity, autonomy, and dignity of girls and women. It is subtle, insidious, and never more dangerous than when women passionately deny that they themselves are engaging in it.[13]

In Australia the media and the position of women have never been more in conflict than during this decade. This is because the conservative status quo has never been more challenged.

Elected office is an important measure of women's empowerment in society. It had been a marathon 41 years between when Australian women were permitted to stand for seats within the Commonwealth Parliament and the first woman attaining a seat. In 2006, women made up just 31 per cent of Australians elected to the Federal Parliament. Canberra ABC journalist and news reader, Virginia Haussegger, believed it was "freakish to see a woman succeed in politics".

> The handful of women-to-watch and women-leaders-in-the-making have all been shot down one way or other as whores, harlots, liars, or lightweights: think Kernot, Kelly, Kirner, Lawrence, Stott Despoja, Bronwyn Bishop.[14]

When Queen Elizabeth II arrived in Australia's national capital in October 2011 she was greeted by Governor-General Quentin Bryce, Prime Minister Julia Gillard and the ACT Chief Minister, Katy Gallagher. It was a unique situation that all were women. In 2012 women made up half of Australia's population yet they made up less than one-third or 29 per cent of all Federal parliamentarians – 66 out of 226. Only seven ministers including the Prime Minister were women, compared with 23 ministers who were men. The number of women in the Senate was 29 or 38 per cent; whilst in the House of Representatives only 37 or 25 per cent were women.[15] The Senate had traditionally boasted a higher proportion of women because it was regarded as less desirable given the lack of direct governance and access to the prime ministership and ministerial positions.

The ANZSOG Institute of Governance, at the University of Canberra, organised a panel of speakers in August 2011 which included ACT Chief Minister Katy Gallagher, former Victorian Police Chief Commissioner, Christine Nixon, and Natasha Stott Despoja. All had been subjected to overt and covert discrimination. Christine Nixon was told she needed to "look tough", to go out and "look like the boys and they'll stop picking on you for being a woman". The ACT Chief Minister recalled how she was once mistaken as the tea lady and that she continued to struggle with the perception that female leaders were weaker than their male counterparts; she had constantly been asked was she "tough enough". Natasha Stott Despoja agreed that because leaders were commonly men, leadership qualities were defined in a masculine manner. She conceded that progress had been made since she entered politics, the percentage of women had risen from 15 per cent in 1995 to 30 per cent. "But 30 per cent, I can't get excited about 30 per cent." Of the 1,595 Australians who have served in both houses of Australia's Parliament since federation only 162 or 10.2 per cent have been women.[16]

Australian National University's Gender Institute School convenor, Dr Fiona Jenkins, is another who believes that women in "leadership are profoundly penalised because 'being a woman' and 'being a leader' are stereotypically perceived as identities in tension". She considers the media is "irresponsible" in its shallow interpretation of gender issues and a deeper discussion was timely because:

> of the deep structural ways in which gender operates
> throughout our society to perpetuate inequalities. Gender
> is about systemic power-relations first and foremost, not
> given identities that set men and women at odds.[17]

The gender agenda encompasses issues that affect everyone's human rights and quality of life.

The unprecedented situation where the highest offices in the nation, Governor-General and Prime Minister (PM), were held by women unleashed an equally unprecedented climate of personal attack and lack of respect for office. Prime Minister Gillard faced a no win situation. When acting in a tough dominant manner she was reviled, when she did not she was ridiculed in a blatant attempt to undermine her authority. A conservative media constantly belittled the PM with dismissive sexist jibes and put-downs. The predominantly male ranks of political columnists denounced her governance and referred to the PM as "Julia" or "her". The vitriolic was unfettered – radio host Allan Jones claimed women "were destroying the joint" and announced that the Prime Minister's father "had died of shame".

ACT Chief Minister Gallagher had been subjected to "overt and subliminal sexism in my working life, most women have", but she had never witnessed:

> The nastiness, the sexism, or the deep intrusion into the
> most personal aspects of my life the Prime Minister has

had to endure. … over the past three years, the simmering undercurrent of sexism has seeped into public life and into accepted national dialogue.[18]

To mark International Women's Day in March 2012 the Australian Graduate School of Management awarded Prime Minister Gillard an "A" for effort. Professor of History Marilyn Lake, would write in *The Brisbane Times* on 25 June 2013, that the achievements of the Gillard government had not been rightfully recognised because of the "relentless persecution by senior male journalists, the vilification, the sexist mockery, the personal abuse and contempt". This was because of "the hysteria of men who could not abide the spectacle of a woman in power".[19]

The climate within Australia's Parliament was no less disrespectful and sexist. On 1 June 2011 Finance Minister Penny Wong was defending the Government's position when Tasmanian Senator, David Bushby "meowed" at her because in his words her reaction "was like an angry cat". Senator Wong reacted:

> It's extraordinary. The blokes are allowed to yell, but if a woman stands her ground you want to make that kind of comment, it's sort of schoolyard politics, mate.

In the larger green chamber, the debate was no less volatile with the Minister for Health Tanya Plibersek responding to a comment with:

> What I am tired of and what so many women are tired of, is that whenever there is conflict, we have the Leader of the Opposition and his senior ministers reverting to this sort of sexist language.

Her Excellency Quentin Bryce, AC, was appointed Australia's 25th Governor-General on 5 September 2008 – the first woman to assume the post in 107 years. It was another first for an Australian with a distinguished career as a lawyer, academic and senior public servant who had advanced human rights and equality, been appointed an Officer of the Order of Australia in 1988 and a Companion of the Order of Australia in 2003; and served as Governor of Queensland. However, *Weekend Australian* columnist Christopher Pearson, showed unprecedented disrespect for the office and for a newly appointed Governor-General:

> Part of Bryce's problem is that she's not especially bright and is prone to saying the first thing that comes into her head. Considering that she was once a legal academic; her grasp of constitutional law in recent years has left a lot to be desired too.[20]

In November 2012 a survey of readers appeared in a *Sydney Morning Herald* special magazine titled – "What Women Want". 1,524 readers had responded to questions including which women they found most inspiring. Dr Fiona Wood headed the list with reader comments such as "incredibly intelligent and driven" and "she appears to just get to work and get the job done". Second most admired was Australia's Governor-General:

> She is a mature woman in a position of great responsibility. She has achieved and demands respect while remaining steadfastly a woman – not aping male characteristics. She's intelligent, driven, competent and likeable.

Third was Australia's Prime Minister with reader comments including: "She is a great role model for a future generation". One 23-year-old reader wrote:

> She epitomises the 21st century working woman, works hard, sticks with her convictions … has been forced to navigate her way through a male-dominated industry and has made sacrifices along the way to be the best that she can be.

Journalist and editor Ita Buttrose, who in 2013 became Australian of the Year, was voted next because "she showed you could be intelligent, successful, tough, caring, as well as feminine". The fifth and final Australian on the most inspiring woman list was Senator Penny Wong:

> She is a strong, principled, articulate and smart woman who also happens to be Asian and gay. And she's doing a great job in a field that has traditionally been male, white and conservative.

Clearly by the end of 2012 there was not general agreement that women were "destroying the joint" and, entrenched beliefs based on biology and the inferior status of women within Australian culture, was clearly under challenge.

A cornerstone of Australian culture is sport. Australian sportswomen have led the world, and accomplished countless physical feats and records; yet read any newspaper, watch any television sports report, or listen to any radio sports summary and sportswomen are all but invisible. In 1996 the Australian Sports Commission found that 95.1 per cent of radio, 56.2 per cent of television and 79.1 per cent of newspaper sports coverage was of men's sport. Once horse-racing and mixed sport team news was removed, women achieved only 1.4 per cent of radio, 2 per cent of television and 10.7 per cent of newspaper coverage. Since 1996 the coverage of women's sports has decreased. The 2010 report *Towards a Level Playing Field: Sport and Gender in Australian media revealed*:

> Television news reports on female sport had the lowest average duration of all the types of sport news analysed; with reports on male sport having an average duration of 30 seconds longer than reports on female sport. Female athletes generally need to win in order to receive media coverage, whereas male athletes tend to receive coverage regardless of their success.

In 2010 male sport occupied 81 per cent of television news and current affairs reporting and 86 per cent of non-news sport coverage on television.[21] In 2011 the Australian Government allocated $1.45 million towards a one-off scheme for women in sport media grants. Under this program funding was allocated to support media exposure of women's sport in Australia. In 2012 the Australian Broadcasting Commission (ABC), the only television station televising live women's sport (soccer, netball and basketball) announced it would "drastically cut back live television coverage of the country's two main women's national leagues".[22]

Australian women have long struggled for their share of the public stage and recognition of their achievements not only in sport but also in literature, art, television and film. A 2010 survey by the group Vida: Women in Literary Arts revealed a gaping disparity in the number of books by male and female authors reviewed in literary journals in the US and Britain. A similar discrepancy was noticed in Australia. After the 2009 and 2011 Miles Franklin Awards had all-male shortlists and with women authors having won only thirteen times (including four times by Thea Astley) since 1957, the inaugural Stella Prize was introduced in April 2013 to recognise women authors.

Similarly in art, the first Archibald Prize was awarded in 1921; artist Max Meldrum was critical when the Archibald was awarded to a woman artist, Nora Heysen, for the first time in 1938. Meldrum believed "women could not be expected to paint as well as men". The harsh comment did him no harm and he won the Archibald the following two years. The next year a woman artist won Archibald was 1960 – Judy Cassab – and she won again in 1967. Janet Dawson won in 1973, Davida Allen in 1986, Wendy Sharp won in 1996, Cherry Hood in 2002, Del Kathryn Barton won the award in 2008 and 2013 – women have won the Archibald nine times in 93 years. Male subjects predominate Archibald finals as do male finalists. The Portia Geach Memorial Award is an annual art prize, established in 1961 to recognise Australian women portraitists.

Since television arrived on our shores in 1956 it has been the major form of entertainment and through the small screen, cultural trends, particular social accents and information, are delivered into households. The role of women on our television screens has taken large strides since the days of older men presenting the news whilst women disappeared as soon as a wrinkle appeared, and when women stood looking glamorous behind male quiz comperes. Jana Wendt broke into the all-male *60 Minutes* in 1982 and was the first woman promoted to commercial prime time. Greater freedom was enjoyed by government-funded television stations which meant that women like Caroline Jones, Anne Deveson and Geraldine Doogue could prosper; SBS TV newsreader Mary Kostakidis presented the evening news for nearly 20 years and Lee Lin Chin has continued since 1992 to the present. Commercial news and current affairs programmes gradually allowed more women to co-compere, but there is a dearth of roles for women in mainstream television and film.

There has been little research done on visual media. A University of Southern California study analysed US and Canadian PG and PG-13 films released between 2006 and 2009. Of the 5,554 speaking roles, 71 per cent of the characters had boys and men's voices. It seems that whether they were animals or people the female characters were sexy, young, beautiful and were passive sidekicks – "eye candy". A quarter of the tiny-waisted female bodies depicted wore sexy attire and one in five was partly nude. Those who created, produced, filmed and directed film were predominantly men: 93 per cent of the directors, 87 per cent of the writers and 80 per cent of the producers. In the early days of cinema films like *The Perils of Pauline* and *The Hazards of Helen* showcased female protagonists. The 1976–79 television show Wonder Woman offered a pretty capable physical "shero" but the creator of *The Bionic Woman* (1976) staring Lindsay Wagner, admitted he was scripting his ideal date rather than an action hero.[23] *Charlie's Angels* flirted their way past the adversaries rather than beat them to death and they worked for a male boss, Charlie. It took another 20 years before western television featured a female who preferred to beat the bad guys rather than bed them, and *Xena: Warrior Princess*, filmed in New Zealand, battled her way on to television screens. Producers believed the show might last more than a season but Xena and her side-kick Gabriel lasted six seasons, the final episode being filmed in 2001. Whilst the stars were attractive they fought their own battles. Other series have succeeded with female main characters but most commonly television and film are dominated by leading men.

Reality television has also spurned many more male characters than female. One of the rare studies into visual media, conducted by Royal Melbourne Institute of Technology University and released in 2012, offered only a small-scale examination. *Women in the Victorian Film, Television and Related Industries* did show that 40 per cent of the women surveyed "saw their gender as a disadvantage". Another interesting finding was that 65 per cent of women believed gender inequality had remained the same over the previous five years, 20 per cent believed it had improved and 13 per cent believed there had been a deterioration (2 per cent "other"). By contrast 57 per cent of men surveyed believed it had remained the same, 43 per cent believed the status quo had improved for women in the film and television industries and none believed there had been any deterioration.[24]

International Women's Day (IWD) each year highlights the degree of discrimination, inequality and violence against women. On IWD 2008 the UN High Commission of Human Rights announced: "Laws that discriminate against women are still to be found on the statute books of virtually every country".[25] A 2012 Human Rights Commission survey found that a quarter of women had been sexually harassed at work in the past five years. The vast majority don't report it, and a third who complain experience backlash – from further harassment to demotion.

Violence against women has taken increased prominence in the international news during 2012 and 2013. In Afghanistan a Taliban-led insurgency keeps girls from attending school. Up to 80 per cent of Afghan women face forced marriage, and nearly two-thirds are married before the legal age of sixteen. In Pakistan honour killings of women and gang-rape punishment of women for their or their family's alleged indiscretions were widely reported. In countries such as Poland and Italy there are few reproductive rights and restrictive abortion law. During the last 12 months we could be forgiven for believing violence against women and girls has proliferated. Headlines tell of too many women killed or injured by male assailants. Millions of girls and women are caught up in conflict in Syria, Somali, Sudan, the Congo, Mali, Papua New Guinea, South Africa, Afghanistan, Colombia, Timor Leste and all over the world. A staggering statistic is that one in three women will be raped or beaten in their lifetime. Violence against women is endemic and undermines social and economic development.

Cultural superiority cannot be assumed by people of the West. If inequality prevails a "rape-supportive culture" exists – a complex of beliefs that excuse, tolerate or even condone violence against women. A "rape culture" is one in which sexual violence is made to be inevitable and invisible. It becomes more about the kind of people who are raped, and the kind of behaviour that "invites" assault – victim-blaming – where we condone offensive behaviour and hold others responsible. In January 2013, in the capital of Australia, three women described as "promotional girls" were mobbed by a group of Summernats patrons, who doused them with water, ripped off parts of their clothing and attempted to drag them from the car. In an average week in Canberra, 150 sexually assaulted girls and women receive emergency contraception at Canberra Hospital. One in five women in the ACT have been the target of physical or sexual violence. The ACT Government took the unusual initiative in 2012 of giving $45,000 derived from confiscated criminal assets to four women's groups: "White Ribbon", the Domestic Violence Prevention Council, the Canberra Rape Crisis Centre and the Women's Services Network. Instead of women being told it is not safe to walk in a certain place, at a certain time, wearing certain clothes or behave in a certain way the accent of blame needs to be moved back to the perpetrators. And a stronger message has to be delivered to publically denounce those who condone harassment and discrimination and shame those who participate in degradation of and violence against women. Culture and faith are not excuses for violence against women.

It is the weekend before Mother's Day 2013. Over morning coffee I peruse the newspaper and accompanying supplements. The *Sunday Canberra Times* dated 5 May 2013 bears the headline "Child Care Fail: Most ACT centres don't meet benchmarks". Is the headline intended to genuinely raise a very important situation or is it intended to set off mothers' guilt? I turn to the back, to the sport pages. I count 14 pages of men's sport, especially football of various codes and standards. There is a very small paragraph on Lauren Jackson continuing to reserve her decision as to when she will next play for the *Canberra Capitals*. Page 7 of the news section is given over to photographs of pencil thin women models in clothes which would never fit or suit the average woman. The Sunday "Relax" supplement is a contradiction of food and diets, of celebrity male chefs and diets and exercise programmes for women. The newspaper is full of catalogues of Mother's Day gift ideas. Household appliances predominate, and the colour pink. At least there are televisions advertised and their promise of relief from all the housework, but then I remember reading a survey which said the man of the house controls the remote.

Most of us are less inspiring and less capable than the six women featured in this book. They demonstrate intelligence, altruism, bravery, ability and most of all enormous determination to be heard and realise their potential and they encourage us to do what we can. Their journeys offer an insight into life in Australia and overseas. They also give rise to the questions: Is it over? Are we there yet? Are Australian women truly represented in positions of power and leadership, free of discrimination, free of detrimental cultural overtones, free to feel safe in their own country? On a good day we can see progress, but sometimes it is hard to convince ourselves we are not going backwards.

And so it was in June 2013 when Australia's first woman Prime Minister, Julia Eileen Gillard, was deposed by her party. For the duration of her Prime Ministership she had faced an unrelenting, undermining campaign by a former Labor Party Prime Minister and his supporters. Their party chose to ignore Gillard Government policy achievements and return to the past for fear of losing the next Federal election. This was shameful. But what more did it say about Australia and Australians? As Anne Summers wrote, "if you are a woman, it is hard not to see parallels in your own life when a female leader is so brutally felled".[26] This nation was clearly unsettled by a woman in the top job. Australian society continues to have a fundamental issue with sexism.

Ngambri elder, Matilda House-Williams, said: "They may win the war but I will win a few battles". Matilda is right but isn't it time the war was over? How much more enriched Australia would be if all individuals were judged purely on merit.

---

1. *The Canberra Times*, 26 January 2008.

2. *The Canberra Times*, 1 Nov 2008.

3. pay, power and position: Beyond the 2008 EOWA Australian Census Of Women In Leadership, www.wge.gov.au

4. The language was now: " (a) to promote and improve gender equality (including equal remuneration between women and men) in employment and in the workplace; and (b) to support employers to remove barriers to the full and equal participation of women in the workforce, in recognition of the disadvantaged position of women in relation to employment matters; and (c) to promote, amongst employers, the elimination of discrimination on the basis of gender in relation to employment matters (including in relation to family and caring responsibilities); and (d) to foster workplace consultation between employers and employees on issues concerning gender equality in employment and in the workplace; and (e) to improve the productivity and competitiveness of Australian business through the advancement of gender equality in employment and in the workplace".

5. *The Australian*, 2 May 2013

6. In 2012, women made up 39 per cent of the Senior Executive Service (up from 28 per cent in 2002). The proportion of women in middle management within the APS was much closer to that of men, with 47 per cent of Executive Level (EL) managers (up from 36 per cent in 2002) being women. The proportion of women in middle management within the APS was much closer to that of men, with 47 per cent of Executive Level (EL) managers (up from 36 per cent in 2002) being women.

7. *The Australian*, 2 May 2013

8. OECD "Education at a Glance 2011".

9. NSW Government, "The NSW Premier's Council on Preventing Violence Against Women", 2012.

10. http://www.wgea.gov.au Australian Government, Work Place Gender Equality Agency. Dentistry (15.7 per cent, $14,400 difference), optometry (8.5 per cent $7,000 difference).

11. *Australian Financial Review*, 5 December 2012.

12. *Sunday Canberra Times*, 23 June 2013.

13. http://ashleyjudd.com/blog/

14. *The Canberra Times*, 7 Oct 2006.

15. www.aph.gov.au Only 36 of the 150 who sit in Australia's House of Representatives in 2012 are women.

16. www.aph.gov.au/About_Parliament/...Library/.../Womeninparliament

17. *The Canberra Times*, 21 June 2013.

18. ibid.

19. The Brisbane Times, 25 June 2013.

20. Weekend Australian, 27-28 September 2008

21. "Australian Government response to the Senate Environment, Communications, Information Technology and the Arts References Committee report: About Time! Women in Sport and Recreation in Australia, Australian Government Department of Regional Australia, Local Government, Arts and Sport, October 2012.

22. *The Australian*, 16 August 2012.

23. http://www.imdb.com/title/tt0073965/ Bionic woman.

24. French, L. Women in the Victorian Film, Television and Related Industries, RMIT, 2012.

25. *The Canberra Times*, 10 March 2008.

26. www.smh.com.au/comment/mad-as-hell-and-not-ready-to-make-nice 13 July 2013.

Bibliography

BOOKS and PUBLICATIONS

Commonwealth of Australia, Senate Hansard, 25 June 2008.

Chipp D and Larkin J. Don Chipp: *The Third Man*, Rigby, 1978.

Cox, Geraldine. *Home is Where the Heart Is*, Pan Macmillan, Sydney, 2000.

Craven, P (ed). *The Best Australian Essays*, Black Inc., 2000, Stretton, H. Leaders.

Flexner A. *Medical Education in the United States and Canada*, New York, Carnegie Foundation for the Advancement of Teaching, 1910.

French, L. *Women in the Victorian Film, Television and Related Industries*, RMIT, 2012.

Grieve, N. and Burns, A. (eds) *Australian Women: Contemporary Feminist Thought*, 1995, Oxford University Press, Simms, Marian. "Women and the secret garden of politics: preselection, political parties and political science".

Henderson, A. *Getting Even: Women MPs on Life, Power and Politics,* Harper Collins, 1999.

Lindsay, P. *Back from the Dead*, Random House, Sydney, 2003.

Lyons, E. *Among the Carrion Crows*, Rigby, 1977.

Mitchell, Susan. *The Scent of Power: On the trail of women and power in Australian politics*, Harper Collins, 1996.

Moses, A.Dirk (ed) *Genocide and Settler Society: Frontier Violence and Stolen Indigenous Children in Australian History*, New York, 2004.

Reddy, Helen. *The Woman I Am*, Harper Collins, 2005.

Sawer, M. Tremblay, M. and Trimble, L. (eds) *Representing Women in Parliament: A Comparative Study,* Routledge, 2006.

Shaw, G.B. *Man and Superman*, Penguin, 1973.

Spurling, K. and Greenhalgh, E. (eds) *Women in Uniform: Perceptions and Pathways*, UNSW@ADFA, 2000.

Ulrich, L. T. *Well-Behaved Women Seldom Make History*, Knopf, 2007.

Virtuosity: Inside the heads of 100 prominent Australians, New Hobsons, Sydney, 1997.

MEDIA

Newspapers, Magazines and Journals

Australian Feminist Studies, Vol.23, No.56, June 2008.

Australian Financial Review, 7 October 2012, 5 December 2012.

Daily Telegraph, 8 March 2007.

Delco Times, 3 July 2004.

Elsevier, vol.2, issue 2.

Herald Sun, 19 June 2008, 27 January 2012.

HQ, March/April 1996.

Jama: the Journal of the American Medical Association, 2 February 2000.

Journal of American Physicians and Surgeons, vol.8 no.2, Summer 2003.

Juice, February 1996.

People, 29 June 1981, 21 March 1983, 16 May 1983.

Savvy&Sage, September/October 2007.

The Seattle Times, 20 June 2004, 24 June 2004, 30 June 2004, 26 September 2008.

Sports Illustrated, 23 July 2004.

Sunday Times, 16 December 2012.

The Sydney Morning Herald, 14 October 2003, 28 August 2004, 13 February 2008, 21 June 2008, 17 August 2008, 12 August 2012, 27 July 2013.

The Advertiser, 4 March 1996, 14 June 2011, 28 May 2012, 28 July 2010, 8 July 2013.

The Age, 17 January 1997, 23 October 2006, 20 March 2007.

The Australian, 27 June 2002, 19 March 2007, 16 August 2012, 2 May 2013.

The Australian Magazine, June 21–22, 2003.

The Border Mail, 14 December 2010, 5 March 2013.

The Bulletin, 23 – 30 January 1996.

The Canberra Times, 2 October 2006, 5 October 2006, 26 January 2008, 10 March 2008, 1 November 2008, 9 November 2008, 16 October 2010, 13 October 2011, 6 October 2012,14 December 2012, 12 January 2013, 19 January 2013, 8 February 2013, 27 March 2013.

The Daily Telegraph, 21 January 2010.

Sunrise Children's Villages, the Australia Cambodia foundation inc., newsletter, October-December 2010, vol.10, issue 4. January-March 2011, vol.11, issue 1. July-September 2011, vol.11, issue 3. July-September 2012, vol.12, issue 4.

Vogue Australia, February 1996, 28 October 2006, 21 July 2008.

The Washington Post, 29 July 2004.

Weekend Australian, 27-28 September 2008.

Who, 4 March 1996.

Television, Radio and DVD

ABC news online, 11 March 2007, 27 November 2009.

AM, ABC, 23 October 2006.

Denton, A. *Enough Rope*, ABC, 21 July 2003, 14 June 2004.

Hosking, J and Lowe, L. *My Khmer Heart*, Direct Cinema, California, 2000.

Grandstand, ABC, 26 January 2003, 27 July 2012, 3 November 2012.

PM, ABC, 24 November 2003.

60 Minutes, Channel 9, 28 September 2003.

7.30 Report, ABC, 21 October 2002, 26 January 2005, 29 April 2008.

Thompson, Peter. *Talking Heads*, ABC, 14 August 2006.

Negus, George. *Tonight,* ABC, 2 April 2003.

Stateline (Cbr), ABC, 28 January 2009.

Webpages

www.abc.net.au/olympics/2008/sports/basketball/media

www.ackworthschool.com

www.ama.com.au

www.aph.gov.au

www.ashleyjudd.com

www.aussiebubblog.wordpress.com

www.australia.gov.au

www.australiandemocrats.org.au

www.australianoftheyear.gov.au

www.australianwomensport.com.au

www.basketball.net.au

www.clinicalcellculture.com

www.crikey.com.au

www.dailymail.co.uk

www.espn.go.com/wnba

www.healthinfonet.ecu.edu.au/health-facts/overviews

www.imdb.com

www.laurenjackson.org

www.laurenjacksonsportscentre.com.au

www.mamamia.com.au

www.motherinc.com.au

www.notebookmagazine.com

www.nswrapecrisis.com.au

www.pembroke.sa.edu.au

www.perthnow.com.com.au

www.preventviolence.org.au

www.quakers.org.au

www.readersdigest.com.au

www.sciencewa.net.au

http://www.smh.com.au

www.StormBasketball.com

www.surgicalcareers.rcseng.ac.uk

www.thinkprogress

www.wge.gov.au

www.wnba.com/storm

www.womenaustralia

Email

Brown, P. 10 July 2008.
Cox, G. 29 March 2012, 5 April 2012.
Lamond, Toni. 28 April 2013.